THE SAMARITAN'S DIL

The Samaritan's Dilemma: The Political Economy of Development Aid

CLARK C. GIBSON, KRISTER ANDERSSON,
ELINOR OSTROM, AND SUJAI SHIVAKUMAR

OXFORD
UNIVERSITY PRESS

This book has been printed digitally and produced in a standard specification in order to ensure its continuing availability

OXFORD
UNIVERSITY PRESS

Great Clarendon Street, Oxford OX2 6DP

Oxford University Press is a department of the University of Oxford.
It furthers the University's objective of excellence in research, scholarship,
and education by publishing worldwide in

Oxford New York

Auckland Cape Town Dar es Salaam Hong Kong Karachi
Kuala Lumpur Madrid Melbourne Mexico City Nairobi
New Delhi Shanghai Taipei Toronto
With offices in
Argentina Austria Brazil Chile Czech Republic France Greece
Guatemala Hungary Italy Japan South Korea Poland Portugal
Singapore Switzerland Thailand Turkey Ukraine Vietnam

Oxford is a registered trade mark of Oxford University Press
in the UK and in certain other countries

Published in the United States
by Oxford University Press Inc., New York

ISBN 978-0-19-927885-5

Acknowledgments

This book is the product of more than four years of work by a team of researchers who were, until June of 2001, all members of the Workshop in Political Theory and Policy Analysis at Indiana University. The initial stimulus for doing this study was a Request for Proposal sent out in November of 1999 by the Department for Evaluation and Internal Audit of the Swedish International Development Cooperation Agency (Sida). In this request, Sida sought an analysis of incentives in the delivery of development aid. We thought the subject matter so intriguing and potentially important that we threw our hats into the ring, and were delighted to have been chosen by Sida for this project in February of 2000.

Our final report—*Aid, Incentives, and Sustainability: An Institutional Analysis of Development Cooperation*, Sida Studies in Evaluation 02/01 (E. Ostrom *et al.* 2002)—was widely distributed to aid agencies and scholars in many countries of the world. We were gratified to see it generate such interest that we received multiple requests to broaden our initial study and rewrite the report as a book. You now hold the fruits of this effort. We have spent the last 18 months broadening the theoretical scope of the report while drawing on our empirical studies of Sida and Sida projects to illustrate our general theoretical orientation.

The overall objective of this book is to introduce a new approach to the study of development aid, an approach that puts the institutional incentives at the center of the development process. We have written this book with the hope that students, researchers, and other individuals who are interested or even directly involved with development aid activities, will learn to apply this approach, and through it gain new insights about the relationships between aid, incentives, and sustainability.

We develop our approach in three stages. First, we review and discuss the state-of-the-art regarding the existing knowledge about incentives and aid. Second, we develop a series of theoretical propositions about the origins of institutional incentives among the different actors who operate within the development aid process. Throughout the book, we draw on these ideas to identify multiple relationships between aid, incentives, and sustainability that are relevant to all aid actors. Finally, we apply and illustrate the theoretical propositions in concrete field settings in Sweden, India, and Zambia.

During multiple visits to Sida headquarters, the Workshop team reviewed more than 100 documents to assess the degree to which the role of incentives is discussed. In Stockholm, we conducted 111 interviews including Sida staff members at all levels, public officials at two Ministries, and consultants familiar with Sida projects. In India and Zambia, we conducted an additional 66 interviews with Sida staff members, recipient government officials, and project organizations associated with the five projects chosen in India and Zambia. The methods used in that initial study are described in E. Ostrom *et al.* (2002, appendix C). There we also reproduced the interview forms that we used for structured interviews and the lists of persons interviewed in Stockholm and related to the projects selected in India and Zambia. We do not make specific references to particular individuals interviewed since we assured each of them of the anonymity of their interviews with us. From these interviews, we gained information on the perceptions of Sida staff and others working closely with Sida regarding incentives and their concerns and consciousness of how incentives are related to sustainability.

Why did We do This Study?

Our main motivation for doing this study, and for allocating some of our own research funds to it, is our deep concern with the long history of frustrated efforts to enhance political and economic development of many of the poorest countries in the world. In our prior "ground-up studies," we had observed a number of instances in which local efforts to create not-for-profit or for-profit organizations providing needed goods and services had been stymied by donor-funded projects of their own national government (E. Ostrom *et al.* 1994; Shivakoti *et al.* 1997; Sowerwine *et al.* 1994). Further, we were already engaged in a number of studies of national-level policy making and its impacts on development processes (Andersson 2003, 2004; Gibson 1999; Gibson and Lehoucq 2000; Shivakumar 2005), and were beginning work on the impact of international assistance in the area of humanitarian aid (McGinnis 1999c).

The opportunity to work with one of the world's leading development assistance agencies—Sida—to examine how incentives could lead well-intentioned individuals to produce results that at times were unintended and counterproductive, also appealed to us. Sida, by simply commissioning this study, signaled that it was willing to consider some of the most perplexing problems facing international development assistance today. Further, Sida and other closely related agencies and researchers in Sweden had already undertaken some path-breaking studies of how institutional structures lead to the potential for perverse incentives (Bräutigam 2000; Catterson and Lindahl 1999; Eriksson Skoog 2000; Sida 1999b). Indeed, it was important to us that our work on this difficult topic—concerning theoretical developments, empirical findings, and policy recommendations—would be taken seriously by the agency requesting the original study. Indeed, in the meetings we have had with Sida after the delivery of our original report, we were very impressed with the depth of their interest in our approach and conclusions.

We hope that other international donors and the scholars who study development will also find the expanded study of value to them. When individuals trying to do good find themselves hampered in these efforts by the incentives they face, it is quite important that one steps back to examine what these incentives are and how they can induce behavior that slows down development rather than enhancing it.

We are deeply indebted to all of the individuals who gave us substantial time when we talked with them or helped to dig out documents, data, and archival materials. At the Workshop, we have benefited greatly by interactions with our larger team including

Professors Matthew Auer, Roy Gardner, Michael McGinnis, and Christopher Waller (now at Notre Dame). We are glad that Matthew Auer could join Krister Andersson in co-authoring Chapter 8 in light of his own extensive prior experience and the large number of interviews he conducted in Stockholm for the original study. We are also glad that Roy Gardner and Christopher Waller were able to revise an excellent technical appendix from the original study for the broadened Chapter 5 of the current book. We thank Eduardo Araral, Sarah Kantner, Shaun McMahon, Esther Mwangi, Amy Poteete, and Enrico Schaar for their useful input. Frank Van Laerhoven drew on his own long experience in development assistance to provide us with effective critiques of all of the chapters in the current book. And, without Patty Lezotte, we could never have survived the fact that we are now separated and located on the opposite coasts of the United States. She interpreted our confused emails and made sense of our contorted files. Her editorial skills are famous, as is her patience.

We are also appreciative of the welcomes we earlier received in Stockholm on multiple occasions from Sida staff—Anders Berlin, Gun Eriksson Skoog, and Ann-Marie Fallenius of UTV—and of the extensive help offered to us by Malin Karlsson, Stefan Engström, and Wendy Fryer. We deeply appreciate the funding provided to us by Sida at the time of our initial study as well as by Indiana University, the Ford Foundation, and the MacArthur Foundation for our broader research mission. We thank the many individuals throughout Sida who took the time to talk to us and who have given us extensive comments on our report. We also received excellent comments on the initial report from Bertin Martens, Mary Shirley, and Ingemar Gustafsson.

For the India case studies, we appreciate the help of Anita Ingevall and Farhad Irani, Lars Lagging, and Elisabeth Ekelund at Sida in Stockholm. We are indebted to Sida's office at the Embassy of Sweden in New Delhi for many kind courtesies extended. Owe Andersson, Jonas Lövkrona, and Ramesh Mukalla were generous with their time and their wisdom in discussing a range of issues relating to incentives and ownership. Also, in New Delhi, Rita Acharya, at the Indian Ministry of Finance and Jagmohan Bajaj, formerly Finance Secretary to the Government of India, took time to inform us on the conduct of bilateral aid.

For the Orissa project, we thank the Orissa Forest Department, in particular P. R. Mohanty and S. C. Mohanty. Neera Singh of *Vasundara* helped us to understand many of the complex issues involved in Orissa forestry. N. C. Saxena was, as always, courteous and knowledgeable. For the Maharashtra project, we appreciate the kind help of Carl-Göte Carlsson of ABB-India, Pramod Deo of the Maharashtra Secretariat, and V. S. Patnai of the Maharashtra State Electricity Board.

The Workshop team that traveled to Zambia received crucial help from both Sida staff and Zambian officials. Ambassador Kristina Svensson allowed her embassy staff the time to help us with both the logistics of this study and to lend their considerable expertise to our work; we would like to especially thank embassy staffers Göran Hedebro, Marie Holmlund, Mulenga Muleba, and Torsten Andersson. In addition to Sida staff, the number of individuals who gave us some of their valuable time and insights include: Peter Aamodt (Zambia Chamber of Commerce and Industry), Peter Agaard (CFU), Kuwana Akapelwa (ZESCO), Cyprian Chitundu (ZESCO), Ian Fraser (Zambian Privatization Agency), Dutch Gibson (CFU), Andrew Kamanga (ERB), Namukolo Mukutu (GART), Teddy Mwale (ZESCO), Jacob Mwanza (Bank of Zambia), J. Mwenechanya, Olle Otteby (Sida consultant), Matthew Phiri (ZESCO), Raphael Salasini (formerly of ERB), Chatis Vlahakis and team (CFU), J. Zyambo (ZNFU), and Moses Zama (ERB). To these individuals, as well as the other 40 people we interviewed in Zambia, we extend our deep thanks.

Even after such extensive help, we are sure that this book still contains errors. To these, we claim complete ownership.

Contents

Part I. Introduction

Part II. Theoretical Foundations

Part III. Case Studies

List of Boxes

List of Figures

List of Tables

List of Acronyms and Abbreviations

ABB   Asea Brown Boveri
AC   Alternating Current
ACF   Agricultural Consultative Forum
Asien   Asia Department (Sida)
BHEL   Bharat Heavy Electrical Limited
BITS   Swedish Agency for International Technical and Economic
         Cooperation
CFLC   Conservation Farming Liaison Committee
CFM   Community Forest Management
CFU   Conservation Farming Unit
CPR   Common-Pool Resource
DC   Direct Current
DEA   Department of Economic Affairs
ERB   Energy Regulation Board
ESW   Economic and Sector Work
EU   European Union
FDCs   Folk Development Colleges
FDI   Foreign Direct Investment
GoI   Government of India
GoM   Government of Maharashtra
GRZ   Government of Zambia
HADO   Hifadhi Ardhi Dodoma
HVDC   High Voltage Direct Current
IAD   Institutional Analysis and Development
IMF   International Monetary Fund
JFM   Joint Forest Management
KGRP   Kafue Gorge Hydropower Station Rehabilitation Project
KGS   Kafue Gorge Hydropower Station
KTS   Contract Financed Technical Cooperation (Sida)
LDCs   Less-developed countries
MAFF   Ministry of Agriculture, Food, and Fisheries
MARP   Millennium African Renewal Programme
MERC   Maharashtra Electricity Regulation Commission
MFA   Ministry of Foreign Affairs
MFi   Ministry of Finance
MOU   Memorandum of Understanding
MSEB   Maharashtra State Electricity Board
Natur   Department for Natural Resources and the Environment (Sida)
NGOs   Nongovernmental organizations

NTFP	Nontimber forest products
NTPC	National Thermal Power Corporation
PFC	Power Finance Corporation
PRP	Power Rehabilitation Program
SEB	State Electricity Board
SEK	Swedish Kronor
Sida	Swedish International Development Cooperation Agency
SIDA	Swedish International Development Authority
SIs	Sustainability Indicators
SMPP	Second Maharashtra Power Project
SWAP	Sector Wide Approach
USAID	United States Agency for International Development
USGAO	United States General Accounting Office
UTV	Department for Evaluation and Internal Audit (Sida)
ZESCO	Zambia Electricity Supply Corporation
ZNFU	Zambia National Farmers Union

List of Contributors

Krister Andersson is assistant professor of political science and environmental studies at the University of Colorado, Boulder, and an affiliated faculty member of the Workshop in Political Theory and Policy Analysis at Indiana University. He studies the politics of international development and environmental governance in nonindustrial societies. His work has appeared in *Public Administration and Development, World Development*, and the *Journal of Environment and Development*.

Matthew R. Auer is associate professor of public and environmental affairs at the School of Public and Environmental Affairs, Indiana University. His research focuses on the politics of foreign aid, international forest policy, and comparative industrial environmental politics. He is editor-in-chief of the journal *Policy Sciences.*

Roy Gardner is Chancellor's Professor of Economics and Remak Professor of West European Studies at Indiana University. He is the author of *Games for Business and Economics* (2004) and co-author of *Rules, Games, and Common-Pool Resources* (1994).

Clark C. Gibson is professor of political science at the University of California and Director of the Program in International Studies. He studies the politics of development, democracy, and the environment. In addition to dozens of articles, he has written *Politicians and Poachers* (1999), and coedited the volumes *Communities and the Environment* (2001) and *People and Forests* (2000).

Elinor Ostrom is the Arthur F. Bentley Professor of Government at Indiana University and Co-director of the Workshop in Political Theory and Policy Analysis and the Center for the Study of Institutions, Population, and Environmental Change (CIPEC). She is the author of *Understanding Institutional Diversity* (2005) and *Governing the Commons* (1990), as well as the editor of several other books on institutional analysis, development, and resource policy.

Sujai Shivakumar is a policy advisor with the Board on Science, Technology, and Economic Policy of the National Research Council, Washington, DC. He is the author of *The Constitution of Development: Crafting Capabilities for Self-Governance* (2005).

Christopher J. Waller is the G. Schaefer Chair of Economics in the Department of Economics and Econometrics at the University of Notre Dame. He specializes in political economy of central banking and his work has appeared in *American Economic Review* and *Quarterly Journal of Economics*.

PART I

INTRODUCTION

1

What's Wrong with Development Aid?

1.1. RETHINKING DEVELOPMENT AID

Development aid is under increasing scrutiny. Many policymakers, aid practitioners, and scholars have called into question the effectiveness of development aid to increase economic growth, alleviate poverty, or promote social development (Adam and O'Connell 1999; Burnside and Dollar 2000a; Cohen et al. 1985; Dollar and Easterly 1999; Easterly 2001, 2003; Martens et al. 2002; Tsikata 1998; World Bank 1998). At the macro-level, only tenuous links between development aid and improved living conditions have been found. At the micro-level, only a few programs appear to outlast their donors' largesse, mocking aid agencies' goals of sustainability and ownership (Catterson and Lindahl 1999; Edgren 1995; Elgström 1992; White 1992, 1998, 1999). And while critiques of development aid are not new, the new chorus of criticism now includes officials of the agencies themselves.

What's wrong with development aid? Almost every part or process of the aid system has been criticized, from the geopolitical agenda of donors to the distributive politics of recipient countries; from the ties that bind aid to procurement from private firms in the donor's country to the constraints on aid bureaucrats' decision-making power; from the type of aid given to the type of accountability demanded. Over the last four decades, hundreds of researchers have identified hundreds of problems.

A number of macro-level studies in the 1990s found little consonance between aid levels and desirable changes in macro-level indicators (Boone 1994; Burnside and Dollar 2000a; Devarajan and Swaroop 1998; Dollar and Svensson 2000; Easterly 2002b, 2003; Feyzioglu et al. 1998; Pack and Pack 1993; White 1992; World Bank 1998). Not all macro-assessments have been negative, and many micro-assessments remain positive. Nevertheless, the widespread perception of aid ineffectiveness has challenged both aid agency officials and scholars.[1]

Donor governments and multilateral financial institutions—many freed from a bipolar geostrategic world of the Cold War that had traded aid allocations for allies—have now begun to demand new, more productive delivery systems for aid. As a result, new concepts have emerged in the day-to-day vocabulary of the post-Cold War development aid agencies. "Development" as a goal of aid has most notably become "sustainable development" (e.g. Government of France 2002; Government of Japan 2002; OECD 2002; United Nations 2002; USAID 2000; WCED 1987). Sustainable development appears to demand a different logic than traditional efforts such as road building and food aid delivery. For one thing, sustainable development seemed to require greater participation of aid recipients: in the terms of some agencies, recipients were to become "owners." Such a shift implied a concomitant decline in a donor's authority over their own aid packages as well as a greater responsibility on behalf of the recipient. The shift also implied a new institutional constellation on both sides of the aid exchange, since sustainable development demands more attention to the long term.

Scholars, too, began to scrutinize the linkages between the micro- and the macro-levels that helped drive outcomes (Hermes and Lensink 1999). Rather than travel the well-worn path of simply blaming corruption (whether on the part of donors, the private sector, or recipients), some analysts shifted their focus toward the institutional settings of aid (Easterly 2003; Martens *et al.* 2002). In this view, the poor outcomes associated with aid do not need conspiracies to flourish, but are quite predictable given the preferences of the individuals involved and the incentives generated by the way in which the aid system is itself structured (Bräutigam and Knack 2004).

This book attempts to build upon this institutional view of development aid—and add to it. While excellent work has begun in this vein (Martens *et al.* 2002), no study that we know of examines the development assistance process systematically from the home offices of the donor agency to the recipients in the field, employing both theory and evidence in its analysis. We seek to do just that. Rather than offer anecdotal evidence to advance a position within the aid debate, we examine the theoretical foundations for development aid's outcomes and apply our theory to study specific projects in the field.

Our study follows the general theoretical orientation of the Institutional Analysis and Development (IAD) framework, which we describe more fully in Chapter 2. The IAD framework focuses on the incentives and outcomes generated by actors in particular decision-making settings. The IAD framework also enables us to use many other theoretical tools in our analysis, including institutional economics, information theory (especially principal–agent approaches), public goods and common-pool resources theory, and game theory.

While the shift in development thinking has affected most agencies and recipients, we focus the empirical parts of our research on the operation of one particular aid agency: the Swedish International Development Cooperation Agency (Sida).[2] Because Sida has long been regarded as an innovator in the aid field, it makes an excellent choice for an institutional analysis of development aid. In addition to our own study, some recent examples of Sida's trendsetting approaches include Sida-sponsored analyses of the shortcomings of their agency's organization and structure (Bräutigam 2000; Catterson and Lindahl 1999; Eriksson Skoog 2000; Sida 1999*b*). A study of Sida can thus serve as a "critical case": if the level, tenacity, and effect of perverse incentives found in Sida are significant, then one may look for other such causes and consequences in other bilateral aid agencies. (Indeed, other agencies have also started to explore the role of perverse incentives in their own operations (AAPAM/Dag Hammarskjold 1995; Bossuyt *et al.* 2000; Ellis and Hilla 2003; Mansuri and Rao 2003; Mohiddin 1998; ODI/ECDPM 1995; Olsen and Udsholt

1995; Platteau 2003; Sterkenberg and van der Wiel 1999; Thomson 1992; USGAO/ NSIAD 1995).)

We believe our study of development aid is timely. The reassessment of aid allowed by the fall of the Berlin Wall has had time to filter through and become part of policy and its implementation. A comprehensive look at the causes of all the relevant outcomes can help us to understand what, if any, real change in aid delivery and impact has taken place over the last decade. It can also help us think about new designs to improve aid's effectiveness. Indeed, significant new approaches proposed for aid from both multilateral (e.g. the UNs Millennium Development Project) and bilateral donors (the United States' Millennium Challenge Account) have already been initi- ated. And at the time of this book's writing, development aid is at the center of US foreign policy in Afghanistan, Iraq, and the countries devastated by the tsunami that hit on December 26, 2004.

This book is organized into three parts. Part I contains our introductory discussion of "What's Wrong with Development Aid?" Part II explores, in detail, the basic theoretical foundations that we think characterize the institutions and relationships found within development aid. Part III discusses the more pragmatic issues of aid in field settings. Part IV presents our own policy recommendations. As academics concerned with improving public policy, we find the linkages between theory, empirical reality, and policy recommendation very important. We hope that our application of theory to fieldwork can lead to a better understanding of why some aid programs succeed to produce sustainable development while others fail. We hope that this book will help construct aid programs and projects that, at least on the margin, do a better job of improving human welfare.

1.2. INCENTIVES, DEVELOPMENT AID, AND THE PLAN OF THIS BOOK

Our research focuses on the incentives generated by the institutions of development aid. We relate these incentives to two core concepts in current aid strategy: *sustainability* AND *ownership*. In general, we argue that a key to understanding the incentives embedded in development aid is to examine collective-action situations through which aid is generated and delivered. We build the book around four important collective-action situations in which perverse incentives may impinge on the success of development aid. First, all citizens face collective-action problems in day-to-day situations. Individuals must construct a variety of institutions at local, regional, and national levels to overcome the perverse incentives that prevent those collective-action problems from being solved. Second, the policy processes in recipi- ent countries can produce their own perverse incentives. Such processes frequently do not lead public officials to search out better ways of improving institutional arrangements facing their citizens in their everyday economic, social, and political lives. Third, the international development assistance system itself is a complex web of relationships that can generate perverse incentives. The problem of accountability pervades the arenas of international relations (Grant and Keohane 2005). Aid sustainability hinges critically on how this system—and the incentives created by it—interacts with the operational and policy-making contexts in the recipient country. Finally, perverse incentives may exist within donor agencies themselves, as well as between these agencies, their contractors, and other donor country organizations. Few incentives may exist for individuals and organizations to produce sustainable development initiatives. We flesh out these four contexts below.

1.2.1. *Perverse Incentives in Day-to-Day Interactions*

People all over the world confront situations where perverse incentives preclude them from realizing the gains from social cooperation. In donor countries, many of these potentially negative incentives are mitigated through institutions that, by restructuring situations of daily life, lead to mutually beneficial outcomes. In recipient countries, by contrast, citizens often continue to face incentives that make it difficult to invest in economic activities, to provide public goods, to manage common-pool resources, and generally to arrive at mutually beneficial day-to-day arrangements.

  These situations are important to economic development, and are so numerous that considerable analytical work has been devoted to understanding their deeper structure. Many of these repetitive situations are poorly solved in countries receiving large quantities of development assistance. Thus, a core problem of development assistance is to understand the structure and incentives generated within these situations. In Chapter 2, we first provide a brief overview of the basic method of analysis we employ in the book—the IAD framework. We then examine a diversity of potentially unproductive daily situations found throughout history and in all countries of the world.

1.2.2. *Perverse Incentives in the Policy Process*

In all of these unproductive situations, participants may be able to achieve productive outcomes if only the incentives could be changed. In those cases where people themselves cannot change the incentives, government policies potentially can. However, the policy process itself faces incentive-related problems. In Chapter 3, we discuss how these incentives at the policy level obstruct institutional reforms needed to improve economic, social, and political conditions. What happens when a donor enters these situations is addressed at the end of Chapter 3 as well as in Chapters 4 and 5.

1.2.3. *Perverse Incentives in the Development Aid System*

In Chapter 4, we examine whether embedding these omnipresent situations in an international development assistance process enhances or detracts from the likelihood of individuals in these situations coming to better outcomes. In Chapter 5, we focus more closely on the negotiation processes between donors and recipients. In Chapter 6, we examine the incentives that are derived from the different kinds of aid—called modalities—used in development assistance.

	More dependent on aid Zambia	Less dependent on aid India
Natural resources/agriculture	Conservation farming unit	Capacity building for participatory management of degraded forests in Orissa
Public infrastructure (energy)	Kafue Gorge Hydropower Station Rehabilitation Project; Energy Regulation Board	Chandrapur–Padghe HVDC Converter Terminal Project

Figure 1.1. *Design matrix for case studies*

1.2.4. *Perverse Incentives in Donor Agencies*

Chapters 7 and 8 examine the incentives within international development agencies, and between these agencies and the contractors they employ. Chapter 7 focuses on one development agency—Sida—to examine the incentives within development agencies themselves. Chapter 8 then examines the incentives facing contractors working on development assistance projects undertaken by a development agency.

1.2.5. *Cases in Recipient Countries*

In Chapters 9 and 10, we apply the insights of the previous chapters to specific aid projects in India and Zambia. To facilitate comparative analysis, we examine projects that were in similar sectors but in countries of high and low aid-dependence. We selected projects in two sectors—public infrastructure and natural resources/agriculture—where we had done extensive prior research. Our research design resulted in the selection of a total of four cases in Zambia and India (see Figure 1.1). Due to its innovative attempt at institution-building, we added the Energy Regulation Board of Zambia to our original selections.

The short-term nature of our fieldwork for each case prevented a fine-grained analysis of these five cases. We felt it important, however, to illustrate the central theoretical findings of our work with reference to extant development aid projects.

1.3. FIVE KEY CONCEPTS FOR THE INSTITUTIONAL ANALYSIS OF DEVELOPMENT AID

This book assesses the current claim of many donor agencies that recipients need to become "owners" of aid in order for development assistance to be sustainable. We examine the assumed linkage between "ownership" and the sustainability of aid by particularly looking at institutions and incentives. Before we dig deeply into the linkage between institutions, incentives, and the sustainability of development assistance, we need to explore the conceptual foundations of five key terms used throughout this book: institutions, incentives, development (and development aid), sustainability, and ownership. Some of the terms have a long history in development studies; others have a more recent origin. We present these histories while clarifying how we will employ these terms in the rest of this book.

1.3.1. *Institutions (and Their Close Cousins)*

Much of this book describes how institutions alter the incentives of individuals. The incentives, in turn, induce individuals to act in certain ways, leading to interactions that affect the productivity and sustainability of efforts in development aid.

Douglass North has made us all aware of the importance of separating the concept of organizations from that of institutions. Organizations can be thought of as "groups of individuals bound by some common purpose to achieve objectives" (North 1990: 5). Organizations are thus the teams of individuals engaged in collective action to produce jointly valued outcomes. Simple organizations can be analyzed as a separate action situation. Complex organizations are simultaneous and sequentially linked action situations. Action situations—as we discuss further in Chapter 2—are the many structured interactions where individuals must make decisions about actions that affect them and others.

Central to many definitions of institutions is the notion of humanly designed constraints (Hodgson 2004). By constraining behavior, institutions increase the predictability of human interactions and thus make possible some activities that would not otherwise occur. Think for a minute about a modern highway system that lacks any accepted and enforced rules of the road. The potential chaos would be so great that few would venture to travel on such a highway no matter how well it was built. Thus, the key aspect of all institutions is their shared rules regarding what actions individuals must take, must not take, or are permitted to take in particular settings (Crawford and Ostrom 2005; E. Ostrom 2005).

Rules are predictably enforced by agents responsible to external authorities or to those directly involved (or both) for monitoring conduct and for imposing sanctions. These prescriptions are the rules of the game that coordinate human interaction. They "structure incentives in human exchange, whether political, social, or economic" (North 1990: 3). We focus primarily on the rules-in-use in particular settings—that is, the rules as they are understood, generally followed by participants, and enforced—rather than focusing only on formal rules written in legislation, contracts, or court decisions that may not be known to participants and affect their incentives and behavior.

Norms are shared and internalized understandings about situations; they address the "do's and don'ts" of individual action. In contrast to rules that are generally enforced, norms are usually not enforced in a regular way by designated agents. Individuals involved in situations with participants who do not follow group norms may gossip about each other and refuse to engage in reciprocity with those who break norms. When rules are accepted as norms in a community, someone who breaks a rule faces a high likelihood of receiving both formal sanctions as well as various forms of disapproval extended to them by others in the group.

Strategies are the plans for action that individuals make within an action situation (or series of linked action situations) produced by rules, physical goods, and attributes of a community. Individuals plan strategies in light of the structure of these situations and the consequent expectations that any one individual has of the likely behavior of others. Strategies are designed based on the individual's perceptions of the likely benefits or costs that they will receive in light of their own and others' actions and the outcomes they jointly reach.

1.3.2. *Incentives*

Most definitions of incentives include two components: an external stimulus and an internal motivation. In institutional analysis, the term refers to rewards and punishments that individuals perceive to be related to their actions and those of others. The payments people receive or costs they have to pay, the respect they earn from others, the acquisition of new skills or knowledge are all external stimuli that may induce more of some kinds of behavior and less of others (Spiller and Tommasi 2004). Donors use a variety of external stimuli in their effort to change behavior of officials and beneficiaries in recipient countries. Some donors may withdraw or allocate additional monies to change incentives. Others may help create an institution that will then provide incentives for certain types of actions.

Perceived rewards and punishments can motivate individuals to take actions that are productive for all involved. A well-structured, enforced, and competitive market for private goods, for example, can lead participants to invest in activities that help them while generating benefits for others. Perverse incentives, on the other hand, lead individuals to avoid engaging in mutually productive outcomes or to take actions that are generally harmful for others (de Soto 2000). Unfortunately, those charged with reforming institutions also face limitations of knowledge and perverse incentives. All institutions are *imperfect institutions* (Eggertsson 2005).

Many of the incentives involved in international assistance programs involve adding funds to government budgets so as to encourage more spending and activities in those domains that a donor perceives to be important. Additional training, supplemental technical assistance, and overseas travel opportunities are examples of aid-funded institutional changes that produce rewards and change behavior. An institutional analysis can help determine whether such short-term changes are real, whether they are congruent with a donor's goals, whether positive changes in behavior occur, and whether they are sustainable.

1.3.3. *Development, Development Aid, and Development Cooperation*

Individuals and groups working in the development field engage in heated discussions over the meaning of foundational concepts such as "development" and "development aid." We generally view development as a process in which individuals, through the design and use of institutions at many scales, increase their well-being by solving more collective-action problems more effectively (see Shivakumar 2005). Given that our empirical referent for this book is Sida, we have paid special attention to how these terms are used in Sida documents and by Sida staff.

Sweden's Parliament has defined development (through development aid) by means of a set of six distinct outcomes:

- economic growth;
- economic and social equality;
- economic and political independence;
- democratic development;
- care for the environment; and
- equality between women and men (Sida 1997*c*: 9 and 10; hereafter referred to as *Sida at Work*).

The Swedish government and Sida expect that these six goals will also produce a seventh and "overall goal" of Swedish development aid: poverty reduction. In this book, we assume that these seven goals provide a general approach to development that many development assistance agencies, in addition to Sida, follow. We define development aid, then, generally as those actions taken by donors and recipients intended to further these seven goals.

1.3.4. *Sustainability*

Another key concept in the current literature on development aid is sustainability. Arriving at a single definition for sustainability is yet another conceptual challenge. A recent effort to examine (and measure) sustainability led Bell and Morse (1999) to conclude that the concept's myriad usages ranged from an empty slogan to a loaded normative term used primarily for political purposes.[3]

Donor governments generally adopt the broad definition as given in the Brundtland Report: "Sustainable development seeks to meet the needs and aspirations of the present without compromising the ability to meet those of the future" (WCED 1987: 40; for Japan, see JICA 2001; for the United Kingdom, see <http://dfid.gov.uk>; for the United States, see USAID 2004: 80). At the operational level, however, we observe a far less unified conceptualization.

In the course of our fieldwork with Sida, we found that even the documents and staff members from a single agency employ different meanings of the term. For example, in *Sida at Work*, we read that development aid projects should be "socially, economically and environmentally sustainable, i.e., lead to results which live on after the support has been discontinued" (p. 51). This definition emphasizes that sustainability concerns the continuation of a project's results. But in the "Analysis Guide" to *Sida at Work*, the questions a staff member should ask about a project include: "Is there policy and legislation in place which is judged to be able to guarantee the continuation of *the project* when Swedish support has been phased out?," "Is it realistic to count on management and institutional capacity and financial resources being available to run *the project* without development assistance?," and "Is the cooperation partner willing and prepared to take on responsibility/ownership of *the activity* in the long run?" (emphases added). Thus, three out of five questions (recommended as a way of determining sustainability) underscore the continued existence of a project or activity per se, and not the results of a project.[4] In *Sida vid Sida*, on the other hand, Sida's mission should contribute to endurable and sustainable effects (see also Sida Director General Tham's preface to the 1989 Sida Annual Report).

The understanding of Sida staff, both in Sweden and in the field, reflects these multiple definitions of sustainability. Some officials thought that Sida's goal of sustainability referred to activities initiated by their projects, others to the projects themselves, and still others to the enduring results of a project. Several staff members listed all three as important. For this book, we refer to the goals laid out by the Swedish Parliament regarding development: clearly, these seven goals refer to the endurance of results and not to projects or post-project activities alone. Thus, we understand sustainability to refer to the longevity of development aid's effects, rather than the existence of particular projects or activities.

Approaching sustainability in this manner frees one from a sense that every project should be continued indefinitely. Applying this particular view of sustainability, we argue that projects, programs, and other modalities are only the means in the effort to achieve the long-term goals of development assistance. Because of their contribution to poverty reduction and the other goals, some projects should continue for a long time and thus be sustainable at the project level. Others may have made their contribution to development goals in their early years, and continuing the project is not necessarily the optimal investment to achieve the broader goals.

1.3.5. *Ownership*

The essential quandary of development has been how to provide assistance that is successful and sustainable in terms of achieving the types of goals that donors desire. In the first several decades of extensive development assistance, the presumption was that donors should take the lead in designing and implementing programs and projects (Morss 1984). By the early 1990s, however, aid critics and practitioners realized that the heavy donor voice in the planning of development assistance deprived recipients of "ownership" over the programs and projects designed for their benefit (Brunetti and Weder 1994; Johnson and Wasty 1993; OECD 1992; van de Walle and Johnston 1996; Wilson and Whitmore 1995). Without such ownership, critics argued, recipients do not make the kind of commitments needed to ensure the realization of the intended long-term results of donor assistance. Critics have urged donor agencies to push the type of institutional development that increases the ownership capabilities of the beneficiaries or else continue the type of unsustainable development aid that has characterized much of recent experience. Several empirical studies underscore this dynamic.[5]

In their review of the sustainability of twelve Sida development projects in Tanzania, for example, Catterson and Lindahl (1999) repeatedly refer to problems of ownership involved in the projects that were not evaluated as sustainable. One example is the Folk Development Colleges (FDCs), whose sustainability had been questioned in project reviews soon after its inception in 1975. Nevertheless, Sida supported the project for 21 years, investing about $15,000,000 over the period. In trying to understand why Sida continued funding the FDCs for more than two decades, Catterson and Lindahl (1999: 77) reflect that

there was a strong sense of Swedish *ownership* of the Programme, both influencing the pattern of support and the phase out problems. . . . The lack of Tanzanian ownership was reflected in the role of Linköping University, which, according to the 1996 evaluation, approached the projects as "missionaries to advocate a purist approach to adult education as seen from a Swedish perspective." (emphasis in original; see also Rogers *et al.* 1997)

In response to the growing awareness of the importance of ownership, many development agencies have formally adopted ideas related to recipient ownership of development assistance. USAID (2000) discusses the idea of "partnerships" in which the "major task must be carried out by the host nation, not the donor."[6] Japan's development agency avers that ownership "relates to the need for developing countries to assume the primary responsibility and role in addressing . . . issues" (JICA 2001). The OECD believes that "partnerships" are key in making aid more effective: "Partnerships are increasingly based on the principle of helping governments and people of developing countries strengthen their capacities to direct their own development initiatives . . . the partnership approach recognizes the importance of a dynamic private sector, local ownership, and participation by civil society" (2002: 66).

Sida, too, has placed ownership at the center of its expressed philosophy of donor assistance. According to *Sida at Work*, a project's owner is "the party which requests support and which is responsible for the planning and implementation of the project, by having, for example, the organization and staff for the task. The project owner finances part, often a large part, of the costs of the project" (1997c: 15). In turn, Sida vests its partner in development aid with full rights to use the resources provided within the framework laid down in the project agreement. Sida understands that this "complete ownership" requires that political bodies, as well as target groups, support and participate in the decision-making process. Through these ideas and procedures, Sida hopes to have the recipient "own" their development processes (ibid.: 17). Further, in the same document, Sida stresses the importance of clear and mutually understood definitions of responsibilities among stakeholders.

Ownership has thus become an important and fashionable concept among many development assistance agencies in the world today. The leaders of recipient countries are also using the term in their efforts to examine critically their post-independence experience.[7] And yet what ownership means remains unclear when reading official documents or talking with officials from either the donor or recipient sides. It becomes even murkier when confronted with the reality of development ownership in the field. As Bräutigam (2000: 32) notes, the question of what "ownership" means in development assistance is not clearly answered in either the scholarly literature or by the donor agencies themselves.

Consider the relatively simple case of a development agency providing technical assistance: the core actors involved in this would be Agency Headquarters, the Agency's field offices, consultants, recipient government ministries, and the groups targeted for the assistance. It is easy to imagine several of these actors "requesting support" and each bearing different types of "responsibility." Each is also likely to have a different interpretation of the distribution of ownership assignments, and the prerogatives and responsibilities that go along with them. We will argue in later chapters that this lack of common understanding of the concept of ownership and the resulting lack of clear responsibility for long-term results lies at the heart of the incentive problem in development.[8]

Development agencies recognize that the concept of ownership in development aid is often complex. Owners of development aid can vary "between different levels and areas, from government policy to different aspects of a project," as well as with different types of aid; ownership "can also lie with different groups of people" (Sida 1997*c*: 18). Development agencies also promote the idea of "popular ownership," which seems to mean that target groups might be allowed some role in the design or implementation of assistance (ibid.). Finally, the staff of a development agency is often encouraged to develop a sense of ownership as "close as possible to the target group and other interested parties" (ibid.).

Tension exists between these different aspects of ownership. For example, the closer the ownership is to the target group for many projects—particularly, large-scale infrastructure investments—the less likely it is that this group will have the finances to underwrite "a large part" of a project. While the target group may be organized for some purposes, it may not always have the staff or organization to implement many types of development projects and their concomitant accounting procedures. Also, because development aid requires approval by the recipient government, these governments will always have a share of the ownership, regardless of the level of the target group. Finally, since the development agency is the source of the aid, it usually retains a great deal of control over the distribution of these resources. Having clarified the meaning and foundations of these five key concepts, we now turn to the question of how these concepts are linked in ways that may or may not promote development.

1.4. PROMOTING DEVELOPMENT

Progress toward achieving the goals of development involves providing many kinds of public goods that are available to individuals within a society, whether or not they contribute to their provision. To stimulate economic growth, for example, one must invest in physical, human, and social capital, including the creation of effective property-rights systems and ways of adjudicating disputes at relatively low costs. Once economic growth is stimulated, more substantial opportunities may become available to all who live in a regime regardless of their prior contributions. In particular, growth provides a better opportunity to address distributional inequities.

Working for economic and social equality and environmental improvement requires finding peaceful means of productively and equitably combining the efforts (and often the unevenly distributed social and economic assets) of individuals. The individuals who are currently most powerful in recipient countries nearly always have the most to lose from changes leading to democratic development. They may forcibly resist such efforts. Achieving economic and political independence and democratic development requires substantial time and energy to be invested by a large number of individuals. Reducing poverty requires investing resources and hard work to create opportunities for the less advantaged.

1.4.1. *Missing Money?*

In the post-colonial period, many researchers studying development, as well as public officials trying to improve economic performance, thought the core problem was a lack of sufficient monetary resources needed to build necessary physical infrastructure and to enhance investment in local economies (see Huntington and Weiner 1987; Prebisch 1970; Rostow 1960). In other words, the problem was "missing money." The proposed solution was a simple and short-term one—"send money."

If this had actually been the core problem and the right solution, the billions of dollars that donor countries have allocated to developing countries over the last four decades should have gone a long way toward solving the problem of underdevelopment (for an extensive review, see van de Walle and Johnston 1996). Many individual infrastructure, health, and educational projects have enjoyed notable successes (e.g. Bosc and Hanak-Freud 1995; Maipose *et al.* 1997). Sending money, however, has not substantially reduced the relative poverty levels of most recipient countries (Blomstrom and Lundahl 1993; Krueger *et al.* 1989). In fact, the problem of poverty in many African and Asian countries is in many ways more severe today, at the beginning of the twenty-first century, than it was half a century ago (Boone 1996). Even in countries with growth, the lives of the poorest members in many societies remain unchanged or, at worst, have deteriorated. "A small elite got richer and richer, but the mass of the people remained as poor as ever" (Elgström 1992: 46).

1.4.2. *Missing Institutions?*

After decades of trying to understand the problems of development, it is now widely accepted that the core problem is "missing institutions" or "perverse institutions" instead of "missing money" (e.g. Burnside and Dollar 1997; North 1990, 1994; World Bank 1998). Rather than emphasizing the lack of material or human resources, an increasing number of analysts examine how certain institutional arrangements—including development aid—may undermine productivity (Bates 1998; Catterson and Lindahl 1999; Killick *et al.* 1998; Martens *et al.* 2002). Their work argues that no matter how well-intentioned those providing assistance are, or how many resources are transferred, development will occur only if political and economic institutions generate incentives that facilitate individuals' achievement of development goals.

As discussed above, institutions are the rules used by individuals in a wide diversity of repeated situations that they confront in life. The rules that individuals adopt, along with other contextual factors discussed in Chapter 2, directly affect their incentives and consequently the likelihood that they will achieve higher levels of productivity in the many collective-action situations faced in everyday life. Thus, institutions help or hinder the efforts of individuals to be optimally productive in the activities they undertake with others.

1.4.3. *Collective-Action Situations and Development*

We argue that collective-action situations lie at the core of development. A *collective-action situation*, as we use the term in this book, occurs whenever a desired joint outcome requires the input of several individuals. Almost all productive relationships involve some form of collective action. For example, while one person can produce agricultural products from a single, small agricultural plot, the amount of agricultural product per amount of inputs is greatly enhanced by creating diverse forms of teamwork through family, community, or corporate arrangements to increase the size of the enterprise. Similar benefits of increasing the number of participants who bring different skills and resources occur in almost all manufacturing or service activities.

Collective-action situations, given this broad definition, pervade both the public and private sectors of all countries. Collective-action *situations* become collective-action *problems* when actors in the situation choose actions that produce outcomes that are evaluated to be less desirable than others available to them. The classic example of a collective-action problem in the public sector is the provision of a public good such as a national highway network or the reduction of environmental harms (such as smog at a local level or global warming at a global level; Sandler 2004). Analysts tend to focus on collective-action problems in the public sector. Yet, as Miller (1992) has clearly demonstrated, simply creating a public bureaucracy to tackle the provision of public goods or the protection of natural resources does not automatically solve the initial collective-action problem and may even foster additional problems.

The core questions faced by the members of any team effort in the public or private sector are who should contribute what, when, and where? Who will coordinate their efforts? How will joint returns be distributed? Unless participants share clear and efficiency-enhancing rules and norms, some may shirk (free-ride) on the efforts of others or try to deflect joint returns primarily to themselves. Once participants hold back on their contributions to joint efforts or allocate considerable time to gaining more than their share of benefits, the level of productive outcomes achieved by their joint efforts starts to deteriorate. Unfortunately, such dynamic processes lead toward lower and lower levels of returns for all involved, and the perverse incentives tend to be self-reinforcing. Thus, problems get worse and worse and it is ever more difficult to reverse the process.

In the 1960s and 1970s, the theoretical presumption was that citizens themselves could not solve most collective-action problems that involved public goods or common-pool resources, and that a centralized government was necessary to impose solutions (Hardin 1968; Olson 1965). Now, in light of considerable theoretical and empirical research, most institutional analysts recognize that individuals are capable of crafting solutions to their own diverse problems of collective action. Such solutions usually require a rich set of general and special institutional arrangements at local, regional, and national levels in both the private as well as public spheres of life (de Soto 2000; Dietz *et al.* 2003; McGinnis 1999*a,b*; Scott 1998; V. Ostrom 1999; V. Ostrom *et al.* 1993). And different sectors likely demand different institutional arrangements: the effective provision of national defense will not look like those that facilitate the protection of natural resources, the construction and maintenance of effective physical infrastructure, the provision of education, and the stimulation of technological innovation.

1.4.4. *Ownership and Collective Action*

Can we, in resolving this problem of multiple definitions, refer to a clear meaning of ownership in the context of development assistance? In economics, ownership generally refers to the rights that individuals possess in relationship to one another with regard to an asset. Full ownership pertains to a bundle of rights attached to an asset (Schlager and Ostrom 1992). These include the rights of access and use, the rights to make management decisions, the rights to determine who else (if anyone) can become a joint owner, and the right to give up or transfer all of these rights (called the "right to alienation").

A clear understanding of ownership and its consequence for aid sustainability must take into account the collective-action problems in development. As we have seen, collective-action problems can occur when individuals receive benefits that are not tied directly to what they contribute to a combined effort. Individuals may hold back on their contribution for a variety of reasons, leading to a deterioration of the productive outcomes of their joint efforts. An individual's reluctance to contribute may stem from the fact that he or she does not perceive a collective activity to be legitimate. An individual may also feel that his or her contribution will have very little impact on the outcome. Such perceptions can be strengthened, especially if the individual was not consulted before beginning a project. Noncontribution to the joint effort, in such circumstances, may seem fair. Yet, because the individual hesitates to exercise ownership, the project is likely to fail.

In our effort to understand collective-action problems as a reflection of inadequate realization of a sense of ownership in a joint project, we have identified four dimensions of ownership: (1) enunciating demand, (2) making a tangible contribution, (3) obtaining benefits, and (4) sharing responsibility for long-term continuation or noncontinuation of a project. Sometimes one or another of these aspects is stressed in official documents. It is important to clarify these components analytically.

Ownership can be viewed as incorporating the following processes:

1. Enunciating demand: Participation in *provision* by articulating what asset, project, or program is needed and deciding how resources should be mobilized.

2. Making a tangible contribution: Participation in *production* by making tangible contributions. Time, effort, and other resources contributed to production are a costly signal that beneficiaries expect to derive benefits from a project.
3. Obtaining benefits: Participation in *consumption* of the benefits if the project is successful and in a share of responsibility if the project fails.
4. Sharing responsibility for long-term continuation or noncontinuation of a project: Participation in decisions related to the *alienation* of the rights to a project (the decision to continue or not continue a project once it has been initiated).

When one is dealing with a strictly private asset, these decisions can be made by a single individual, family, or firm. But when examining the type of projects involved with development assistance, all of the above processes tend to be collective in nature. Further, they tend to be shared by local beneficiaries, an implementing agency, national government officials, and the officials of a donor country. The relative mix of contributions by multiple parties varies in each project or program.

In the early years of development assistance, local beneficiaries were expected to participate in the consumption of benefits (the third aspect discussed above), but not much more. The recent focus on ownership stresses their role in one or more of the other three aspects of this concept.

Some development projects enhance ownership by having beneficiaries more actively engage in both provision and production processes. By making investment in these processes, beneficiaries are not simply consumers of someone else's largesse. They have had to articulate their own preferences and allocate their own resources. Projects that require beneficiary participation in provision and production activities usually involve considerably more time and effort by the staff of an implementing agency. If a donor is willing to pay the full costs of a project, it is easier and faster for the implementing agency to design the project and arrange all aspects of production. Once the implementing agency has gone to the effort of designing and producing the project, however, it (or the consultant it hires) becomes more of an owner than the beneficiary (Catterson and Lindhahl 1999).

In regard to private goods, the key attribute of ownership stressed in the analytical literature is the right to alienate (or give up) all rights to a good (Alchian and Demsetz 1972; but see Larson and Bromley 1990, who challenge this narrow view of ownership). At first glance, any of the actors could be seen as having a potential veto over continuation of any project. The donor country could withdraw funding, government officials cancel permits, and local people stop participating. (Note that the consultants and other implementing agencies that formally enter at the production stage—but may also play an unofficial role at the provision stage—have less control over alienation, since other actors could always be selected to implement a given provision decision.) This is where a development agency's goal of sustainability becomes crucial. Projects may be sustainable if local (or government) participants may continue it even after donor funding ends. At a deeper level, each project should enhance a society's capacity to sustain progress on the goals of economic growth, equity, etc. Since any particular aid project will have a limited duration, the expected situation at the end of the project should be a focus of its design in the first place.

Any one project should be terminated whenever its continuation detracts from the realization of any of the basic goals of a development assistance program. Does it foster an attitude of dependence? Does it further the career goals of staff members of a recipient or donor government (or of a contractor) rather than enhance local capacity? Deciding when and how to terminate projects turns out to be a critical issue, one that is highlighted by an emphasis on ownership and sustainability.

Complex institutional arrangements, tailored to the exigencies of particular situations, generally require the voice and role of targeted beneficiaries in all aspects of ownership. Without policy to the contrary, the agency responsible for most of the funding will be heavily involved in the provision and alienation processes—while also helping to choose the implementing agency that engages in production. Without ownership of provision/production/alienation, beneficiaries will only consume benefits in the long run.

To be effective and sustainable, a donor's intervention has to help solve underlying collective-action problems, not just provide another project and the temporary infusion of funds and jobs associated with a project. This response, in turn, should incorporate the local knowledge about the needs, preferences, and problems of target beneficiaries that only they themselves possess. Access to this localized knowledge requires active beneficiary ownership—meaning a role in all four aspects of ownership—rather than just the consumption of whatever is produced. Ownership is a necessary, though not sufficient, condition for aid sustainability.

1.5. CONCLUSION

Development aid is not likely to end in the foreseeable future. Moved by strategic, political, economic, and normative reasons, individual countries will likely continue to shift resources to other countries through bilateral and multilateral aid organizations to achieve some mixture of goals. If we are to explain the outcomes of development aid, we need strong theoretical and empirical studies that, ideally, address many links in the aid chain. The next chapter begins to lay the theoretical foundation for our work by presenting our theoretical framework and by exploring the collective-action problems that lay at the heart of development.

NOTES

1. Hansen and Tarp (2000) argue, for instance, that most of the macro-studies over the last 30 years do in fact support the idea that aid helps national-level growth (see also Hansen and Tarp 2001). Other scholars still question the findings of these efforts, claiming that the two-gap theory upon which many statistical studies are based remains fundamentally flawed (Easterly 1999, 2003). While aid can certainly boast notable achievements (Levy 1987; van de Walle and Johnston 1996), most scholars and practitioners would at least agree that it is too often ineffective (Edgren 1995; Elgström 1992; White 1992, 1998, 1999).

2. This book evolved from a Sida-funded evaluation study (E. Ostrom *et al.* 2002). To improve the effectiveness of their own aid delivery system, Sida wanted advice regarding how their operations might generate incentives inimical to good outcomes. Sida also wanted practical suggestions regarding techniques that might help to overcome such incentive problems. Sida's commitment to our enterprise was demonstrated by their support of a 2-year research project that included intense scrutiny of both their headquarters in Sweden and five cases drawn from their efforts in India and Zambia. Sida offered something essential for a detailed study of development aid: nearly unfettered access to their staff and agency data. We interviewed over 100 Sida staff members in three countries, poured over budget and personnel data, read dozens of internal documents and published books, and examined projects and programs first-hand. Only with such extensive support can research into development aid hope to be accurate and useful.

3. See, for example, Salmi (1996), who identifies nine major contexts within which the concept of sustainability is invoked, including allocative efficiency, intergenerational equity, resource substitutability, externalities, and property rights. In dealing with its Agenda 21, the United Nations has developed 132 Sustainability Indicators (SIs) measuring driving forces, states of the world, and responses. See discussion of the United Nations and other efforts to develop systematic SIs by Bell and Morse (1999), who present an in-depth treatment of the concept of sustainability and the grave problems of its measurement.

4. Catterson and Lindahl also define sustainability by project: Sustainability is "the capacity of an aid support project, institution, or programme to continue to function post-aid" (1999: 25).

5. For a discussion of the importance of institutional development and *project* sustainability see Cernea (1987), who evaluated 25 World Bank projects that had originally been judged to be successful at the time of project completion and to have good prospects for long-term sustainability. Only 12 of the 25 projects actually achieved long-term sustainability. At the design stage, all of the sustainable projects involved very specific efforts to enhance the institutional capacities of beneficiaries (ibid.: 3).

6. USAID (2004: 80) advises Operating Units to "discuss Strategic Plan direction and content with host country counterparts early and often to confirm host country support and sense of ownership." Of course, allowing a "sense of ownership" is not exactly the same thing as ownership.

7. The President of South Africa, Thabo Mbeki, and other African leaders have developed the Millennium African Renewal Programme (MARP) in which they call for all African leaders to "take ownership and responsibility for the sustainable economic development of the continent" (reported in *The Economist*, February 24, 2001, p. 17).

8. This is illustrated in Chapters 8, 9, and 10 of this book.

PART II

THEORETICAL FOUNDATIONS

2

Laying the Theoretical Foundations for the Study of Development Aid

2.1. INTRODUCTION

In Chapter 1, we argued that the incentives generated by development aid's institutions are important in explaining its lackluster outcomes. Understanding the incentives that confront donors and recipients requires knowledge of the fundamental collective-action problems that these actors face. Such problems may lead individuals seeking to improve their lot to choose actions that actually undermine their well-being. Even before aid flows into a country, these basic, day-to-day problems need solutions if foreign assistance is to produce successful and sustainable results.

In this chapter, we focus on the problem of collective action as it relates to development, especially at the day-to-day or what we call the operational level. Why do people fail to contribute to the production of joint benefits? We first explore how individuals' motivation may hamper their incentive to work together. The collective-action literature identifies several types of motivation problems under concepts such as common-pool resource problems, public goods problems, the Samaritan's Dilemma, and asymmetric power. We then focus on how missing or asymmetric information about the actions or characteristics of individuals may also inhibit their cooperation. Researchers identify several situations of information constraint, such as principal–agent problems, moral hazard problems, and signaling problems.

We undertake this exploration of collective-action problems using the Institutional Analysis and Development (IAD) framework. Used as the analytical foundation for scores of empirical studies, the IAD framework employs a multidisciplinary approach that presents a practical method for dealing with multiple levels of analysis. It also enables the investigation of configural or interactive processes, such as the multiplicity of collective-action problems and various systems of development aid.

This chapter, then, lays the theoretical foundation for the book's study of development aid. In Section 2.2, we provide the history and capabilities of the IAD framework. Section 2.3 examines the process of doing institutional analysis and the working parts of an action arena. Section 2.4 focuses on the context for analyzing action arenas: rules, the community, and the physical world. Section 2.5 begins our study of motivational problems at the operational level that tend to haunt many collective-action situations, including public goods and free riding, common-pool resource problems, the Samaritan's Dilemma, and asymmetric power relationships.

We devote Section 2.6 to a discussion of informational problems at the operational level including missing information, local knowledge, monitoring to establish trust, moral hazard, principal–agent problems, adverse selection, and signaling problems. In the last section, we begin a discussion about how the citizens and officials of recipient countries can tackle these problems and how donors can try not to increase the difficulty of surmounting these obstacles; this discussion will carry on throughout the remainder of the book.

2.2. AN OVERVIEW OF THE INSTITUTIONAL ANALYSIS AND DEVELOPMENT FRAMEWORK

Since its formation in 1973, scholars affiliated with the Workshop in Political Theory and Policy Analysis at Indiana University have developed a useful theoretical tool called the IAD framework (E. Ostrom 2005; E. Ostrom *et al.* 1994; Kiser and Ostrom 1982; Oakerson 1992). The IAD framework has been employed in a large number of empirical studies, including those that measured the impact of metropolitan-area governance structures on urban service delivery, gauged how institutional incentives affect infrastructure sustainability in developing countries, examined how diverse forms of organization affect irrigation system performance, and explained how ecological conditions combined with institutional structure affect land use change dynamics (particularly changes in forest cover, extent, and composition; see E. Ostrom *et al.* 1993; Gibson *et al.* 2000; McGinnis 1999*a,b*, 2000; Shivakoti and Ostrom 2002). The IAD framework highlights how physical and material conditions, rules-in-use, and the attributes of community jointly shape policy outcomes.

The IAD framework provides an excellent tool for the study of a wide variety of puzzles related to development aid for several reasons. First, multilevel and broad analyses of development demand a multidisciplinary approach. Economists are concerned with the efficient use of resources. Anthropologists and historians have developed tools to analyze the context within which a situation is located. Political scientists tend to examine the power relationships among actors. While providing a more general language than any one discipline (but one compatible with them all), the IAD framework can draw on the insights of most fields to address development aid puzzles.

Second, IAD presents a practical method for dealing with multiple levels of analysis. IAD uses three levels: operational, policy-making, and constitutional. When individuals interact in repetitive settings that directly affect physical outcomes, they are in an *operational* situation. All production and consumption activities exist at an operational level of analysis. The construction and operation of a power plant or the planting of an agricultural field are examples of operational situations. The rules that affect the structure of an operational situation are themselves designed and agreed upon in *policy-making* situations (also called collective-choice situations). Elected officials in legislative or executive bodies in both donor and recipient countries make policy decisions about rules that affect the structure of many operational situations. These policies are themselves made within *constitutional* rules that affect who will make policy decisions using what type of rules and procedures.

Third, IAD allows for investigating configural or interactive processes. Configural processes occur when two or more variables are dependent upon the values of at least one other variable. In other words, the outcome of a configural process is not a simple additive process. Many of the causal processes related to the study of incentives in development are configural or interactive in nature. This is particularly the case with the rules that affect incentive structures. In order to understand the effect of changing one rule, we often must know other rules in effect.[1] The configural nature of rules makes institutional analysis a more difficult and complex enterprise than studies of phenomena that are strictly additive; and requires an approach like the IAD.

The study of institutions and incentives depends on theoretical work undertaken at three levels of specificity: frameworks, theories, and models. Frameworks are metatheoretical schema facilitating the organization of diagnosis, analysis, and prescription. The IAD framework provides a general compilation of the types of variables that should be used to analyze a relevant problem. In other words, the framework identifies the universal elements that studies of incentives need to include.

Theory enables the analyst to specify which elements of the framework are particularly relevant to specific kinds of puzzles and to make assumptions about these elements. After using the framework to ensure that the important questions are asked, an analyst needs to utilize theory to put the answers together, explain processes, and predict outcomes. Economic theory, game theory, the theory of complex adaptive systems, transaction cost theory, and theories of public goods and common-pool resources are all compatible with the IAD framework; we make use of all of these theories in this book.

Models make precise assumptions about a limited set of parameters and variables and enable one to make precise predictions for a limited set of specific settings of relevant variables. Game theoretical models are particularly useful tools for institutional analysis when it can be reasonably assumed that actors have a high level of common knowledge, the capability of processing information, and strategically choose actions to achieve the desired goods, as is illustrated in Chapter 5.

2.3. DOING INSTITUTIONAL ANALYSIS

When conducting an institutional analysis, the analyst needs to identify the arena that is of direct relevance to the problem being examined, the context that frames and affects that arena (including other relevant arenas), and the behavioral interactions and outcomes that are likely. The context of a situation provides the initial conditions or "the environment" that structures the efforts to achieve outcomes (Ashby 1960). It is within that context that an analyst can identify an action arena and its incentives. Actors facing these incentives interact and generate outcomes. The analyst may apply one or more evaluative criteria in addition to examining the likely set of outcomes that will be achieved.[2] Evaluative criteria that are frequently used in evaluating international assistance are efficiency, accountability, sustainability, and equity (see discussion below and E. Ostrom *et al.* 1993). At the broadest level, these elements of institutional analysis are related as shown in Figure 2.1.

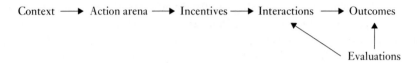

Figure 2.1. *The most general elements of institutional analysis (E. Ostrom et al. 2002: 23)*

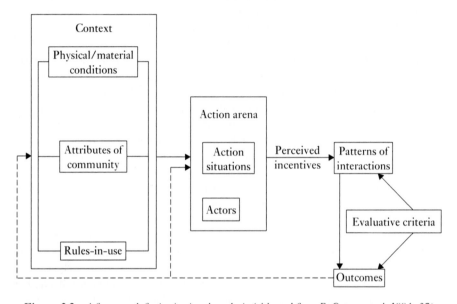

Figure 2.2. *A framework for institutional analysis (Adapted from E. Ostrom et al. 1994: 37)*

When actually conducting a specific analysis, all of these elements are decomposed into finer categories of analysis, as displayed in Figure 2.2. The context is set by configurations of physical conditions, rules-in-use, and the attributes of a community. In examining any kind of problem or puzzle, the analyst first needs to identify a relevant action arena, which is a complex conceptual unit containing one set of variables about an action situation and a second set of variables about an actor. An actor can be either a single individual or a group of individuals who have a regularized way of making decisions, such as a firm or a government (see Martens *et al.* 2002). The concept of an action situation helps the analyst isolate the immediate structure affecting a process so as to explain why particular outcomes tend to occur and potentially identify ways of reforming them.

The structure of an action situation is composed of variables including the actors, their actions, and the outcomes associated with those actions. We explain the full set of variables below. An action situation that occurs only once may generate different outcomes than one that is finitely or indefinitely repeated.

The actors in a situation can be characterized by four sets of variables:

(1) The resources (time, energy, finances) that an actor brings to a situation;
(2) The internal valuation that actors assign to actions and outcomes (including pride and shame);
(3) The way actors acquire, process, retain, and use knowledge and information; and
(4) The processes actors use to select particular courses of actions.

Before we discuss each of the above working parts of a particular action arena, it is important to mention that there are two additional and important steps to conducting an institutional analysis if one is interested in doing policy analysis and in recommending ways of improving outcomes. First, besides learning about the structure of a particular action arena, the analyst wants to know the factors that affect the structure of the arena itself. To do so requires that one digs into the physical and material conditions that are involved, the specific rules being used to structure the arena, and the nature of the general community within which any particular arena exists. Second, one may want to examine how an arena is linked to others. Both of these steps are important in the analysis of development assistance processes.

Having gained an overview of the IAD framework, we will now venture a little deeper into the basic elements and begin to unpack some of these into specific variables.

2.3.1. *Actors and Action Situations*

The *actor* in a situation can be thought of as a single individual or as a group functioning as a corporate actor. The term *action* refers to those human behaviors for which the acting individual attaches a subjective and instrumental meaning. All analysts of micro-behavior use an implicit or explicit theory of how individuals make decisions in order to derive inferences about the likely behavior of each actor in a situation (and, thus, about the pattern of joint results that may be produced). The analyst must make assumptions about what and how actors value; what resources, information, and beliefs they have; their information-processing capabilities; and the internal mechanisms they use to decide upon actions (or strategies involving plans for future actions to be taken) given the expected strategies of others.

For many problems, it is useful to accept the view that an actor's choice of strategy in any particular situation depends on how he or she perceives and weighs the benefits and costs of various strategies and their likely outcomes. The most well-established model of the individual used in institutional analysis is the rational choice model. The rational choice model frequently involves the assumptions that actors have complete and well-ordered preferences, complete information, unlimited computational capability, and that they maximize the net value of expected returns to themselves.

All of these assumptions are controversial and their empirical validity is being challenged on many fronts (see, for example, Camerer 2003; Hammerstein 2003). These assumptions are, however, extremely useful for analyzing situations in which considerable competition exists and when the competitive process generates survivors whose behavior is consistent with these assumptions. For field settings that approximate this kind of competition, these theories generate empirically confirmed predictions. Further, these assumptions can be used analytically—in game theoretic and other micro-institutional models—to generate specific and testable hypotheses. These assumptions are also useful when one is interested in knowing what results to expect when individuals are short-sighted and competitive. The formal models of problematic situations, on which our discussions later in this chapter are largely founded, use this model of the individual. It is the base model used initially by most political economists to capture the core incentives of a particular situation.

Once the stark features of a situation are understood, many institutional analysts prefer to use a broader conception of individual actors. For example, some scholars stress that perceived costs and benefits should include the time and resources devoted to establishing and maintaining relationships (Williamson 1979, 1994), as well as the value that individuals attach to reciprocity and being able to establish a reputation for being reliable and trustworthy (Breton and Wintrobe 1982; Oakerson 1993). Many of the situations of interest in understanding collective-action problems are uncertain, complex, and lack the selective pressure and information-generating capabilities of a competitive market. Therefore, one can substitute the assumption of bounded rationality—that persons are intendedly rational but only limitedly so—for the assumptions of perfect information and utility maximization used in axiomatic choice theory (see E. Ostrom *et al.* 1994: chap. 9; Simon 1965, 1972; Williamson 1985).

Information search is costly, and the information-processing capabilities of human beings are limited. Individuals, therefore, often must make choices based on incomplete knowledge of all possible alternatives and their likely outcomes. With incomplete information and imperfect information-processing capabilities, all individuals may make mistakes in choosing strategies designed to realize a set of goals (V. Ostrom 1986). Over time, however, they can acquire a greater understanding of their situation and adopt strategies that result in higher returns. Reciprocity may develop rather than strictly narrow, short-term pursuit of self-interest (Hyden 1990; Oakerson 1993).

Not all individuals in an interaction have access to the same information. Literacy makes available to some individuals much more information than to others. The contribution of any one individual to a joint undertaking is often difficult for others to judge. When joint outcomes depend on multiple actors contributing inputs that are costly and difficult to measure, incentives exist for individuals to behave opportunistically (Williamson 1975). Opportunism—deceitful behavior intended to improve one's own welfare at the expense of others—may take many forms, from the inconsequential and, perhaps unconscious, to a carefully calculated effort to defraud others with whom one is engaged in ongoing relationships. The opportunism of individuals who may say one thing and do something else further compounds the problem of uncertainty in a given situation. Moreover, the level of opportunistic behavior that may occur in any setting is affected by the norms and institutions used to govern relationships in that setting, as well as by attributes of the decision environment itself (Eggertsson 1990). Boundedly rational individuals may learn from the institutional setting in which they find themselves how to make reciprocity work for them over time or how to act opportunistically so as to achieve more than others in the same situations. Different types of individuals learn from situations, which strategies pay off in the long run.

More broadly, one could assume that individuals calculate benefits and costs but do so as fallible learners. Fallibility and the capacity to learn can thus be viewed as assumptions of a more general theory of the individual (V. Ostrom 1987; Simon 1985, 1997). Fallible learners can, and often do, make mistakes. Mistakes are, in fact, essential for learning to occur (Ashby 1960). Whether incentives encourage people to learn from these mistakes, or to continue to make the same mistakes, depends on the particular institutional setting. And, whether incentives encourage the adoption of a reputation for being reliable and trustworthy or the seeking out of short-term benefits without taking into account the effect on long-term patterns of interactions, also depends largely on the rules structuring particular situations.

Viewing actors as fallible learners within specific institutional arenas leads to the conclusion that the institutional arrangements that individuals use in governing and managing problematic situations offer different incentives and opportunities to learn. In some settings, incentives lead them to repeat the mistakes of the past or to seek only short-term advantages. In these settings, individuals learn to become more opportunistic over time. In other settings, actors learn quickly from their past actions and can adopt more effective strategies over time. They may learn the importance of a reputation as a trustworthy participant and norms of behavior that, when adopted by most participants, leave them all better-off. Further, in all cases, the repertoire of institutional design principles known to individuals and their past experience in crafting their own rules also affect their capacity to change their institutions in order to improve learning and other outcomes when faced with repeated failures.

When fallible, learning individuals interact in frequently repeated and simple situations, it is possible to model them as if they have complete information about the relevant variables for making choices in those same situations. In highly competitive environments, mentioned above, we can also assume that the individuals who survive the selective pressure of the environment, act as if they are maximizers of a key variable associated with survival in that environment (e.g. profits or fitness: Alchian 1950). When individuals face a relatively simple decision situation where institutions generate accurate information about the variables relevant to a particular problem, that problem can be adequately represented as a straightforward, constrained maximization problem.

Game theorists tend to assume that actors are, in addition to having complete information, narrowly selfish and do not adopt any internal norms that would constrain their maximizing of personal gain. Actors who enter and succeed in highly competitive situations can be modeled successfully using this narrow conception of individual morality. In many settings relevant to the study of development aid, however, actors vary in regard to the extent to which they care for others' well-being and in terms of their personal commitment to keeping promises and honoring forms of reciprocity extended to them (E. Ostrom 1998). Even within private profit-making firms, individuals need to establish reputations for being trustworthy. Cultural norms develop within firms that reduce problems of shirking and untrustworthy behavior (Kreps 1990).

Assuming variation in the types of norms that guide individual behavior adds substantial complexity to formal models. Recent work drawing on evolutionary theory has begun to provide some analytical tools that can be used to manage this complexity (Boyd and Richerson 1985; Güth 1995; Hammerstein 2003). What is most important, however, is to recognize that humans are capable of adopting norms about the actions that they must, must not, or may choose to take. Given this capacity for reflection and choice of personal norms, groups that develop a shared understanding of the "do's and don'ts" that they all agree to follow are able to deal more effectively with many of the collective-action problems discussed in Chapter 3. Designing rules that enhance the likelihood that actors may come to know one another, interact at least occasionally on a face-to-face basis, detect when others fail to conform to group rules and norms, and encourage learning about the importance of shared norms, greatly increases the sustainability of collective action (E. Ostrom 2000).

Individuals in society, from both developing and developed countries, behave for the most part within the bounds of their own institutional framework. Though we rarely reflect consciously on this, the question of whether we as fallible learners learn from our mistakes or keep repeating them depends on whether the particular institutional settings that we find ourselves in are suited to the problems we face.

The appropriateness of these institutional settings for development, in turn, depends on the repertoire of design principles we possess and on our own past experience in crafting rules to adapt to contemporary challenges. Indigenous institutions contain a wide variety of normative prescriptions that are expressed in ways resonant to us in our own social context. As such, they help to constitute a basis for an adaptive community of understanding, and, in this way, can contribute to the wealth of social capital (Shivakumar 2003).[3]

While such institutions have enabled groups to solve collective-action problems in the past, they may not necessarily (1) be applied to new situations in socially beneficial ways or (2) be legal in a contemporary setting. Further, they may have been perverted over time for partisan purposes, through negligence, or as a result of misunderstandings by external authorities, and thus produce poor outcomes. In developing countries, aid projects and programs frequently address the manifestations or outcomes of such institutional failures. However, interventions by a foreign donor introduce additional actors and rules to the action arena. These often reflect institutional understandings formed within the cultural context of the donor's own community. New rules and constraints are necessarily interpreted, however, by the developing country learner within the context of his or her own institutional context.

Unless external aid initiatives build on existing institutional understandings and hence "improve" them in terms of their ability to overcome particular collective-action problems, learning on the recipient side will not occur or the lessons learnt may hinder rather than promote development. Without learning, any resolution to the underlying problem will be unsustainable. Indeed, ownership in aid takes meaning when the individuals confronting a collective-action problem are poised to modify an institutionalized system of incentives by drawing on past learning to change the structure of the incentives they face. Ominously, however, aid can erode or undermine local social capital when the rules and constraints that come along with it are placed carelessly in inappropriate interaction with other elements within the local structure of social capital (Morss 1984). When this happens, social capital is destroyed, learning is inhibited, and the developing society is left poorer for the aid it has received.

The term *action situation* refers to a concept that enables an analyst to isolate the immediate structure affecting a particular process in order to explain regularities in human action and results. The common set of variables used to describe the structure of an action situation within a particular context includes:

1. the set of actors;
2. the set of specific positions to be filled by actors;
3. the set of allowable actions and their linkage to outcomes;
4. the potential outcomes that are linked to individual sequences of actions;
5. the level of control each actor has over choice;
6. the information available to actors about the structure of the action situation; and
7. the costs and benefits—which affect perceived incentives—assigned to actions and outcomes.

Also affecting individual strategies is whether a situation will occur once, a known finite number of times, or indefinitely. When explaining actions and accumulated results within the framework of an action arena, these variables are the "givens" that one works with to describe the structure of the situation. These are also the common elements used in game theory to construct a formal game. We will illustrate several action situations below that are frequently found in development aid settings.

2.3.2. *Explaining Outcomes Within an Action Arena*

Depending upon the analytical structure of a situation and the particular assumptions about the actor used, the analyst makes strong or weak inferences about results. In tightly constrained, one-shot, action situations under conditions of complete information, where participants are motivated to select particular strategies or chains of actions that jointly lead to stable equilibria, an analyst can frequently make strong inferences and specific predictions about likely patterns of behavior and outcomes.

Many action arenas, however, do not generate such clear results. Instead of completely independent decision making, individuals may be embedded in communities where initial norms of fairness may change the structure of the situation dramatically. Within these situations, participants may adopt a broader range of strategies. Further, they may change their strategies over time as they learn about the results of past actions. The institutional analyst examining these more open, less-constrained situations makes weaker inferences and predictions on the patterns of outcomes that forecast greater variation in the likely result from a particular type of situation.

In field settings, it is often difficult to tell where one action arena stops and another starts. Life continues in what appears to be a seamless web as individuals move from home to market to work (action situations typically characterized by reciprocity, by exchange, or by team problem solving or command). Further, within arenas, choices of actions within a set of rules as contrasted to choices among future rules are frequently made without recognizing that the level of action has shifted. So, when a "boss" says to an "employee," "How about changing the way we do X?," and the two discuss options and jointly agree upon a better way, they have shifted from taking actions within previously established rules to making decisions about the rules structuring future actions. In language of the IAD framework, they have shifted from an operational arena to a collective-choice arena.

In addition to explaining outcomes, the institutional analyst may also evaluate the processes and outcomes that are being achieved. Most development agencies, for example, identify a number of different goals for their projects and programs; high on the official list of many agencies are sustainability and recipient ownership. In addition, analysts frequently use some combination of five other criteria: economic efficiency, equity (through fiscal equivalence or through redistribution or a search for just remedies), accountability, conformance to general morality, and adaptability.

How these frequently used criteria in the evaluation of public programs are themselves related to sustainability needs to be examined rather closely. Obviously, a donor-funded program or project that is not considered efficient, in the sense that costs exceed benefits, is immediately suspect in regard to its sustainability. When the most important overall goal is poverty reduction, however, some projects that are not immediately efficient, but do benefit the needy (and would be evaluated positively in regard to redistribution), may be considered sustainable so long as those who would pay for the activities after donor funds are withdrawn are deeply committed to the goal of redistribution. A donor may contribute to the construction of a major infrastructure project in the first place due to its own commitment to redistribution (from its taxpayers to the poorest in the recipient country). It is difficult to imagine how such a project would be sustainable in the long run, however, if operating costs are not assigned roughly in proportion to those who receive benefits from the continuing operation of the project.

Recipients in developing countries may invest time or effort in a way that might be judged wasteful in a donor's society, but that may be sustainable if they simultaneously satisfy other criteria such as conformity to local traditions or perceptions of fairness. If they lead to an agreement that most perceive as fair and appropriate, the time spent in deciding various aspects about a project may add to the social capital of those involved by re-enforcing the legitimacy of shared norms and the long-term sustainability of a project. Given the importance of solving the information problems discussed below, some local practices are very effective in sharing information about the input of all participants even though it would be possible to design a more efficient practice if solving information problems was not so difficult.

As we will see, one of the most difficult problems facing donors is finding ways of shifting the support of an ongoing project from revenue provided by the donor to revenue provided by the beneficiaries. The criterion of accountability is clearly related to sustainability. Ensuring that (1) funds are used for the purposes they were allocated, (2) corrupt practices are revealed, and (3) procedures for reviewing practices are institutionalized, are all necessary conditions for any investment to be sustained over the long run.

We have now completed a brief overview of the working parts of an institutional analysis applied to any particular action arena. Underlying the conceptualization of action arenas are implicit assumptions about the context in which the decision making occurs. In IAD language, the context consists of the rules-in-use individuals use to order their relationships, about attributes of states of the world and their transformations, and about the nature of the community within which the arena occurs. Rules, states of the world, and the nature of the community all jointly affect the types of actions that individuals can take, the benefits and costs of their attributes to these actions and resulting outcomes, and the likely outcomes achieved.

2.3.3. *The Concept of Rules*

In the IAD framework, we use the term "rules" rather than the term "institutions" since the latter term is frequently used to refer to organizations as well as to the rules that individuals use within and across organizational boundaries. Rules are shared understandings among those involved that refer to enforced prescriptions about what actions (or states of the world) are required, prohibited, or permitted. Rules also establish the position of enforcers of the rules themselves who have the power to coerce conformance. In a democratic society, rule enforcers must follow agreed-upon procedures for the enforcement of rules. In an authoritarian society, enforcement may be quite arbitrary. In studying these development assistance processes, one needs to ask where the rules that individuals use in given action situations originate.

In an open and democratic governance system, there are many sources of the rules that individuals use in everyday life. In many instances, individuals may legally self-organize in voluntary associations and craft their own rules of interaction. Individuals are authorized to adopt specific rules regarding who is a member of the firm or association, how profits (benefits) are to be shared, how decisions will be made, and are prohibited from adopting others (e.g. in some countries, rules that would exclude someone from participating on the basis of race). Even each family constitutes its own rule-making body or is organized in relation to a patriarchal or matriarchal extended family. Of course, formal rules—laws and regulations—are most likely to be agreed upon within central, regional, local, and special units of government.

Many of the multiple layers of rules are written down in literate societies. Many rules, however, emerge as individuals work together to figure out solutions to commonly faced problems. Working rules may come about "informally" to serve illegal or immoral purposes. For instance, institutional arrangements among politicians, allowing them to behave as organized bandits (McGuire and Olson 1996) and prey on the citizenry, do not promote the overall prosperity of societies. In some bureaucracies, officials have set the price that they must be paid by an applicant in order to receive a position in the bureaucracy (Wade 1985). Here, the rules by which positions are to be purchased are well-known, as are the rewards and punishments for observing or violating these (usually illegal) rules and norms. Although such rules and norms create incentives that promote cooperation and coordination within the rent-seeking bureaucracy, the corruption and ineptitude sponsored by this institution inhibit the development of the larger society (de Soto 2000; Tanzi and Davoodi 1998).

If development agencies and governments seek sustainable solutions to problems, then they will have to focus on more than just altering the biophysical/material world or a community's attributes (the latter being very difficult to change anyway). For example, building a pipeline to provide potable water to a village does change the material world, but such a fix will soon face the collective-action problem of maintaining the tap over time. In addition to the tap's construction, rules will need to be constructed and enforced. Few governments—especially the poorer ones who receive development assistance—have the resources to maintain by themselves the entire infrastructure they build (E. Ostrom *et al.* 1993). Without a change or creation of rules-in-use, the potable water solution will eventually disappear. The creation of such rules is a collective problem in itself, influenced by the biophysical/material conditions and community attributes.

2.3.4. *Biophysical/Material Conditions*

The biophysical/material world is central to much of human decision making. The problems facing farmers learning how to improve their soil (see our analysis of the Conservation Farming Unit in Zambia (Chapter 10)) are far different from those faced by officials constructing an electricity distribution system (see our analysis of the Chandrapur–Padghe HVDC Converter Terminal Project in India (Chapter 9)). The characteristics of the biophysical/material world produce incentives that affect the set of choices available.

As part of identifying the biophysical/material world, the analyst decides what type of goods and services are central to their investigation, for example, private goods, common-pool resources, club goods, or public goods. Different types of goods demand different types of institutional structures for their production and allocation. Private goods are individually consumed and can be easily excluded from potential beneficiaries. Repeated analyses have shown that market institutions are the most efficient institutional arrangement for making provision, production, and allocation decisions related to strictly private goods. Of course, market institutions operate efficiently only in the context of effective laws giving individuals clear property rights to the relevant goods and services, of adequate policing, and of a fair and accessible court system. Many of the goods involved in development aid programs are public goods or common-pool resources. Both of these goods are far more difficult to exclude from potential beneficiaries, making market institutions unsuitable in many situations (see section 2.3.2 above). Creating effective rules to achieve the efficient and fair provision and production of these goods is always a challenge.

2.3.5. *Attributes of a Community*

The third part of identifying the context of a situation is related to the attributes of a community. Communities differ along numerous dimensions: population, assets, history, ethnicity, education, etc. These factors affect individuals' capacity to self-organize, although the importance of any single attribute, or mix of attributes, will likely vary from context to context. For example, communities that have had a long history of solving their collective-action problems will likely have a better chance of doing so again when they confront another such problem. This community might be able to piggyback new solutions on existing institutions, might have a larger reservoir of trust upon which to draw, and it may have a longer time horizon than other communities without such a history (E. Ostrom 1990).

All parts of the IADs context—working rules, biophysical/material conditions, and community attributes—provide the initial conditions or "the environment" that structures efforts to achieve outcomes. It is within this context that an analyst can identify an *action arena* and its incentives for an individual's choices. Action arenas are composed of the incentives generated by the situation's context, and the incentives of the particular actors involved (see the middle "box" in Figure 2.2). Finally, these actors, operating within the incentives produced by action situations, interact and make choices to generate outcomes.

An infinite number of action situations inhabit the world of development aid: from the day-to-day actions of development agency staff in their home office, to the actions of the officials in a recipient country's ministry, to the actions of locals in an aid-targeted village. We explore a number of different operational-level action situations later in this chapter, including a wide variety of production, exchange, gift, and consumption activities. At the policy level, which we examine in Chapter 3, participants in action situations make decisions about the rules used in operational situations. In Chapter 4, we explore how the many recurrent action situations found in development aid link across national and organizational boundaries. In Chapter 5, we illustrate the kinds of questions that an institutional analyst would use in starting to undertake an explanation of outcomes—in this case, focusing on the negotiation arena between a donor and recipient government.

2.4. MOTIVATIONAL PROBLEMS AT THE OPERATIONAL LEVEL

In this section, we provide a brief introduction to the core dysfunctional problems that, while present in all countries, tend to exist at an even greater extent in aid-receiving countries. We focus first on problems stemming primarily from an individual's inadequate motivation to contribute to the production of joint benefits, even when the actor has complete information. These problems include the incentives in situations with public goods, common-pool resources, and the Samaritan's Dilemma. And when power is asymmetric between actors, the powerful may resist more efficient arrangements due to their privileged, status quo payoffs.

We then focus on those problems with missing or asymmetric information about the actions being taken by actors or about the characteristics of these actors (or both). Both types of missing information create or exacerbate motivation problems (Arrow 1985; Campbell 1995), and have labels such as principal–agent dilemmas, moral hazard, adverse selection, signaling, and corruption.

2.4.1. *Public Goods and Free-Riding*

Public goods (and services) are those that are (1) consumed jointly by individuals, (2) difficult to exclude consumption by noncontributors, and (3) one person's consumption does *not* subtract from the availability of the good to others. In a basic public goods problem, a set of actors, who are all in similar positions, must decide whether or not to take costly actions that generate a net loss for each individual but produce a net benefit for the actors as a group. When the individual costs of providing a public good are less than the individual benefits derived from it, even though when many contribute they are all better-off, standard theory holds that public goods will be underproduced. Mancur Olson argues that "unless the number of individuals is quite small, or unless there is coercion or some other device to make individuals act in their common interest, *rational self-interested individuals will not act to achieve their common or group interests*" (1965: 2, emphasis in original). Not contributing to a joint effort when others do is "free-riding," as the noncontributor benefits. Of course, if no one contributes, there is no benefit on which to free ride.

When scholars analyze public good problems formally, they generally assume:

1. All participants have common knowledge about the costs of action and the distribution of benefits.
2. Decisions about contributions are made independently—frequently simultaneously.
3. No external authority enforces potential agreements among actors.

As shown in Chapter 5, public good situations formalized as a finitely repeated game with complete information generates actors that have a dominant strategy not to provide the good. Under the specified conditions, thus, the predicted outcome is that no one contributes and the public good is not produced (Roberts 1979). This outcome repeats in all finite repetitions. If uncertainty exists about the number of repetitions, formal analysis generates a very large number of potential outcomes including zero contributions as well as full contributions. But the lesson from these formal analyses is that unless the participants themselves are able to find ways of reaching enforceable agreements, or external authorities enforce effective rules, we should expect an inefficient provision of most public goods.

In many contemporary settings, individuals have created a wide diversity of institutional arrangements that allow them to provide local public goods through various forms of organization, from voluntary associations, to informal arrangements that closely approximate those found in the official public sector, to governments. For large-scale public goods—such as national defense—national governments are the prime mechanism used to provide (and produce) these goods. Mixed public and private systems exist for the provision of many goods, such as public radio, where government subsidies supplement voluntary contributions made by citizens. Where communities create local public goods, one usually finds some complex of government and private organizations that have evolved or been self-consciously designed to overcome the perverse incentives that would otherwise lead to underproduction. One of the most solid and empirically supported findings from the collective-action literature is that without the development of adequate rules governing who (and how) will provide the good, public goods will be undersupplied.

Donors frequently fund projects that provide public goods, such as school construction. As we discuss throughout the rest of this book, while donors may be able to finance the short-term provision of public goods, donor efforts often fail to address the underlying incentive problems, and thus do not help generate sustainable solutions. Schools, for instance, need maintenance and repair. While each member of a village would like their school to be in good working order, each member also has the incentive to let another villager, or another infusion from a donor, do the work. Thus, the donor would have solved one collective-action problem by providing the school, but would also have created others that can lead to poor outcomes over time. In fact, education is an example of a public service, which requires the active participation of both engaged parents and the students themselves in order to produce a good quality result. A donor has to be careful not to crowd out such necessary local engagement by providing too much support and thereby creating incentives to be passive observers among local people.

2.4.2. *Common-Pool Resource Problems*

Similar to public goods, excluding potential beneficiaries from the use of common-pool resources is difficult. Unlike public goods, however, one person's use does subtract from the resources available to others. Thus, in the absence of effective institutions, users will overharvest common-pool resources; natural resources such as forests, fisheries, and grazing areas may even be destroyed.

Garrett Hardin (1968) paints a grim picture to characterize the "tragedy of the commons," thought by many to occur whenever multiple actors jointly use a single common-pool resource. Hardin's metaphor so dramatically captured the imagination of scholars, activists, and officials that major policies related to natural resources have been based on the presumed helplessness of the users themselves to change the structure of incentives they faced. For example, the Hifadhi Ardhi Dodoma (HADO) Regional Soil Conservation Project in Tanzania assumed that the growing population of domesticated animals in the district was causing the area's severe soil erosion. Donors supported the activities of the Ministry of Natural Resources, which included tree planting, construction of bunds, and the "temporary" destocking of all animals in one region. No investment was made, however, to help the beneficiaries of the aid project to develop more effective rules related to stocking densities. Subsequent evaluations of this top-down, national government approach questioned the extent of benefits achieved. In particular, evaluators faulted the program for its lack of attention to more sustainable solutions, such as those that took a longer view and included thinking about local incentives (see Catterson and Lindahl 1999; Erikson *et al.* 1995).[4]

People may also create common-pool resources such as the treasuries of a national government or a private firm; similar tragedies of the commons can occur in these resources too. Increased pressure on a public treasury can lead to irresponsible budgetary behavior. The "harvesters" in this case are bureaucrats, local and national politicians, and interest groups who keep taking from a recurrent budget by calling for increased spending for their particular issue. The government budget is a common-pool resource since they can consume parts of the treasury at little cost to themselves (Campos and Pradhan 1996). Donor largesse, can, in some cases, create a fiscal commons that is ongoing and subject to few constraints and therefore are likely to produce inefficient and inequitable outcomes (see Eriksson Skoog 2000).

Theoretical and empirical findings, however, demonstrate that Hardin's predicted outcome does not hold in many cases. A large literature has identified many common-pool resource situations in which users of the resource have developed effective rules for governing and managing it over time (Bromley *et al.* 1992; McCay and Acheson 1987; E. Ostrom 1990). Institutions that limit harvesting exist in situations from rural watersheds to national budgets. Of course, the particulars of any specific harvesting situation differ dramatically from one location to another. Such research makes it important for donors to determine what the good is and, if it is a common-pool resource, not automatically disregard local level institutions that may be operating effectively already.

2.4.3. *The Samaritan's Dilemma*

Another situation that pervades development aid is the Samaritan's Dilemma (Buchanan 1977). An actor deeply concerned about the well-being of others—the Samaritan as per the parable in the New Testament—confronts situations in which other people might be in need of help. In Buchanan's formulation, the Samaritan chooses between helping and not helping. The recipient, on the other hand, decides how much effort he or she must make to obtain the Samaritan's help, high or low. If the Samaritan extends help and the recipient exerts high effort, both the Samaritan and the recipient benefit—but the recipient receives even higher benefits when expending less effort. Figure 2.3 shows this dilemma as a two-person game with ordinal payoffs.

		Recipient	
		High effort	Low effort
Samaritan	No help	2, 2	1, 1
	Help	4, 3	3, 4

Figure 2.3. *The Samaritan's Dilemma (Adapted from Buchanan 1977: 170)*

Samaritans face a fundamental problem: they are better-off helping no matter what the recipient does; in game theory terms, extending help is a dominant strategy. Once the recipient understands this, then its own dominant strategy is to expend a low level of effort. The Samaritan prefers that the recipient puts in high effort, but the structure of the interaction guarantees the recipient gives only low effort.

Ian Fisher, the Nairobi bureau chief for *The New York Times*, describes a proto-typical description of a Samaritan's Dilemma in his "Can International Relief Do More Good than Harm?" He tells of interviewing a Nuba rebel leader who describes a trip he made in 1993 to an area in southern Sudan that had been receiving considerable food aid from the United Nations. "The people of the area are great farmers," he says, "but because there is this relief food, they did not farm for three years. I could see the difficulty. It was spoiling people. They just sleep and have food. It is very bad" (Fisher 2001: 74). Many examples of the Samaritan's Dilemma can be culled from development agencies' experiences: Bossert (1990) discusses the negative effects of donor-supported health projects in Central America and Africa. Eriksson Skoog (2000) observed that soft budget constraints occurred when kind-hearted government officials repeatedly bail out state-owned enterprises, which then repeatedly spend more than their budgets. Maren's polemical *Road to Hell* (1997) argued that the supply-driven aid to Somalia in the 1980s led directly to famine in the 1990s. The Samaritan-donors in these cases produced poor—and sometimes catastrophic—outcomes, despite their desire to help.

When analyzed formally, this problem is strictly a "motivational" problem and does not depend on the absence of information or the asymmetry of information. The recipient knows from the structure of the situation that the Samaritan is going to help. The Samaritan knows that the recipient is unlikely to put out high effort. From an external view, the joint situation may be efficient if the payoffs are similar to those chosen by Buchanan, since both the lower left and lower right-hand cells are equal in value. The matrix in Figure 2.3 shows the subjective preference ordering of the two players. Most likely, however, the equilibrium outcome of the Samaritan offering help and the recipient undertaking low effort will be inefficient when measured in terms of material well-being. The distribution of benefits, in any case, is skewed to the recipient. Moreover, if the situation is repeated—as it often is in the development aid process—the donor may be creating a situation where the recipient actually loses skill and motivation over time.

Infrastructure constructed with donor assistance is often another classic case of Samaritan's Dilemmas. Modern power stations, for example, should last 50 to 60 years without major rehabilitation if routine maintenance is performed (Catterson and Lindahl 1999). In many recipient countries, however, power stations need major rehabilitations every 10–15 years "mainly since the politicians cannot see the point of putting limited amounts into maintenance over time when, free of charge, they can have a totally rehabilitated or new plant within a few years" (ibid.: 145). A very similar situation exists in the Zambian power sector, as we explore in a later chapter and in many— if not most—other infrastructural projects (E. Ostrom *et al.* 1993). Given the values of the donor-Samaritan, there is little choice but to help maintain these large works.

There are some fixes for such situations, as we explore in more detail later. A more sophisticated Samaritan might try to condition their aid on meaningful participation by the recipient. Alternatively, truly joint ownership (as defined in Chapter 1) of a project may induce higher efforts from the recipient.

2.4.4. *Asymmetric Power Relationships*

Although power may be distributed in a relatively equal manner, as is frequently assumed in public good and common-pool resource problems, it is usually skewed. From small rural communities in developing countries to the bureaucracies of aid agencies, individuals often face other actors with greater command over key resources. Such unequal distribution can have serious effects on the ability of governments or citizens to solve collective-action problems.

The farmers located at the head end of any irrigation system, for example, have considerably more power to affect what happens downstream than the farmers located at the tail end. Empirical studies of irrigation systems in Nepal find that when the head-enders use a farmer-constructed irrigation system that does not need much maintenance, they tend to take most of the water and leave only what they cannot use for tail-enders (see E. Ostrom and Gardner 1993). In these cases, tail-enders invest little effort in maintaining the system. On the other hand, most farmer-constructed irrigation systems do require substantial maintenance. When the farmers themselves have created rules about how maintenance is to be supplied, tail-end farmers have considerably more bargaining power. They often demand, and obtain, a fair share of irrigation water in return for their contribution to the maintenance of the system (see Lam 1998). These systems also tend to produce the higher agricultural yields. When donors invest in irrigation systems without an understanding of these dynamics, they may reduce the bargaining power of the tail-enders leading to substantially lower levels of production and increased greater distributional problems (E. Ostrom 1996).

Many other sources of asymmetric power exist besides sheer location. Most collective-action problems occur within the context of a pre-existing distribution of economic and political power. If that distribution is highly unequal, economic or political elites have likely ensured that past decisions distribute assets disproportionately to themselves. Solutions to collective-action problems can produce low productivity, but still generate enough advantage for those with asymmetric power to remain in place. If changes increase the joint outcomes for all, but leave the elite with less, they may resist them.

Olson, on the other hand, theorized that groups with some advantaged members (privileged groups) may in fact have an easier path to solving their collective-action problems. The better-off individuals may contribute more than their fair share to solve the dilemma. But the solution reached may not benefit all equally or even in proportion to contribution. Empirical evidence for this contention is mixed.[5]

The solution to some collective-action problems may require the leadership and example of entrepreneurs who are willing to take initiative and invest more than an equal share of the effort needed to make the collective process work (Kuhnert 2001).

When some individuals within a group have a disproportionate and larger stake in the solution of a particular collective dilemma, these individuals may be prepared to facilitate the solution of the problem. Although everyone will be better-off if the problem is solved, everyone but the entrepreneur will have an incentive to shirk on the efforts of others. The entrepreneur, on the other hand, will be motivated to monitor the compliance of the group members. Although the presence of an entrepreneur may provide a solution to the motivation problem inherent in many collective dilemmas, it does not provide a solution for all of them. For instance, as the entrepreneur tries to monitor the behavior of other group members, information asymmetries often complicate the effectiveness of such efforts. Information problems are discussed below.

2.5. INFORMATION PROBLEMS AT AN OPERATIONAL LEVEL

All the problems discussed above stem primarily from the underlying motivation structures of collective-action problems. Most models of these situations, however, also assume that all actors have perfect information. We now turn to a set of problems generated from missing or asymmetric information, for example, even if all actors rank joint outcomes in the same order, lack of information may still prevent solutions to the collective-action problem. Missing or asymmetric information also create structures of incentives that produce moral hazard, principal–agent problems, and adverse selection (Holmstrom 1982*a,b*; Miller 1992; Moe 1984). And when the motivational problems discussed in the previous section combine with the information problems discussed below, the difficulty of overcoming collective-action problems escalates.

2.5.1. *Missing Information and Local Knowledge*

Solving most public good and common-pool resource problems at the operational level requires considerable local knowledge. Hayek (1948) recognized a body of important but unorganized knowledge that individuals, each in their particular circumstance, possess about their own time and place. This knowledge by its nature cannot be tabulated, and thus is difficult to use systematically. Often individuals acting within a particular situation over a long period of time hold the most local knowledge. For example, farmers who have used a stream to irrigate crops are usually well aware of where the stream crosses solid rock as contrasted to where the stream crosses a long section of sandy and unstable soil. If the engineers designing a donor-funded irrigation project do not learn this information, the canal may wash out after only a few years of operation, as Hilton (2002) graphically describes in an analysis of some donor-funded projects in Nepal.

Such specific time and place knowledge contrasts with objective scientific knowledge, which emphasizes the placement of observed regularities within some theoretical context. Hayek (1952) stressed that given the issue of time-and-place knowledge, methods of scientific analysis appropriate for physical phenomena cannot be uniformly applied without qualification to understand the social–economic nexus.[6]

Building sustainable projects with development aid will likely require a combination of scientific and time-and-place knowledge. If farmers attempt to construct roads suitable for heavy traffic or an irrigation system in difficult terrain, they may not have sufficient scientific and technical knowledge to build a sustainable project. Similarly, engineers who do not obtain reliable information about a locality may construct an extremely sophisticated physical infrastructure, only to have it washed out later because they did not know enough about local soils or microclimate. Significant asymmetries of both time-and-place knowledge and scientific knowledge exist in the context of development aid, and thus a central challenge in aid is incorporating both. While increasing transaction costs in the short run, using both knowledge types would likely enhance sustainability and thus efficiency over the longer term. Additionally, designs that allow beneficiaries joint ownership over a project or program would likely be able to integrate local knowledge more easily.

Development aid is plagued by situations of asymmetric information, in which two or more individuals interact without fully knowing the other's deeds. Asymmetric information about actions characterizes a series of problems referred to as *moral hazard*. Originally analyzed in regard to insurance problems, moral hazard problems are found whenever an actor is protected against risk partly resulting from the same actor's own behavior. Another common situation characterized by asymmetric information is the *principal–agent* problem. Principal–agent problems are found whenever individuals work within a hierarchy.

Moral hazard

Moral hazard problems exist in a wide variety of settings where individuals contract to indemnify themselves against loss regardless of their efforts to avoid such loss.[7] The concept originates from the difficulties of insurance companies to create effective insurance institutions. At least some individuals will be more careless after obtaining insurance, and insurance companies cannot afford to monitor each individual's behavior at all times. Since observing actions is costly, and since the individual is now protected from loss, the protection itself may reduce the likelihood that the actor takes preventive measures.

The term *moral hazard* has come to be used as the general term used for hidden action problems (see Campbell 1995). An example from development aid is a donor government's budgetary relationship with its aid agency. The government would like the agency to make good investments in aid projects and programs, that is, ones that are the most efficient in terms of "development" per "dollar." But the agency knows that its government has difficulty in judging the agency's efficiency. Further, the agency also knows that if it chooses an inefficient project, the government is likely not to reduce its budget. This relationship creates an incentive for the agency to invest in relatively riskier projects than if it had to bear the financial consequences of a bad decision.[8]

Another example of moral hazard caused by development aid is when recipient governments promise to take costly future actions to reform political or economic institutions in exchange for immediate financial support from a donor. The aid itself, however, can encourage the recipients to delay these reforms even longer than they would have in the absence of aid (Eriksson Skoog 2000; Gibson and Hoffmann 2005; van de Walle 2001). "The indiscriminate availability of aid creates a moral hazard, where aid availability, by 'insuring' incompetent governments from the results of their actions, allows governments to postpone reform efforts and weakens their incentive to find alternative revenue sources" (Bräutigam 2000: 24).

Principal–agent situations

Much of productive life is organized in hierarchies in which individuals in decision situations are arrayed in a series of superior–subordinate positions. All development agencies are organized hierarchically (even when there is a sincere effort to reduce the number of levels in the hierarchy). In the idealized hierarchy, a superior defines what, how, when, and where a subordinate works. She also evaluates the subordinate in light of these instructions. Implicitly, this model assumes that the superior can know the actions of the subordinate and can thus reward performance. Until recently, this simple model was part of most recommendations made by donors to developing countries to generate better policy outcomes (V. Ostrom 1999; Wunsch 2000).

Work in the political economy tradition has found this simple model of hierarchy—and thus bureaucracy—fundamentally flawed. Numerous scholars have shown that such institutions are riddled with problems of asymmetric information, generated by their inherent principal–agent relationships (Alchian and Demsetz 1972; Bickers and Williams 2001; Tirole 1986). In a principal–agent relationship, the principal is the individual (or the representative for an organized set of individuals) who benefits from the outcomes achieved by the agent, while the agent is offered a contract to take the appropriate actions to achieve these outcomes. A problem occurs in this relationship since the agent may have different preferences than her principal, and the principal has only coarse information about the agent's actions (Rasmusen 1989).

The simplest example of an isolated principal–agent situation occurs when an individual consults a doctor or a lawyer. The individual is the principal who is asking an agent for professional services to increase the principal's welfare. The individual, however, does not have a guarantee that the professional will thoroughly consider their interest and provide them the best service. One of the mechanisms used around the world to reduce the difficulties in principal–agent problems is to create professional associations that monitor the performance of their own members. It is in the interest of the professionals to be able to claim higher reliability in serving the interest of their clients by having adopted a professional code and being a member of a professional association. The ability to bring lawsuits for malpractice is another mechanism available to principals who believe they were not well served. (Such professional associations are weak to nonexistent among many recipient countries (Narayan 2000).)

In larger organizations, hierarchies contain a series of principal–agent relationships, breeding both an incentive problem and an ever-increasing problem of missing information and of asymmetric information. At each level there is a reduction in the level of information passed along to superiors; the larger the chain of staff, the smaller proportion of the information known to those at the bottom will reach the top (Williamson 1967, 1973). This reduction of information becomes magnified by the subordinates' incentive to pass information favorable to their own performance. Those at the top of the chain consequently receive limited and biased information. Organizations have designed a variety of institutions to mitigate these problems. Private firms attempt to tie work and pay tightly together through such arrangements as piecework contracts, commissions, and bonuses or stock options for firm profitability (Milgrom and Roberts 1992). Entry-level staff members in organizations may be motivated to work hard by the promise of promotions to positions with more responsibility, status, and pay based on performance. But given the complexity of work assignments, no complete contract can be written covering all exigencies and specifying what will happen to the agent under each circumstance, even in the private sector (Grossman and Hart 1986).

Solving the problems resulting from asymmetric information in public bureaucracies such as an aid agency is much more difficult than in private sector firms. Governments charge public agencies with a variety of objectives that are difficult to measure, making equally difficult the evaluation about an agency's efforts (let alone any one staff member's contribution to outcomes) (Easterly 2002a; Tirole 1994). The kind of contracts offered to employees of government agencies is also much more limited. In developing countries, the pay of public employees is frequently much less than the competitive wage—offset by a promise of a relatively long-term contract. Civil service regulations often create barriers to firing a government worker for lack of performance. While citizen organizations are able to monitor some aspects of the work of street-level public servants, the work of most public employees is carried out far from public view. And although schools of public administration stress the professional nature of public service, no professional association has taken on as strong and active a role regarding public officials as have associations of medical doctors and lawyers.

The combination of low pay and long-term employment also exacerbates the severity of moral hazard problems faced in public bureaucracies, particularly in developing countries. Public employees may devote their working time to a wide diversity of private activities such as running their own private businesses. Where the "privatization" of a public office has gone too far, jobs are bought and sold, as described by Wade (1985, 1989) in India. Instead of just the shirking associated with principal–agent relationships, public employees may need to find ways of gaining private returns to make their investment in obtaining a public position worthwhile, such as extracting side payments from citizens wishing to obtain a license or who are suspected of committing a crime.

2.5.2. *Asymmetric Information About Characteristics*

Actors' characteristics, in addition to their actions, can be private information. As analysts begin to develop models of situations where there are multiple types of actors—rather than a single type which has characterized much of the political economy literature until very recently—a core question arises as to the difference this type of asymmetric information makes in the incentives facing individuals.

Adverse selection

An adverse selection problem occurs when an individual knows their own characteristics but others do not share this private information. The individual may have private knowledge about an object that the individual would like to sell (Akerlof 1970) or about his or her own skills as a worker (Spence 1973). Adverse selection problems occur whenever the selection of beneficiaries or future employees is a nonrandom process that tends to select for the least-productive individuals. This logic helps explain why it is so difficult to devise a sustainable, private health insurance or unemployment insurance scheme. The problem facing health insurance or unemployment schemes is that those least likely to need the insurance are the most likely to opt out of the system. That makes the pool of individuals remaining in the insurance scheme even more likely to incur sickness or unemployment. The rates must then increase. This leads again to a dropout of the individuals who are least likely to draw on the insurance at the new price. Over time, the scheme's costs become ever higher, and those that remain are ever more likely to draw on benefits. This structure of incentives prevents private markets from solving adverse selection problems. Putting the insurance scheme in the public sector may solve the adverse selection problem by greatly expanding the pool of insured to include healthier, as well as less healthy individuals—but it may not solve the moral hazard problem.

Similar processes occur in development aid. As donor agencies ratchet up the conditions (analogous to the costs in the insurance example) to be met by recipients in exchange for aid, those in least need of aid (analogous to the healthy) will opt to leave the pool of possible recipients. This leaves those less able to meet the conditions in the pool, and seeing this, creates incentives for the aid agency to increase the conditions on receiving aid. Eventually, the riskiest projects will remain.

Signaling problems

The private information that is held by individuals and leads to adverse selection problems may be discovered by others involved in an ongoing situation at some cost. Before hiring a new employee, for example, firms try to obtain relevant information about education, skills, and past work performance. Some of this may be acquired by testing; the rest by various screening processes. This information, however, is always an imperfect indicator of the quality of a future staff member. This is a particularly puzzling problem for agencies working in recipient countries that want to hire local staff members. How excellence is signalled in one culture may differ substantially from the signals that an individual would use in another culture. It is even a problem for how staff members within a development agency itself signal their skills to superiors.[9] If they are too overt in trying to show their skills, other staff members may resent their efforts. If they are too humble, they may be overlooked when a promotion opportunity occurs.

2.6. SOLVING OPERATIONAL-LEVEL PROBLEMS

If so many of these operational-level problems exist in developing countries, how is it that individuals can get *anything* done? By relying on family, kin, and friends, individuals in developing countries are able to resolve many of these problems, and do undertake a wide variety of small-scale activities that enhance their economic well-being. These arrangements, however, are frequently limited to the "informal sector" and to relatively small-scale enterprises. As Hernando de Soto (2000: 153) expresses

Box 2.1. *General questions all development projects should ask*

The theories presented in this chapter generate questions that we would ask of any project or program designed as part of development aid.

✓ *What underlying collective-action problem(s) do beneficiaries face?*

- Is it a public-good problem/free-rider problem/tragedy of the commons problem?
- What are the basic incentive problems facing beneficiaries at an operational level? Motivational? Missing information? Asymmetric information? Other?
- What are the developmental implications of this collective-action failure?
- What rules or norms have been used in this cultural tradition in the past that may be the source of modern rules that resonate with beneficiaries as fair and can be understood easily?
- Are needed institutions missing or weak, or are perverse institutions in place?
- Would a modification in rules affecting this underlying problem be threatening to the power elite of this country?

✓ *In what ways have previous aid interventions altered similar collective-action problems?*

- Did development aid abet or exacerbate power or information asymmetries or adverse selection?
- What ownership attributes do the targeted beneficiaries possess?
- Have aid interventions affected the capacity of the beneficiary group to address the collective-action failure?
- Have they exacerbated existing perverse incentive structures?

✓ *What are the implications for sustainability?*

- How will the underlying collective-action problems be addressed by a planned future aid project or program?
- Who will be the owners of this intervention?
- Given the roles of the beneficiaries, contractors, development agency personnel, and recipient government officials, are the prospects for an appropriate solution to the underlying collective-action problem enhanced or reduced?

Answering these questions helps a development practitioner to confront the serious impediments at the heart of collective-action problems. Answering these questions should also point the way to overcoming these problems, and to the design of solutions that would be more efficient and sustainable.

it: "Nearly every developing and former communist nation has a formal property system. The problem is that most citizens cannot gain access to it. . . . Their only alternative . . . is to retreat with their assets into the extralegal sector where they can live and do business—but without ever being able to convert their assets into capital."

Small-scale problems of motivation and information can thus be overcome with the built-in reciprocity and trust of social networks. Indeed, we would argue that the higher failure rate (especially in terms of sustainability) that characterizes large-scale development projects and programs is at least in part due to this lack of effective, large-scale institutions.

We think understanding the theoretical underpinnings of the collective-action problems that occur in all societies is key for all development organizations interested in producing better outcomes. We provide a short list of questions in Box 2.1 that we urge all to use in the design of aid projects. Achieving increasing economic productivity and poverty reduction requires helping beneficiaries and their leaders to understand and change the structure of the situations they face to overcome these fundamental motivation and information problems.

NOTES

1. To predict the outcome of a voting process at a policy-making level considering a change in the rules affecting an operational situation, one needs to know about at least three rules: (1) the rule prescribing the proportion of individuals who must agree prior to changing a rule (e.g. 50 per cent plus 1, 2/3, or unanimity); (2) the quorum rule (e.g. how many must be present at the time of the vote?); and (3) the reversion rule (e.g. what happens if agreement is not reached?). The effect of changing one rule depends on the specific attributes of the other two rules.
2. Sida has, for example, identified the evaluative criteria of sustainability as being of major interest in sponsoring this study (E. Ostrom *et al.* 2002).
3. Indigenously evolved institutions may not be efficient, given a current problem situation. They do, however, provide a set of understandings from which to draw on in crafting better adapted solutions to extant problems of collective action (see Shivakumar 2003).
4. Ngaido and Kirk (2001) provide an excellent review of the failed efforts of many African countries to solve rangeland problems through centralized interventions as well as the recent paradigm change to radical decentralization, which they argue will also be an inadequate institutional structure for a phenomena that is complex and many layered.
5. Part of the problem with applying this theory to the real world is the operationalization of privileged groups. All communities have relatively richer and poorer members, but which should be considered privileged? How much should the difference in assets be to earn the attribute of privileged? These are challenging problems in operationalizing these concepts.
6. Hayek (1952), in his essay "Scientism and the Study of Society," refers to "Scientism" as the uncritical application of the methods, or of the supposed methods, of the natural sciences to problems for which they are not apt.
7. These problems are sometimes referred to as "post-contractual opportunism."
8. Campbell (1995: 339) points to an interesting example of the use of small fees to reduce moral hazard problems in Canada.

In 1992 Quebec introduced a $1.60 charge per prescription for residents over sixty-five. This group had been receiving free medicine. The fee was expected to save the province $16 million a year, but the annual savings have been closer to $40 million. A resident who had been customarily getting refills "just in case" would now wait until it was clear that the medication was needed—and so on.

9. The "career concerns" models of Holmstrom (1982*a,b*) and the multitask model of Holmstrom and Milgrom (1991) examine what happens when agents are motivated more by the hope of demonstrating their abilities than by immediate monetary rewards. As Seabright (2002: 29) argues, the strategic selection of which tasks to do and how to do them "is particularly applicable to the case of aid agencies whose staff tend to be salaried rather than paid in a manner directly linked to ostensible performance." Convincing superiors that work is outstanding leads to an input bias—which is more easily monitored— as contrasted to focusing on outcomes such as sustainability—which is far more difficult to monitor.

3

Better Development Through Better Policy?

Development Aid's Challenges at the Collective-Choice Level

3.1. INTRODUCTION

One of the arguments in the last chapter was that some social networks can overcome particular information and motivation problems of joint action: "It takes a village" can be true for issues at a local level. To achieve broader development goals, however, generally requires collective-action institutions at a higher level of social organization. Work in the new institutional economics has begun to provide theory and empirical evidence demonstrating that clearer property rights, better-functioning courts, more accountable governance, and more transparent economic systems generate more productive outcomes over time (Martens *et al.* 2002). These institutions require decisions to be made at the collective-choice—or policy—level. In aid-recipient countries, however, such institutions are often missing, weak, or bad. This chapter shifts the focus from the operational-level challenges of development aid to the collective-choice level, where individuals make decisions about these crucial institutions.

The collective-choice level presents obstacles both similar and different to the operational level. Similar to the operational level, motivational and information problems haunt the efforts of policy-making bodies at the collective-choice level. In addition to these problems, policymakers also have relationships with the public at the operational level, which can allow officials to impose costs (corruption, poor policy, etc.) on citizens. Changing the rules (institutions) at the policy-making level may potentially improve joint outcomes substantially. However, perverse incentive structures at this level can just as well throw up sizeable barriers to solving the collective-action problems of development. Depending on their actions, international development agencies can exacerbate these obstacles or help to reduce them.

In this chapter, we explore the obstacles and possibilities for development at the collective-choice level. In Section 3.2, we discuss the collective-choice level and the difficulties most likely to thwart efforts to solve collective-action situations in recipient countries. Section 3.3 examines how the reality of weak, bad, or missing institutions hampers development efforts. We unpack the particular challenges arising at the collective-choice level in Section 3.4, emphasizing the (by now) familiar categories of information and motivation problems. In Section 3.5, we pay particular attention to how donors change the development context. As in Chapter 2, we conclude with questions to be asked about development aid in an effort to improve its design and outcome.

3.2. CHANGING UNPRODUCTIVE SITUATIONS AT THE COLLECTIVE-CHOICE LEVEL

Chapter 2 described many unproductive collective-action situations that are often found in aid-receiving countries. Using the Institutional Analysis and Development (IAD) framework, we can expect to find the causes of the unproductiveness of these situations in (1) the particular configurations of the underlying material or physical events (the "nature of the goods" involved), (2) the specific sets of rules-in-use affecting the structure of the situations (number of participants, their actions, information, outcomes, payoffs, etc.), (3) the community attributes, and/or (4) the resulting action situation. To change poor outcomes, therefore, requires either a change in the context and/or the direct modification in the action situation (by changing the specific actors, for example). Few of these changes are "quick fixes" that can be imposed from the outside without the informed agreement and active participation of those involved. Since it is difficult to change the nature of the goods or the attributes of a community, most efforts to improve the outcomes of operational situations involve efforts to change the rules affecting these situations. This is the realm of the collective-choice level.

The collective-choice level is where individuals create rules that govern operational-level behavior: both a village council and a government ministry can be considered collective-choice level arenas. At this level, individuals can, for example, solve operational-level collective-action problems through the creation of new rules that facilitate or promote informal face-to-face discussions at the micro-level. But coordinated strategies and shared norms may not solve many collective-action problems, especially those that encompass large numbers of heterogeneous actors or goods, or that require complex organization between different groups of actors. Such situations call for collective-choice level decisions to be made within different groups, such as a government or nongovernmental agency. The distribution of authority to engage in collective-choice arenas results from an amalgam of decisions made at what we call the constitutional-choice level: this is the level where individuals produce rules about who participates over what decisions at the collective-choice level. (We generally do not discuss the constitutional level in this study since most development assistance agencies avoid projects that might incur constitutional changes in a recipient country.)[1]

In seeking solutions to problems of collective action, policymakers and development agency staff face three general types of problems. First, a solution is unknown; second, a proposed solution may not work (or even backfire); third, a solution may exist but is not adopted.

In the first problem, solutions may not be obvious to either an analyst or a decision maker. One example is designing institutions so that forest users are sufficiently motivated to undertake sustainable resource management (harvesting at sustainable yields, protecting biodiversity, and conserving other ecosystem services). Forests produce different types of goods at different rates. The end consumers of forest goods and services may live right next to, or thousands of miles from, the forest itself. While both benefit from forest products, it is the local user who bears the lion's share of the costs of sustainable management. How the distant beneficiaries can be involved in providing the local users with sufficient benefits to motivate them to continue investing in sustainable harvesting practices is an extremely challenging problem of institutional design. Considerable controversy currently exists regarding the most appropriate mix of rules, and about which public and/or private organizations would be most likely to accomplish these difficult objectives (see Gibson *et al.* 2000). Such collective-action problems have no agreed-upon policy solution; they are likely to persist until more experience and research can help guide future policies.

A second problem occurs when actors implement policies that create incentives that lead to perverse results. Some putative solutions can themselves trigger dysfunctional processes where, for example, a few benefit at the expense of many others. Those who favor strong state intervention to cure unproductive situations sometimes find that such "solutions" only lead to the problem re-emerging, making this state-centered approach ephemeral.

Pritchett and Woolcock (2004) point out that, all too many times, the focus on a single solution as a panacea can instead be the source of even further problems. They illustrated the overreliance on top-down planning that developed a "needs–supply civil service solution" in the rural water supply, irrigation, education, agricultural extension, and family planning sectors of many recipient countries. Having detailed the many failures of these development projects, they conclude that:

> The same thing happened in all these sectors because the common structure of the solution created the common conditions for its failure—namely, the lack of feedback mechanisms and modes for engagement of citizens in either controlling the state or directly controlling providers allowed systemic problems of organizational design to overwhelm logistics. But the logic of the solution is so seductive to governments (and donors) alike that it has taken decades of painful and expensive failures in sector after sector to see that the problem is not just a few mistakes here and there, but that as an approach to development, it can be fundamentally wrong-headed from top to bottom. (ibid.: 199)

They point to many reasons for the overreliance on this type of top-down project design including the appearance of rationality, modernity, and legibility of such projects. Another reason pointed to is that "complete government control from the top down meant the central government was able to reward supporters and punish detractors" (ibid.: 199).

A classic case of perverse incentives is using the state as a monopsony for staple foods. While this strategy might decrease the volatility of prices that farmers receive for their crops, it may also destroy the incentives for farmers to grow crops if the price is set too low (e.g. Bates 1981). The unintended consequence of this policy could be insufficient food to meet the demand of a country's citizens over the long term.

Food relief programs similarly face the problem of possibly destroying the market for crops while trying to alleviate hunger.

Development assistance in some countries has created moral hazard problems at the collective-choice level. Dependence on external funding enables recipient governments to greatly expand their spending and their size without establishing new policies to expand the productive sectors of a country that would eventually generate a stronger tax base and revenue to the government. Dependence fosters further dependence—the so-called "flypaper effect." In a study of the expenditure patterns of 120 lower- to middle-income nations from 1970–1999, Remmer (2004) finds strong evidence that aid dependence is related to increased national government expenditures in lower- to middle-income nations. Even more unsettling is her finding that "aid dependence is linked with reduced revenue generation. The implication is that aid dependence fosters more aid dependence, rather than the realization of the developmental goals sought via development assistance" (ibid.: 87).

The third problem occurs when the solution technology is well-known but not adopted. If the solution is not too costly, then nonadoption generally occurs when decision makers fear the loss of substantial personal benefits (monetary or political) by making the change. Take, for instance, the case where a donor constructs large-scale, power-generating facilities in a developing country (as in the case in India, which we examine in Chapter 9). Upon a project's initiation, recipient country politicians face few incentives to price electricity to cover the costs of operation, maintenance, and replacement over the long run. In their early days, the facilities run well, industry responds to the availability of power, and low-cost access to power by the urban poor is immensely popular. Later, however, power failures become increasingly frequent due to inadequate levels of maintenance, repair, and reinvestment. The benefits of the donor's investment prove to be unsustainable due to government officials' disinclination to charge the true costs of the facility to its users.

The basic solution to the lack of funds to sustain power and other utilities in developing countries is relatively well-known: power needs to be metered and charged to its users. Such a scheme leads to more efficient power use, so that the government (or private supplier) can cover its marginal and fixed costs of producing and distributing electricity. However, in cases where users have been subsidized for a long period of time—and when an economy does not generate a high standard of living—users of electricity, from the poor to the rich, strongly resist any effort to "get the prices right." Further, as long as an external donor is willing to provide new funds to maintain, refurbish, and rebuild power facilities (i.e. as long as the donor faces a Samaritan's Dilemma as described in Chapter 2), national leaders face high costs and few immediate benefits moving to a more economically efficient policy. The difficult questions in resolving inadequate pricing arrangements concern how to get broad agreement supporting an economically efficient solution and how to determine who pays which costs.

Recent studies by scholars at the World Bank (Dollar and Levin 2004) do allow for a somewhat more optimistic picture for the future. Dollar and Levin (2004) examine the allocation of aid for 41 donors using a policy selectivity index. The index is intended to measure the extent of targeting of aid to countries that have adopted policies evaluated as leading to sustainable development. Dollar and Levin conclude that "aid was earlier allocated indiscriminately but that today, there is a clear tendency to allocate more assistance to poor countries that have reasonably good economic governance" (ibid.: 13). They point out, however, that some of the larger donors, including the United States, do not use selectivity in their aid decisions.

3.3. MISSING, WEAK, OR BAD INSTITUTIONS

Many scholars argue that development results from a broad set of institutional arrangements that facilitate a wide diversity of enforceable contractual arrangements (e.g. de Soto 2000; North 1990, 1994). When embedded in an open public realm with an effective property-rights system, and an available and fair court system, individuals can build trusting relationships that enable them to increase the benefits that they jointly obtain. When trustworthy behavior and a reputation for being fair and honest can make a difference in long-run opportunities for individuals, strong norms reinforcing these behaviors grow and develop over time.

In contrast, in most countries receiving large amounts of development aid such institutions are missing, weak, or bad. In countries with missing institutions, individuals must deal primarily with their own family and networks of friends and neighbors to solve some of these basic problems. Pockets of highly productive and ingenious solutions to some of these problems exist. As we have discussed, however, such solutions are usually limited in scope and time.

In countries with weak or bad institutions, there may be an extensive public sector with many formal laws that purport to help solve some of these problems. Rather than facilitate solutions, however, such public sectors may use their authority against those who are trying to create productive opportunities for themselves and others. For example, underpaid public servants may resort to obtaining additional funds from side-payments extracted from citizens who need official approval for some action; the more steps required to comply with formal laws, the more opportunities exist for citizens to become discouraged (and for public officials to extract side-payments). In a sobering example of this problem, de Soto (2000) documents the 728 different bureaucratic steps required by the city of Lima for a resident to obtain a legal title to a home.[2]

Why are institutions sometimes bad, weak, or nonexistent? Changing the rules used at an operational level may improve joint outcomes substantially. However, if the incentives are perverse in the collective-choice arena, then it will be difficult to create policies (collective choices) that can solve these problems. Here, we again find basic problems resulting from motivational and informational sources. Informational problems may be especially difficult given the uncertainties associated with major institutional changes.

When a public authority enforces rules, individuals have an incentive to propose rules that give them advantages over others. Profits greater than those that would be available from an open, competitive process are referred to as *rents*; the process of seeking rules to give these advantages is *rent-seeking* behavior. Successful rent-seeking strategies may lead to substantial costs imposed on others. Those who have been successful in the past in obtaining privileges may then become entrenched in a patron–client system whereby the elite keep themselves in an advantaged system by distributing rents to their clients in return for their support. Reaching agreement on an appropriate change in rules and then monitoring and enforcing those rules in an efficient, fair, and open manner is thus an extremely challenging task at the collective-choice level. It may require defining new positions of authority and ensuring that actors in these new positions face appropriate incentives and have sufficient information to act in a manner more consistent with reaching the goals spelled out in public policy. (We illustrate this process in Chapter 10 with our case study of the Zambian Energy Regulation Board.) Making these changes sustainable over time is an even more difficult challenge. (We take up the problem of holding public officials accountable in Chapter 7.)

3.4. MOTIVATIONAL PROBLEMS AT THE COLLECTIVE-CHOICE LEVEL

As discussed in Chapter 2, development agencies and analysts trying to understand where and when projects and programs can lead to sustainable outcomes must understand the motivational and informational problems that beneficiaries face at the operational level. They also need to grasp the motivational and informational problems at the collective-choice level.

3.4.1. *Rules as Public Goods*

The new or reformed rules intended to govern an operational situation can have the characteristics of a public good. That is, the use of a rule by one person does not subtract from the availability of the rule for others, and all actors in the situation receive the benefit in future rounds regardless of whether they spent any time and effort trying to devise new rules. Thus, devising new rules is a second-order, public-good problem. Even when the actors who are directly involved have the authority to make their own collective-choice rules, one cannot automatically presume that they will invest in this costly effort (all those meetings) and reach agreement on a new set of rules to improve their joint outcome.

Several factors may help overcome this collective-action problem. Actors who have interacted with one another over a long time period and expect to continue these interactions far into the future—in other words, they do not heavily discount the future—are more likely to invest in the time and effort to propose, discuss, argue, and eventually reach an agreement on a new or revised set of rules. Repeated interactions also allow actors to gradually adjust the rules to produce better outcomes (Andersson 2004; Kanbur and Sandler 1999; E. Ostrom 1990). Groups communicating with others facing similar problems can learn a larger repertoire of actions. Public entrepreneurs play a particularly important role by investing their time and energy exploring the advantages and costs of diverse rules (Kuhnert 2001). The possibility of creating a formal, compensated leadership position in the future affects the likelihood of their willingness to invest resources in these costly transactions (Ueda 2001).

3.4.2. *Rent Seeking*

Rules may be public goods, but they also have distributional consequences at the operational level. Such consequences do not go unnoticed, and they complicate the design of new institutions greatly (Knight 1992). Rent-seeking individuals may create rules that augment their fortunes, while hindering the economic development of the broader society.

Rents are returns to activities that cannot be competed away in an open competitive process (Krueger 1993). In an open competitive market for homogeneous private goods, the first entrants may be able to capture substantial rents, but eventually these will be competed away. If one producer can obtain a monopoly on the right to produce a product, however, this artificial scarcity can be exploited by charging higher prices than would occur under competition. Governments create barriers to trade that confer considerable benefits to protected sectors and thus motivate them to engage in rent-seeking behavior.

Rent seeking occurs on both sides of the donor–recipient relationship. For donors, tied-aid—aid that requires the recipient to contract with the donor country for supplies and staff—constitutes rent seeking. By offering tied-aid to recipient countries, the donor country is effectively subsidizing their export of goods and services since the recipient country must purchase these from the donor country (P. Jones 1995). Producer groups actively campaign in the donor country for international assistance to be in this form. Exporters are also likely to adjust their pricing policies when supplying recipient countries. Because of the rent seeking involved in tied-aid and the consequent loss of value of this form of assistance, many (but not all) donor countries have attempted to reduce this form of international assistance.

Problems of rent seeking in development assistance have plagued multinational, as well as bilateral, donors. James Putzel (1998) reports that the office of the UK Permanent Representative to the European Union (EU) encourages British citizens and firms to propose development projects that will generate revenue for them. The framework contracts used early in the cycle of identifying EU development projects, Putzel argues, also encourage extensive rent seeking by EU community businessmen leading to inefficient outcomes in regard to project choice.

3.4.3. *Corruption*

Another challenge facing the collective-choice level is the official who may hold up the creation or implementation of rules unless illegal rewards are made available to them. The level of corruption in a country has not generally been taken into account in planning development assistance, at least not formally. Van de Walle (2001: 188) has pointed out that Cameroon, in spite of being one of the most corrupt countries in the world, was rewarded with a major benefit by the donor community:

In events a couple of weeks apart in the fall of 1999, the Western donors announced that Cameroon was slated to be among the first nations to receive significant debt relief in the context of the revised highly indebted poor countries (HIPC) initiative; and Transparency International (TI) announced that Cameroon had for the second year in a row received the dubious distinction of ranking as the most corrupt nation in the world in the annual TI Corruptions Perceptions Index.

Robert Klitgaard (1988, 1995) has also looked closely at the problem of aid and corruption. He argues that it is neither inevitable nor intractable. He stresses, however, that understanding incentives, monopoly, openness of information, and accountability is needed to reduce corruption to a low level. (An immense literature exists on the problem of corruption in both donor and recipient countries, but time and space limitations force us to recommend that the interested reader consult Shleifer and Vishny (1998), NORAD (2000), Wade (1985, 1989), and Chambers (1988).)

3.5. INFORMATIONAL PROBLEMS AT THE COLLECTIVE-CHOICE LEVEL

In addition to the motivation problems identified above, collective-choice decisions also face the possibility of substantial missing and asymmetric information.

3.5.1. *Missing and Asymmetric Information*

Actors directly involved in an operational situation often organize themselves to make collective choices. When close to the operational situation, actors receive feedback more rapidly; they do not need to have it conveyed to them by others. In turn, they can respond quickly. In this way, the learning process can be brisk and increasingly efficient.

When those who make the collective-choice decisions are not directly involved, they instead depend on various mechanisms for conveying information. The further away these decision makers are from the situation, the more are the number of links through which information must pass. Not only is there a loss of information from these links but there is also the possibility for some individuals to be strongly advantaged by one set of rules as contrasted to another; they would seek to convince legislators and others involved in distant collective choices to pass rules advantageous to themselves. Often such "favors" can be bought.

Fiscal illusion

When obligations to a collectivity are collected in the form of monetary resources, rather than as labor or material inputs, knowledge of how these funds are spent and what they produce is extremely difficult to gather. A fiscal illusion can be created that the government is doing great things—in the next locality or district—even though little can be observed in a home district. Cynical taxpayers may seek ways to reduce their tax burden, as they do not see real benefits coming from their payments. Thus, if public sector collective choices lead to a serious fiscal illusion, the long-term process leads to an impoverished public sector.

3.5.2. *Translating Preferences into Outcomes—The Impossibility Theorem*

Many collective-choice action situations use a decision rule that aggregates individual actions (such as votes) into a summary action for the group as a whole. While voting is indeed an essential mechanism to give voice to a large number of people about the rules that they themselves will be governed by, all voting systems are, themselves, besieged by various difficulties in aggregating individual preferences into a stable, efficient outcome (Monroe forthcoming). Kenneth Arrow (1951) established in his famous impossibility theorem that no voting rule could take individual preferences, which were themselves well-ordered, in a transitive manner and guarantee to produce a similar well-ordered transitive outcome for the group as a whole.[3]

When groups have very similar preferences, choosing an action or policy may not be too difficult. But in groups with considerable disagreement regarding the benefits and costs of different actions and outcomes, there may be no rule that will guarantee a "final" settlement of a dispute. The outcome is highly dependent on the order in which alternatives are presented for a vote and the extent to which voters misrepresent their true preferences by strategic voting. Therefore, we cannot simply rely on a mechanism like majority vote to ensure that stable efficient rules are selected at a collective-choice level. Thus, once an agreement has been reached that collective decisions will be made according to majority rules (or any other voting rule that might be selected), all voting institutions can be manipulated by those who control the agenda (Baumgartner and Jones 1993; Riker 1982; Romer and Rosenthal 1978; Shepsle 1979).

3.6. ENTER THE DONOR

We have now examined many of the typical operational and policy situations that exist everywhere in the world. Many of the unproductive outcomes that can happen in these situations have been improved in developed countries due to the inclusion of citizens in choices about the rules that affect them. Because rules influence the distribution of costs and benefits, the process of changing rules is never a one-way street toward ever-more efficient and fair outcomes. The broad trajectory in more developed countries has been, however, toward creating nested sets of institutional arrangements that together tend to create many situations that generate positive outcomes for most participants.

One of the major differences between developed and developing countries is the prevalence of dysfunctional situations in the latter. When a donor enters a recipient country to try to help, it enters a diversity of operational and policy situations that may be difficult to change. Aid agencies "are not just rational, neutral tools of policy makers and as such external to the problems of development" (Quarles van Ufford *et al.* 1988: 11). As demonstrated by Gardner and Waller in the formal game-theoretical analysis in Chapter 5, the entry of a donor into ongoing situations of the type outlined in Chapters 2 and 3 can lead to an improvement, no change, or a deterioration of the base situation.

The donor always adds at least a second layer to the original action situation. Donors do not often choose to be a participant in the base situations, but only after the foundational collective choices have been made. The donor's presence always alters, for better or worse, existing incentives. And even if the presence of the donor can shift incentives toward more productive outcomes in the short run, the perverse incentives generated by the domestic institutions may be resistant to long-term change.

One of the counterintentional impacts of development assistance can be the result of moral hazards introduced by the aid process itself. Financing gap models have been used by many donors, including Sweden (Andersen 1996), since they were so strongly recommended in the development economics literature. These models are the academic foundation for a method used by advisors to calculate the estimated amount of support needed by a recipient country to achieve a targeted level of growth (Chenery and Strout 1966). The underlying financing gap model has been questioned by empirical evidence that external aid funds have not led to a significant and positive effect on investment.[4] This method of calculating aid also tends to generate a moral hazard. "There is also a moral hazard problem with giving aid on the basis of a 'financing gap.' Recipient countries will have an incentive to maintain or increase the 'financing gap' by low-savings (i.e., high consumption) so as to get more aid" (Easterly 1999).

At a collective-choice level, aid may be allocated to certain sectors, allowing recipient country officials to decide on the merits of alternative projects. (After all, this is what devolving some ownership over aid to recipients means.) But, of course, these officials have their own interests at heart, which may or may not facilitate the long-term development goals of the donor. Sweden's aid agency—Sida—often attempts to avoid "power asymmetries" in bilateral relations with aid recipient countries by vesting project ownership with recipient country ministries and bureaucratic agencies. And yet, such a policy can exacerbate already acute power asymmetries within the recipient's own political economy by giving the resources to the most powerful, and, in so doing actually undermine sustainability.

In fact, politicians in highly centralized political systems without the check of meaningful democratic elections and governance arrangements at multiple levels are more likely to use their power over the distribution of development aid to enhance or maintain their status as patron (e.g. Coolidge and Rose-Ackerman 2000; Gibson and Hoffmann 2005; Joseph 1987; Robinson 2003). In such cases, politicians will use aid to distribute as rewards to clients and followers. In countries where representative elections are seen as legitimate, politicians may seek to target development projects in certain electoral districts—a phenomenon better known as pork-barrel politics (Mayhew 1986; Stein and Bickers 1995). If, on the other hand, ethnicity is important in national politics, politicians may try to deliver the benefits of development aid to their clan or tribe. In each case, politicians exercise power over the nature and distribution of aid. The important finding in all these cases is that politicians have an incentive to target development aid to their followers and supporters, who in turn are defined by the particular economic, political, and cultural institutions of a country.

We have mentioned—and will explore in greater detail in Chapter 9—the example of how the price of electricity is used distributively by politicians. In addition to electric power, elected politicians also "play" around with the prices established for water used for irrigation. During elections in the Philippines in the early 1990s, several candidates for office made a pledge to farmers that they would vote to eliminate the irrigation service fee that was at that time charged to all farmers. "They said farmers were too poor and shouldn't have to pay the fee" (Vermillion 2001: 188). Quite surprisingly, in this instance, there were large demonstrations of farmers in Manila soon thereafter who protested against the elimination of the fee. The farmers argued that "their payment of the fee was their only basis for demanding an acceptable irrigation service from the government. In their minds, payments of the fee established their right to an acceptable service" (ibid.: 188). In this case, the farmers were asking to be real joint owners of systems rather than just dependents on the generosity (or the receipt of illegal payments) of others.

Politicians in Taiwan, however, did not learn from this lesson. In the early 1990s, politicians argued that farmers were facing hard times and had difficulty making a living. They also argued to eliminate the small fees that the farmers were paying. "In 1993, after much political negotiation, the government agreed to pay the irrigation fees on behalf of the farmers" (Lam forthcoming: ms. p. 8). Raised at first by politicians from one party, both parties joined the campaign and the fees were cancelled soon after the next election. At an earlier juncture, Taiwan irrigation systems were among the most efficient in Asia (Wade 1995). The cancellation of the fees led to a steady decline in the maintenance of the systems, and the cost of water supply is on the rise. Systems that had been noted for their efficiency were being destroyed because politicians wanted to "help" the farmer as a way of gaining electoral support. As one local official expressed it: "The problem facing irrigation management at the field level is not simply a matter of finding one or two farmers to serve as [local group] leaders, the more serious challenge is that nowadays fewer and fewer farmers have good knowledge of their own systems and understand how to engage with one another in organizing collective actions" (quoted in Lam forthcoming: ms. p. 12).

Bureaucrats also hold preferences over the types of aid given by donors. The kinds of aid preferred relate to the incentives that specific bureaucrats face in their various positions (Moe 1990*a,b*). In general, top-level bureaucrats are interested in expanding their power. Thus, they are more interested in projects that extend their duties, staffs, and budgets. Lower-level bureaucrats, meanwhile, see donor-funded aid projects as career opportunities, and as opportunities for getting extra (legal or illegal) income (Gibson 1999).

Given the problems outlined in this chapter, creating rules at the collective-choice level to improve the operational situations beneficiaries face in recipient countries is difficult due to extant motivational and informational incentives. In the hopes of helping the many recipient country officials, donors, and policy analysts who are trying to improve the outcomes obtained from development assistance, we have summarized some of the lessons of this chapter into a set of questions in Box 3.1.

Box 3.1. *Specific questions all development projects should ask regarding the collective-choice level*

Below we try to incorporate the lessons of this chapter into a series of questions that donors (or analysts) can ask about the collective-choice level to improve the outcomes from their development aid:

- What incentives have precluded beneficiaries from resolving their own collective-action problems at a collective-choice level in the absence of aid?
- What is the structure of incentives generated by the extant government institutions for the actors involved with the proposed aid (government, donor, beneficiary)?
- Which form of aid will most likely succeed in achieving long-term development given the baseline institutions already extant in the recipient country?
- Is there a possibility for aid to improve a poorly functioning baseline institution? Or could aid help to produce an important policy that had not been created due to its status as a public good?
- How might the aid be designed to mitigate the worst effects of its distribution as a political good?
- What is the structure of information flow and how might it be redesigned to increase its volume and accuracy to the donor (and government and beneficiary)?

NOTES

1. Constitutional processes, however, have received considerably more attention since the influential book *Calculus of Consent* by Buchanan and Tullock (1962). The journal *Constitutional Political Economy* contains important contemporary work on this level of analysis.
2. De Soto (2000) also clocked the amount of time that it takes a typical entrepreneur in Lima to get through all of the legal steps required to set up a sewing machine garment factory in Lima. "We discovered that to become legal took more than 300 days, working 6 hours a day. The cost: thirty-two times the monthly minimum wage" (p. 189).
3. By transitive, one means that if A is preferred to B and B is preferred to C, A is preferred to C. A well-ordered preference function meets these criteria as well as the criterion of being complete. A complete ordering is nothing more than stating that an actor can completely rank all outcomes as either preferred one to another or in some cases as being equally desirable (or undesirable).
4. Easterly (1999) shows that only 6 out of 88 countries receiving aid from 1965 to 1995 show a significant, positive relationship greater than one (meaning that there were at least some funds added to investment beyond the aid itself) between Overseas Development Assistance and investment/GDP. What is quite disturbing is that 36 out of 88 countries show a negative and significant relationship between gross domestic investment and Overseas Development Assistance.

4

Sorting Out the Tangle: Incentives Across Action Situations in Development Aid

4.1. INTRODUCTION

In Chapters 2 and 3, we identified many of the hurdles that confront development aid by our initial analysis of separate action situations. Of course, international development aid is really a set of linked action situations, with multiple actors and arenas that cross national borders. How these action situations are linked also greatly affects the outcomes of development aid since the effectiveness of a given system depends on the way its action situations are linked together (Simon 1965, 1972). An effectively structured federal governance system, for example, links national, regional, and local units so that each can undertake those activities for which it is most efficient (V. Ostrom 1997). When this is the case, each unit provides goods and services complementary to those provided by other levels of government. Information flows can lead to greater accountability than could be achieved in the absence of an overall system. Of course, it is also possible to link units of government in a federal system so that these benefits are not achieved, and the overall results are less than could be achieved by either a fully centralized or a fully decentralized system of governance.

The conventional way of thinking about the linkages among action situations involved in development assistance is as a "chain of aid delivery," which we will discuss in Section 4.2. This stresses the primacy of the donor as a principal who must work through a series of hierarchically organized agents to reach the final beneficiary (see Figure 4.1). In an era when most donors are stressing the importance of ownership, however, this top-down way of thinking about a chain of relationships is a particularly inappropriate representation. In fact, the only two-way relationships in the chain of aid are those between an individual donor and other donors. Even the recipient government is viewed here as being no more than an agent of a donor government. While this may be, in fact, how some view the process of development cooperation, we think it is more valuable to think about a set of nested situations that may take on any of a variety of productive or unproductive relationships.

In our effort to understand the complexities of development cooperation, we have developed a schema that we call the International Development Cooperation Octangle—or "the Octangle," for short. Section 4.2 derives the Octangle from its component parts. In essence, we scale up our analysis so as to look at linked action

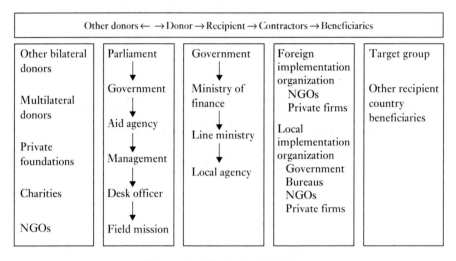

Figure 4.1. *The chain of aid delivery*

situations rather than isolated situations. We identify eight important actors within the development cooperation system and place each one in their appropriate set of relationships. Rather than the metaphor of the aid delivery chain, which brings to mind linear linkages from one actor to the next, the Octangle shows the more realistic tangle of relationships involved in aid. For example, whereas the donor pays for the services of a contractor, the nominal principal is the recipient government. Meanwhile, the consultant, typically, has more information about ground realities than do officials of the donor or of the recipient agencies—or of the citizens of either country. The result of this tangle of relationships facilitates a situation in which many individuals may have *de jure* responsibility for ensuring the effectiveness of aid, even using language in aid contracts like "ownership" and "sustainability," but no one is actually held accountable for its performance.

4.2. THE CHAIN OF AID DELIVERY

The aid delivery process is often perceived as if it were a linear chain that links a donor government to a recipient country beneficiary via various concatenated intermediary organizations. According to this interpretation, the intermediaries then would include (an assortment of) recipient government ministries and agencies, nongovernmental organizations (NGOs), other donors, and private implementation contractors. As schematized in Figure 4.1, international development cooperation involves a very large number of actors.[1] In this representation, the internal workings of the donor government and agency appear remote from the problems beneficiaries face in the recipient country. By conceiving of development cooperation in this way, donors may infer (incorrectly) that the incentive structures of their internal aid-disbursing operations are far-distanced, and thus insulated and largely unrelated to problems of aid sustainability on the recipient side.

Figure 4.1 portrays how aid funds and responsibilities are transmitted, left to right, from the donor to the beneficiary through intermediary organizations. It highlights, mainly, the principal–agent relationships involved in development cooperation. While many of the links in aid do involve a principal–agent structure, other types of relationships—including Samaritan's Dilemmas, along with the whole host of other collective-action problems identified in Chapter 3—are also often involved. The perception of aid being delivered in a chain-like fashion, thus, does not fully reveal the varied institutional contexts within which each of these multiple actors in development cooperation interact, in practice, to each other.

To understand how incentives enhance or detract from aid sustainability, we first need to identify the major types of actors involved in the aid system. Eight types of actors (many of whom are themselves composed of multiple actors) have a repeated strategic role to play in a series of linked action situations. The eight major actors are:

(1) the donor government;
(2) the recipient government;
(3) other donors;
(4) the donor's international development agency;
(5) sectoral ministries and agencies within the recipient government;
(6) third-party implementing organizations, including NGOs and private consultants and contractors;
(7) organized interest groups and civil society organizations within the donor and recipient countries; and finally
(8) the target beneficiaries.

Second, we need to see how these actors in their situations are connected to each other. Beyond the internal structure of any one of the situations involved in development aid, each situation is complexly interlinked to others. The nature of each linkage affects the incentives of those involved and the sustainability of the programs they design or implement. Our Octangle captures a simplified picture of the configuration of linked individual situations among these eight major actors.

The sustainability of aid depends on how incentives structure interactions between or among the key corporate and individual actors involved in development cooperation. These structures may result from a conscious effort to design and impose rules governing donor–recipient relations, or from an evolutionary process designed by no one in particular. They may involve asymmetries in power or asymmetries in information, pose moral hazard problems, or yield a Samaritan's Dilemma. (Chapter 2 provides a discussion of these basic problematic situations.)

4.3. THE INTERNATIONAL DEVELOPMENT COOPERATION OCTANGLE

The International Development Cooperation Octangle—by which we intend to convey the tangle of interrelationships among the important aid actors—provides an alternative conceptual scheme to that of the Chain of Delivery image.

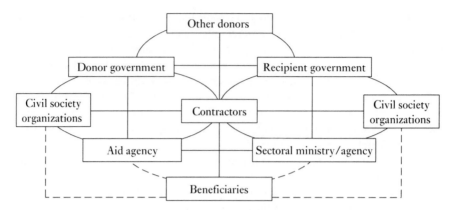

Figure 4.2. *The international development cooperation octangle*

4.3.1. *The Full Octangle*

Figure 4.2 brings together the full set of linkages among all eight types of actors involved in the system of international development aid. The reason for exploring the full set of relationships among the major actors involved in international assistance is to examine whether "the system" as a whole creates positive incentives that counteract some of the negative incentives that exist in many of the individual action arenas examined in Chapters 2 and 3. We are responding to the call of many scholars to examine the linkages *among* the major actors in development aid and not just *within* any one agency (see Tendler 1975, for example). As Quarles van Ufford (1988: 13) expressed the need: "It is vital to study the nature of the inter-organizational linkages between the different levels. In what ways do the agencies influence each other? How autonomous are they, how much do they depend on the others? How is the policy process changed, adapted or even blocked as funds flow from one level to the next?"

While the potential for counteracting negative incentives does exist, it appears that instead of reducing the severity of problems, many of the problems of collective action are accentuated within the larger system of the Octangle.

When conducting an analysis, one may be able to examine only one or two linkages from any node in the Octangle in relative isolation from others. In fact, most actors in development cooperation, surveying the world from where they stand, do not see the full Octangle. Yet, in practice, the actions of all actors (and their component parts) influence each other over time. Each type of actor may thus be able to play a major role in determining whether the results of aid are sustainable over time. We will explore this question as we explore some of the dyads and triads contained within the overall Octangle. We begin our discussion of the Octangle with the donor–recipient dyad—and we will return to a more detailed analysis of this dyad at the end of this chapter.

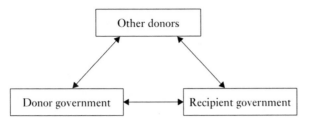

Figure 4.3. *The donor–recipient bargaining arena*

4.3.2. *The Donor–Recipient Negotiation Arena*

In the modern world of sovereign states, donor governments must gain the formal approval of recipient governments for any official bilateral assistance undertaken within a developing country (see Pedersen 1998). Thus, as depicted in Figure 4.3, a core action arena at the international level is that between a donor and the recipient government. The nature of this relationship varies with the power asymmetry between the donor and recipient government, and with the availability of alternative donors. We distinguish three basic configurations of donor–recipient relationships, based on the relative bargaining power of each government.

Strong donor—strong recipient
A relationship between a strong donor and strong recipient can exist if power asymmetries between the recipient government and the donor government are not too significant. Such a relationship can occur in several contexts.

One context is where the recipient government retains strong institutions but requires help to rebuild its physical infrastructure. Here, the recipient government is aware of its needs and the conditions it is willing to accept in negotiating a framework for development cooperation. After the Second World War, for example, the countries of Western Europe, facing massive destruction of their physical infra-structure, received reconstruction aid from the United States. However, many of them had effective systems of government and property rights that survived the war. When strong principals, as in this case, face one another in negotiations, they are frequently able to search out mutually satisfactory outcomes. In such a situation, both countries may find mutually agreeable arrangements that help the recipient country to recover faster and return to being a productive partner with the donor country.

In a second context, a recipient's negotiating strength is improved if it can choose among competing donors. If one donor is not able to meet its needs or its terms, a recipient government can approach others, effectively decreasing the effect of power asymmetries. During the Cold War, for example, many recipient countries sought to augment their bargaining strength by threatening to seek development aid from the other bloc.

The Cold War has ended, but alternatives do exist for recipients to threaten to defect to other donors. Recipients that are less aid-dependent—India, for example—can negotiate from a position of greater strength, particularly vis-à-vis small donors. Donors, though, are increasingly cooperating with each other to regain negotiating strength in this regard. For example, OECD rules, set out in the Helsinki Protocol, attempt to deter donors from bidding against each other to fund large infrastructure projects (OECD 1992).

Of course, a recipient's increased negotiation strength (resulting, say, from the presence of multiple donors) may have nothing to do with increasing the probability that aid will lead to sustainable outcomes. When the recipient country is governed by officials who are primarily interested in seeking out opportunities for private gain, and few institutions are in place to keep these motivations in check, moral hazard problems can become substantial. Take, for example, a case where a strong recipient bargains for financial assistance to reduce pressing budgetary constraints. A donor obliges, but on condition that the recipient takes up certain reforms. The aid immediately relieves a budget constraint faced by the agents of the recipient government. Yet, without this constraint, the recipient government may not implement needed reforms—even when these reforms were included in the aid agreement. There is, as a result, no increase in the productivity of operational situations throughout the private and public economy of the recipient (see Eriksson Skoog 2000: chap. 5).

Strong donor—weak recipient

A weak recipient government is one that may have grown entirely dependent on external assistance, especially if the bulk of that aid is provided by a single donor. A weak recipient that lacks sufficient capacity in economic planning and project administration may not make much effort to prioritize its needs in seeking assistance and will initially accept most plans presented by the donor (Strategy A discussed below—see Figure 4.6). Often in cases where a strong donor faces a weak recipient, most of the initiative in planning development aid must be undertaken by the donor. Negotiations between the two nominal sovereigns can be turned into a principal–agent situation where the donor, as principal, specifies what the recipient country, as agent, must do if it wants to receive development aid. In some cases, where the recipient fails to cooperate to the donor's satisfaction, the donor may impose conditionalities.

This situation can lead to several undesirable outcomes. Reforms attempted by the donor may not be sustained after funding is terminated due to both a lack of commitment and a lack of local credibility (Brunetti and Weder 1994; Johnson and Wasty 1993). The moral hazard problem, implicit in a situation where a recipient government becomes dependent on a donor, may again lead to promises of reform made at the time of aid financing, but then not kept as the donor's attention is diverted to other problems. Still again, the donor could take advantage of the weak position of the recipient and push toward an unfair bargain—including loans given at excessively high interest rates, demands for priority access to key natural resources, and excessive levels of tied-aid.

Even when a donor does not try to take economic or political advantage of a weak recipient, the donor may try to use its position as principal and specify what the recipient government must do to qualify for development aid. Alternatively, the recipient government may grow increasingly dependent on the donor government prolonging an unhealthy relationship between the two countries (Bräutigam 2000; Lensink and White 1999; Sida 1996*a,b*). For a weak recipient, being dependent on a large infusion of foreign aid may also reduce the accountability of its government to its own people, since the leadership is not fiscally accountable to them. An administration that is highly dependent on aid is also more susceptible to top-down decision making within its own governmental apparatus. Consequently, aid projects may not enhance the capabilities of the final beneficiaries or even officials located in local or regional governments. (See our discussion of the Sector-Wide Approach (SWAP) in Chapter 6.)

Several recent studies of aid and economic policy making in recipient countries have stressed, however, that even weak recipients are stronger than expected given their capacity to ignore conditions after agreeing to them in the first place (Devarajan *et al.* 2001; Goldsmith 2001; van de Walle 2001).

Policy processes within recipient countries are driven heavily by domestic factors that have sometimes been consistent with conditions that donors have wanted to place on recipients. Frequently, domestic politics have "trumped" donor efforts to obtain policy reforms. Further, both donors and their critics have avoided discussing the accumulating evidence that donors rarely have asymmetric power to impose policies on reluctant recipients. As Collier (1997: 57) expressed it:

Obviously, the donors did not wish to admit that their conditionality was a charade. Equally, the critics of market-friendly policy reforms—largely Marxist academics and the nongovernmental organization (NGO) community—wanted to attribute the impetus to reform to imperialist donors rather than to African governments. Donors and their critics thus connived at exaggerating the power of donor conditionality out of proportion to its true effects.

Thus, even "weak recipients" have had more power than often thought due to their capacity to continue to receive international assistance from some donors even after not performing on previous agreements.

Enlightened donor—weak recipient

Over the past decade, many donors recognized that recipient reliance on prolonged aid processes induces perverse incentives. As a result, these enlightened donors have tried to change the structure of the aid relationship. According to their official policy, an official recipient owner is designated for each aid intervention. Such owners often are the recipient country ministry or government agency in charge of the sector of aid activity. The purpose of vesting such ownership is to build local capacity and to foster commitment. In this way, development projects and programs are intended to be sustainable after external assistance ends.

While this idea of ownership is commendable, its meaning and interpretation are often lost when translated into development practice. In Chapter 1, we saw that the theoretical conception of ownership is often not very clear. In our effort to define the concept of ownership we presented four dimensions that are involved in the concept. First, the owner needs to enunciate a demand for the provision of financial, material, or technological inputs to be used in their own efforts to find better institutional arrangements for their own problems of collective action. Second, the owner needs to allocate at least some of their own assets to the production of a project or program so that they have a real stake in the way their own and other actors' assets are used. Third, the owners need to consume some of the benefits of a successful project or to share responsibility if the project fails. Fourth, the owner needs to participate in key decisions about continuing or not continuing a project. In practice, all four of these conditions are rarely exercised by the beneficiaries or found together within a single organization, even when a donor sincerely believes that ownership is an essential condition to sustainable development. Consequently, for participants to have a clear picture of who the co-owners of a project are, the parties involved need to have a clear assignment of responsibility as well as knowing the repercussions if they do not discharge their responsibilities. This does not always happen.

Indeed, the current emphasis on "ownership" by nearly all major donors, highlights a tension present in bilateral and multilateral aid processes. This tension arises from the fact that the interests of donors and recipient governments usually do not fully coincide. In the early years of aid, the dominance of donor plans highlighted both the divergence of interests between donor and recipient as well as the weak position of recipient governments. Contemporary policies that stress recipient ownership have neither removed these tensions nor the implicit power that recipients have to renege on a contract. In fact, aid practices of many donors and recipients have not substantially changed (e.g. Mule 1996).

Many donors have tried to avoid playing the strong donor–weak recipient game by encouraging ownership of development projects by recipient governments through the establishment of "country frames" for long-term investments, and by providing technical assistance so that recipients can build their own competence over time. This has worked well in some relationships but less well in others. It turns out to be extremely difficult to engage in dyadic negotiation processes where the donor has access to the funds that the recipient really wants while, at the same time, providing full ownership to the recipient. Sophisticated donors do not want to be Samaritans, repeatedly giving aid to recalcitrant recipients. To avoid the Samaritan's Dilemma, donor governments need to have more control over the process. How can recipient ownership be reconciled with donor control? Indeed, having an official policy to encourage ownership and actually carrying this out within real programs and projects are quite different activities. The specific structure of donor–recipient and donor–recipient–donor relationships varies substantially across projects and programs within the different recipient countries. At the end of this chapter, we expand on the analysis presented above to apply the Institutional Analysis and Development (IAD) framework more specifically to the donor–recipient negotiation arena.

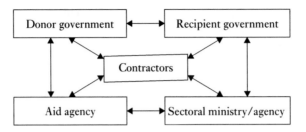

Figure 4.4. *Principal–agent relationships within donor and recipient governments*

4.3.3. *Principal–Agent Arenas Within Donor and Recipient Countries*

In addition to the dyadic and triadic relationships among sovereign governments, there are a series of principal–agent relationships within the ministries of the donor and recipient governments. All of these, in turn, have additional principal–agent relationships with those contractors that are responsible for carrying out a particular project (see Figure 4.4).

In many donor countries, the Finance Ministry and the Foreign Affairs Ministry play a major role in developing foreign aid policies and disbursement priorities. In turn, the domestic donor agency responsible for international aid assumes major responsibility for managing development programs. The recipient country, correspondingly, may specify a single agency, such as the Indian Department of Economic Affairs in the Ministry of Finance, or authorize several internal ministries or agencies to coordinate its aid policy and to undertake the detailed negotiation and oversight of foreign aid programs and projects.

The likelihood of asymmetric information problems within the involved donor agency is often more severe than for other public sector bureaucracies. As we elucidate in Chapter 7, this occurs because there is little correlation between the level of individual effort of the donor agency staff and the effectiveness and sustainability of aid. Gaining a valid and reliable measure of how the entire agency is doing in regard to sustainability in particular, as well as in regard to other broad goals, let alone how one's own contribution is making a difference to the donor agency's mission, is difficult. We focus on these problems in Chapter 7.

Thus, unless the evaluation department of the donor agency has a substantial budget and an imaginative and rigorously trained staff, there will be little systematic feedback to the rank and file. Evaluations undertaken only upon the termination of projects cannot fully serve their purpose unless substantial effort is devoted in the home office to organizing seminars to study project evaluations, to discuss their central lessons, and to build these lessons into the design of new projects. And without such efforts, a donor agency as a whole is not learning much from its own activities. When there is little connection between project evaluations and the work of personnel connected with the project, recipient ownership can come to be a way for donor agency personnel to fault the owner for things that go wrong with the project.

Two of the most important sets of principal–agent relationships within the Octangle occur between (1) politicians and bureaucrats, with the latter less directly dependent on electoral success and (2) contractors and bureaucrats, with the former often being responsible for the implementation of aid activities agreed to by the donor and recipient governments.

Principal–agent relations—politicians and bureaucrats

Principal–agent relationships also occur between political leaders and bureaucrats, where the politicians, as principals, are supposed to make policies and the bureaucrats, as agents, are supposed to carry them out. As in all principal–agent relationships, there is the potential for substantial divergence of preferences and behavior between the principal and the agent. As in all incomplete contracts, therefore, substantial room exists here for moral hazard and other adverse incentive situations (Tirole 1994).

The political leaders of a recipient country may wish to conduct public affairs in a way that benefits a small clique of influential supporters, as Bauer (1971) recognized years ago. Politicians who are worried about political survival may want bureaucrats to implement policies in a way that benefits their own supporters (Geddes 1994). Meanwhile, bureaucrats are more likely to be worried about their own career development. This is especially the case in many recipient countries where bureaucrats are paid poorly and face insecurities of tenure. In such cases, accepting bribes for speeding up licensing procedures or approving projects may become the accepted way of earning sufficient income. Those who resist such practices, where they are common, may find themselves given assignments that lower their chances for upward mobility.

In the donor country, politicians may be interested in their political survival and in convincing the public that taxpayer money is being spent in a wise and efficient manner. Politicians tend to stress the progress that foreign aid is achieving. Officials in a donor country's development agency face their own set of incentives. While they may be protected from arbitrary dismissal, they are charged with administering a set of programs for which there are no known "sure" technologies to achieve economic, political, and social development. Thus, it is difficult for anyone to know if progress is really being made.

Development organizations are directly affected by the basic contradiction of development goals. . . . They are placed between different publics: (a) the public which is at the receiving end of aid, and (b) those who are allocating funds. These two parts of the environment are segregated from each other and do not overlap. The ambiguity greatly affects the ways development organizations operate. (Quarles van Ufford 1988: 21)

A nearly universal pressure exists within almost all development agencies, however, to spend the money that is allocated in one budgetary cycle, as parliamentarians are likely to interpret unallocated funds as evidence that the funds are not needed (Catterson and Lindahl 1999; E. Ostrom *et al.* 1993). Indeed, this need to "move the money" is a universal incentive in all public bureaucracies. Such an incentive can lead to particularly perverse outcomes in the context of development cooperation where projects are sometimes selected by the donor country's agency because they involve a large sum of money without the need for an equivalently large amount of time and energy on the part of an agency's officials. As Lavergne (1988: 60) reflected, drawing on a study of Canadian development aid:

Aid agencies are far removed geographically, administratively, and politically from the people of the Third World, the intended beneficiaries of their activities. As a result, the role of aid agencies is, to a large extent merely that of channeling aid funds to other bureaucracies or agencies responsible for the actual implementation of aid projects and programs. Hence, Donors do not so much manage development projects as development funds, and one of the prime objectives is to allocate these funds with as little administrative cost as possible to the government.

For this reason, large infrastructure projects involving donor country contractors are usually more attractive to top management at a donor agency than small projects involving extensive participation of beneficiaries. Large projects move more money. There is political support in the home country for projects undertaken by donor country contractors. In addition, these projects make lower demands on scarce staff time.

Principal–agent relations—owners, donor agencies, and contractors
While ownership may be vested by the donor agency in a ministry or agency of the recipient government, third-party contractors and consultants are often brought in to assist the owner in implementation. Such contractors and consultants may be selected for the project by the donor country's development agency or by a recipient country ministry or agency, or by both. The relationship between these third-party implementing agencies and the donor/recipient ministries is another principal–agent relationship where the interests of all parties have some overlap but also have considerable divergence. Incomplete contracts also characterize all of these relationships (see Murrell 1999 for an extended analysis of the incentives for donors, recipients, and contractors). Ministry officials typically consider projects that proceed according to plan and meet deadlines as successes.

   In the donor country, contracting with an implementing organization may be seen as a way of reducing the influence of unsavory interest groups in the recipient country and reducing the level of corruption. Further, the suppliers of aid services in the donor country—private for-profit firms, NGOs, individual consultants, and some academic institutions—may have close connections to the political leaders of the donor country and may have strongly articulated the need for international assistance in general. Officials in the implementing organization may also share some of the interests of the donors and recipient governments, but also may be interested in expending less effort or resources on this project in order to retain budgetary slack (Salanié 1997). It is also possible that "development bureaucrats can hide behind their consultants" (Epstein 1988: 206) when they turn questions from their own political principals to their long-term consultants to answer.

In some cases, the initiative for an aid-supported activity at a donor agency may have actually come from the potential contractor as this organization, as a business, faces a need to continue implementing projects in its area of expertise. Frequently, the same contractor who designed a project is contracted to carry it out. Given that the officials in both countries' ministries are unlikely to have time to spend informing themselves about the day-to-day problems of implementation, there is considerable asymmetry of information between the implementing agency and the ministries (Laffont and Tirole 1993).

Given the wide diversity of projects funded in a large number of countries, the staff of international development agencies is often stretched to the limit in their effort to stay on top of what is going on. It is almost impossible to achieve the level of monitoring of individual projects that would actually be needed to be completely knowledgeable of how they are operating. The tendency in many development agencies is to rely on certain contractors and NGOs[2] who have developed a reputation for doing good work. It is difficult, moreover, for the staff at the development agency to know what is going on in the field for many of the projects in their portfolios.

Taken together, these considerations can tangle the principal–agent relationships among the development agency, the recipient owner, and the third-party implementer. For example, whereas the development agency pays for the services of a contractor, the nominal principal is the recipient owner. Meanwhile, the consultant, typically, has more information about ground realities than do officials at the development agency or recipient agencies. Such consultants may consequently take on, in effect, some of the development agency's administrative responsibilities. In this case, the nominal owner may look to the consultant as its *de facto* principal. The upshot is that, while many individuals are responsible for ensuring the effectiveness and sustainability of aid, no one is really held accountable.

4.3.4. *Beneficiaries*

The size and definition of aid's beneficiaries vary with the type of assistance provided. In the case of project aid, the beneficiary is most narrowly defined to involve those who are supposed to be helped most directly by the donor intervention. In humanitarian assistance, beneficiaries are those who are displaced or who otherwise suffer the consequences of natural or man-made disasters. Beneficiaries in program aid presumably are a larger group including the ones that benefit from the marginal impact of the increase of spending. Beneficiary groups, thus, can be small or large, and be composed of well-defined or amorphous groupings. As a result, they may have varying degrees of success in recognizing themselves as a part of an identified group and in recognizing the collective-action problems they face. In many recipient countries, however, a large part of the population does not see much of the aid spending at all, or even know of its existence.

Improving the welfare of beneficiaries is the ultimate goal of the donor agency, but feedback links between beneficiaries and a donor are weak to nonexistent. Many activities do not focus on beneficiaries as much as on policy goals. Donor officials find that they are rarely held accountable for the performance of particular projects (see Chapter 7). Media publicity about a particular project can bring unwelcome attention in some cases. Donors frequently fund studies and evaluations of projects, but these occur after the project is completed, are frequently seen as routine exercises that are required for bureaucratic purposes, or do not systematically include the responses of beneficiaries. Discussing the findings of evaluations with the beneficiaries is even rarer (Sida 1999*a*).

In the case of Project Aid, development agencies interact with beneficiaries through contractors and the recipient's ministries and agencies. In the case of humanitarian assistance, for example, the development agency may be directly linked to the target beneficiaries or through a United Nations or NGO relief organization. In the case of program aid, those who actually do receive benefits are only indirectly linked to the donor and recipient governments.

Links between beneficiaries and government

Individuals in beneficiary groups, in theory, are most closely connected to their own governments. The *raison d'être* for government, after all, is to help citizens to work together to recognize and overcome problems of collective action and in this way improve their welfare. Of course, in reality, recipient governments are often not accountable to their citizens. Indeed, many governments may be structured so that those working within it face incentives to act in ways that deter beneficiaries from solving their collective-action problems; other governments exacerbate existing collective-action problems. When a donor provides aid in such a setting—unless the aid itself creates appropriate institutions—it is likely to be unsustainable.

Linking governments to citizens and interest groups

Besides the major actors we have discussed above, the citizens living in both the recipient and donor countries may participate in the aid process in a variety of ways (see Figure 4.5). Organized interest groups are particularly likely to participate in

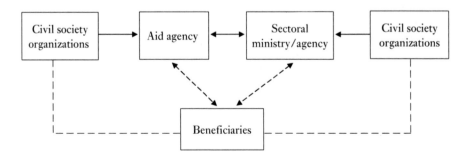

Figure 4.5. *Beneficiaries in development cooperation*

both the donor and recipient countries. Business interests within the donor country have frequently pressured the donor government to negotiate tied-aid, whereby the funds given to the recipient country are used to purchase goods (e.g. tractors, turbines, and other equipment), services (such as training and consulting), and/or staff from the donor country. Now that the Cold War is over, there is less pressure to support political clients of donor countries, but there is increasing pressure to distribute aid in ways that interest groups—for example, family planning advocates, environmentalists, etc.—within the donor country support (see Lancaster 1999*a,b*).

International assistance policies within the donor country are quite different from domestic policies that may be extensively monitored by a variety of groups. Many citizens in the donor country have a sincere interest in redistributing resources from their affluent incomes to help alleviate poverty in recipient countries. There is, however, very little feedback from the supposed recipient country beneficiaries to the donor country taxpayers. As an economist with the Evaluation Unit of the European Commission in Brussels has reflected:

> This lack of direct information feedback makes foreign aid programmes particularly vulnerable to manipulation of information and facilitates the use of persuasion as a political instrument in foreign aid, especially because politicians have privileged access to project evaluation information. Only an explicit information feedback mechanism, labeled generically as "evaluation," can correct information asymmetries in foreign aid. (Martens 2000: 28–9)

Some donor governments, however, have instituted innovative funding mechanisms that seek to strengthen the links between government and civil society in development aid. In the Netherlands, for example, the government channels about 14 per cent of its ODA through Dutch NGOs with activities both in the Netherlands and in developing countries. The government's support is a matching grant, calculated as a percentage of the funds that the NGO raises among its members for a particular project activity. In Sweden, a similar funding scheme provides 80 per cent of total project costs that Swedish NGOs and their counterparts implement in developing countries, leaving the remaining 20 per cent to be covered by the funds raised by NGO members. One of the advantages of such arrangements is that they narrow the distance between citizens and their government in the donor country at the same time as they provide direct support to civil society organizations in recipient countries.

The linkage between government and "civil society" is also one of the important relationships in the building of more effective governance in developing countries. Facilitating ways for citizens to make their voice effective is one of the important steps that both donor and recipient countries need to undertake. However, for some recipient governments, this is a risky step as it means opening political discourse to those who oppose government programs. It also provides opportunities to those who wish to undertake many kinds of local development. As this can strengthen local leadership capabilities, it may be threatening to those in central leadership positions. This link, therefore, may be relatively weak in many developing countries.

4.3.5. *Competition Among Donors*

Even though many donor–recipient negotiations are strictly dyadic, many are, in effect, conducted in a strategic environment where the recipient government can elicit competition among potential donors. Such competition among donors can exacerbate incentive problems among recipients. When the recipient knows that other donors will step in to fund a project even if one threatens credibly to withdraw based on its recipient's poor show of effort, there are few consequences for putting in less effort (or conversely few incentives to change strategies).

Schmidtchen (2002), discussing Buchanan's Samaritan's Dilemma, notes that "enlightened" Samaritans could overcome this dilemma by delegating their decision to assist to an independent arbiter who is required to take into account the overall strategic context. "However," Schmidtchen concludes, "if the population of Samaritans is heterogeneous, 'enlightened' Samaritans, which have hired an agent, might now have to compete with those having chosen the 'soft option.' With 'potential parasites' preferring to get help from the latter group, something described by Gresham's law result. 'Bad' Samaritans drive the 'good' ones out of the market" (ibid.: 483).

In the Orissa Forestry case study (taken up in Chapter 9), for example, the development agency has threatened not to continue funding for its project, citing repeated lapses in follow-through on its agreements by the project's nominal owner— the Orissa Forest Department. Yet, this does not appear to have affected the strategy of the Forest Department; in interviews, its officials hinted that aid can be sought from the Japanese—who they claimed were less picky—should Swedish International Development Cooperation Agency (Sida) decide not to resume funding of its project.

The presence of a large number of donors trying to provide aid to a single country can also affect the bureaucratic capacity of the recipient country. Knack and Rahman (2004) have recently completed an empirical analysis of the adverse effect of large amounts of development assistance as well as donor fragmentation for a 96-country sample. They argue that multiple donors in a recipient country may lure recipient county officials to serve their projects rather than building recipient country capabilities. Their study finds that: "Competitive donor practices . . . erode administrative capacity in recipient country governments. In their need to show results, donors each act to maximize performance of their own projects, and shirk on provision of the public sector infrastructure essential for the countries overall long-term development" (ibid.: 25).

4.4. APPLYING THE IAD FRAMEWORK TO ANALYZE THE DONOR–RECIPIENT DYAD

Foreign aid involves multiple interlinked action situations as discussed above. Among all of them, the dyad between the donor and recipient is most crucial as the rest of the Octangle would not exist if a donor government and a recipient government were not in a bargaining mode. For development aid to flow, both actors in this dyad must reach a basic agreement about the level and content of any assistance package.

In this section, we focus on this critical part of the Octangle to begin a more detailed institutional analysis. We provide a sketch of how an analyst would approach a more extended examination of this particular action situation using the IAD framework. We present a series of general questions that an institutional analyst should ask when they analyze a specific case of donor–recipient interactions. These questions seek to reveal who the actors are, what factors affect their incentives and strategies, and the likely outcomes of their interaction. In Chapter 5, Roy Gardner and Christopher Waller dig further into this dyad and provide a more technical, game-theoretic analysis of the strategic interactions between donor and recipient governments. The case studies in later chapters illustrate many of the characteristics analyzed here in Chapter 4 and in Chapter 5.

To understand the structure of the negotiations arena between a particular donor and recipient dyad, one needs to ask many questions. The following questions provide an initial general guide to the kinds of questions one needs to ask. In light of the answers obtained, one can begin to lay out the structure of interaction between these two actors as shown below. The first step, however, is to ask at least the following broad questions:

1. *Which actors are involved in this particular negotiation process? Who is directly or indirectly involved in this negotiation?*

A. Are there representatives from two countries, one a donor country and one a recipient country? Or, are one or more actors from a multilateral donor?

B. Is there more than one bilateral donor providing aid to the recipient?

C. If there is more than one donor involved, have the bilateral donors developed mechanisms to avoid being played off against one another—so that they can be considered a coalition rather than single players?

D. Are these governments starting a new relationship or continuing a long-established one?

These questions establish who the actors are within the action situation in order to understand the structure of the relationship and thus the choices that each actor confronts. With just two actors, the donor and the recipient, it is generally easier to analyze the information and strategies of each than if more actors are involved. Further, some scholars have argued that the presence of a single donor (or a dominant one) leads to higher levels of success (see Bräutigam 2000).

2. *What are the positions of the officials representing the recipient government and donor government within their own countries and in regard to each other?*

A. How are the recipient government leaders chosen in their home country? In open, democratic elections or by authoritarian means?

B. How recently have the recipient government leaders assumed office? How close was the contest for national office (if there was a contest)?

C. How dependent are recipient government leaders on entrenched interests who, in turn, receive benefits from the status quo?

D. Have recipient government leaders been selected for their reform policies?

E. How are donor government leaders chosen?
F. Do donor government leaders represent a new coalition or one that has been in power for some time?
G. How secure are donor government leaders if they pursue aid programs? (e.g. how committed is the donor country population to aid?)
H. How dependent are donor government leaders on domestic coalitions that benefit from some kinds of aid (e.g. tied-trade) but not others?
I. Can these officials make final decisions for their respective governments or do they have to submit proposed negotiated settlements to others in their government?

This set of questions begins the task of identifying the incentives of each actor in the context of their own political institutions. Whether leaders are elected or not, how aid-related policies may affect their power, and the nature of the politician-aid bureaucrat relationship affect actors' incentives before aid programs are even chosen.

3. *What are some of the key actions (sets of strategies) that donors and recipients can take in the planning and negotiations stage of the process?*
The specific actions will always have to do with the issues that are involved in a particular case. To illustrate the method, however, let us outline a stylized version of some of the types of strategies that donor and recipient governments have taken in the past. The actual array of potential strategies is much larger than the strategies outlined here and will depend in a particular instance on many contextual variables. For example, bilateral donors could form a coalition and provide untied funding to support a portion of a broad development plan proposed by a recipient government (see Kanbur and Sandler 1999). We focus, however, on well-known strategies to illustrate how the broad method helps to identify general relationships.

In negotiating either a development program or a particular project, the *recipient government* needs to decide which of the following general strategies to pursue:

A. Say yes to any development program or project proposed by the donor without investment in planning and a commitment to follow through. (Get the project.)
B. Say yes to all programs and projects with strong commitment to follow through on those proposed and supported by own ministries and little commitment otherwise.
C. Say no to proposed reforms, programs, or projects not consistent with own development policies and plans of recipient government, say yes to those that are consistent.

For the *donor government*, it must decide which of the following strategies to pursue:

A. Make annual project-by-project decisions.
   (1) Support proposals designed primarily by own donor agency and contractors or by other donor agencies and international finance institutions.
   (2) Support proposals designed primarily by recipient government participants.

B. Make long-term commitments to support reforms, programs, and projects for 3–5 years.

  (1) Support proposals designed primarily by own donor agency and contractors or by other donor agencies and international finance institutions.
  (2) Support proposals designed primarily by recipient government participants.

4. How are these actions linked to potential outcomes?
Many specific outcomes are related to the type of agreements reached that can result from this kind of negotiation process. Each outcome can be evaluated using any of the criteria discussed above. First, we want to examine whether an agreement is likely or not, whether the agreement will be for a short-term project, or whether the agreement will span a long time horizon in which both the donor and the recipient government can gain substantial information about performance and be able to adapt the assistance to local needs and capabilities. Then we will ask which of these outcomes is more likely to be sustainable over the long term. In the second part of this chapter, we will focus on a more specific formulation to examine a game-theoretic analysis.

One way of showing the action–outcome linkage is illustrated in Figure 4.6. In regard to the immediate outcome of achieving an agreement or not, given the specified strategies, we would expect a negotiation process structured in this manner to achieve agreements in two-thirds of the possible combined strategies. Of those eight potential outcomes, half are likely to be of short-term duration and half are likely to be of long-term duration.

A donor may be in the situation of facing a recipient government that cannot do anything other than select Strategy A given that it does not have a skilled bureaucracy to design and follow through on programs and projects. The recipient government may be eager or even desperate to receive foreign assistance and will agree to any proposal. No matter what strategy the donor adopts, if the recipient government chooses Strategy A, either there is no agreement and no foreign assistance, or the projects that are funded are unlikely to be sustainable, given the lack of commitment by the recipient government. If the donor is highly motivated to provide assistance to this particular country, the donor will find itself in a true Samaritan's Dilemma.

A recipient government, on the other hand, may design some programs or projects on its own and have a real commitment to them, but still agree to any proposal made by the owner (Strategy B). In this case, an agreement is likely, but if the donor funds only proposals that it has confidence in because of its own efforts in their design, the ensuing activities are not likely to be sustainable. If the donor adopts either a short-term or long-term strategy to fund projects where the recipient country shows real ownership, then agreement is likely and those funded under a long-term commitment by the donor are more likely to be sustainable due to the increased knowledge that the donor has about the recipient and the increased confidence that the recipient has that risks that may need to be taken as a result of a foreign assistance may be compensated for over the long run.

	Recipient country strategies		
Donor country strategies	A. Say *yes* to all, but no involvement or commitment	B. Say *yes* to all; Commit to own	C. Say *no* to proposals outside own policies; Say yes and commit to own

A. Short-term

A1: Fund own or other donor-designed proposals	1-1 Short-term agreement	1-2 Short-term agreement	1-3 No agreement
A2: Fund recipient-designed proposals	2-1 Nothing proposed	2-2 Short-term agreement	2-3 Short-term agreement

B. Long-term

B1: Fund own or other donor-designed proposals	3-1 Long-term agreement	3-2 Long-term agreement	3-3 No agreement
B2: Fund recipient-designed proposals	4-1 Nothing proposed	4-2 Sustainable long-term agreement	4-3 Sustainable long-term agreement

Figure 4.6. *Action–outcome linkages for simplified donor–recipient negotiation situations*

From the evidence offered by the World Bank (1997, 1998), Sida (1996*a,b,c*, 1997*a*), and others (Bräutigam 2000; van de Walle and Johnston 1996), projects designed primarily by a donor country's own development agency and its own consultants (or by other external international finance institutions that have defined a major reform program) are less likely to be sustainable than projects where the recipient government has a greater voice in the design and has a commitment to long-term sustainability. In other words, when the recipient country is the "real" owner of a program or project, in the sense that they have had an active voice in the design of the project and have made a commitment to the activities involved in the project, the probability of sustainability is presumed to be much higher than if the donor country is the effective owner of the program or project. Projects that are undertaken with a longer time horizon are likely to be more sustainable—in the sense defined in Chapter 1—than those undertaken with a short time horizon.

If the recipient government adopts Strategy C and is actually willing to say no to some programs and projects as being outside its own plans, a stalemate is likely to follow if the donor is committed to its own proposals. The tougher stand of the recipient, however, leads to a chance of receiving foreign aid for programs and projects that fit well into its overall development program. Thus, when a donor faces a somewhat tougher recipient country and makes a long-term commitment to support proposals that fit into a recipient country's policies, there is a higher probability of achieving sustainable projects.

Thus, as shown by the shaded cells in Figure 4.6, two out of the twelve possible outcomes are more likely to be sustainable than the other outcomes. And, if Outcome 4–3 is reached in a recipient country that has adopted major political and economic reforms, the result may be highly beneficial for all. Unfortunately, there are many reasons why donors and recipients do not choose the strategies leading to Outcome 4–3 and that recipients do not adopt political and economic reforms. Many of these relate to the costs and benefits involved.

5. *What are the costs and benefits assigned to actions and outcomes?*
In simple situations, it may be possible to find a way of assigning costs and benefits to all actions and outcomes using a single metric, such as a monetary unit, and derive a clear-cut overall assessment of the net-benefits present in all action–outcome combinations. For this analysis, we can only illustrate the types of benefits and costs that may be involved for different kinds of participants in this bargaining situation. One of the key problems in assigning benefits to outcomes of foreign aid is the problem of its fungibility (Cassen 1994; Feyzioglu *et al.* 1998; Gibson and Hoffmann 2005). A donor country may have as a high priority supporting education or health projects and be willing to invest substantially in such projects either designed by itself or designed by the recipient government. The donor country hopes that its investment will be added to the investment in health or education that the recipient country already plans to make. The recipient country, however, may have other priorities.

In some cases, the recipient government may actually reduce its own spending levels after receiving a grant or loan below what it had earlier allocated.[3] Of course, the donor country may support a reduction in a government budget that reduces deficits as part of an overall reform package. Even if the amount of aid provided is translated into an equivalent increase in the recipient government's budget, a further question is whether the aid results in higher spending in the sector supported. Governments receiving foreign aid to support education, for example, may decrease their spending on education and allocate extra funds to other sectors (Pack and Pack 1993). Since foreign aid is frequently fungible, it can crowd out domestic sources of funds—a phenomenon that is often observed in regard to the allocations made to a particular sector by a national government. Thus, regardless of whether the total government budget increases, decreases, or is unaltered after donor funding, there is usually some level of crowding-out taking place.

Given the difficulty of assessing the overall benefits of programs or projects, let us instead assume that any of the projects funded would bring at least substantial short-term benefits to the recipient country. If any of these projects were sustained, we would further assume that they would generate more benefits than costs and thus be evaluated as both sustainable and efficient in the long-term. This allows us in this illustrative example to proceed with an initial analysis of the costs of diverse strategies to the participants. Since the costs are proximate to those involved and the benefits are diffusely spread across many others and in the future, the costs to participants may be the more relevant factor that affects strategic choice in this type of bargaining situation.

If the government of the recipient country is a relatively entrenched authoritarian regime that owes its continuity in office to its distribution of benefits to key supporters, the costs of the three strategies vary rather substantially. Strategy A is the lowest cost strategy. No investment has to be made in establishing a strong, independent, public service capable of making coherent long-term policies and designing and implementing good projects. So long as donor countries are willing to lend funds, the recipient can get by with promises of commitments, without any real commitments to any externally or internally imposed reforms (see Pedersen 1996, 1998). If the government is relatively corrupt, then the benefits from diverting funds either directly from the project or through the fungibility of the national budget allows the government to siphon funds that are made available to top government officials and to enter issue-attractive contracts favored by supporters.

This strategy has been adopted so often over the past 40 years that many stories are told about countries that make promises during negotiations but do not carry them out during the implementation phase. These stories illustrate what is meant by the term *moral hazard*. The "dance" between the donors and a recipient was well-captured in a 1995 story in *The Economist*:

Over the past few years Kenya has performed a curious mating ritual with its aid donors. The steps are: one, Kenya wins its yearly pledges of foreign aid. Two, the government begins to misbehave, backtracking on economic reform and behaving in an authoritarian manner. Three, a new meeting of donor countries looms with exasperated foreign governments preparing their sharp rebukes. Four, Kenya pulls a placatory rabbit out of the hat. Five, the donors are mollified and the aid is pledged. The whole dance then starts again. (August 19, 1995, quoted in Dollar and Easterly 1999)

The "dance" continued for some time—only with a slightly different tune. In 1997, the IMF did stop paying out a large loan it had approved in 1996. With a bad drought in both aid funds and weather, President Daniel Arap Moi became quite desperate about this situation and was now willing to promise to meet the toughest set of conditions ever imposed by the International Monetary Fund (IMF). This set of promises did open up the flow of $18 million during the summer of 2000 to help relieve the drastic effects of the recent drought (see *The Economist*, 5 August 2000).

For a corrupt government, Strategy C is very costly, as it involves at least some level of political and economic reform. Such reforms may lead to the end of the regime itself and are rarely adopted by entrenched authoritarian regimes. Strategy B may be less costly than C, but even this strategy involves some reform efforts in order to come up with programs and plans that a donor would be willing to fund and to commit oneself to follow-through when funding is completed. Most corrupt governments do not have the capacity or desire to make such a commitment. Consequently, a donor can expect that authoritarian regimes are most likely to adopt Strategy A and at most Strategy B. Trying to impose conditions that would move the recipient country closer to institutional and policy reform is unlikely to work. The World Bank, reflecting on its own experience, reports that "policy reforms rarely succeed unless the government is genuinely convinced that the reforms have to be implemented and considers the reform program its own" (World Bank 1997: 37).

Governments more likely to adopt Strategy C are those that must rely on a broad constituency, rather than a narrow clientele base. They are also more likely to resist large government deficits, avoid overdependence on loans, and invest more heavily in elementary and secondary education (Bueno de Mesquita and Root 2000). Countries with newly elected reform governments are more likely to be committed to reform than even democratically elected governments that have been in power 10 or 15 years (Dollar and Svensson 2000). If Strategy C is adopted, a donor that makes long-term commitments to provide aid and develops some mutually agreed-upon conditional loans may help achieve Outcome 4–3. Such loans enable the reform government to make a public commitment to its reforms and send a signal to private investors that it is now safer to invest in the recipient country.

For the donor country, expending funds to design projects themselves is more costly than relying on design prepared by recipient governments. Thus, assuming equally attractive benefits, a donor would always prefer the second option under either short-term or long-term strategies. Consultants often prepare project designs for recipient governments and it is difficult for a donor to know whether the design represents a genuine interest by the recipient government or a project that a consultant thinks the donor will find attractive. We discuss this puzzle further in Chapter 8.

6. What is the information that is available to each participant about the situation?
A major problem facing both donor and recipient governments is determining which strategy the other will adopt and then choosing their own best response to that choice. Both participants have a considerable amount of private information about the level of benefits and costs of diverse actions and outcomes. In general, there is more information about the donor's costs and benefits than about the recipient's. The asymmetry of information is largely a function of the fact that in most donor countries a free press exists, and considerable information exists about public opinion and government policy regarding aid.

What the recipient country has a hard time knowing, however, is the strength of the donor government's determination to withdraw further funding if the recipient country does not keep its commitments. As the story in *The Economist* quoted above illustrates, many donor countries have found it difficult to withhold funds from a recipient country that does not keep its promises to perform in certain ways. Once funds have been committed in a donor government's budget, there are potential risks to the donor country's future aid budget of withholding funds to a recipient. Funds that are not spent during one budgetary period are sometimes viewed by legislative bodies as "surplus" to be retrieved from an ineffective agency (see Wildavsky 1984). Once a donor has been forgiving in the past, however, it has a hard time convincing a recipient country that it will be tough in the future (see the discussion of the Samaritan's Dilemma in Chapters 3 and 5).

The donor country, on the other hand, has a hard time knowing whether a recipient has chosen Strategy A or Strategy B. A donor country that thinks a recipient has chosen Strategy A should withdraw entirely from the situation. With Strategy B, there is at least a little hope. A clever recipient government that wants to choose Strategy A, however, only needs to hire a consultant who has good knowledge of the donor and wants to implement a funded project. The government asks the consultant to devise a credible proposal likely to attract the donor's interest (and offers to pay the consultant only if the project is funded). Thus, the simple presentation of plans and proposals by the recipient does not provide credible proof of the real commitment of the recipient and does not help the donor sort out between Strategy A and Strategy B. (If one wanted to analyze this situation closely, one would need to add one more strategy to Figure 5.1 where a consultant's plans were put forward without a strong commitment to follow-up.) Thus, determining when a government *really* has a sense of ownership for reforms, programs, or projects turns out in practice to be extremely difficult. And, given the high volume of demands on the officials in a donor country's development agency, actually determining what strategy the recipient government is likely to choose may not be feasible in many donor–recipient bargaining situations.

7. What is the level of control that participants have over the choice of strategy?
For the donor, one needs to ask whether ambassadors or heads of development cooperation agencies in the field are authorized to make independent decisions or whether they must carry out policies designed by the Foreign Ministry, Ministry of Finance, or the cabinet. For the recipient, one needs to ask what decision rules recipient government officials must use before coming to a decision about choice of strategy.

In the initial negotiations over an aid agreement, one can think of the direct participants in the negotiation process as agents of their own country's government. Where the level of control that these agents possess can be very important is when there are disagreements about whether one or the other government has lived up to its "agreements." This can happen, for example, when a recipient government has agreed to conditions attached to a foreign assistance grant and the ambassador for the donor country thinks that the recipient government is not keeping its agreement. An important aspect of the ongoing action situation is how much freedom has the ambassador—who has more direct information about the ongoing strategies of the recipient—been given to cancel future payments due to nonperformance of the recipient government. If the ambassador has little control over continuing payments, a recipient government uninterested in keeping reform commitments may find itself in a setting with more freedom to adopt Strategy A while professing to have adopted

Strategy B or even Strategy C. This problem is exacerbated due to the severe information constraints and asymmetries that frequently characterize this situation.

4.5. CONCLUSION

The International Development Cooperation Octangle is a schema to assist in an examination of the system of relationships that exist among many individual situations that are frequently examined in isolation. It represents an initial effort to "scale up" to a different level of analysis that encompasses the entire development aid process within both donor and recipient countries.

Some conclusions can initially be derived from the discussion above. For starters, donor-country citizens—altruistically motivated to transfer resources to recipient country citizens—are, by and large, not able to monitor the performance of their own government's stewardship of international development aid. As discussed above, the feedback loop is often broken. Basic agreements, between the donor and the recipient governments, as agents of their people, are hammered out in negotiations outside the limelight of media coverage. While these documents nearly always contain buzzwords like "sustainability" and "ownership," they often put little of this rhetoric into practice. Nothing in the rest of the Octangle seems, at present, to correct for this inability to monitor what is really happening in the field, although there is potential for interest groups in the donor and recipient country to highlight such problems.

Contractors, whose services are paid for by the development agency, stand in the middle of the Octangle and have considerable control over the flow of information in all directions. Officials in the recipient countries often treat them as donor representatives. Moreover, they are the only ones who deal directly with beneficiaries in many projects. Meanwhile, the beneficiaries have little voice or control (except in rare circumstances) as to what will be undertaken in a development project. In some instances, the contractors design a project that they themselves are in a unique situation to carry out (see our further discussion in Chapter 8).

Encouraging programs that place the beneficiaries, rather than contractors, in the center of the linked arenas is an obvious step to give more emphasis to the role of beneficiaries in the ownership of projects. Projects that have involved the beneficiaries in all four processes involved in ownership—provision, production, consumption, and alienation—have been shown to be sustainable long after a project itself has ended (Shivakoti *et al.* 1997). Putting the beneficiaries in the center, however, requires quite different project designs than have been the predominant pattern in development aid. For one, they require substantial time and effort by those helping to put beneficiaries in the center to overcome the skepticism and suspicion of the expected beneficiaries who have often been told in the past that they should "participate" only to find that this meant showing up at meetings and accepting the ideas of those designing projects.

The Octangle provides, we argue, a useful way of perceiving the system of aid. A further step in examining the impact of this system is to examine the bilateral relationships between donor and recipient governments more intensively.

As one can see from the above, analyzing the structure of interactions between a donor and a recipient government (ignoring for the moment the discussion of embedding of bilateral negotiations in the context of many other donors interacting with the same recipient) involves bringing together a diverse set of analytical elements. These elements include those related to the context including the nature of the physical world being acted upon, the kind of rules that are involved, and the broad sense of community involved within the donor and recipient countries and between them. Further elements have to do with the structure of particular types of situations such as the types of actors, the positions involved, the actions or strategies that can be adopted, the outcomes that are likely, the control, the relevant information, and the payoffs. Perceived incentives are the result of how all of these elements combine to create a particular structure. And, to make analysis more difficult, the result of changes in any one element frequently depends on the particular values of the other elements.

The specifics of each donor–recipient bargaining situation will differ, depending on a large number of factors having to do with political relationships and dependencies in each country, the history of the interaction, and the subsequent principal–agent relations with those who implement funded programs or projects. But three broad lessons can be gleaned from the analysis of this generalized situation. And, the posited relations are based on the empirical evidence presented by many scholars linking effective ownership and a long-term perspective to an increased likelihood of sustainability (see discussion of sustainability and ownership in Chapter 1, as well as in the concluding chapter). Assuming that these hypotheses are correct, we reach three expectations that are relevant for a bilateral donor.

1. Adopting a policy that foreign aid will largely be allocated to programs or projects where the recipient government is committed or "owns" the proposed activity is generally more sustainable (two out of twelve possible outcomes with at least some probability of sustainability) than when the recipient does not have real ownership.
2. The best outcomes are achievable when a long-term commitment to a recipient country is made. If recipient governments are not committed to institutional and economic reform and accept aid without a firm commitment to sustain them, then long-term commitments can involve substantial investments that produce few desirable results. This could lead to the least efficient and sustainable foreign aid.
3. When facing recipient governments whose leaders are not themselves benefited by institutional reforms and effective economic policies (due to their reliance for continuance in office on supporters who are advantaged by the status quo), donors are faced with a choice between helping a few citizens with short-term gains versus pulling out and waiting for a more auspicious opportunity. Pulling out may be the only way to help those citizens in the long run, especially if donors can form alliances with other donors to hold firm, but may make it more difficult to obtain large aid budgets in the future as such actions bring public attention to the strategic actions of authoritarian and corrupt recipient regimes.

In all cases, however, considerable knowledge about the history and current political context of a regime is needed to apply these tentative lessons wisely in settings where information is scarce about the strategies adopted by a recipient government. Before aid can achieve beneficial outcomes for the citizens of the recipient country (and, if successful, for the citizens of the donor country), further analysis is needed of the role of special interests, of principal–agent relationships between both countries and with implementing organizations, and of their relationships with the citizens being served. All of the actors involved in the Aid Octangle have some impact on the sustainability, efficiency, and growth-enhancing capabilities of foreign aid. And, all of these actors are involved in potentially difficult collective-action problems and principal–agent relationships discussed earlier.

These tentative lessons help to summarize the specific findings for many studies, but each should be viewed as a hypothesis for which some initial empirical support exists. Further testing of these hypotheses will be important as a foundation for future aid policies. Now let us dig even further into the important relationship among donor and recipient countries in the game-theoretic analysis presented in Chapter 5.

NOTES

1. Figure 4.1 can be drawn from the descriptions of the project cycle and of processes in development cooperation presented in *Sida at Work* (Sida 1997c).
2. Many developing country NGOs dedicate themselves and their resources to their mission of development, rather than organize themselves mainly to obtain donor funds. Many successful projects have been undertaken by NGOs that have a firm commitment to empowering local citizens and to achieving real growth and sustainability. However, not all NGOs have such effective records of accomplishment (see Grindle 1997; Lancaster 1999a; Lindahl *et al.* 1999).
3. Studies of how much impact foreign aid has had on recipient government budgets have come up with varied responses as one would expect, but studies of a large number of countries have most frequently shown that development financing does not translate uniformly into an increase in funding. Feyzioglu *et al.* (1998), for example, found that $1 in concessional loans led to 63 cents in additional government spending for the 38 countries in their sample. Cashel-Cordo and Craig (1990) found no effect of bilateral loans on government spending in their study of 46 countries. Studies of individual countries have not found as much fungibility. Pack and Pack (1990), for example, found that $1 in aid to Indonesia led to $1.50 in additional spending. Thus, one cannot make any firm estimation of how much fungibility there may be in a particular setting, but has to be wary that the amount of foreign aid spent does not automatically translate into added government spending.

5

A Formal Analysis of Incentives in Strategic Interactions Involving an International Development Cooperation Agency

ROY GARDNER AND CHRISTOPHER J. WALLER

5.1. INTRODUCTION

To set the stage for the analysis that follows, we first consider initial conditions in a recipient country. Prior to a donor agency involvement in the recipient country, we already have a difficult setting. Initial conditions in the recipient almost always reflect tragedies of the commons, public good problems, and principal–agent problems. Given the incentives present in such problems, a donor has an unenviable task at the outset. Donors do not operate in countries like Denmark, Finland, Sweden, and New Zealand (among the top countries in the world on the Transparency International ratings), where corruption is lowest. Donors tend not to operate in countries that have good investment climates and high per capita GDP. Instead, donors operate in countries exhibiting bad circumstances—terrible investment climate, high levels of corruption, and low per capita GDP. Most donor programs are committed to poverty-reduction efforts in less-developed countries (LDCs), but the very inability of LDC governments to address governance problems associated with practically all forms of government intervention, and poverty-reduction programs in particular themselves, complicates the task of the donor. Recall the Octangle in Chapter 4 and, in particular, the donor recipient bargaining arena, to better fix ideas of the discussion that follows.

We identify two broad motives/mechanisms behind the decision on the part of a developed country to enter a recipient country with aid. The first of these is *altruism and warm glow*. Caring about those less fortunate than ourselves is a commonly held value in most societies. Development aid is an expression of this value. Even in the harshest budget battles, development aid is almost never singled out for a zero–option. Of course, to be effective in addressing altruistic motives, such aid must achieve verifiable results. Even if results are not verifiable, warm glow may be enough. Economic experiments as well as a vast literature in sociology and social psychology have identified the existence of warm glow—that donor governments, donor personnel, and citizens will feel good simply from the act of giving, whether they get any results or not. To the extent that warm glow drives public support for donor activities, development results are simply a fringe benefit.

The second of these is *increased per capita GDP, via growth factors, including essential capital investment, overcoming market failure in the recipient countries.* Given poor investment climate and underdeveloped internal financial markets in recipient countries, the private sector, even at the global level, will not provide the capital necessary to fuel growth. In addition, governments with poor credit ratings, rife with corruption, will also not attract growth capital, even at extraordinary interest rates. Thus, unless a donor offers aid to such a country, growth will be negligible, if at all. To the extent that growth in poor countries enhances growth of donor countries, such growth provides an incentive for aid. Moreover, all economies face externality problems, such as public good problems, arising from the provision and maintenance of public goods; the tragedy of the commons, afflicting common-pool resources (CPR); and principal–agent problems, which often manifest themselves in market failure, or inefficient market outcomes. Externality problems are especially intense in LDCs. The view of many donors is that, without donor programs targeting these problems, national governments and national markets will not solve them.

We now turn to the strategic implications of this mix of initial conditions and donor motives on donor outcomes. In particular, we demonstrate that aid dependency is a likely outcome of this mix.

5.2. STRATEGIC IMPLICATION OF ALTRUISM FOR RESULTS

5.2.1. *Aid in a One-Shot Game: The Samaritan*

Aid is often intended to serve as a means of helping those less fortunate than oneself. As discussed in Chapter 2, developed countries are "Samaritans" that give help to the less-fortunate countries. For example, drought and resulting food crises are simple but common examples in which foreign aid alleviates the temporary misfortune of a country in crisis. Developed countries give food aid to the affected nations to alleviate hunger. The drought-stricken country accepts the food and distributes it to the starving citizens. The world media broadcasts pictures of starving children eating food to the citizens of the developed countries. In this "good" equilibrium, the hungry are fed and the senders of the food feel good about their help in alleviating starvation. Both sides benefit from the aid of food.

5.2.2. *Aid in a Repeated Game: The Samaritan's Dilemma*

The paragraph above is a description of a "one-shot" aid game between donor and recipient. It is also a stylized description of how one would like to think that the aid game is played and the outcomes that *should* occur. In many aid games, however, this type of equilibrium does not arise. The reason is that foreign aid can alter the incentives that recipient countries face. In the story above, the aid is viewed as a "one-shot" game or one-time event. But in many aid situations, the game is repeated again and again. The mere fact that the game is repeated allows the players of the game to base current actions on past behavior and expected future behavior. Consider the same game above in a repeated environment. A developing country knows that if it experiences a food shortage, developed countries will provide food. They then view developing countries as subsidizing domestic food production and this gives them an incentive to reallocate their own scarce resources away from agriculture to alternative, and not necessarily productive, uses. As a result, the country does not produce enough food and a "crisis" arises that requires food transfers from the developed countries to the developing country. Consequently, a "bad" equilibrium can arise in this repeated version of the food aid game in which the recipient country consistently underproduces food and developed countries consistently send food to prevent starvation. Thus, the fungibility of aid (i.e. the ability to reallocate resources to other uses) creates a situation of aid dependence.

Fungibility of aid is not the only problem that can arise in this simple aid game. The objective of donor countries is to get the food to the starving citizenry. However, the food must be received and distributed by an intermediary of some sort. It is often the case that the control of the resources allows the intermediary to take actions that ultimately cause food to be reallocated to alternative uses than to feed citizens. In Somalia, for example, in some cases, intermediaries directed food toward warring clans who then used the food to buy weapons or coerce young men to join the clan militias in return for their families receiving food. Thus, food aid essentially became a resource for extending civil war and misery (see de Waal 1997).

Clearly the donor country would like to ensure that these undesired outcomes do not arise. But how does it do so? The donor countries would have to monitor the behavior of the recipient countries to ensure that reallocation of resources does not occur. This requires a substantial amount of information. Second, the donor country must then be able to affix blame on who is responsible. This requires accountability. Then, if reallocation of resources or food is detected, the donor country must be able to take action to "punish" errant behavior on the part of the recipient country. This typically requires some form of legal recourse within the country or threatening the loss of future aid if the problem is not resolved in a satisfactory manner. But as we mentioned above, the initial conditions in aid-recipient countries prevent such courses of action—information is scarce, accountability of bureaucrats is often limited, legal recourse is unlikely due to ineffective judicial systems, and the Samaritan donor is incapable of credibly threatening to withdraw future aid.

The examples above suggest that a key problem is that the objectives of the donor are not compatible with those of the recipient. These problems are referred to as principal–agent problems in the economics literature (see Chapter 2). Indeed, these problems are likely to be encountered at almost every level of society, from personal interactions to the interaction between the central government and a ministry of that government. In the next two sections, we present generic game-theoretic models of principal–agent problems in both "normal form" (payoff matrices) and "extensive form" (decision trees with payoffs) to illustrate how game theory can be used to model actors' strategies and equilibrium outcomes.

5.2.3. *Principal–Agent Problems in One-Shot Games*

In Chapter 2, we have explained that in generic terms a principal is a person or organization that hires another person or organization to perform services. An agent is any person, firm, or organization hired to perform services for a principal. A homely example is a person with a legal problem (the principal) who hires a lawyer (the agent) to solve that legal problem. In precisely the same sense, in a parliamentary system the parliament is the principal and its Minister of Foreign Affairs (and his or her ministry) is its agent to conduct its foreign policy in the desired manner (see Gardner 2004: chap. 11 for detailed analysis).

The reason relationships between a principal and an agent can lead to problems is that often the interests of the principal and of the agent do not coincide. A person with a legal problem may want his or her lawyer to work harder than the lawyer wants to work. A central government may want to implement a certain policy with regards to another country, while the Ministry of Foreign Affairs prefers that another policy be implemented with regards to that country.

Figure 5.1 shows a simple, but typical, principal–agent problem in extensive form. The principal moves first in this decision tree diagram. At first move, the principal either offers the agent a contract, or not. If the principal does not offer the agent a contract, then the game ends with the payoffs:

(0,0) = (0 for principal, 0 for agent).

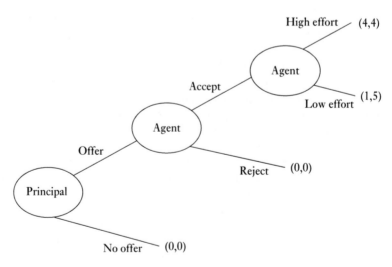

Figure 5.1. *Principal–agent problem, extensive form game*

0 is a normalization of payoffs, representing no relationship or a worthless relationship.

Throughout this chapter we will use integers for payoffs. The exact numbers are not nearly as important as the strategic considerations they represent. A detailed analysis will yield actual payoffs to any desired accuracy.

If the principal offers the agent a contract, then it is the agent's turn to move. The agent either accepts the contract or does not accept the contract. If the agent does not accept the contract, then the game ends with the payoffs:

(0,0) = (0 for principal, 0 for agent).

Finally, if the agent accepts the contract, the agent again has to decide whether to expend high effort or low effort in fulfilling the contract. This decision by the agent is the crux of the principal–agent problem.

In Chapters 9 and 10, we will come across case studies to which this structure can be argued to apply. For example, in the Maharashtra power station case (discussed in Chapter 9), effort is characterized by expending resources to monitor theft of electricity from the power grid—high effort corresponds to reducing theft but at a cost of policing effort, low effort is simply doing nothing and thus maintaining the status quo. Also, expending effort to reduce costs, firing workers to trim the labor costs, and giving up political patronage all correspond to generating high effort. Hence, effort is simply a short-cut method for capturing disutility of undertaking reforms—a metaphor if you will, but a metaphor that can be measured in actual payoffs.

Return to the situation portrayed in Figure 5.1. The optimum choice—the first-best arrangement—is for the agent to expend high effort. This yields the payoff vector:

(4,4) = (4 for principal, 4 for agent).

With a total of 8, this score represents the largest available in the entire diagram.

However, the agent, whose choice it is to respond to the agent's offer, prefers to expend low effort. This yields the payoff vector:

(1,5) = (1 for principal, 5 for agent).

With a total payoff of 6, this score constitutes the second largest available in the entire diagram. What is 25 per cent better for the agent (5 > 4) is 33.3 per cent worse for society (6 < 8).

In this case, the principal–agent problem leads to a loss in efficiency of 25 per cent relative to optimum. It is obvious that if the agent could commit to putting forth high effort, society would be better-off. But perfect commitment is very difficult to do in general. Hence, alternative methods are needed to improve on the low effort equilibrium.

We have considered a very simple principal–agent problem here. More complicated problems can arise. For instance, one can work out the implications of a three-player interaction, where one player is overall principal, one player is agent to the overall principal and principal to the third player, who is agent to the intermediate principal. One can show that increasing the number of players in such linked manner reduces overall efficiency—precisely the same number-of-players effect as in public goods and commons problems (see Svensson 2000*b* for a treatment of such complications).

Whereas even in the most advanced economies, principal–agent problems pose challenges, these challenges are especially pressing in countries targeted as recipients by donors. The issue for the principal is to design an incentive mechanism to induce the agent to behave in the manner desired by the principal. In this example, the principal wants the agent to put forth high effort. So consider the following contract offer to the agent: If the total output is observed to be 8, the agent will receive 75 per cent of total output rather than 50 per cent of total output. Now the agent's best response is to put forth high effort, which pays him 6 instead of 5. The principal is also made better-off because he receives a payoff of 2 rather than 1. Thus, by offering the agent more than a 50–50 split, the principal can alter the agent's incentives in such a way as to produce the optimum. This contract is a form of aid conditionality—aid is given conditional on a particular outcome being observed. Consequently, this hypothetical approach would require the donor to commit more funds to a project than they would like to as a way of enticing the recipient country to put forth high reform efforts.

5.2.4. *Principal–Agent Problems in Repeated Games*

The key feature of the incentive contract above is that it is conditioned on the history of play in the game. While one-shot games are interesting, most donor/target recipient relationships are long-lived, 3 years appears to be a minimum, with some lasting 20 years or more. Thus, long histories of play and behavior can be used to design contracts. In this case, history of play is valuable information for trying to obtain the best equilibrium. In game theory, long-lived relationships are modeled as repeated games (Gardner 2004) or as time-dependent super-games (Herr *et al.* 1997). There is a set of famous results for such games, called Folk Theorems—since they were widely known to be true long before proofs appeared in print. A finitely repeated game can model the relationship between a donor and a target recipient. Let G be such a game. The relevant Folk Theorem for such G says:

"Good" Folk Theorem. If G has a good Nash equilibrium and a bad Nash equilibrium, then finitely repeated G has, for any Pareto optimal outcome, a Nash equilibrium outcome in the vicinity (in outcome space) of that Pareto outcome. This would seem to be good news for a donor. The trouble is, with incentives, as often arise in a donor/target recipient relationship, we can get the *"Bad" Folk Theorem*. Suppose the donor is a passive player in G, while local officials and donor personnel in-country are active players in G. If the interests of the donor and the active players clash, then a nearly Pareto optimal outcome for active players can be payoff minimizing for the donor.

To foreshadow our main point here:

Repetition of a game with incentives for a donor can lead to even worse outcomes than playing the game only once.

		Player 2's strategies	
		High	Low
Player 1's strategies	High	(2.4,2.4)	(1,4)
	Low	(4,1)	(1,1)

Figure 5.2. *Game G: Principal–agent problem, normal form game*

To see this, consider the one-shot normal form game G (Figure 5.2), which will be played between local officials (player 1) and donor personnel in-country (player 2). High and Low refer to effort levels by the two players, respectively. The most value in the game G is created by high effort on the part of both players. We can think of this as stemming from a principal–agent problem. In-country donor personnel (player 2) act as principal; local officials (player 1) as agent. The best outcome for donor personnel, assuming they put forth high effort, occurs when the local officials put forth high effort also. However, local officials get even higher payoff by putting forth low effort. So incentives to "cheat" are present in G. The task for the donor is to design an incentive scheme that induces the agent to behave in the desired fashion.

The game G has three Nash equilibria:

1. (Low, High) paying (4,1). At this Nash equilibrium, the local officials put in low effort, while the donor personnel in-county puts forth high effort. This outcome is best for local officials. The efficiency of this equilibrium is $(4 + 1)/(4 + 1) = 100$ per cent; a good equilibrium.
2. (High, Low) paying (1,4). At this Nash equilibrium, the local officials put in high effort, while the donor personnel in-country put forth low effort. This outcome is best for donor personnel in-country. The efficiency of this equilibrium is again 100 per cent; another good equilibrium.
3. (Low, Low) paying (1,1). At this Nash equilibrium, both local officials and donor personnel in-country put forth low effort. The outcome (1,1) pays the least for both players. The efficiency of this equilibrium is $(1 + 1)/(4 + 1) = 40$ per cent; a bad equilibrium.

Although two of these equilibria achieve 100 per cent efficiency, they divide payoffs very unevenly, with the player putting forth low effort getting the lion's share of the gains.

Now suppose the game G is played many times. Repeated play gives the players much more latitude for designing "reputation" strategies that reward and/or punish the other player based on the history of play. One simple way for the two players to interact in this relationship is to alternate between (High, Low) and (Low, High). By playing in this fashion, they average $(1 + 4)/2 = 2.5$ each. The only problem with this rotation is if some player would deviate. When it is player 1's turn to put forth high effort, he gets the same payoff by putting forth low effort. Thus, a reputation strategy must be employed by each player to ensure that the other player puts forth high effort when he is supposed to.

Consider the following reputation strategy in which deviating does not pay: The play rotates between (High, Low) and (Low, High). If either player ever deviates, then the players play (Low, Low) from then on until the end of the game. This strategy will produce a Nash equilibrium. Furthermore, not only is it a Nash equilibrium but also a sub-game perfect equilibrium (see Gardner 2004: chap. 8 for details).

To verify this, suppose player 1 puts forth high effort in odd-numbered periods, player 2, in even-numbered periods. Suppose player 1 considers deviating in the very first period. Deviation yields no gain, since $1 - 1 = 0$, but a long-run loss of -3 every other period, since $1 - 4 = -3$ in subsequent odd-numbered periods. The long-run loss overwhelms the short-run 0 gain; deviation does not pay. The same holds true for player 2. Hence, we have a Nash equilibrium.

So by adopting strategies based on the history of play, the donor country can ensure better performance on the part of the recipient country. Again, this is essentially a form of aid conditionality, the condition being that the game ends upon repeated deviation.

Now that we have outlined a two-player principal–agent game, we want to consider how adding a third player can affect the game. We add a third player (player 3), the donor home office, which is passive. Player 3 has no strategic choice, and simply gets a payoff from the game played between players 1 (local officials) and 2 (in-country donor personnel). We represent this configuration in Figure 5.3 and will call this game G+. The donor home office payoff is 0 in the event of low effort by both players—this corresponds to not even entering the target recipient's country. The donor home office payoff is 1 in the event of low effort by exactly one of the players— this corresponds to partially successful development. The donor home office payoff is 3 in the event of high effort by both players. This corresponds to successful development.

Here comes the Bad Folk Theorem. G+ and G have the same active players and the same set of Nash equilibria. According to the Bad Folk Theorem, local officials and in-country donor officials can achieve the payoffs (2.5, 2.5) by rotating between (High, Low) and (Low, High) effort every period. Since (2.5, 2.5) dominates (2.4, 2.4), we hardly expect the local officials and in-country donor officials to put forth (High, High) efforts. What is good for players 1 and 2 guarantees a payoff of

		Player 3's strategy: Passive player 2's strategies	
		High	Low
Player 1's strategies	High	(2.4,2.4,3)	(1,4,1)
	Low	(4,1,1)	(1,1,0)

Figure 5.3. *Game G+: Normal form game with a passive player*

1—partial development success—for player 3, the donor. This is an embedded principal–agent problem with a vengeance.

This is one of the many forms that aid dependency can take. The target recipient wants to continue the relationship, as do donor personnel in-country. However, the personnel at donor headquarters would very much like better results from the relationship. At a bad Nash equilibrium, however, better results are not forthcoming. In addition, if a player in a game is passive—here, the donor headquarters with no strategies to choose from—then there is nothing that player can do to change the outcome. The bad equilibrium does not go away by itself, and the active players have every interest in seeing that equilibrium persist. This is a mechanism for supporting aid dependency in the long run. A comparable point is made, in a rather more complicated way, by Pedersen (1996) and Murrell (1999).

5.3. FOREIGN AID AS A SUBSTITUTE FOR BORROWING IN CAPITAL MARKETS

Information problems, lack of credibility, and poor legal structures make borrowing on internal and world capital markets impossible for many developing countries. Consequently, developed countries may opt to indirectly lend to developing countries via foreign aid. However, aid takes on the properties of a lending contract in these situations rather than a form of charity.

Countries tend to borrow in capital markets to finance major capital or infrastructure projects. Power stations, highways, airports, shipyards, water treatment facilities, and housing are all examples of major capital projects that need major financing and engineering skills to accomplish the project.

With these types of projects, the Samaritan's Dilemma is at the forefront. Consider the production of a power plant. A donor country may well see this as a "one-time" expenditure, much like food aid during a drought. The donor provides funding, via a loan, and engineering expertise to build the power station. Once the power station is built, the donor's job is done and the recipient country is now better off by having a new reliable source of power supply. However, like all capital, power stations must be maintained. Maintenance requires resources being allocated to it. The recipient country may not allocate the resources or have the technical expertise to run the power station correctly. In the end, the power station deteriorates and forces the donor country to assume long-run responsibility for the upkeep of the capital stock, the collateral on its loan, so to speak. Thus, large, technical capital projects are ripe for generating aid dependence.

In addition to these maintenance problems, as in the food distribution story, significant principal–agent problems exist with the distribution of electric power. We will address this issue in Section 5.4 on market externalities, since electrical power takes on the properties of a "public good" or "common-pool resource." Furthermore, corruption on the part of local bureaucrats can lead to underprovision of productive capital due to resource extraction in the form of bribes and the disincentive effects for private investment. We will return to the issue of corruption and private investment in Section 5.4.

Thus, by taking the place of capital markets, donors take on the role of lenders for capital projects in developing countries. As with any lenders, setting up the correct incentives to ensure borrower compliance requires substantial information and means of enforcing the "loan contract." In the next sections, we outline how principal–agent relationships and mechanism design can be used to enforce desired outcomes.

5.3.1. *Aid Conditionality*

In the previous section, we saw the baleful effects that a repeated relationship can have on the part of a donor home office, when that home office is a passive player. This could be the equilibrium corresponding to maintaining a power station or policing power theft from the power grid. We now consider how a more active donor home office (player 3) can affect the aid relationship. Through the use of appropriate threats, the donor can improve on bad equilibrium outcomes. (For a more complicated version of this result, see Drazen 1999.) To anticipate our result, we show that: "An active donor home office can neutralize the worst effects of the Folk Theorem by a credible strategy of withdrawal."

Recall the 3-player game described in Section 5.2.4. Let the matrix G+ in that section correspond to the strategy for player 3 called "passive." In that equilibrium, the two players had to devise strategies to try and improve on the low–low equilibrium. In this section, we consider the donor as playing the role of an "enforcer" of good behavior (Figure 5.4). Let the matrix, G++, correspond to the strategy for player 3 called "active."

What player 3 has done is zero-out the game—all payoffs at zero correspond to terminating the aid relationship. It is a very blunt instrument, to be sure, but it has the effect—quite beneficial for player 3—of preventing negative payoffs. The following is a Nash equilibrium for the game consisting of matrices G+ and G++:

> Players 1 and 2 rotate between (High, Low) and (Low, High) every period.
> Player 3 plays "passive."

This Nash equilibrium corresponds to the donor settling for partial development success, so as not to "rock the boat," and yields an average efficiency per period of $(1 + 4 + 1)/(2.4 + 2.4 + 3) = 77$ per cent, not especially bad.

Fortunately for the donor, there are other Nash equilibria—in particular, one that achieves 100 per cent efficiency (of course, this is theorists' contrivance, but theoretical efficiencies in the nineties should be our goal—why settle for less). Here it

		Player 3's strategy: Active player 2's strategies	
		High	Low
Player 1's strategies	High	(0,0,0)	(0,0,0)
	Low	(0,0,0)	(0,0,0)

Figure 5.4. *Game G++: Normal form game, player 3 is active*

is: "Players 1 and 2 play High all but the last period, when they play any Nash equilibrium of the one-shot game. Player 3 plays 'passive' throughout the game. If any player ever deviates, players 1 and 2 play (Low, Low) forever, while player 3 plays 'active'."

Notice the efficiency of this equilibrium, per play, is $(7.2)/(7.2) = 100$ per cent, except in the last period. As the number of periods T gets large, the weight on the last period $(1/T)$ vanishes. This equilibrium gains credibility because player 3—the donor home office—is prepared to shut down the relationship in case of partial development success, when full success is attainable.

In projects supported by one donor country, such as the case of the power station in Maharashtra described in Chapter 9, the use of reputation strategies can enforce "good play" of the game by the participants. However, credibility is always an issue with reputation strategies; the donor must be willing to carry out threats to terminate the aid relationship. In the case of the power station, the donor country must be willing to let the capital stock deteriorate to ensure good play by the participants in the recipient country. The donor country must view its expenditures on the power station as a "sunk cost" that cannot be recouped. Thus, all that should matter to a donor country is current and future expenditures, not past expenditures.

However, despite the logic of ignoring sunk costs in economic decision making, it is difficult to get individuals to ignore sunk costs. Thus, despite its threats to withdraw maintenance funds for a capital project, recipient countries know that the threat is not credible. In these situations, the donor country may opt for an institutional arrangement as a substitute for credibility. For example, borrowing from the central banking literature on delegating monetary policy to a "conservative" central banker, Svensson (2000*b*) argues that donors should turn over their aid powers to a "tough" international organization that is willing to reduce aid if certain events are not realized. This is similar to a bank turning over its collection activities to a "mafia" bill collector who threatens to break your legs if you do not repay your debt. Thus, viewing aid in this form is similar to a bank loan that must be collected on somehow. While this idea is a clever theoretical construct, we doubt that individual countries will turn over the aid decisions to an independent international organization. Nor is it likely that recipient countries would comply with the threats of such a "tough" international organization.

5.3.2. *Aid Tournaments*

In most of the aid stories discussed so far are bilateral aid arrangements—there is a single donor and a single recipient. Due to this bilateral relationship, the recipient country has substantial "bargaining power" over how aid is to be used and results are measured. Furthermore, the risk of losing aid from putting forth low reform efforts is low. Thus, donors could employ "aid tournaments" to allocate aid among a group of countries. Tournaments have been shown to be effective ways to elicit high effort from participants. In effect, countries have to compete for foreign aid rather than negotiate for it. "A donor can forestall the worst effects of the principal–agent problem by conducting tournaments among target recipients for an aid project."

This works as follows. Return to the situation in Figure 5.1; only now suppose that the principal has two agents, each exactly like the one in Figure 5.1 with whom to deal. The principal is the donor; the two agents are two target recipients.

The donor, if it plays the game depicted in Figure 5.1 twice—that is, enters both countries—gets the same second-best outcome in each: low effort, partial development success. Contrast that rather unsatisfactory outcome to the following sub-game perfect equilibrium outcome. The donor says to the first target recipient:

I know how your competitor for this project will operate. They will put in low effort, and the project will be a partial success—a payoff of 1 for me. If you commit to high effort, and allow me to observe your effort, then I will give you the project, and I will guarantee that you get a payoff 10 per cent higher than 5, 5.5. I will take the extra out of my payoff from the first-best outcome.

This speech contains a Nash equilibrium—one that is quite acceptable from the point of view of both the donor and the lucky country that wins the competition for the aid project, by committing to high effort. This is what it takes to win the tournament being conducted by the donor, and this is what it takes to achieve complete development success.

Moreover, this strategy is eminently playable (see Svensson 2000*b* for a detailed treatment of how the donor can commit to such a strategy). Consider the set of countries in a region. Even when one is talking about very large countries—Russia, China, or Brazil—there are still other countries in the region. So there is always another target recipient in the region of the one a donor is dealing with. And since donors are usually organized by region, such a strategy is completely consistent with internal organization.

An alternative way of using a tournament is much like a lender asking for the borrower to put up collateral for a loan. An aid tournament could consist of a qualifying round and a final round. In the qualifying round, countries would have to undertake a certain amount of reforms to qualify for the actual aid tournament. In this way, they are putting up collateral to get a chance at the aid funds. In game theory, this is referred to as the "stick and carrot" strategy—the recipient must incur some costly activity in order to be rewarded.

An extra benefit of a tournament is that the donor shields itself from being subject to "hold-up strategies" on the part of the recipient. Hold-up strategies can be used when the donor country has no recourse but to comply with the recipient's demands. For example, in banking relationships, major borrowers can use the threat of nonpayment to take the bank hostage. In foreign aid, an example would be an aid recipient threatening to form political alliances opposed by the donor country. In these situations, the donor is essentially taken hostage by the recipient country. The best response on the part of a donor to avoid this situation is to have a regional alternative lined up—what we have called here a tournament.

Although we have talked about aid tournaments exclusively in terms of between countries, they might also be conducted within countries, just as open tenders might be conducted. The same logic applies to the within-country case.

5.4. EXTERNALITIES AND MARKET FAILURES

A standard economic reason for government intervention in the private provision of goods and services is that the market "fails" to provide the good efficiently (social marginal benefit equal to social marginal cost). Classic economic examples of market failure involve public goods and common-pool resource problems. In these situations, government intervention to improve the allocation of resources is a common method for overcoming the market failure. However, in many developing countries, weak governments or conflicting objectives require the input from a "neutral" third party to help solve the problem. Foreign aid is a form of third-party intervention to solve market failures.

5.4.1. *Public Good Problems*

A phenomenon that pervades target recipient countries is the public good problem. As explained in Chapter 2, public good is defined by two characteristics: exclusion is prohibitively costly, and consumption is nonrivalrous. Thus, public goods are polar opposites of private goods. While private goods only rarely exhibit inefficient outcomes when markets are effective, public goods almost always exhibit inefficient outcomes. The inefficiency associated with public good problems is observed the world over, in often more pronounced form in target recipient countries. Here are just three examples:

1. *Law and Order.* The provision of law and order is the fundamental public good underlying all civil societies. This public good is underprovided, especially in target recipients that are, or have been, torn asunder by civil strife and armed insurrection (Rwanda, Haiti, Afghanistan).
2. *Trust.* Without trust, most social arrangements, including economic ones, are hard to sustain. Lender/borrower relationships are a good example. It rarely pays to lend to someone who is untrustworthy. At the same time, the presence of trust makes possible the play of good equilibria that would not otherwise be possible.
3. *Technology Transfer.* Once a technology has been developed, it represents a public good to the rest of the world. The transfer of such technologies plays a major role in donor success. However, developing a technology is costly, and pricing it as a public good (if a market for such a good exists at all) does not cover cost, so technologies tend not to be developed solely for transfer.

All these examples have the feature that the public good is underprovided: There is not enough law and order, too little trust, and not enough technology transfer. Here follows a simple game model (a parable, if you like) to illustrate the incentives behind the underprovision of public goods. This model has been shown to have considerable explanatory success in the classic experiments run by Isaac and Walker (1988).

Consider a set of n players. Each player has a single indivisible unit of human resource at his or her disposal. If the player devotes that unit of human resource to private sector activity, the player gets the return w. If the player devotes that unit of

A Formal Analysis of Incentives

Player 2	Private sector	Public sector
Player 1		
Private sector	1,1	1.75,0.75
Public sector	0.75,1.75	1.5,1.5

Figure 5.5. *Public goods game in normal form*

human resource to public sector activity, every player in the game gets the payoff $3w/4$. The game matrix in Figure 5.5 shows the situation for $n = 2$, and $w = 1$.

Thus, if player 1 invests in the private sector while player 2 invests in the public sector, player 1 gets:

$1 + 0.75 = 1.75.$

The first term equals the return from private sector investment, the second from player 2's public sector investment. From the same investment, pattern player 2 gets the payoff:

$0 + 0.75 = 0.75.$

This matrix is an example of a Prisoner's Dilemma, a game the unique equilibrium of which is inefficient. The unique Nash equilibrium has each player investing in the private sector, so there is zero provision of public goods. The payoff to this equilibrium is $1 + 1 = 2$. The optimum, where the sum of payoffs is maximized, has each player investing in the public sector, so there is maximum provision of public goods. The payoff to the optimum is $1.5 + 1.5 = 3$. (Each player receives the return of his or her own investment plus the return of the investment in the public sector by the other player.)

The efficiency of the Nash equilibrium is $2/3 = 67$ per cent, an already considerable efficiency loss with just two players. Worse yet, the efficiency loss increases as does the number of players—a result reminiscent of the Tragedy of the Commons. For instance, with three players, the optimum pays $2.25 + 2.25 + 2.25 = 6.75$, while the equilibrium pays $1 + 1 + 1 = 3$, for an efficiency of $3/6.75 = 44$ per cent. This efficiency approaches zero as the number of players approaches infinity. The payoff to the Nash equilibrium with n players equals n; the payoff to the social optimum with n players equals $0.75n^2$, so the efficiency in the limit is

$$\lim \text{efficiency} = \lim n/[0.75n^2] = \lim 1/[0.75n] = 0$$

as n goes to infinity. The public good problem can be very serious.

One might say that the technology assumed here is extreme (linear), and this accounts for the optimal solution at a corner of the problem, with each player investing all resources in the private good. Although this is certainly true, the decrease in efficiency of a public good Nash equilibrium as the number of players rises is a very general result.

Most countries identified as a target recipient by donors reflect the short- and long-run inefficiencies associated with public good problems. There is a real and persistent market failure here, reflected in underprovision of law and order, trust, and technology transfer, among others. This market failure opens a window of opportunity for donors to enjoy development success. Donors need to address the public good problem in the target recipient country.

5.4.2. *Common-Pool Resource (CPR) Problems*

Consider next a common-pool resource, or commons. A commons is defined by two characteristics: exclusion is costly, but consumption is rivalrous (see Chapter 2). Thus, commons are polar opposites of club goods, where exclusion is costless but consumption is nonrivalrous. Club goods can be local (as in country clubs) or global (the European Union (EU)). Clubs exclude nonmembers from benefits (compare the Netherlands to Norway with regard to EU membership), while one member's consumption of benefits from club membership does not reduce another member's consumption of benefits from membership (compare the Netherlands and Finland). While club goods rarely if ever have tragic outcomes, commons are plagued by outcomes exhibiting short-run inefficiency and long-run unsustainability (destruction)—a phenomenon popularly known as the Tragedy of the Commons. This tragedy is often observed the world over, especially in target recipient countries. Two classes of examples where tragic outcomes have been or could be observed are (1) deforestation of tropical forests throughout the world, forests being a commons and (2) electrical power generation, with power grids acting as a commons.

Two of the case studies in this book (Chapters 9 and 10) exemplify commons problems: the Orissa forestry management project and the Maharashtra electrical power project. E. Ostrom (1990) contains many more such examples of tragic outcomes, as well as many examples where the users of a commons have organized themselves so as to overcome the strong temptations to overharvest and have sustainably used commons for many centuries. E. Ostrom *et al.* (1994) study commons from the point of view of game theory, institutional analysis, empirical political science, and experimental economics. (See also Svensson 2000*a* for an application of the concept of commons to foreign aid and rent seeking.)

To fix ideas, suppose there are n players, each having the same access to the commons, say a forest. (We sacrifice no generality by calling the commons a forest.) The production of forest output is given by a concave production function $F(X)$, where X is the number of players using the forest. Each player has one of two choices:

(1) use the forest, in which case the player's payoff is $F(X)/X$; or
(2) do not use the forest, in which case the player's payoff is w.

(1) follows from the equal access assumption; (2) represents a fixed outside opportunity, w, available to all potential users.

Forest production is shown on the vertical axis of Figure 5.6; inputs X into production, here the number of users, on the horizontal axis.

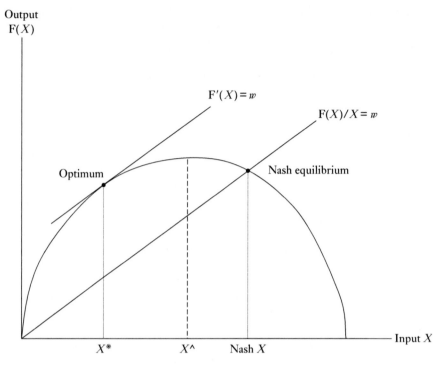

Figure 5.6. *Tragedy of the commons*

First, we can determine the Nash equilibrium of the game played by the n potential users of the forest, the players. A player will use the forest in the event that (1) pays better than (2):

$F(X)/X > w$ then use the forest.

A player will be indifferent between using the forest and exercising his outside option when (1) and (2) pay the same:

$F(X)/X = w$ then use the forest or exercise outside opportunity.

A player will exercise the outside opportunity in the event that (2) pays better than (1):

$F(X)/X < w$ then exercise outside opportunity.

At a Nash equilibrium, each player individually has maximized payoff; hence, this is a number of players X using the forest commons such that

$F(X)/X = w$ or $F(X) = wX,$

the point labeled Nash equilibrium in Figure 5.6.

Next, consider the optimization problem posed by the forest. One wants to maximize net output, which is the difference between forest output and opportunity cost:

Maximize $F(X) - wX$.

Using the theorem of the mean value from calculus, it is clear that the above maximum occurs at the point marked Optimum in Figure 5.6.

It follows from concavity of the production function that the number of users at Optimum is always less than the number of users at Nash equilibrium. So the situation portrayed in Figure 5.6 is completely general. Thus, we have as an immediate implication that the forest is overused at a Nash equilibrium.

This already implies an inefficiency. Define efficiency to be

Efficiency = (total payoff at Nash equilibrium)/(total payoff at Optimum).

This definition is a literal rendition of Debreu's coefficient of resource utilization (Debreu 1951). For the case shown in Figure 5.6, we have

Efficiency = $wX/[F(X^*) + w(X - X^*)] < 1$.

Indeed, this efficiency will be well below 100 per cent, since commons production in Figure 5.6 occurs in the counterproductive zone, where marginal product is negative. As long as average product is positive, no matter how low, one may get a Nash equilibrium at that level—all it takes is a low enough outside opportunity w.

Here is the recipe for ultimate tragic outcomes: w near 0 (low value outside opportunity) and large X (many potential users, for whom the commons is the best thing they have). This is the situation in many developing countries, such as the state of Orissa in India (see Chapter 9), where property rights to forested lands are ill-defined or where large-scale, government-owned forests are not guarded effectively and are *de facto*, open-access forests. In some cases, the property rights to such forested areas were relatively well-defined and enforced prior to colonization but not understood or recognized by colonial powers. Thus, earlier systems of property rights to forests were destroyed by external governments leaving many resources to be effectively open-access resources that had earlier been regulated by those who have communal rights to their use. Where the economic opportunities that local residents face outside an unprotected forest are very low and the population of local users is growing, the level of inefficiency can get worse and worse. The outcome is very low efficiency, as the Nash equilibrium is driven further and further toward zero—which must be reached in the limit as X grows large, again by concavity.

The study of the Maharashtra power project (Chapter 9) is another example of a commons. The power grid covers a wide area, is relatively easy to tap into, and power theft is rivalrous since it prevents others from consuming the electricity generated. Agents illegally tap into power grids, thereby making it nearly impossible for private electricity suppliers to cover production costs. Furthermore, the state electricity board used access to the power grid as a means of generating patronage. Since one bureaucrat's decision to hand out cheap (or free) electricity to his patrons does not incorporate how such a decision affects other users on the power grid, the grid is similar to a fishery (another classic example of a commons) that is "overfished" by the bureaucrats.

Returning to our mathematical model, in the limit for large X as w goes to zero, efficiency is driven to zero:

$$\text{Lim Efficiency} = \lim wX/[\text{F}(X^*) + w(X - X^*) = 0/\text{F}(X^\wedge) = 0,$$

where $X^\wedge$ is the X satisfying $\text{F}'(X^\wedge) = 0$, where maximum commons output occurs.

We identify low efficiency of commons utilization as a short-run tragedy. However, overuse also has long-run implications. Indeed, if overuse is not sustainable, then the commons will inevitably degrade, and may even be destroyed as a result. We identify destruction of the commons as a long-run tragedy.

Most countries, identified as target recipients by donors, reflect the short- and long-run tragic outcomes associated with commons. There is a real and persistent problem of property rights that have not been well-specified. This problem opens another window of opportunity for donors to enjoy development success: address the tragedy of the commons in the target recipient.

One might move toward the optimum with some kind of management scheme, for instance management by the central government, or even by the donor. The trouble with management by the donor is that it might infringe on widely held conceptions of sovereignty; thus, the donor would most likely be represented by a consultant. In either case, management by the central government or by a consultant representing the donor, an efficiency problem could arise if the agent who coordinates or monitors these management functions is corrupt. We now turn to the consideration of corruption.

5.4.3. *Corruption*

Corruption pervades the target recipients where donors operate. In the phenomenon of corruption, market failures come together in an especially perverse configuration. First, we can think of (and usefully model) foreign direct investment (FDI) as a fiscal commons, which is plundered by corrupt officials seeking bribes to invest in an economy—this is a Tragedy of the Commons. Second, we can think of corruption as a breakdown of law and order—this is a public good problem. Third, we can analyze corruption as a conflict between the citizenry (the principal) and its government officials (the agent)—this is a principal–agent problem. There is no guarantee that the donor will be able to overcome the configural nightmares posed by embedded corruption. To anticipate our main result: "Corruption represents the configuration of commons, public good and principal–agent problems. Corruption is a pervasive problem in target recipients where donors operate. Entry by a donor into a corrupt situation does not guarantee development success."

To make this point as vividly as possible, consider the case of FDI, where corrupt officials charge bribes so that FDI can take place. This turns out to be a commons problem in the extended sense, and game theory can treat it (see Waller *et al.* 2002 for more details). According to this view, bureaucrats view the private sector as a CPR that can be "harvested" via bribes. Corruption is a common feature in most recipient countries and it is one of the fundamental guarantors of bad initial results in such countries. We model corruption as a public official using public office for private gain. In particular, suppose a public official can give or deny permits for a foreign investor to invest in a given country—think of licenses, permits, fire inspections, tax inspections, and the like. The public official does not distribute permits on the basis of merit. Rather, the public official asks for a bribe, which is the price a foreign investor must pay to get this permission. The more permissions a foreign investor must get, the higher the price in terms of total bribes.

To take a concrete example of configuration, consider the decision by a donor to invest in the infrastructure of a country by building roads. Then the problem consists first in getting the necessary construction permits (the above CPR problem). But the problem is compounded by the need to hire local contractors to build the road (a principal–agent problem). Local contractors have an incentive to put forth low effort, by skimping on costly inputs if they can get away with it. So the donor requests government inspectors. However, if inspectors can get a bribe for looking the other way (a public good problem) then the new investment by the donor has fueled opportunities for bribe-taking and poor work. Many of the roads built in developing countries 20 or even 10 years ago have deteriorated very rapidly due to this problem (e.g. *The Economist*, 21 August 2002).

The basic situation before the donor enters the country is shown in Figure 5.7. Quantity of FDI, denoted Q, is shown on the horizontal axis; the price in terms of total bribes, B, is shown on the vertical axis. The demand for permits is the piecewise linear function with vertical intercept at

$$Q = 0, \quad B = k$$

and horizontal intercept at

$$Q = 1, \quad B = 0.$$

The vertical intercept represents the willingness of the foreign investor with the highest value investment project to invest. We denote this willingness by the parameter k. The higher this parameter, the more investment demand there is, for a given slope (which we hold constant). For simplicity, we assume linearity of demand in the figure. However, the main result is true for any demand function that displays monotone elasticity of demand—demand elastic at high prices, inelastic at low prices.

Depending on how corruption is organized, various outcomes along the demand function are possible:

1. *First-best*. The country has no corruption; or if it once had corruption, an anti-corruption drive has succeeded in wiping it out. In either case, $B = 0$, no bribes are taken, and all willing FDI enters the country. This case is represented by the horizontal intercept in Figure 5.7. We normalize $Q = 1$ to mean that 100 per cent of all willing FDI enters the country.

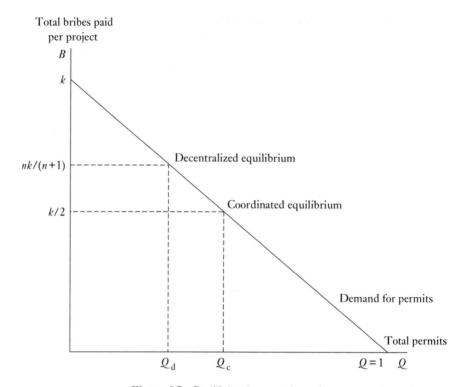

Figure 5.7. *Equilibrium in corruption regimes*

2. *Second-best.* The country has corruption, but that corruption is coordinated. For instance, the coordinator may be the president or prime minister, or some family member of the above. The coordinator sees that the most money possible is raised from bribes. This outcome is denoted Coordinated Equilibrium in Figure 5.7. The Coordinated Equilibrium is precisely what a monopoly public official would charge if he or she were handling bribes. This sort of equilibrium is encountered in one-family states or kleptocracies, such as Indonesia or Azerbaijan.

3. *Third-best.* The country has corruption, indeed is rife with it, and the corruption is decentralized. That is, there are n corrupt officials, with n being large, and each corrupt official charges a bribe on his or her own. This is just like many users, each using a CPR on his or her own, and not internalizing the implications of that use on the entire set of users. Just as in any CPR, one gets overuse of the CPR, much higher bribes in total are charged, and much less FDI enters the country, compared to either first- or second-best. This outcome is denoted Decentralized Equilibrium in Figure 5.7. Russia and Ukraine, the countries rated as the very worst in the world for investment climate according to the World Competitiveness Report (HIID 1999), exhibit the Decentralized Equilibrium. A typical value of n for Ukraine is 30—a typical firm can expect to be asked for bribes 30 different times in the course of a business year.

The above rankings are based on an efficiency measure, namely how much FDI is achieved relative to the optimum of 100 per cent. There is another commonly used measure of corruption, namely how much is the total value of bribes collected. In terms of Figure 5.7, this is the difference between the quantity axis (Q) and total revenue (BQ). In the event that Coordinated Equilibrium falls in the elastic range of market demand for permits, the rankings given by total bribes rate Coordinated Equilibrium worse than Decentralized Equilibrium, the opposite of the rankings given by efficiency.

If this is a commons, we should expect a potentially tragic outcome. And, true to form, here is how the Tragedy of the Commons arises. As n goes to infinity, the bribe charged at the Decentralized Equilibrium, $B = nk/(n + 1)$, approaches k, the reservation price of the most willing investor. That is, with enough corrupt public officials making enough inspections, FDI is completely discouraged. As an example of this, consider a country with an extremely poor investment climate, Russia, thanks in part to corruption. Very few foreign investors are found in Russia. At the same time, the biggest component of FDI into Ukraine comes from Russian investors, for whom Ukraine offers a better investment climate than home.

The initial situation facing the donor before entry into the target recipient is bad, especially if it faces the Decentralized Equilibrium. Generally speaking, three things can happen when the donor enters the country in the role of investor. However, it would not be correct to assume that donor investment simply adds to that of the rest of the market FDI. Below are three scenarios for what can happen to market demand as portrayed in Figure 5.7.

1. *Crowding-In.* This is the best scenario. Donor investment signals to the rest of the market that reform is underway. This signal is credible when donor investment is tied to reform, and that tie is known to other investors. In this event, donor investment encourages more FDI, the demand for permits shifts outward and upward (larger value of k), both B and Q rise. The rise in Q has beneficial micro- and macro-economic effects, contributing to overall development success. As a practical example, if donor investment in power generation leads to sector-wide reforms, then private investment is also encouraged.
2. *No Change.* Donor investment neither encourages nor discourages FDI, and the demand for permits does not change. Since B and Q do not change, there is no contribution to overall development success.
3. *Crowding-Out.* This is the worst scenario. Donor investment merely replaces existing local investment, while having no effect on FDI. For example, by providing electrical power to the state of Maharashtra, the case treated in Chapter 9, via foreign aid, private investment in electricity generation was driven out. In this case, the demand for permits shifts inward and downward (smaller value of k), both B and Q fall. The fall in Q has deleterious micro- and macro-economic effects, detracting from and possibly reversing overall development success.

The donor is confronted with a three-scenario analysis: these occur over and over again, quite naturally, in real-world decisions. To determine which of these three scenarios is most likely, and to what extent that scenario is realized, requires a great deal of further data (country-specific, especially), as well as a close analysis of potential FDI. In the best case, donor entry may even reduce corruption (here modeled by a lower value of n) as part of an overall reform package.

Traditionally, donors have focused on improving the capacity of official government agencies. This focus has been reinforced by the priorities of officials in target recipient countries. A more efficient government can also more efficiently extract rents (raising corruption), while aid that more directly enhances the capacity of local communities to coordinate their own actions might be more efficient (lowering corruption). In terms of the contrast between Nash equilibrium (3) and social optimum (4), an increase in corruption lowers the value of (3), while leaving the value of (4) unchanged.

The inefficiencies caused by corruption only get worse with a greater number of levels of corruption. For instance, if corruption is also present at the local community level, then the efficiency gain pointed to above may not materialize. A donor will have to put up with some level of corruption—this is present in all target recipient countries—although there is no doubt a threshold above which they would prefer to deny aid (following the logic of Section 5.3). This suggests that a rational government in a target recipient country will find that threshold value, and extract just as much as possible without causing the donor to pull out completely. If so, this is a certain invitation to continued dissatisfaction on both sides.

Sometimes training government officials to be more efficient makes them more efficient at seeking and finding rents. As long as a government cannot credibly threaten to fire such officials, the problem of corruption will be present forever. The key to the solution of this problem is adding some government levels that truly are responsive to a public. Local democratic systems where voters do have some chance to vote out corrupt local officials can at times improve the situation. So even though adding more government levels may make the situation regarding corruption worse, it may also bring with it the means of a solution to the problem.

5.5. COORDINATED AID

So far, we have considered a single pair of countries, one represented by the donor, the other represented by the target recipient. There are also interesting strategic aspects when there are two or more countries represented by donors.

As we pointed out in the previous section, donors typically encounter corruption in the target recipient country. Corruption can encompass CPR problems, public good problems, and principal–agent problems. Put all together, these encounters can utterly vitiate all results of development activity. Even worse, it may seem there is nothing the donor countries can do about this unfortunate situation.

Here is a simple model of the phenomenon. Suppose two donors, each representing a donor country, face the payoff matrix $G+$ (recall Section 5.2.4.). There is a single target recipient, and for each donor, the interaction inside the target recipient should the donor enter looks like $G+$. Given passive donors, either donor country can expect the payoff 1—partial development success—from entering, or staying in, the target recipient.

Now suppose that donor country A has entered the target recipient country, and decides to improve the situation by getting tough with the target recipient, playing actively. This means A credibly threatens to withdraw, with the payoff consequences given by G++.

What does the target recipient do in a case like this? It turns to the second donor country B, which has not entered the target recipient country, and invites B to replace A in the donor/recipient relationship—often with (noncredible) promises of development success. (We heard this repeated in numerous interviews.) This is precisely exercise of an outside opportunity by the target recipient—the outside opportunity being the country not currently operating in the target recipient country.

So it would seem that the donor countries are stuck, strategically speaking, in partial success equilibria with their attendant aid dependency—and no way out to complete success.

In a situation like this, it is often useful to change the rules of the game. This is precisely what the OECD donor countries did when they ratified the OECD Treaty against Corruption in 1999. By providing the possibility of taking legal actions against OECD firms that pay bribes, OECD members essentially ruled out scenarios like the above, where a single corrupt target recipient plays off one donor against another. It is too early to tell whether the OECD treaty is actually working.

Even better from the standpoint of the donors, with this rule change the equilibria of the form (High, High, passive) are restored to viability, unless there is a deviation. Instead of having to settle for partial development success, the donors can demand (and come very close to getting) complete development success. Their interests are best served by crafting the rules of the game in such a way that bad (for them) equilibria are ruled out.

The main point here is: "Coordinated commitment on the part of donor country donors can forestall the worst effects of the Bad Folk Theorem."

5.6. EQUITY CONSIDERATIONS

To this point, we have considered only efficiency gains as a desired consequence of donor activity. It would be an oversight not to say something about distributional consequences from external aid. Here we show: "External aid not only changes economic incentives, it also changes the distribution of payoffs. Such changes may jeopardize the sustainability of efficiency gains."

Here is a simple game sketch of this process. Prior to entry by the donor, the players in the target recipient country are playing a symmetric equilibrium—everyone uses the same strategy and receives the same payoff, 1. With two players, this is the distribution:

(player 1, player 2) = (1,1).

So, one starts with a situation of complete equality. Suppose this total payoff, 2, represents 50 per cent efficiency.

Now external aid enters the country, making government officials more efficient at distributing that aid—but also more efficient at channeling that aid to groups whose support the government wants to court. Such is often the case when a developing country is monetized. The mere institution of money is sufficient to create winners and losers, depending on access to money and credit. It is worth noting that in some of the poorest countries, money as a medium of exchange is not prevalent, and most exchange is carried out by barter. North Korea is an example of this.

Suppose that as a result of the aid process, the initial total of 2 $(1 + 1)$ becomes 4, to be distributed over the two players. In the distribution process, player 1, favored by the government, gains while player 2 loses:

(player 1, player 2) = (3.1, 0.9).

Now the pre-existing but inefficient situation has been replaced by a very asymmetric but efficient situation, where one player (think of this as representing a large constituency) is a winner and another player is a loser. Clearly, such distributional asymmetries may not be sustainable—they may be upset by social unrest, even revolution.

We suspect that donors often have very specific distributional objectives in mind. Improving the lot of the poorest might be seen as a success from some perspectives, and could be touted as such. From such a standpoint, the above example of raising efficiency from 50 per cent to 100 per cent would not be counted as a success. In any event, equity successes of that sort are very likely to clash with efficiency—a familiar result from the debate over Rawls's theory of justice.

5.7. WARM-GLOW EFFECTS

We have so far presumed that the donor country was altruistic, that is, it received utility only if the aid provided generated results in terms of improving the standard of living in the recipient country. The disturbing fact of foreign aid, documented in Burnside and Dollar (2000*a*,*b*), is that aid does not seem to generate the desired results. As we have argued in this chapter, this may be the result of donor country donors not using the appropriate mechanisms to provide the appropriate incentives for recipient countries to reform. But an alternative view comes from the evidence from economics and social psychology on charitable giving. It is well-documented that people like to give to charities regardless of whether or not the aid accomplishes anything. This is called the "warm glow" effect (see the classic paper by Andreoni 1990). For example, it appears to be a major reason that people vote in national elections even though the paradox of voting suggests that it is not individually rational to expend private resources to vote.

If one views foreign aid from a "warm glow" perspective, then all that matters to aid givers is the act of giving itself. If the aid actually accomplishes something, they are happy; but if it does not, they do not care since it is the act of giving that matters. In this situation, expending resources to actually achieve results is not necessarily desirable—what matters is simply making sure that the aid money is spent, that is, that bureaucrats "move the money." If donor countries care only about giving and not what the giving produces, one should observe considerable amounts of aid being given to countries with little effort being expended to ensure that the giving accomplishes something. This prediction is clearly consistent with the data of foreign aid. While clearly a cynical view of foreign aid, it seems to fit the facts and is supported by considerable experimental and empirical data (see Burnside and Dollar 2000*a,b* and the vast literature inspired by this article). Furthermore, voters may base election votes on how much aid a politician is willing to spend rather than how it is spent or what it produces. Consequently, to give voters their desired "warm glow" effect, politicians have incentives to put pressure on donors to "move the money" for political reasons rather than humanitarian reasons. If the warm glow effect is what drives foreign aid decisions, then designing appropriate incentive mechanisms for recipient countries is a moot point.

5.8. CONCLUSION

In this chapter, we have presented the kind of insights into the strategic interactions facing a donor agency that game theory makes possible. In the interest of clarity, we chose to use simple models that serve as good illustrations to our main arguments. At the same time, the models have been rather abstract. The reason for this was to make the most general points possible, and generality would be compromised by overly specific examples.

In the next chapter, the focus is on different kinds of aid and the incentives of different forms of international assistance. Many of the theoretical findings of this chapter will be illustrated there and subsequently in the third part of the book, which draws on empirical studies of the aid process ranging all the way from headquarters to the field.

6

All Aid is Not the Same: The Incentives of Different Types of Aid

6.1. INTRODUCTION

Different types of aid can generate different incentives. In this chapter, we look at how the modalities, means, and conditions of aid can produce different kinds of incentives and, in this way, engender a variety of outcomes. *Modalities* refer to broad instruments of aid, such as Project Aid, Program Aid, and Sector Program Support. The *means* of aid refer to whether the aid is delivered in the form of credits, grants, or guarantees. Finally, *conditionality* refers to how donor-imposed constraints on the delivery of aid might persuade a recipient government to behave in certain ways. We begin this chapter by briefly reviewing the most common interpretation of aid as an incentive to spur policy change in the government of an aid recipient. We then examine some of the rules embedded in the modality, means, and conditions of aid, and consider how these in combination might generate incentives within specific contexts of aid delivery.

6.2. AID AS "CARROTS AND STICKS"

Early conceptions of aid held that substantial transfer of assets were needed to jump-start the development process. The "gap theory" stressed that foreign assistance could infuse the capital, infrastructure, and technical assistance absent in developing countries. Official capital flows—facilitated through grants and credits, and financed by the governments of developed countries and multilateral donor organizations—were to make possible this developmental transformation.[1]

In many situations, however, aid transfers have not been effective in stimulating development. In the case of Project Aid, this low level of return on the aid-dollar has been linked to three fundamental problems (Collier 1999; Stiglitz 1997). The first problem is that aid projects are often not *scalable*, which means that projects that are successful in one context may not be in others, limiting the replicability of a project model. The second problem is that project funding is often *fungible* (Feyzioglu *et al*. 1998; van de Walle 2001; World Bank 1998), which means that donor financing of a project can potentially release resources of the recipient government for other more marginal projects. In effect, therefore, donors do not finance the project they appear to pay for, but rather the one that the recipient government, for whatever reason, chooses to undertake with the resources freed by aid. The third reason given for the relative ineffectiveness of aid is the poor quality of the overall *policy environment*.

Donors have found the problems of scalability difficult to overcome, but they have attempted to tackle the fungibility and policy environment problems with the tool of aid conditionality. Different types of aid conditionality, often focusing on macro-economic or Program Aid, emerged in the 1980s as a way of using the carrots and sticks of providing or withholding aid dollars to extract desired policy reforms from recipient countries. Conditioning aid in return for explicit negotiated commitments to reform means that policy change is the price that recipient governments, in effect, pay in exchange for aid. This leads to several incentive-related problems, according to Collier (1999).

First, if donors have "bought" reforms with program aid, they become the owners. Donors, realizing this peril, have sought to portray aid in exchange for policy reform as the "costs of adjustment." Despite such creative labeling, recipient governments can threaten (and have threatened) to rollback previously undertaken reforms as a way of countering donor pressure. Such threats show that recipient government leaders know who really owns the reforms.

Second, a recipient country's leader may not be motivated to take on the respon-sibilities of ownership. Instead, by vociferously protesting the conditions being imposed by donors, hardships caused by the reforms can later be blamed on the donor. Popularity at home can be gained by making the donor out to be the "bad guy." When it is polit-ically expedient to identify ownership of reforms with the donor, leaders are less motivated to develop the domestic consensus needed for reform, restructuring, or belt-tightening to be effective.

Third, recipient government officials can affect a reluctance to reform as a way of wringing more concessions in the aid bargaining process. Donor-negotiating teams, meanwhile, see their purpose as extracting the maximum reform for a given amount of aid. Thus, even if the recipient government believes in the reform, there can be an incentive to impede rather than assist the reform process.

Aid conditionality can also fail when the conditions for aid are weakly enforced by the donor agency. Stone's (2004) model of IMF funding finds that governments that were receiving significant funds from the United States, France, and Great Britain were for-given faster than others and the new IMF funds started even when they really had not met the conditions previously laid down. Stone (ibid.: 590) notes that "IMF program conditions are enforced less rigorously when borrowing countries receive large amounts of US aid, belong to post colonial institutions that link them to France or Great Britain, or have voting postures in the UN similar to France," revealing that these large donors trade off developmental objectives for geopolitical gain, even in the post-Cold War era.

Additional reasons exist why a donor's offer of aid for reform may not induce a supply response. An injection of aid may, in some cases, alleviate the immediate fiscal crisis of the recipient government, and hence the urgency for change, delaying needed reform. Some recipients may also see little downside in failing to deliver on aid-conditional policy reform because they expect that donors, reluctant to concede a failure or fearful of the fallout from failure, will continue to provide aid.

Short-term political and commercial goals pushed by interest groups in the donor country also help undermine the discipline of donor conditionality (Collier *et al.* 1997). As we note in our case study of the Indian power sector in Chapter 9, keeping domestic firms profitable and workers employed through tied-aid procurement can be politically persuasive. Another contributing factor from the donor's side is that Desk Officers in some donor agencies find their career advancement linked to the number of projects signed and funds disbursed; maintaining restraint, on the other hand, may not be perceived as career-enhancing.

One outcome of this set of incentives is the "promise now but delay delivery until later" strategy of aid recipients that is described in *The Economist*'s (August 5, 2000) Kenya-Fund Dance, where the donor keeps extracting new promises from the recipient in order to maintain a flow of donor funds.

6.3. THE CONFIGURATION OF AID CAPITAL

Understanding incentives in aid requires that we move beyond a focus on a single action situation—that between donor government and recipient government—to consider more complex and configural relationships. The Octangle, developed in Chapter 4, provides a representation of the connections among the primary actors in this system of aid. Incentives derived from actors' interactions emerge, partly, from the presence of given modalities and means of aid. These characteristics can affect the effectiveness and sustainability of aid.

Characteristics distinguishing any particular initiative in aid include the sector of activity, the modality of assistance, the form of finance, the nature of the contract, and the channel of implementation. In turn, these categories each imply the presence of certain rules and conditions that circumscribe the context within which aid takes place. Any particular aid intervention represents a bundle of rules and incentives. Such rules will also interact with diverse endogenous rules and localized contextual understandings. Given that incentives arise from the interaction of individuals within the bounds of formal and informal understandings, the nature of these aid characteristics and their interaction with existing institutional arrangements is important to any understanding of how aid, incentives, and sustainability are related.

The economist Ludwig Lachmann (1971, 1978) refers, in his studies of capital, to a morphology of relevant forms that the structure of production assumes in a dynamic environment. As a form of social capital, institutions are also composed of various elements or rules (E. Ostrom 1999). Among all of the rules that might apply in a particular situation, only some are feasible. A further subset of these may be meaningful for sustainable development. To take a bricks-and-mortar analog, only certain architectural designs—those that specify the strategic location of load-bearing walls, for example—will support the construction of viable buildings. Further, only certain types of buildings will be suitable for a given purpose—say, as a house or a factory. Similarly, only particular configurations of characteristics will be feasible in aid. Of these, some may be more relevant for a particular collective-action problem than others in developing the types of incentives needed for project success and sustainability.

To improve the institutional contexts of aid, we must come to grips with what each of these characteristics represent, and with how each might work in conjunction with others.

Numerous combinations and permutations are possible among the categories and rule features of aid. Take, as an illustration, a *project* in the *natural resources sector*. The project contract is based on principles of *ex ante conditionality*, and is financed by a *grant*. It is *implemented by a partner country organization*. All these factors have associated rule implications that take on additional meaning in their combined context and in the context of endogenous rules and localized arrangements. Understanding the incentive properties that each of these factors represent—both singly and together, as invoked in the design of any given aid intervention—can make us more aware of the incentive consequences of aid and, hence, the prospects of sustainability.

Untangling these incentives for all possible combinations and contexts is of course too large a task for this book; our ambition in this chapter is to provide brief descriptions of the various characteristics and modalities of aid, indicate the incentives they generate, and draw out some likely consequences, especially for sustainability.

6.4. THE CHARACTERISTICS OF AID

The characteristics of aid shape the institutional context of aid. Below, we review three basic means of aid finance—*grants, credits,* and *guarantees*. Following this, we take up some specific conditions attached to such aid. *Tied-aid* conditions specify a locus of procurement—usually in the donor country itself—and *Aid Conditionalities* specify what is required of the recipient in order to qualify for the aid disbursement. We explore how these characteristics of aid yield incentives that can have important consequences for aid ownership and sustainability.

6.4.1. *Grants, Credits, and Guarantees*

Grants, credits, and guarantees are three ways in which a donor conveys financial assistance to a recipient. Each is characterized by particular incentives, where the incentive effects emerge under specific conditions.

Grants
Grants are transfers made from the donor to the recipient in cash, goods, or services for which no repayment is required.[2] Grants are attractive in our everyday understanding since they do not have to be repaid. Here, potential grantees may modify their behavior to make themselves eligible for a grant. This incentive effect of grants, however, can evaporate in the aid context, when a recipient government swaps all or some portion of its own contributions to the organization carrying out the project with that derived from donor funding—the issue of fungibility.

An interest in maintaining a good reputation may also motivate the prudent use of grant funds by an awardee. Research scientists, for example, are repeatedly motivated to face up to the tedium of writing grant proposals that set out detailed representations of intended activities. Ownership through accountability is ensured in this case by the researcher's stake in the outcome of the funded work. Among other considerations, this includes the need to build a reputation among his or her peers, and the need to attract similar funds in the future. In the aid context, responsible use of grants is enhanced when recipient governments need to maintain credibility with their donors and creditors. However, if the donor faces a Samaritan's Dilemma, or if competition exists between donors, there may be fewer stakes for a recipient in maintaining a good reputation. In the case of Project Aid, it is also possible that local-level officials in charge of implementation face fewer repercussions for irresponsible project owner-ship, facing a different reality than officials at the finance ministry.

Credits
Credits (or loans) are fund transfers for which repayment is required and where the terms of repayment vary with the rate of interest and the length of the repayment period.[3] Among other factors, these terms depend on how the United Nations clas-sifies a recipient country, with those in the "Least Developed" category—a select list—receiving a higher rate of concessionality.[4]

The incentive value of credits, as per our everyday experience, depends on how well recipient ownership is rooted. If we take an everyday case of a bank financing an entre-preneur with credit, the borrower has a stake in his or her own success since this enables repayment of the loan. In this way, he remains creditworthy—that is, able to take out further loans if needed.[5] The bank correspondingly has an incentive to screen loan applicants carefully as it stays in business through recovering its loans plus interest.

However, when ownership is separated from its associated responsibility, as often happens in aid, the incentive effects of credits become obscured. If repayments of credits taken to finance particular development projects in recipient countries are derived from the country's general tax base (as is usual) rather than earmarked from the income generated by the funded project, there are fewer financial stakes for the project owner or recipient government in the success of a given development project. This is particularly so for relatively small projects.

Incentives also weaken when donors extend credits as program assistance. Macro-economic Program Aid credits are designed to prompt recipient governments to adopt good policies and to make national investments needed for high rates of economic growth and human development. The repayment schedules here are usually extended over periods of up to 20 or more years. However, the short-term political imperatives of recipient country officials may overtake the objectives of such long-term financing, leading recipient government officials to make promises to donors to secure the credits only to later backtrack on these commitments.[6]

When, for this or other reasons, the expected growth from macro-economic Program Aid does not materialize, repayment cannot be made and the debt burden can accumulate. This stock of outstanding debt then will deter both domestic and foreign investment. When donor involvement crowds out private investment, a recip-ient can become more dependent on donors and this can negatively affect prospects for sustainable development (Bräutigam 2000).

Guarantees

Guarantees facilitate the financing of projects (often large infrastructure projects) that use private sources of capital. Such capital can be drawn from domestic capital markets or from abroad. High risks, however, can inhibit private investment. Guarantees help overcome these risks, making privately financed investments possible.

There are three basic types of guarantees covering three basic types of risks: Investment Guarantees cover the political risks in share capital, Credit Enhancement Guarantees overcome the credit risks developing-country borrowers pose, and Performance Guarantees mitigate the risks to investors from the shortcomings in regulation, legislation, and project execution capacities of the developing country in question (Sida 1999e).

While guarantees reduce the risk involved for firms from donor countries to invest in specific projects in the recipient country, these selected investments can postpone the need for fundamental institutional reform required of the recipient country to deal with the presence of these risks in the first place. A recipient government will be less compelled to face up to its responsibilities—in terms of maintaining credible systems of governance, regulation, and adjudication—as a way of attracting needed private investment as long as donors compensate for these shortcomings through pro-viding guarantees. The Moral Hazard problem presented here is illustrated in a case study of power infrastructure development in Chapter 9, where Swedish guarantees helped finance power-transmitting equipment in India, postponing the reckoning for needed reforms.[7]

6.4.2. *Tied-Aid—Issues and Incentives*

Donor aid, whether in the form of credits, grants, or guarantees, is considered "tied" when goods and services associated with the project must be procured in the donor country.[8] In general, tied-aid can limit a recipient country's ownership of aid since it denies the prerogative to make decisions regarding the aid.[9] There are three more specific arguments made in the literature that are critical of tied-aid.

First, tied-aid requires the use of the donor country's technical and/or material resources where these resources may not be the most appropriate. Being forced to buy a cutting-edge generator, for example, may be worse for a recipient than buying less sophisticated gear that can be installed and repaired locally. Tied-aid can threaten the long-run success of a development project when the recipient does not have the skills or means to maintain the project. A case study in Chapter 10 describes how tied-aid from Sweden was used to buy electricity-generating equipment for Zambia's power company, virtually assuring that Sida (Swedish International Development Cooperation Agency)-paid Swedish companies would be required to provide support for decades to come.

Another problem with tied-aid is that it runs the risk of reducing competitive pres-sure in procurement. In this way, it can hamper the efficient use of aid resources. Jepma (1991) notes that using tied-aid to protect domestic industries results in higher procurement prices than when aid is untied. Relatedly, Hayter and Watson (1985) have calculated that the price of goods financed by aid exceeds world market prices by 25–30 per cent.

Tied-aid also dilutes the central purpose of aid when it is used to channel funds drawn from general taxes in the donor country to specific donor country enterprises. Philip Jones (1995: 369) notes in this regard that "the decision to provide tied-aid depends on political pressures in the donor country and the willingness of donor tax-payers to fund it." The scope for rent seeking is broadened when taxpayers support government-funded altruism and there are few alternatives for delivering this aid. This donor country rent seeking can negatively influence the potential for sustainable development.

Indeed, tied-aid has long been a way for donor governments to pursue mercantilist policies. While subsidizing exports is not allowed by the World Trade Organization, purchasing or financing the purchase of goods to be sent to recipient countries under the guise of aid can amount to the same thing. Various donor governments have, in the past, subsidized exports by guaranteeing loans below market interest rates. Donor governments are also keen to promote their national companies in competition with those of other countries, "especially when big infrastructure contracts are at stake in emerging markets" (*The Economist*, February 1, 1997). In this regard, a 1994 report by the United States General Accounting Office (USGAO) on tied-aid noted (based on averages for the 1988 to 1991 period) that other Western donors linked between 45 and 91 per cent of their tied-aid to capital projects (USGAO 1994).

The trade effects of tied-aid can be long-lasting. Since tied-aid is most common in the sector of infrastructure—which includes projects in telecommunications, power generation, construction, and transportation—the loss of an initial contract usually implies the associated loss to the contracted firm(s) of very lucrative follow-on sales of spare parts and maintenance contracts.[10] In order to discourage the use of such trade-distorting tied-aid, the OECD in 1992 established the "Helsinki Package." This rule prohibits the use of tied-aid for projects in recipient countries whose per capita income is sufficiently high to make them ineligible for 17–20-year loans from the World Bank. It also restricts the use of tied-aid for projects that are otherwise commercially viable. Finally, the Helsinki Package seeks to improve transparency in the provision of tied-aid by fortifying notification and consultation procedures (OECD 1996).

While the Helsinki Package requires individual members of the OECD to adhere to the rules on tied-aid, the agreement specifically excludes aid programs of multi-lateral or regional institutions. United States officials have suggested that some European countries are circumventing the protocol by channeling tied-aid through the European Union (USGAO 1994).[11]

Jakob Svensson (2000*a*) argues that the conventional wisdom on tied-aid—that tied-aid is bad for the recipient country and that it is mostly a way to increase the commercial impact of an aid project—does not look sufficiently at incentive structures inherent in donor–recipient interactions. He holds that recipients may overcome moral hazard problems inhibiting the implementation of needed structural reforms in cases where donors possess a credible means of committing themselves. Donor-imposed conditionality often does not work, says Svensson, citing *The Economist*'s (August 5, 2000) Kenya-Fund Dance. Instead, such commitment can come, he notes, through tied-aid, among other mechanisms.

This commitment technology is introduced since a tied-aid project is contractible within the donor country, in contrast to an untied-aid project where there is no independent framework for enforcement. Tied contracts, he notes, can be enforced by the legal institutions of the donor country. Here, donor country courts could hold the donor agency's feet to the fire. As Svensson concludes, "this in turn constrains the donor's *ex post* incentives, thereby providing the necessary incentives for the recipient governments to induce effort" (2000*b*: 64). Svensson argues that through this pre-commitment, the donor government's strategy is made credible to the recipient government. As such, the recipient government is further induced to make the needed effort on its part to help improve aid sustainability. In this way, he notes, the potential commitment properties of tied-aid can overcome the other drawbacks of tied-aid.[12]

Svensson's recommendations, if adopted, would undercut the Helsinki Package. Given this, more thought has to be given, among other issues, to the conditions under which donor country firms will seek legal recourse. Indeed, it is possible that both the donor agency and the donor country firm can have good reasons to avoid court proceedings. Inhibitions in this regard may stem, for example, from the fear of unfavorable media attention. Such bad press can increase critical scrutiny of donor organizations and dissipate public support for aid.[13]

6.4.3. *Aid Conditionality*—Ex ante *Versus* Ex post

In a speech at the Bank-Fund annual meeting in 1999, Joseph Stiglitz, then the World Bank's chief economist, observed that traditional *ex ante* conditionality—aid contracts with strings attached—has not worked. He noted further that democratic accountability and economic sustainability require that the recipient country take ownership of its development strategy. In carrying this theme further, Gilbert *et al.* (1999) argue that conditionality should be *ex post*: countries that have adopted good policies and have used past aid well should be rewarded with aid without conditions. Here countries that have demonstrated accountability would be given the full responsibilities and rewards of ownership. An *ex post* certification regime would also encourage private investment. In theory, this would signal recipient governments that they would be rewarded for good policy behavior while giving poor reformers a greater incentive to change (van de Walle 1999).

Ex post conditionality, however, raises several incentive-related issues.[14] First, the varying levels of selectivity among different donors can create strategic openings for recipient country agents. What level of performance should donors reward? If some donor governments are less selective than others, they may snatch away the political, strategic, and commercial rewards of providing aid from donors that are more stringent. This can create a race to the bottom. Without sufficient coordination among donors, incentives will be created for aid recipients to play one donor against the other, leading to no improvement.

Second, donor funding under an *ex post* regime creates fewer rewards for the donor country and the donor agency. *Ex post* conditionality will require less donor supervision and project appraisal since these responsibilities are passed on to the recipient owners. When ownership is truly exercised by the recipient, donor countries lose the advantages that providing aid confers them in realizing their own strategic and commercial goals. Donor agencies will also likely lose power and influence—important rewards for donor agency officials—particularly in recipient country polities.

Third, existing incentive structures within donor agencies may not support *ex post* conditionality. Van de Walle (2001) notes that donor agency staff sometimes lack the discipline to lend to temporarily virtuous countries, or resist lending to marginally professional ones, when advancement is related to the size of their portfolio of projects.

Fourth, foreign aid becomes less publicly defensible to donor country taxpayers when it is disbursed only to countries that, through responsible government, have improved their own level of development.[15] Such countries are more likely to attract private investment and are not as reliant on aid funds. Humanitarian motives underlying public support for aid in donor countries will be undermined when countries dealing ably with their own challenges in development are the ones receiving most of the aid.

While strategies related to conditionality are most commonly associated with incentives and aid, the nature of aid can also give rise to incentives that affect its sustainability, as we see next.

6.5. THE MODALITIES OF AID

We now examine the rules embedded in the major modalities of Project Aid, Program Aid, Sector-Wide Approaches (SWAPs), Humanitarian Assistance, and Technical Cooperation. In each case, we briefly describe the modality, introduce the actors involved, and describe the linkages among them. Finally, we highlight selected issues related to incentives and sustainability that might arise in the context of the given modality.

6.5.1. *Project Aid*

Project Aid concerns support by a donor for specific short- to medium-term interventions in the recipient country. Project funds typically cover such expenses as procuring capital, paying contractors, and training local officials. Although Project Aid encompasses a very large variety of activities, the interventions are relatively distinct and limited. The beneficiaries they target are also relatively well-defined. The usual purpose of a donor project is to set in place physical and human capital inputs that the recipient is otherwise thought not willing or able to procure or fund.

Bilateral Project Aid usually proceeds within a framework drawn up by the *donor government* and accepted through negotiations with the *recipient government*. Such "country frameworks" are usually presented by the *donor's foreign ministry* to the counterpart *ministry of the recipient government*. A country framework, as in Sweden's case, sets out the budget and focus of activity for a period of time. This country framework guides the individual projects of the *donor's aid agency*.

Once the donor agency finds a project it wants to fund, it proceeds to identify an owner within the recipient government. This often is the agency or a *line ministry* that holds the portfolio most relevant to the project, although ownership can also be vested in quasi-governmental and *nongovernmental organizations*. These owners may implement the project although, frequently, added inputs—equipment, advice, and training—are contracted through third-party organizations. In the case of tied-aid, procurement is linked to donor country firms and service providers.

Interest groups in both the donor and recipient countries may also be involved. *Contractors* that are to provide equipment or services for a donor-funded project may, for example, lobby the donor government in this regard. On the other side, *civil society organizations*, whether within or outside government, may argue for or protest a project's funding. Targeted *beneficiaries* are those who are supposed to benefit most directly from the project. These groups may be large or small and may be scattered or concentrated. The degree to which their interests are represented in a project's design and execution can vary. *Recipient governments*, in many developing country contexts, poorly represent beneficiary interests unless these beneficiaries are able to coalesce into effective *interest groups*.

Any particular initiative in Project Aid involves, in one way or the other, all the main actors of the Octangle. Analyzing the incentives that structure each of these actors and further those that structure interactions among particular subsets of these is particularly complex. (The project case studies in Chapters 9 and 10 provide concrete examples of these inter-linkages.) The more specific a project is in terms of who it will benefit and how they are to be assisted through aid, the clearer it is for agents of the donor government to patronize (potentially) selected domestic firms or other organizations for this purpose. Donor country interests, in this case, face incentives to lobby for such projects (Jones 1995). In our case study of a Sida-financed power project in India, for example, ABB (a Swedish company) lobbied Sida to provide the aid funds to procure its high voltage transformers (see Chapter 9).

Another interaction in Project Aid is that between the donor agency, the sectoral ministry or agency that is designated the recipient owner, and the beneficiaries. Donor funds sometimes pay for cars and office equipment needed to facilitate implementation of important components of the project. These inputs are often viewed by recipient country officials in charge of the project as perquisites, leading some to prolong the project as a way of continuing with their use. Arguments can be made to prolong a project as long as the beneficiaries continue to face problems. There may be, thus, few incentives for recipient country officials (the formal owners) to help beneficiaries develop sustainable solutions to their collective-action problems unless there are mechanisms in place for citizens to hold their government accountable (Smith 1994).

6.5.2. *Program Aid*

Program Aid generally dispenses large lump sums of aid in pursuit of general policy objectives, often related to realizing desired macro-economic conditions. It includes such instruments as debt relief and budget support.[16] These instruments are usually linked by donors—often explicitly as incentives—to foster economic and governance reforms by the government of the recipient country.

Program Aid links the *donor government* and the *recipient government*, usually in coordination with *other bilateral and multilateral donors*. The ostensible *beneficiary* of Program Aid, the population of the recipient country as a whole, does not directly participate in the negotiation process.[17] *Special interest groups* from within the recipient country, which hope to gain differentially from an increase of spending in public expenditures as a result of such aid, can seek to influence the negotiation process for Program Aid. Similarly, interest groups from donor countries may also get involved. In general, however, Program Aid involves links only at the top of the Octangle.

For the donor, Program Aid has two appealing aspects. First, it can be used as an instrument in foreign policy. This is reflected, for example, in the fact that the Swedish account for Economic Reform and Debt Relief is ultimately responsible to the Ministry of Foreign Affairs, rather than to Sida (1999*a*). With such control, modifications to Program Aid allocations (or threats to that effect) can serve as a handy way for Sweden to signal its pleasure or discontent with the policies of a recipient government. Program Aid is also used as a lure by Sweden to encourage its development partners to support its positions in the UN General Assembly and other international forums (Sida 1999*b*). Second, Program Aid can expend a donor's foreign aid budget much more quickly than other modalities. Whereas Project Aid, for example, requires significant commitments of time and effort in management and follow-through, Program Aid dispatches large sums of a donor's budget allocation for aid with far less administrative exertion. Program Aid is thus a more efficient money-mover than many other aid modalities.

For a recipient government, Program Aid offers a way of meeting its obligations to its creditors in exchange for promises to reform government or change policies. When, for example, the regime of a recipient state is threatened with internal unrest because it does not have the funds to pay public sector wages, it can have a strong incentive to make assurances to donors on reforms in exchange for the large sums that Program Aid offers. Further, there are generally weak incentives to follow-through on these conditions once the funds have been disbursed. The literature is replete with stories about how skilled recipients are at the "promise now but delay delivery until later" strategy of securing Program Aid. Indeed, this strategy underpins the donor community's efforts to construct meaningful oversight institutions for their aid.

6.5.3. *Sector-Wide Approaches*

The SWAPs are an attempt to move away from directing aid through isolated projects and toward building an integrated and long-term approach to donor–recipient development cooperation. Formally, a SWAP defines a working relationship between a *donor government* with *other donor governments and organizations*, and the *government of an aid-dependent recipient* country. They are usually set up within a national-level Medium Term Budget Framework, where this framework outlines the overall national goals, budgetary resources, and expenditure priorities. The framework is designed to build the needed organizational capacity to carry out the chosen policies, and to coordinate the joint allocation of government and donor funds accordingly.

SWAPs are supposed to foster strong national ownership and political commitment through common goals and a common policy framework for a joint program of work.[18] They are designed to overcome the problem of development projects that fail to be sustainable because they lack an overall supportive policy environment. While SWAPs are an attempt at coordination to come to terms with the diverse social and economic realities that exist in developing countries, the strong donor involvement required can lead to "top-down delivery systems" (Norton and Bird 1999). SWAPs can also lead to the creation of a donor-dominated shadow ministry that develops policy for a particular sector and allocates budgets accordingly. Local ownership is also adversely affected when policy and funding coordination among donor agencies breaks down, as can happen when donors are driven by their own various timetables. As a report by the World Health Organization notes, these coordination pressures among donors "can lead to Government signing up to policies and programs which have not been widely enough discussed to ensure local ownership, or which have not adequately recognized constraints in implementation" (WHO 1999: 5).

SWAPs can also promote greater administrative centralization. Enhancing the capacity of a sectoral ministry to make policy in the capital city reduces localized beneficiary participation in crafting the rules that govern their use and distribution of resources and instead strengthen the ownership position of the governing elite. Since such groups traditionally draw their support from urban constituencies, policy initiatives taken by them are susceptible to be at the expense of the rural beneficiaries (Lipton 1993). In fact, few SWAP efforts have emerged through broader national debate. As the World Health Organization's (WHO 1999: 9) report notes, "There is as yet little experience of how to implement a SWAP using a decentralized local government structure." When local decision making and accountability are diminished through a centralization of policy making, local ownership is reduced and the incentives for such target beneficiaries to sustain projects introduced on their behalf become weak.

The relative permanence of overall donor commitment expected within a SWAP framework may also lead an aid recipient to contribute less effort. A donor agency's long-term commitment to national sector-wide initiatives may generate expectations among recipients that continued support is forthcoming regardless of their own level of effort. This effect will be particularly acute in cases where inputs and outputs are difficult to measure, where monitoring by the donor agency is difficult, and where the donor agency finds exiting a difficult or costly option. Discontinuing bilateral support is often a "big deal" with significant diplomatic and commercial repercussions and is rarely taken in response to a single breach of contract.

Finally, there may be fewer professional incentives for aid officials to deal with SWAPs. Several Desk Officers at Sida noted to us that there is often more job satisfaction and greater prospects for professional advancement from administering short-term projects, rather than in overseeing complex integrated long-term processes such as those involved with sector-wide programs. With well-defined and short projects, the Desk Officer has a greater opportunity to create signals that can be noticed by his or her superiors. Larger and more complex programs, by contrast, involve more group effort, with less tangible correspondence between individual effort and overall positive outcomes.

6.5.4. *Humanitarian Assistance*

Humanitarian assistance programs can take various forms, including responding to and taking steps to avoid natural and man-made catastrophes. Conflict-related humanitarian assistance is a key example of humanitarian assistance. This often involves the delivery of massive quantities of food and emergency supplies to areas where transportation infrastructures have been disrupted by some past disaster or ongoing natural or man-made emergency. Such efforts present severe challenges. Refugee camps, for instance, are often established in areas where there are limited facilities and where access is difficult. Moral and political dilemmas are often associated with the delivery of humanitarian assistance. In conflict-related humanitarian crises, combatants can treat the supplies provided by humanitarian aid organizations as a potential resource that can be exploited for their own strategic purposes (MacRae *et al.* 1994; McGinnis 1999*c*).

Humanitarian aid involves *donor governments* seeking to reach *beneficiary groups* that are in dire need of emergency assistance. Many international donor agencies, like Sweden's Sida, channel their humanitarian assistance through *other donors*, notably specialized UN agencies like UNHCR and international NGOs like the Red Cross. These organizations, in turn, often work with local and international *contractors* to procure and deliver relief materials and services. In some cases, aid can also be channeled through the central or local levels of the *recipient government*.

The fundamental impulse behind the international humanitarian community remains the widespread desire to help fellow human beings facing almost unimaginable conditions. Even so, the presence of aid resources often provides other motivations to involved actors. Below, we highlight some possibilities—both positive and negative.

Nongovernmental organizations play critical roles in alerting attention to disasters and are often in the forefront, helping to address pressing needs. Humanitarian crises elicit public concern in donor countries, particularly in the face of stark television news coverage and many NGOs tap into this concern to publicize their efforts and to draw in contributions. Many NGOs are innovators in humanitarian assistance and donor agencies often draw on their experience in promoting developmental humanitarian assistance (Sida 1999*d*). Other NGOs may be motivated to publicize the worst crises, in hopes of attracting higher donations. Given that it is exceedingly difficult to evaluate the effectiveness of humanitarian aid programs, some relief organizations can face incentives to exaggerate the need for their services (Maren 1997).

Donor governments often provide humanitarian relief for a combination of reasons. The US government, for example, donates large amounts of food as an instrument of its agricultural policy. Humanitarian relief can be one way to dispose of excess crops purchased from domestic farmers in order to support higher levels of domestic production and prices sought after by some farm lobbies. In some cases, donor governments focus their humanitarian efforts on particular regions of concern. Sweden, for example, focuses most of its humanitarian assistance to countries and regions in Africa (Sida 1997e: 10). This focus can promote more effective results to the extent that the donor gains, or already has, experience and local credibility in the particular disaster area.

Recipient government leaders or others holding local political power or advantageous economic positions sometimes act to take advantage of humanitarian emergencies (Keen 1994). For example, aid may be routed to those segments of the population supportive of the current government, while disfavored groups may be forced to relocate to government-controlled camps. These officials may exaggerate the number of refugees serviced in each camp, hoping to attract higher levels of aid that they can divert to other purposes (including military operations).

Beneficiaries, which in humanitarian crises are often refugees, face strong incentives to resume productive lives in their own lands, but are, often, understandably reluctant to return to their home areas as long as the conflict that first caused them to leave remains unresolved. In some cases, humanitarian emergencies can become institutionalized, with refugee camps remaining in place for decades. Semi-permanent camps, once established, make it harder for refugees to return home. Life in such a refugee camp, though miserable, often provides a greater level of security, food, and medical attention than life back home; the beneficiaries of humanitarian assistance may prefer the devil they know to ones they do not.

Humanitarian assistance has implications for sustainability as well. Efforts to alleviate suffering in the short term may inadvertently undermine the capacity of local communities to cope with less severe conditions over the long term. The regular arrival of tons of food to be distributed free of charge, for example, can severely lower local food prices, giving local producers less of an incentive to plant or harvest their own crops.

Although all viable communities develop means to cope with minor problems, any local community, no matter how successful, can be overwhelmed by sufficiently dire circumstances. This may not become a national problem as long as neighboring communities remain unaffected, provided relations between communities support mutual assistance. However, in times of severe and widespread environmental disruption (or conflict), national governments have an important role to play.

Unfortunately, many governments in less developed parts of the world have shirked on this responsibility, preferring instead to concentrate their meager resources on those groups whose support is most vital for their continued existence in power. Why should such leaders bother to develop a national-level capacity to respond to natural disasters if they can rely on the speedy delivery of emergency supplies from the international humanitarian community? Some national governments may come to rely on donor organizations to fulfill basic aspects of governance. Some critics of the humanitarian aid community argue this practice has the effect of legitimizing governments and rebel organizations that routinely violate basic principles of human rights (de Waal 1997).

6.5.5. *Technical Cooperation*

Technical Cooperation facilitates the transfer and adaptation of ideas, knowledge, technologies, or skills to foster development. It covers a wide array of aid activities designed to enhance human resource development in particular recipient countries. Donor agencies foster technical cooperation through a variety of means. As a particular example of technical cooperation, we focus on Sida's Contract Financed Technical Cooperation (KTS), which finances contracts between recipient country partners and Swedish consultants, particularly where Swedish expertise is found to be relevant. By dispatching Swedish experts and consultants to a local partner's project, KTS aims to transfer the necessary technical expertise and skills—and in this way promote Sweden's objectives in international development.

The role of a *donor agency* in Technical Cooperation is to finance the contracts between donor country *contractors*—who supply the skills, technology, and other learning services—and recipient country *beneficiary organizations*. Sida, through KTS, selects projects for funding based on an evaluation of the local beneficiary and its ability to make good use of the technical assistance. Proposals requesting Swedish know-how in a specific sector are officially transmitted by the *government of the recipient beneficiary* to the *Swedish Government*, which passes them on to its *donor agency*, Sida. Sida also cooperates with *other donors*, such as the World Bank and the UNDP, where funds provided by Sida make it possible for these multilateral organizations to use Swedish expertise within the framework of technical cooperation activities they oversee.

KTS is supposed to contribute to the objectives of Swedish international development by transferring Swedish knowledge to developing countries. Transferring this knowledge also works to achieve international exposure for Swedish companies, agencies, and institutions, providing strong commercial motivations for KTS (Schedvin 2001). Training programs also offer an opportunity for academics and consultancy organizations in Sweden to develop contacts with decision makers and other influential persons in the recipient country. Building such networks between the Swedish and developing country counterparts can be helpful in developing further business opportunities for Swedish industry and service concerns. It can also be a tool for Swedish diplomacy. Forss *et al.* (1996: 38) note in this regard that the initiative for many projects in Technical Cooperation often lie more with Swedish firms and Sweden's embassies than with recipient country organizations.

Recipient country actors also have interests in mechanisms for Technical Cooperation like Sida's KTS. The training associated with technical assistance provides opportunities for selected individuals to learn new skills, to travel abroad, and to network internationally. Being selected for such a program, in many cases, is also a matter of considerable personal prestige.

Sida vests formal ownership responsibility for KTS projects on the local partner and in this way seeks to secure a greater prospect for sustainability. To overcome potential Moral Hazard problems, Sida also requires the developing country participant to share in the costs of training: Related equipment and operating costs are not normally financed by Sida, and local costs are usually expected to be borne by the local partner. Sida also limits the duration and financial volume of KTS projects, with the aim of avoiding aid dependency.

While Sida is not a signing partner in KTS contracts, it necessarily maintains relationships with both the local partner and the Swedish partner. Sida provides the funds that enable the developing country participant to pay for the Swedish consultant's services but Sida also participates in the choice of the Swedish consultant, thus taking on some ownership prerogatives. Beneficiary ownership is further diffused when important decisions about the project require the approval of officials in a recipient country ministry, where such officials can and often do have objectives ancillary to those of the local partner.

6.6. CONCLUSION

Most current analyses on aid and incentives focus on donor–recipient negotiations. This chapter has looked more broadly on how the rules embedded within frequently used modalities, means, and conditions of aid interventions, and affecting actors from various parts of the aid Octangle, can create incentives that affect the short-term and long-term outcomes of aid. If one is interested in how aid affects outcomes, it is essential to understand the broader foundations of aid.

What types of incentives might arise, for example, from a grant-financed project in natural resources, based on *ex ante* conditionality, and implemented by a partner country organization? And how might the rule properties inherent in this combination of features affect a project's sustainability? Our case study of a project in Orissa forestry (Chapter 9) considers this mix of variables. Alternatively, what might be the incentives for a loan-financed program aid for the electricity sector that is essentially a tied-aid project? Our case study of the Zambian power sector (Chapter 10) takes up these questions. These are just two typical examples from the world of development aid. Studies of aid more narrowly focused than this book would do well to heed the importance of the modalities, means, and conditions involved in the focus of their work.

NOTES

1. This view of aid as instrumental in overcoming the development trap remains widespread (e.g. Sachs 2004).
2. Definitions are based on those of the OECD (see http://www.oecd.org/home/).
3. Ibid.
4. The classification of a country's development status is critical to the considerations it can receive for exemptions in tariff reduction agreements, pollution quotas, terms of credit, etc. under the prevailing international welfare system organized by the United Nations. For example, exemptions for developing countries from having to reduce tariff rates are often desired by domestic industries seeking protectionist shelter. This system creates incentives to maintain or even foster a recording of those economic and social features that enable the state to be categorized as worse-off in the developmental league tables maintained by the United Nations. There are clear disincentives to "graduate" from a lower development category to a higher one as this implies a loss of various "privileges."

5. Sound lending institutions, at the same time, are aware that a very high rate of interest will attract only the cocky entrepreneur who is willing to take very high risks. They also know that if it lends a very large sum to the borrower, then it can itself become vulnerable to the borrower's threats to default. When a donor country offers credits to a recipient country, it is less financially dependent on repayment of the debt. As such, it can be less discriminating of the creditworthiness of the recipient than private lenders most often are.

6. The incentive effect of program aid leads recipient governments to adopt the "promise now, delay delivery until later" strategy with donors. An exemplar of this relationship is that between the Government of Kenya and the IMF—the Kenya-Fund Dance (see *The Economist*, August 5, 2000).

7. See the analysis of Sida's Chandrapur–Padghe project in Chapter 9 of this report.

8. Although guarantees are formally untied in the case of Sweden, they are required to address a "Swedish interest"—meaning that "Swedish exporters shall have the opportunity of winning contracts in international competition, that the project is a part of Swedish aid in that country, or that Swedish parties are involved in the project."

9. Agents of recipient governments prefer untied-aid to tied-aid since, with untied-aid, they can independently contract through international bidding the best contractor or, at least, one of their own choice—for a development project. However, when such ownership is not sufficiently constrained, it broadens the potential for extra-contractual negotiations between recipient country officials and suppliers.

10. *The Economist* recently reported on the sophisticated mural defenses against the rising ocean that was constructed, at $13,000 per linear meter, around Male, the capital of the Maldives.

   It is interesting to know how Maldives could afford this. As an official explains, the Japanese government was generous enough to pay for it. He hesitates. Yes? He goes on: the aid was linked to a contract award for a Japanese firm, which used patented technology. To extend or repair the wall, the official complains, they must buy from the firm at outrageous prices (*The Economist*, May 13, 2000).

11. Sweden, in the past, has gone ahead with tied-aid for an infrastructure project despite a decision by the OECD that the offer does not conform to the rules of the Helsinki Package. Our study of the Chandrapur–Padghe power project, set out in Chapter 9, describes the circumstances of this case. Sida officials we interviewed insisted that such derogation will not occur again and that Sweden will, in the future, follow a multilateral approach in promoting large infrastructure aid projects.

12. The credibility of this commitment can be further enhanced, notes Svensson, by channeling the disbursement of tied-aid through multilateral agencies that have a stronger reputation for being conservative and inflexible in interactions with recipient governments. This, he concludes, will elicit more *ex ante* effort on the part of the recipient government in putting in place required reforms.

13. Another point to consider here concerns heterogeneity among donors. Bad Samaritans crowd out Good Samaritans. If so, commitment technologies related to tied-aid, as adopted by Good Samaritans, may be ineffective.

14. There are still others, such as those relating to luck (see Bigsten 1999), but our present discussion is limited to those relating to incentives.

15. Aid has, as van de Walle (2001) notes, two supporting constituencies within the donor's polity—the taxpaying public, which has to be sold on the humanitarian aspects of aid, and the business and foreign policy communities that see direct benefits from providing aid. Need-based aid is only superficially attractive in political terms. It allows governments to play up the humanitarian dimension of aid while defusing the criticism that aid is in effect "taxing the poor people in rich countries on behalf of rich people in poor countries."

16. Each of these possesses still further particular characteristics.

17. Unrest, rioting, etc. by segments of the population often do have an effect.

18. The World Bank's Comprehensive Development Framework is a key example of a SWAP approach.

PART III

CASE STUDIES

7

Applying the IAD Framework: The Incentives Inside a Development Agency

7.1. INTRODUCTION

The Institutional Analysis and Development (IAD) framework enables an analyst to break up examinations of incentive structures into separate components as well as to examine linkages among them. In Chapters 4 and 5, we examined the linkages among operational action situations within the Octangle and focused particularly on the bargaining linkages between a donor and a recipient. In Chapter 6, we examined how the diverse modalities of aid produce diverse sets of incentives leading to both positive and negative outcomes. We noted that it is possible to examine three different yet inter-connected analytical levels: the operational, policy, and constitutional levels of analysis.

A major contribution of an IAD framework–guided analysis is that the observed results at the operational level of analysis in the field can be linked to decision-making processes at the collective-choice and constitutional levels in the respective govern-ments' national capitals. In other words, to fix an undesired outcome in a field activity may require adjustments in the rules-in-use or other contextual factors at a collective-choice or constitutional level in the decision-making hierarchy. These rule adjustments are often related to the decision-making process inside the development agency's headquarters, but may also involve decisions by other actors who have the authority to limit the powers of the aid agency.

More fundamentally, to fix such problems, decision makers must first be able to diag-nose *what* to fix and then know *how* to fix it in a reasonable way. To develop that kind of knowledge requires an active learning process about field activities and about insti-tutional responses to undesired outcomes at headquarters and in the field. We argue that incentives for an aid agency's staff to learn about sustainability of field activities is one of the most fundamental factors in that agency's quest for sustainable development outcomes. We suggest that it is essential for agencies to base their decisions about devel-opment cooperation programs on an ongoing learning and adjustment process. For this to happen, it is paramount that the incentives of agency staff are aligned with the goal of strengthening both individual and organizational learning processes. The purpose of this chapter is to assess these incentives and their alignment.

As a donor trying to help the population of a recipient country, an aid organization's staff members face a diverse set of multilevel action situations. First, they confront the structure of the multiple underlying operational problems existing in the recipient countries. To achieve sustainable development in the recipient countries, the staff members have to affect these underlying situations. To do so requires substantial knowledge about the history and context of these situations as well as about the way operational, policy, and constitutional choices are made in that cultural context. Second, a donor agency's staff members face a set of principal–agent relationships within their own organization and with contractors. Even when aid organization staff are enthusiastic and hard working, they may still find themselves in situations complicated by many of the motivational and information problems identified in Chapter 2.

This leads us to the core message of this chapter: Precisely because it is so difficult to construct effective institutions to address collective-action problems on the ground, *continuous learning* about why some past efforts succeeded while others failed is essential. Without such learning, the portfolio of a development agency will continue to have the same success and failure rates. Thus, the incentives for learning from experience within a development agency are crucial to improving its performance over time.

The inquiry below suggests that this ongoing learning and adjustment process within an aid organization's headquarters is necessary in order to enhance the support to institutions that could solve the collective-action problems in recipient countries. Drawing from the general discussion of collective-action problems in public organizations in earlier chapters, we now employ the IAD framework to identify and analyze specific collective-action problems within the Swedish International Development Cooperation Agency (Sida) and its relationships with counterparts and contractors both at the Stockholm headquarters and in the field.

7.2. METHODS

This chapter focuses on the collective-choice institutions within Sida, and draws on archival research as well as semi-structured interviews with 95 individuals involved with activities at the Sida headquarters in Stockholm. To obtain accurate information about incentives in development aid, it is essential to talk with the staff involved in development cooperation at all levels. Although one can learn a great deal about incentives by studying the formal structure and archival records of an organization, it is essential to obtain good information about the perceptions of those working in a process about the incentives they face. Our team interviewed staff members working at all levels within Sida headquarters in Stockholm. Our sample included all 14 members of the Sida management team, 18 key informants selected by Sida, as well as 63 randomly selected Desk Officers and support staff. For the randomly selected staff, we constructed a semi-structured interview that addressed the perceptions of a variety of incentives that the staff faced, as well as some of their own career patterns (reproduced with other methodological information in appendix C of E. Ostrom *et al.* 2002). We recorded these interview data in both structured and standardized responses, as well as in long text form. With members of the management team and the key informants selected by Sida, we carried out more qualitative, in-depth interviews.

7.3. USING THE IAD FRAMEWORK TO STUDY THE ORGANIZATION OF A DEVELOPMENT AGENCY: SIDA

The IAD approach starts by identifying the relevant action arenas, where different actors interact in a series of action situations. We are particularly interested in this chapter in how a donor organization's internal organization affects the prospects for sustainable outcomes in the field. Consequently, we define the focal action arena to encompass the web of interactions between the donor headquarters and the different actors in the field.

Serious information asymmetries frequently plague the interaction between headquarters in the donor country and the main actors in the field. One way of dealing with these information asymmetries is for headquarters personnel to interact with actors in the field to learn about the field actor's actions and strategies. Such interactions, if structured in a meaningful manner, can lead to an improved understanding of the possible causes of observed outcomes in donor-sponsored activities. We start by describing the general context and structure of the situations in the action arena, the participating actors, and the central challenges they face in terms of solving embedded collective-action problems.

7.3.1. *Sida as an Agent of the Swedish Government and Its People*

The structure of the immediate action situations in which the staff members of Sida find themselves during most of their working hours is that of a series of principal–agent situations. Sida itself is an agent for the government of Sweden, which is in turn an agent for the people of Sweden. The people of Sweden say: "Do something about poverty in developing countries." The elected officials in Parliament and the government tend to agree that this is an important task. (When a government allocates close to 1 per cent of a country's GNP to an activity, it is assigning a high priority to that activity.) The outcome of this large investment occurs over a long period and in places far away from Stockholm. Neither the Swedish people nor the government of Sweden has full information about the specific activities undertaken by Sida and the difference they are making in the lives of people.

Therefore, while the principal in this case (the citizenry of the donor country) wants something done, it generally does not know how to make it happen and has few tools to discover if and how it has happened. This principal–agent relationship is different from that of a patient going to a doctor to seek advice on how to get well. While the patient does not know how to get well, the patient does get direct feedback about what the doctor recommends and can determine whether it makes a difference or not. To supplement this direct feedback, the patient can discuss the doctor's prescriptions with friends who have faced the same problems and with other doctors. In the case of development assistance, the principal rarely gets direct feedback about activities or outcomes. Thus, the principal rarely knows whether the life prospects of others have been improved or not. The citizens of a donor country receive only brief hints in news reports and official documents about whether the "cures" applied by its agent seem to be working, or not.

Further, as we discuss below, given the time frame and the action space of a donor staff member working on any particular problem, even the agent is uncertain about whether the activities undertaken by implementing organizations are making a positive and sustainable difference. In the three or four years that a staff member may be assigned to a task (see below for a discussion of average length of assignment), she may be able to see some projects proceed from the initial design phase to some outcome in the field. Such a time frame is insufficient, however, to ascertain whether the constructed road, school, or power plant is being used and maintained, or allowed to disintegrate through a lack of proper use and maintenance.[1] If the project involves building of a new institution that requires developing expertise by users to use it effectively, the time frame needed to determine sustainability might be decades.

Thus, in the principal–agent relationships in which Sida staff members engage, the "ultimate" principal is the Swedish public that has minimal information about what Sida does, what it could do, and what difference it makes. Martens (2002) stresses that this broken information feedback loop is one of the most distinctive—and important—aspects of developing assistance:

However, a unique and most striking characteristic of foreign aid is that the people for whose benefit aid agencies work are not the same as those from whom their revenues are obtained; they actually live in different countries and different political constituencies. This geographical and political separation between beneficiaries and taxpayers blocks the normal performance feedback process: beneficiaries may be able to observe performance but cannot modulate payments (rewards to the agents) in function of performance. (ibid.: 14)

To keep their own positions, however, Sida staff members need to keep the relevant parts of the Swedish government informed and satisfied that their general goals are being achieved and that more support is needed over the long term. Given the nature of development assistance, this is a challenge. Little is reported in the media about successful projects. Hints of a scandal related to corruption or an obvious egregious error of judgment will be reported by Swedish media as well as coups d'état or eruption of protest movements. Scandals, coups, and other "newsworthy" stories make both citizens and government officials in the donor country nervous about spending more money on development assistance.

One of the "facts," or quantitative indicators, that can be observed by government officials and ultimately the people of Sweden is whether Sida (or any other government agency) has spent all of their allocated funds in the corresponding budgetary period. Given the competing needs for public funds, any evidence of the nonexpenditure of funds can be used in debates to argue for budget reductions. All public agencies face the need to spend allocated funds within their budget cycles in order to justify receiving further budgetary allotments (Seabright 2002; Wildavsky 1984).

Under such circumstance, one should expect to see Sida staff members spending substantial time reviewing a continuing stream of paperwork related to project design and negotiations, specifying contracts with implementing organizations and consultants, as well as reviewing reports and accounts. Major attention is likely to be paid to what is observable—submission of proper project documents, expenditure of funds as specified in project documents, and demonstration of skills and knowledge in meetings.

Considerable uncertainty exists as to whether activities are leading to desired outcomes. The specific way this "task environment" is established within Sida will affect the level of uncertainty, the types of behavior that are rewarded, the perceived incentives of staff, and the impact of these on the sustainability of development activities undertaken by Sida.

So far, we have treated the donor agency much like a black box. In order to understand how the aid agency staff itself interacts to address the observed collective-action problems, however, we need to develop a more fine-grained appreciation of the internal dynamics of the aid agency. In this section, we present the main Sida actors within their main action arenas. We discuss what positions they hold and what their functions are according to the internal staff structure.

7.3.2. *Looking Inside Sida*

Sida, in its present incarnation, was established in 1995. Before that date, various bureaucracies within Sweden worked to further development cooperation. The component agencies amalgamated within Sida included: (1) the Swedish International Development Authority (old SIDA), which conducted regular project and program aid and currently forms a major part of the new Sida organization; (2) the Swedish Agency for International Technical and Economic Cooperation (BITS), which dealt with technical support; (3) SwedeCorp, which pertained to support for private sector development initiatives; and (4) the Department for Research Cooperation (SAREC), which focused on cooperation between research organizations in Sweden and recipient countries. Many of the senior staff at Sida today originally joined SIDA and the other predecessor agencies prior to 1995 (see discussion of age distribution below). There were around 650 staff members working for Sida in the spring of 2000 when we conducted our empirical research at Sida headquarters.

A General Director heads Sida, and serves as the Chairman of its Board (see Figure 7.1). The Sida Board is made up of representatives from the political parties currently in Parliament, NGOs, the government, and the private sector. This Board is responsible for approving the annual report, annual budget proposals, annual audit and evaluation plans, measures and responses to the internal audit reports as well as to the annual, external audit report from the Swedish National Audit Office. Most

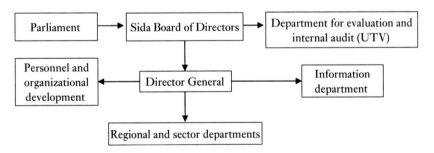

Figure 7.1. *Sida top-level organizational chart (Adapted from Organization Chart provided by Sida Information office.)*

important, the Board is Sida's voice to the government. Although it does not involve itself in the day-to-day management of Sida, the Board maintains general oversight. There are 14 different departments within Sida. The Department for Evaluation and Internal Audit (UTV) reports directly to the Board. As such, UTV has substantial autonomy within Sida.

The fourteen department heads constitute the Executive Committee and play a central role in the internal planning of activities such as allocating human and financial resources within Sida. To ensure the prosperity (or survival) of their own department as well as their own career advancement in the Sida hierarchy, each department head faces incentives to secure their own department's programs and projects and maximize its funding. Apart from the political priorities defined at the constitutional level, several Sida staff members with whom we talked (at both management and Desk-Officer levels) perceive these allocations to reflect (1) how well the particular departments have addressed past priority areas as set forth by the Parliament and (2) how well they have disbursed funds allocated in previous years.

Sida is a relatively flat organization, at least on paper. Starting from the top and moving down from the General Director, there are Department Heads, and at the level below are the Division Heads. Under the Division Heads are the Desk Officers, who represent the largest group of Sida employees with almost two-thirds of the total number of employees. Finally, there is the Administrative Support staff, which is the second largest group of employees, 25 per cent of the total. That means that only about 10 per cent of Sida's staff holds management positions.[2]

Figure 7.2 shows that Sida staff members participate in a series of action situations with multiple actors at many different levels. In each one of these relationships, asymmetries of information are present. Many different actors in the field—such as consultants, recipient government agencies, and colleagues at the Swedish Embassy—report to a Sida staff member in Stockholm. Therefore, reported information is seldom complete. Pieces of information are lost in each of the interactions shown in Figure 7.2. This information loss is the product of a *selection process* of the information that each actor chooses to communicate to another actor. Each actor has an incentive to select and transmit primarily the information that will benefit him or her personally. This asymmetry and loss of information are a common problem in all hierarchies and constitute a fundamental principal–agent problem for aid agencies as well.

The multiple layers of international development cooperation activities aggravate information asymmetry and loss problems. The many layers of intermediary actors between the Desk Officer at headquarters and the intended beneficiaries in the field complicate the decision-making process for the Desk Officer. Before making crucial decisions about future activities, a Desk Officer relies on the input from a variety of consultants and national government officials.[3] Seldom do these intermediary actors have direct contact with the ultimate beneficiaries of the development cooperation. Thus, they also have to rely on secondary sources for beneficiary-level information. Broken feedback loops repeatedly occur throughout these layers of activities.

The multilayered action arena makes it very difficult for a Desk Officer to gain accurate information about what is really going on in the field. In our interviews with Sida

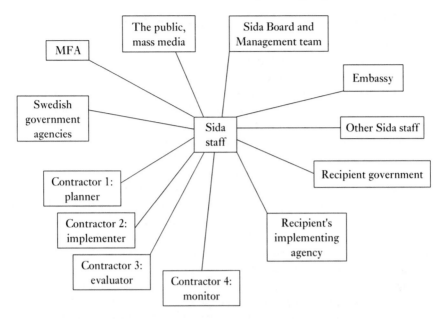

Figure 7.2. *Multiple action situations of development cooperation from the perspective of a Sida staff member*

staff, they repeatedly reflected on the information deficit at the Desk-Officer level. The implication of this finding is rather serious for the prospects of achieving sustainable outcomes, because even if the Desk Officer has the best of intentions to achieve sustained improvements in the welfare of the intended beneficiaries, it is extremely difficult for her to make adequate decisions without access to accurate, timely, and reliable information about the beneficiary-level reality.

The challenge for any development agency to address the information asymmetry problem is to create an environment in which its staff members are encouraged to find ways to acquire essential information from interactions with their colleagues at home and in recipient countries.

7.4. CONTEXTUAL VARIABLES AND THEIR INFLUENCES ON ACTION ARENAS

Having identified the main action situation of interest as *Sida's efforts to learn how to address collective-action problems both at home and in partner countries*, we now turn to examine what contextual factors might influence the outcomes of these efforts. The types of contextual factors that tend to influence the outcomes of the interactions between actors in the action arenas can be divided into the *institutional, cultural, and biophysical* characteristics of human interactions. These three factors, in turn, may come into play at all three levels of human interactions: constitutional, collective-choice, and operational.[4]

7.4.1. *Institutional Factors Influencing Action Arenas*

As a government agency, Sida is embedded in a set of constitutional, policy, and operational rule structures—many of which exist in the form of written documents. In Figure 7.3, we present a brief overview of the levels of policy making and rules that affect the structure of principal–agent relationships within Sida or with contractors. The constitutional rules-in-use, represented by the fundamental laws and policies of the government, define the competence and responsibilities of the different government agents associated with international development cooperation. The very creation of the new Sida in 1995, and the mandate given to Sida by Parliament, are examples of a constitutional-level rules-in-use related to Sida itself.

The rules-in-use at the *collective-choice* level regulate primarily how to organize the development cooperation system. The Ministry of Foreign Affairs (MFA) has largely delegated this policy responsibility directly to Sida. The top management within Sida decides how to organize the day-to-day operation of Sida. The *operational* rules that affect particular situations are themselves the result of decisions made in collective-choice situations as discussed in Chapter 2.

According to Sweden's official aid policy the size of the Swedish aid budget should represent approximately one per cent of country's Gross National Product. It is the task of the Swedish parliament, however, to determine the actual volume of Sweden's overall aid budget. It does so by allocating funds to proposals put forward by the government. Swedish aid contains three parts: multilateral aid, bilateral aid, and "other." Of the total aid budget of 13.6 billion Swedish Kronor (SEK) in 2001 (about 1.8 billion US dollars with December 2001 exchange rate), Sida disbursed around SEK 9.6 billion in bilateral aid.

Level of interaction	Rules affecting action arenas	Examples of instruments	Main actors
Constitutional	The laws and policies that define the fundamental purpose and rationale of Swedish aid.	The seven objectives of the Swedish aid program, bilateral framework agreements, expenditure ceilings, 1% of GNP aid target, etc.	Parliament, MFA, Sida
Collective-choice (policy)	Procedural rules that define and change operational rules.	Country strategy documents, internal budgets, administrative guidelines, work plans.	Parliament, MFA, MFi, Sida
Operational	The rules that define the format and content of specific activities.	Contracts, terms of reference with staff, consultants, and counterpart organizations.	Sida and Embassy staff, consultants, recipients

Figure 7.3. *Type of rules affecting Swedish aid*

During the period between 1995 and 2000, several changes in the rules-in-use at the constitutional level impacted the decision making within Sida. In 1995, the strict implementation of budget ceilings in all Swedish government agencies induced a very conservative and cautionary planning approach for government managers. As a result, unspent funds would frequently exist at the end of the year—the difference between the amount of the budget ceiling and the amount actually spent. In addition, situations existed where money already approved could not be disbursed because of unforeseen events. Until 1997, Sida could carry over these unspent funds into a reserve fund from which the organization could draw during the next budget year.

By the end of 1997, Sida had built a reserve of over SEK3 billion. As these reserves piled up, they sparked the attention of Parliament and the public who wanted to know why Sida was not using up its budget allocations. The natural question was whether these funds could be used elsewhere if Sida could not use them. Sida management successfully convinced Parliament to allow it to keep the funds it had in reserve under the condition that it worked out a strategy for successively reducing the size of the reserve funds. Sida management responded by instructing their desk officers to over-program activities (much in the way airlines overbook passengers) in the expectation that some percentage of projects would not be funded. Using such strategies, as one staff member pointed out, Sida accelerated its funding commitments (but not their disbursements) during the first part of 1998 in order to try to spend more by the end of 1998. But in December of 1998, due to a general budgetary squeeze, the government changed the budgetary rules again. The new rules eliminated the reserve fund and forced each Sida department to comply with strict budget ceilings. This severe cutback was a difficult challenge to face, and Sida quickly adopted budget-cutting measures, such as reducing staff travel and hiring temporary rather than permanent staff.[5]

Table 7.1 presents the disbursement pattern between 1997 and 2000. Note that in 1997, the last year with a tight ceiling, disbursements in the fourth quarter were 39 per cent of the total for the year. Sida's total disbursements fell in 1998 as the new constitutional rules forced several readjustments, while managers made plans for accelerated disbursements in 1999. Examining the limited time series of disbursement data and taking into account the atypical conditions of the 1998–1999 period,

Table 7.1. *Total disbursements of Sida budgets for 1997–2000 by quarter*

Quarter	1997	1998	1999	2000
1st	1,267,025,432	1,372,360,129	2,866,072,552	2,302,032,160
2nd	2,089,850,692	1,849,667,065	1,686,893,222	2,497,049,205
First half	3,356,876,124	3,222,027,194	4,552,965,774	4,799,081,365
3rd	1,600,213,330	2,091,751,397	1,829,923,050	2,079,786,305
4th	3,120,446,858	2,093,224,836	2,096,431,879	3,385,428,692
Second half	4,720,660,188	4,184,976,233	3,926,354,929	5,465,214,997
Per year	8,077,536,312	7,407,003,427	8,479,320,703	10,264,298,362

it becomes clear that disbursements tend to increase during the last quarter of the budget year. Later in the chapter, we draw on the results of our survey with Sida staff to explore how the changes in budgetary rules impact the Desk Officers' decision making and what these changes imply for sustainability.

7.4.2. *Cultural Factors Influencing the Action Arenas*

A widely shared moral commitment exists among Swedish citizens to assist the less fortunate in developing countries. This deeply rooted view underpins much of the widespread public support in Sweden for development aid. This sentiment has been consistent since the 1960s and remains a relatively fixed feature in Swedish politics. The official Swedish government policy to earmark 1 per cent of the GNP to be used for foreign assistance continues to receive strong support from public opinion polls. Indeed, there is even a sense of disappointment or shame when the government fails to meet this target.

The geopolitical strategic interests of Sweden also provide support for an elaborate aid program. Swedish aid has traditionally been a tool for expressing solidarity for political movements with which the public and governments in Sweden have sympathized. Sweden had been a strong, long-standing, and consistent supporter of past socialist regimes such as Vietnam, Tanzania, and Nicaragua. The Olof Palme Government (1969–1976; 1979–1986), in particular, supported a series of development projects in countries that shared the fundamental notions of the Swedish government's social democratic ideology. For example, the Bai Bang paper mill project in Vietnam, conceived and designed during that country's war with the United States (and built shortly after), was a way of showing Sweden's solidarity to the government in Hanoi (Sida 1999c).

In addition, in keeping with the strategic use of aid, Swedish development cooperation has focused on a relatively small number of countries. Sweden, as a middle power, has sought to be a niche player, concentrating its resources and attentions to gaining influence in particular regions such as southern Africa (Schraeder *et al.* 1998). Sweden's international reputation is one of a loyal donor that remains engaged over the long haul (Lumsdaine 1997).

Given a strong public and government commitment to development assistance, the mass media in Sweden takes a keen interest in the disbursement and administration of aid. Sida is a well-known organization in Sweden, representing the Swedish aid establishment. As a result, Sida is the focus of much critical scrutiny in the Swedish mass media. In the past, Swedish investments in large-scale projects, such as the Bai Bang project in Vietnam, generated a great deal of controversy. Sida has consistently been open in acknowledging the challenges it faces in development cooperation and, in this way, strives to maintain its reputation and credibility.

Apart from public interest and support, the Swedish private sector is also a strong advocate for aid. As Sida itself reports (Sida 1997b: 17), around 60 per cent of Swedish aid funnels back to Swedish firms and consultants. Several of the Desk Officers with whom we talked believed that many Swedish corporations view development cooperation as a way to gain a foothold in foreign markets.

While the influence of the cultural norms may often be hard to quantify, they are critical factors that help explain the nature of interactions both within Sida and between the organization and its many different counterpart organizations and contractors. The incentives for Sida staff to learn about the sustainability of aid program outcomes must be viewed in light of the cultural expectations that Sida's principals—the Swedish government and taxpayers—place on aid programs. By recognizing this cultural dimension to the operation of aid programs, it becomes clear that sustainability is only one of the evaluative criteria that the principals use when assessing the performance of Sida. The Sida case shows us how geopolitical considerations, the benefits to a country's economy, and the actual volume of aid can in some instances be more important determinants of aid allocation than formally stated objectives of aid, such as the sustainability of aid.

7.4.3. *Biophysical Characteristics Influencing the Action Arenas*

One of the major influences on the incentives generated in an operational-level action situation is the nature of the good that the interaction revolves around. As we have discussed in Chapter 2, when operational situations involve public goods or common-pool resources, specific attributes of the good strongly affect incentives.

Those involved in natural resource management have to understand how various institutional arrangements enhance or detract from the incentives of field managers and users to build, maintain, and sustain resource systems. Those involved in educational projects need to understand a different set of institutional arrangements and how they affect the incentives and behavior of teachers, school administrators, and students. Furthermore, those involved in humanitarian aid, building institutions, or still other projects have to understand how diverse biophysical characteristics in each sector and in different parts of a recipient country change the nature of interactions and thus affect outcomes.

We now move to explore this argument in more detail within the institutional context of Sida headquarters. In Sida's many activities, there is a large variety of biophysical characteristics present. This variety affects the capability of Sida staff to learn how they can enhance the sustainability of different types of projects. The higher the variety of biophysical characteristics, the more complex it is for Sida staff to learn about sustainability.

7.5. PATTERNS OF INTERACTIONS: INCENTIVES FOR LEARNING ABOUT SUSTAINABLE OUTCOMES

Over time, actors interact with each other in repeated action situations. They position themselves and find strategies that seem to work best for them; thus, patterns of interactions emerge. It is by studying these patterns of interaction that we are able to identify the main institutional incentives influencing each actor. We start this part of the institutional analysis by identifying the particular incentives that affect agency staff for individual learning about sustainable outcomes.

A word of caution: Identifying an incentive is one thing, but to assess the incentive compatibility and to predict the net effect of the identified incentives is a much more challenging task. The main difficulty concerns reliable methods of measurement: It is difficult to measure accurately the relative strength of one incentive compared to another since the result of the internal process that actors use to weigh incentives against one another depends on each actor's individual preferences.

Another problem facing the study of incentives is that even if one can detect the existence of positive incentives, these may be overpowered or counteracted by institutions that generate negative incentives. At the end of the day, the individual staff member will act upon the net effect of a mix of positive and negative incentives, which are different for each individual. To measure this net effect accurately is a complex task and it is beyond the scope of this book to do so. Nevertheless, as a result of our extensive interviews with Sida management, with a random sample of Sida employees, and reading dozens of internal documents, it is possible to discern the predominating patterns of the incentive structures within Sida.

Our main argument in this section is that donor agencies would increase their prospects for achieving sustainable outcomes by investing in a robust system of learning about how to achieve sustainable outcomes in the field.[6] We believe that when such a system forms the basis for the continuous adjustments and fine-tuning of institutional factors, a donor agency will become better at contributing to collective-action solutions both at home and in partner country institutions.

7.5.1. *A Highly Motivated Staff*

For people visiting the Sida home office in Stockholm, one of the most noticeable aspects of the general atmosphere within the home office is the number of highly motivated members of the staff. In the over 90 interviews we conducted with Sida staff members, we found them engaged and more than willing to talk with us about their perceptions of Sida's work and their own incentives.[7]

One of Sida's own surveys (Sida 2001)[8] confirms our research team's general impressions.[9] The survey asked a variety of questions related to Sida staff commitment to working at Sida and their general evaluations of their working environment. The results established that (1) more than 70 per cent of the respondents strongly agreed or agreed completely that they felt engaged by and committed to their work, and (2) more than 70 per cent were also willing to "stand up and push for Sida's goals and vision, even outside of Sida." The top management of any agency would be pleased with receiving such a strong endorsement from the staff.

The question must be asked, however, if a highly motivated staff is sufficient to foster the sustainability of development assistance. Given our theoretical analysis in earlier chapters, our answer is that it might be a necessary but not a sufficient condition. The devotion and hard work of the Sida staff do overcome many of the problems of moral hazard found in organizations where low morale and shirking are common.

The problems of missing and asymmetric information discussed in Chapter 2, however, still affect the likelihood of designing international assistance programs that lead to sustainable results.

A major problem facing the staff of all international development agencies who try to strengthen institutions in recipient countries is the problem of gaining sufficient information about what works well to overcome collective-action problems in particular cultural and historical contexts. This location-specific contextual information tends to change over time with political changes, the appearance of new constellations of actors, and the changes in the rules-in-use that emerge from the interaction within new constellations of actors. Any donor-supported intervention designed to facilitate the solution of a particular collective-action problem must therefore construct mechanisms that can acquire timely and reliable contextual information. Time and distance represent substantial constraints, especially for donor agency staff working in the home office and who may visit their partner countries perhaps only one or two weeks per year. To overcome these constraints, the donor agency may provide incentives for staff to acquire essential contextual information. Here we consider the incentives for two kinds of learning: individual and organizational learning about donor agency strategies and outcomes in the recipient country related to the sustainability of project activities.

Individual learning about sustainability
The question is: How do individual staff members learn which kinds of projects or programs are most likely to lead to sustainable outcomes? One way of learning is entirely personal. If this were the primary way to learn about sustainability, individual staff members would need to be assigned to individual projects and programs for a very long period of time so that they could observe what works and what does not seem to work well in a particular socioeconomic and cultural setting. Individuals would need to be motivated to learn effectively about the sustainability of development assistance. This learning entails a constant evaluation of how one's own activities are related to project outcomes. The clearer this relation between personal action and project success, the easier the learning process will become.

While Sida promotes the idea of recipient country ownership of activities, this does not mean that the agency simply funds any project that the recipient would like to see funded. Neither does it restrict funding to those organizations with a strong record of past successes, as this would rule out some of the neediest recipients. Sida strives to strike a balance between local demands, needs, and capacity in their decisions to support development activities. The outcomes of these decisions, therefore, depend largely on the ability of Sida staff to evaluate the likelihood that a future project would lead to sustainable results. Moreover, rewarding staff who have contributed to the design, technical advice, and successful implementation of activities that have a sustainable impact on the goals of development would be an important step to encourage staff members' investment into this kind of individual learning.

If an organization composed of several levels of principal–agent relationships had created incentives for individual learning about sustainability, one would expect to find at least some of the following conditions:

1. Long-term assignments of staff to overseas positions where they could observe projects from the initial design through sufficient years of operation to learn which kinds of projects had the highest probability of being sustainable.
2. Careful efforts to ensure that individual staff, who were shifted to other assignments, were able to obtain continuing information about projects with which they had an earlier association so that they could learn whether any sustainable results had been achieved.
3. Strong efforts to retain younger staff, who have had opportunities for substantial learning and promoting long-term contracts for junior positions and relying less on temporary contracts.
4. Career advancement criteria based to some extent on past participation in projects that had proven to be sustainable—particularly for advancement to managerial staff.

Each of these conditions would critically affect the level of feedback that an individual staff member would receive about the factors that affect sustainability in specific activities.

Empirical evidence on the conditions for individual learning about sustainability

We did not find much evidence to support an argument that the incentives inside Sida are strongly oriented toward learning about sustainability and rewarding efforts that lead to sustainability of development assistance efforts. Many of the incentives that we identified above as being of particular importance for the learning about what it takes to guarantee the sustainability of projects appear to be missing or have a different structure in Sida's contemporary organization and budgetary structure.

The lack of strong incentives for learning from past projects and the field shows up in Sida's own Web-based survey. Almost one-fourth of the Sida staff members who responded to the survey chose not to give a rating to the statement: "I feel Sida is good at harnessing knowledge from the field and the experience acquired by embassy personnel." Of those who did respond, over 50 per cent *disagreed* with the statement. A majority of respondents also disagreed with the statement that "I perceive Sida as a workplace where it is self-evident to question the established thought-patterns and working routines." These data help to provide a general overview of a staff that is less certain about knowledge transfer and learning from the field and who are under considerable pressure at work.

Short-term assignments

Instead of long-term assignments that would enable Sida staff to learn from their own prolonged experience in a particular socioeconomic and cultural environment and from projects that they have seen through an entire project cycle, Sida staff typically rotates quickly between different postings both among departments and divisions at headquarters as well as between headquarters and the field. Rapid movement from assignment to assignment promotes greater integration among staff, and exposure to a variety of experiences. It also fosters the development of generalists rather than those with deep knowledge of the particular circumstances and culture of the recipient and beneficiaries.

Through our interviews, we found that the length of time in an assignment varied from 5 months for one staff member to another who indicated serving 18 years with one department at Sida headquarters. The average length of time in an assignment in the field or at headquarters is only 4 years. One staff member who has worked for Sida for 25 years had the following pattern of assignments:

30 months in Field assignment 1
28 months in Field assignment 2
27 months in Field assignment 3
23 months in Field assignment 4
12 months in Field assignment 5
72 months at Headquarters
12 months in Field assignment 6
36 months in Field assignment 7
42 months in Field assignment 8
18 months at Headquarters

With work experience like this, an individual gains a good overview of Sida operations in many locations and has much to offer Sida in terms of accumulated wisdom about the inner workings of Sida. But, few of the field assignments lasted long enough for the staff member to see all phases of a set of projects. Rarely is a project completed from the initial idea, through the design and implementation stage, to a stage at which its sustainability can be assessed during a 4-year period. Thus, Sida staff members tend to be joining departments or field offices when some projects are just beginning, others are midway through (and their beginnings can only be guessed at from massive files), and others are just ending.

Many of the staff with whom we talked reflected on this problem. Of the 50 Sida staff members who expressed their opinion regarding the effect of frequent changes in personnel on the performance of Sida projects, 75 per cent of them indicated that the rapid turnover of assignments had a negative impact on performance. Only 16 per cent thought that turnover brought positive results due to the introduction of new skills and insights, and 8 per cent thought it had no impact.

Communication after an assignment
One way of encouraging staff to learn about the sustainability of past projects is to facilitate communication between the staff who have shifted to a new assignment and those staying behind. We did not find much evidence of the transmission of learning

from prior projects to staff members shifted to work in another location. A consistent message from our interviewees was that they view field assignments as highly desirable since they enable staff to participate "in the action" as well as to live a more comfortable lifestyle and earn more money.[10]

Sida staff assigned overseas received thorough orientations to current activities in their new overseas assignment but not when they returned to Stockholm. Staff returning from the field possess valuable insights about the posts they have just left. This knowledge is rarely utilized by staff who continue to work in their former posts. Of the 48 Sida staff members who had worked on multiple projects, 47 per cent responded that they had *no* contact at all with the projects on which they had worked earlier. Only 33 per cent indicated a limited level of contact (around once a year), and 19 per cent indicated a fair amount of contact (around one to three discussions per year). Indeed, the practice is to shift to a different area of work as a way of diversifying one's job portfolio. When such information is lost, opportunities for learning from experience are reduced; less learning takes place; lessons are not transmitted about how to avoid making the same mistakes or to achieve good performance and, thus, how to realize more sustainability in project outcomes.

Temporary contracts

There has been considerable stability in the size of the permanent staff at Sida. At the same time, a significant number of Sida employees do not have permanent positions. The number of permanent staff slowly grew from 677 in 1995 to 711 in 1999, the last year complete data was available to us. During the same time, the number of temporary staff has grown from 90 in 1995, to 126 in 1999 (with a dip to 73 in 1996). The proportion of temporary staff to permanent staff shifted over this 5-year period, from 11.7 per cent to 15.1 per cent (Figure 7.4).

Most temporary contracts are substitute positions for vacant Desk Officer posts or for staff on leave. The length of temporary contracts typically ranges from 3 to 12 months. If Sida extends a person's contract to more than 3 years over a 5-year period, Sida is obliged to offer an employee a permanent employment agreement according to the

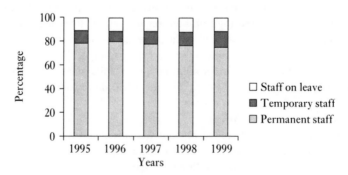

Figure 7.4. *Distribution of permanent and temporary staff at Sida from 1995–1999*

applicable Swedish labor protection laws (Government of Sweden 1982: 80). Other types of contracts are project contracts that are temporary posts associated with a specific activity rather than a vacant post within Sida. The length of this contract must not exceed the lifespan of the project. It is also possible for Sida to hire temporary relief staff during seasonal peaks of workload, such as during the end of the book-keeping year when it is time to balance the books (maximum length for this type of contract is 2 years).

At the time of our visit in the spring of 2000, a very large proportion of the Desk Officer positions within the Africa and Latin America Regional Departments held temporary contracts. In the Latin American Department, for example, 4 out of 6 Desk Officers working in March of 2000 held temporary contracts—all four with less than 1-year's experience.[11] In the Africa Department, 8 out of 12 Desk Officers had temporary employment agreements. In the Asia Department, 1 out of 6 Desk Officers was a temporary staff member. These employees were hired and frequently then rehired on 3-month contracts.

While these individuals may have considerable knowledge and skills, such short contracts inhibit staff from absorbing detailed knowledge about the societies in which their projects are to be applied. Staff performance frequently depends on how well they interact with their coworkers. We can expect temporary workers to be less likely to invest in relationships with others in their group leading to a reduced level of learning from communication with coworkers. Temporary staff also have fewer incentives to object to instructions and more incentives to do as they are told.

Retention and recruitment of younger staff
The random sample of staff members that we interviewed had, on average, worked at Sida for 10 years. Having lost full-time, permanent staff following the 1995 consolidation and reorganization, and having not recruited actively for many years, the age distribution within Sida is skewed toward the older age groups. The current age distribution poses a potential problem for Sida's future performance. This problem was recognized in the Personnel and Organization Development Department's *Annual Report for 1999* (Sida 1999c: 5) where it was noted:

Between the years 2000 and 2005, 72 members of the staff will retire. A further 222 persons will retire between the years of 2006 and 2011. This will be an extremely serious loss of skilled personnel. In response to the departure of such a large number of staff and to bring new skills into Sida, Sida has recruited younger staff during the last three years, in particular young program officers.

Instead of a large number of younger staff members vying for more senior positions, it would appear that the ranks of the 40 to 50-year-old staff are relatively small, while many of the younger staff members leave during their first decade of employment. This portends of a loss of institutional memory likely to happen in the next decade or so.

Further, given that a large proportion of staff in Stockholm's regional departments consists of temporary staff, considerable demand has been placed on Desk Officers with permanent posts, who tend to represent the department's institutional memory and have an intimate knowledge of current and potential future collaborating institutions in priority sectors and countries. This may leave the permanent Desk Officers with little time to monitor and follow up the quality of work carried out by temporary staff or contractors. This is particularly serious when the budget increases without proportionate increases in personnel.

Part of the reason for the relatively rapid turnover of younger staff is their perception of limited opportunities for promotion. When asked about their perceptions of "in-house advancement or promotions," 68 per cent of the 60 staff members who responded to this question indicated that they perceived it to be rather poor to very poor. *No one* responded that they perceived the advancement potential to be very good. While currently motivated to work hard, many of the younger staff members indicated to our research team that they planned to work for Sida for 5 years or so before going on to a different position in another organization.

Career advancement criteria related to performance of past projects
Success or failure in the initiatives taken in development cooperation has little perceived bearing on the careers of involved Sida staff. There was almost universal acknowledgement on this point among our interviewees. Only one respondent indicated that promotions relate to the performance of the projects on which individuals have worked. Sixty per cent of the 47 respondents who had been at Sida long enough to have an opinion about the promotion process thought that promotions are *not at all related* to the past project performance. The rest thought that perhaps some aspects of past project performance were taken into account indirectly.

Respondents advanced several reasons for this: first, there are so many factors that go into the success or failure of a particular project that it is difficult to see clearly what difference the involved Sida official made. There are so many other players, and so many other inputs, as well as external factors—natural disasters, war, etc.—that a relationship cannot meaningfully be established between sustainability and effort. Second, the outcome of many development initiatives is so general in scope and it may take so long before that outcome comes to fruition that the concerned officer would have well moved on by then. Further, outcomes of some projects, such as in drug prevention, where success is perceived as the absence of particular conditions— for example, addiction—are difficult to measure.

It is obvious that Sida has an outstanding Personnel and Organization Department that invests heavily in recruitment, training, and career development. It is, however, also obvious that the record that a Sida staff member has in managing his or her portfolio of projects (including monitoring the performance of contractors and coun- terparts) that are evaluated as sustainable is not included in the criteria for promotion to (or evaluation of) management positions.

Sida's relatively flat hierarchy means that aspiring Desk Officers do not have many opportunities to be promoted to higher-level posts. While about two-thirds of all professional positions are Desk Officer positions, less than 10 per cent are managerial ones. Indeed, several of the young Desk Officers we interviewed noted that they are not interested in a long-term commitment to Sida precisely because the chances of moving up the professional ladder appear to be so slim.

On the other hand, those in management pointed out that there are many opportunities available for young, aspiring Desk Officers. First, it was pointed out that Sida's flatness was not particularly out of the norm in Sweden—that enterprises in Swedish industry and the public sector frequently adhere to this model. Second, due to the demographic peculiarities, as already noted, many of the older staff members will be retiring soon, creating vacancies and, thus, incentives to stay on within Sida. Third, it was noted that the pay disparity between the professional staff and management was not that different, particularly after taxes. (A division head earns only about 30 per cent more than a Desk Officer.) At any rate, we were informed, a Desk Officer has plenty of interesting things to do and lots of responsibility to go with it. Thus, it was argued (by those in management) that there is a great deal of satisfaction in remaining a Desk Officer.

We were also able to observe that though there are few official levels in the organization, there are several subtle gradations in salary, power, and perks. First, we noted that salaries are individually negotiated (although Sida's unions prefer that these remain within certain bands for each type of employee and level of seniority). Second, some types of jobs were seen as more interesting or prestigious. Jobs in the Director General's secretariat, for example, are highly prized. In addition, jobs in the sector departments are valued over the regional ones for these offer junior officers more opportunities to shine in the eyes of their bosses. Most senior management are old Africa hands. This leads also to a greater attraction for working on projects in that continent. This is where the action is perceived to be.

In short, few Sida staff members whom we interviewed believe that the fate of their project will influence their career, since there is no effective tracking mechanism that links project success or failure with the individual contributions of Sida staff members and, as we discuss below, evaluations do not capture the effort or insights of staff members involved in a project. Further, promotions or other incentive schemes are not based, as a rule, on an employee's contribution to the sustainability of a portfolio of development projects.

In sum, we do not find evidence that Sida has attempted to create any of the four institutional conditions that we posit above as ways to enhance individual incentives to learn more about how to achieve more sustainable projects. As important as it would be for Sida to create institutional arrangements that are more propitious for individual learning, it is also necessary to acknowledge the difficulty in doing so. Developing new institutional incentive structures is a complicated collective process in its own right. This collective endeavor is unlikely to happen without changes within Sida's internal institutional arrangements for organizational learning.

7.6. ORGANIZATIONAL LEARNING THROUGH FORMAL EVALUATIONS

When principal–agent relationships are organized within a permanent organization, learning does not need to occur at the individual level alone. As Carlsson and Wohlgemuth (2000: 9) point out, learning in development assistance activities is complex and difficult largely due to the fact that individuals in multiple organizations that are geographically separated must learn from each other. "Knowledge is generated and learning takes place in parallel processes in the aid agency and in the organizations in the home country." A key problem is how to get these processes integrated. The processes "have to be married at some point if the parties are to be able to work together and learn from each other" (ibid.). Information from scattered sources needs to be aggregated and made comprehensible so that future designs can be improved in light of past experience. Efforts can be made to undertake formal reviews or evaluations that provide information to a large number of staff members about the kind of projects that have proved to be successful and sustainable in coping with particular types of problems in specific socioeconomic and cultural contexts. The evaluation processes could become a crucial strategy for ensuring that many people are learning from the experience of their colleagues and can thus avoid the same errors repeating. Unfortunately, a large number of evaluations are *undertaken* but are seriously *studied and discussed* by only a very small number of staff members.

If an organization had created positive incentives to learn about factors leading to sustainable development outcomes, one would expect to find:

1. Mechanisms to ensure that evaluations were read, discussed, and considered as a basis for future planning in all departments.
2. The staff should feel that formal evaluations were useful and that serious attention was paid to them.
3. The evaluation process would put considerable emphasis on the factors identified *a priori* as important for achieving sustainability. If ownership, for example, is considered a necessary (but not sufficient) condition for sustainability, then one would expect to see that evaluators were instructed to examine the level of ownership in a project or program and that its impact on sustainability would be seriously discussed.
4. A formal evaluation process that occurred prior to the completion of a project so that project participants would learn more effectively about their own activities and be able to adjust strategies mid-project in order to enhance the sustainability of at least the investment made in that activity.
5. Those affected by projects (the beneficiaries) would be involved in the evaluation of projects so that learning would occur for the beneficiaries, the supposed "owners" of the supported activities, as well as the donors and contractors.
6. The existence of general agreement about the criteria for success.

These factors would help to enhance the learning process about sustainability as well as developing a reliable and valid evaluation process that is important for the beneficiaries as well as for the Sida staff. Next, we examine to what extent these factors exist within Sida's organization.

7.7. EMPIRICAL EVIDENCE ON ORGANIZATIONAL LEARNING THROUGH EVALUATIONS

While there is considerable emphasis on learning in the official documents issued by the Department of Personnel and Organization Development, our findings do not provide strong evidence that the individual learning process within Sida is oriented to learning *about the factors that lead to sustainability*. Although there is evidence of high morale of Sida staff members, and most of the staff feel that their managers listen to them, and allow for individual growth, this does not necessarily mean that the incentives within Sida are conducive to increasing the sustainability of development assistance investments. Clearly, there are individuals at Sida who are *motivated* to learn more about sustainability, but the incentives created by the general structure and personnel policies of the organization do not stress paying close attention to the sustainability of aid investments. Thus, the official evaluation process becomes even more important as a greater weight must be placed on it as a way of encouraging learning about sustainability.

The usefulness of evaluations has already been the subject of studies within UTV/Sida (Sida 1997*d*, 1999*a*). A recent study (Sida 1999*a*), for example, presents a very frank picture of evaluations. The authors state:

It is no exaggeration to say that there is still some way to go before the typical evaluation process provides a good starting point for a broad utilization of evaluations results. There is, across the board, a significant disregard of the critical factors which determine whether an evaluation will be relevant to all stakeholders. An evaluation continues to be a concern for a very limited proportion of all those who have an interest in a project and are affected by its outcome [. . .] It is discouraging to find that the general pattern has been that *the further away you are from the centre of the project in terms of power and involvement, the less information you receive on evaluation recommendations and findings.* (Sida 1999*a*: 1, emphasis in original)

These internal studies confirm information we gained through interviews—that staff do not view the formal Sida evaluations in general as useful. Of the 60 staff members who discussed this topic with us, only 15 per cent considered formal evaluations effective in providing projects and programs with useful information, while 85 per cent considered them ineffective. On a related question, 41 per cent of all staff interviewed considered evaluations to be irrelevant to the assessment of the success of a project. Evaluations are generally seen as onerous administrative chores and are completed only as a required exercise. Consequently, evaluations are not embraced as opportunities to pass on learning or insights on the practice of development.

Others focused on the effectiveness of the evaluation process. A Department Head commented that the "program evaluation process is not very effective in changing the ways things are done around Sida." Others commented that the evaluations cover only the tangible, readily available, and measurable information from a project rather than trying to get at deeper reasons for successes or failures. They are often written to justify decisions that have already been made and to represent the vested concerns of various interested parties, and thus, are rarely perceived of as objective. Further, the UTV studies found that evaluations were not widely shared and discussed—that is, used as tools for learning (Sida 1999*a*).

Because of Sida's own recognition that ownership is one of the essential components of sustainable development outcomes, we were particularly interested in examining how evaluations addressed the question of ownership. To get a sense of the role owner-ship issues play in formal evaluations, we examined a sample of ten evaluation reports, which according to UTV was a representative sample of recent formal evaluations. We read these reports carefully to assess their content regarding each report's analysis of the ownership of a project as well as the degree of its sustainability.[12]

All evaluations must assess sustainability, and all ten reports did so. Since several of the projects contained an infrastructure component, the key question was whether the physical infrastructure would survive, rather than whether institutions created to govern and manage the infrastructure over time would survive and flourish to encour-age long-term sustainability. Most of the reports contained no discussion of ownership as a factor leading to project outcomes or sustainability. One document did contain a significant discussion of ownership. The evaluation of *HESAWA, Health through Sanitation and Water*, (97/12) devoted section 4.2 (p. 17) to a discussion of the active participation and village/user ownership that had been established as part of this pro-ject. In a sympathetic discussion of the problem of finding appropriate technologies that would effectively involve women and other beneficiaries from the villages in the provision, production, and consumption of improved water and sanitation, the evalu-ation reported that user groups were sometimes presented with inappropriate options. The report urged that more emphasis be given to augmenting local capacities to con-struct, monitor, and maintain sanitation and water systems.

The evaluation of the *Pahal Project—India: Participatory Approach to Human and Land Resource Development* (97/17) focused extensively on participation without tying this concept to ownership. It evaluated the level of participation in the project on an ordinal scale from one (involving manipulative participation—or a pretense at involving users) to seven (involving the affected beneficiaries taking initiative to change systems and control how resources are used). The report found that participation was just above four and pointed out that the high subsidy levels in this project were eroding the level of participation of users. The concept of ownership is briefly mentioned in *The Bank of Zambia—Way Forward* (98/32). In this case, there was only a short para-graph on the last page indicating that there appeared to be a strong commitment to change by the Bank management and employees. The other reports were even less specific on the subject of ownership. We find that the content of these reports makes it very difficult to learn about how to build ownership or to what extent the project promotes local ownership and whether this is contributing to achieving sustainable investments.

With regards to the timing of evaluations, many staff members perceive them as coming too late in the process. A staff member who had earlier worked in the Infrastructure Department indicated that they used to require every project to have an annual independent review, which he felt allowed project staff and recipient government officials to take corrective action immediately if needed. As the staff member reflected: "The way evaluations are currently run in Sida do not play the role that they should. Many program staff have left the project by the time it is evaluated. They don't absorb any lessons from the evaluation. Thus, very little learning is really gained from evaluations."

One of the most serious constraints to effective organizational learning is the lack of beneficiary and citizen participation in formal evaluations (for reviews, see Martens 2002; Gordillo and Andersson 2004). The authors of the above Sida report (1999*a*) were deeply concerned that stakeholders—particularly those who were not directly involved in a contractual relationship with a project—had little or no voice in its evaluation. They could not therefore, use the evaluations to further their own learning. Further, this evaluation of the evaluation process concluded that there were "few examples of evaluations actually contributing something new in terms of knowledge" (Sida 1999*a*: 2).

Finally, many staff members perceive a lack of an agreed-upon criteria within Sida for project success. Of the 64 responses to our question about which criteria are used to evaluate project success, 38 per cent responded that there were no well agreed-upon criteria, 22 per cent responded that improved institutional capacity was the major criterion, 17 per cent indicated that the disbursement rate was the prime factor, 5 per cent indicated that poverty reduction was the main criterion, and 12 per cent cited a variety of other criteria. A similar ambiguity surfaced concerning the reasons that some projects fail. Of the 38 Sida respondents who ventured an opinion about the major reasons for failure, 40 per cent thought most projects failed because of design flaws, 11 per cent thought it was due to recipient lack of follow-through, and 50 per cent cited a variety of other reasons. This finding underscores the importance of establishing an effective learning process because if design flaws are frequently involved in failed projects, it is all the more important to stimulate a learning process that will improve the design of future projects.

7.8. A FORMAL EVALUATION PROCESS WITHOUT MUCH LEARNING

We did not find any of the indicators outlined above (Section 7.6) that a donor agency might adopt if it wanted to stress incentives for sustainability. The formal evaluation process now occurs only after a project has been completed, while earlier mid-term evaluations did occur for some projects at an earlier date so that learning and adjustments could be made. According to Sida's own evaluations of its evaluation process (Sida 1999*a*), the beneficiaries of projects are not involved in the evaluation process nor do they learn the outcome of an evaluation effort. Of the evaluation reports that we sampled, only one paid serious attention to ownership—a factor that has been identified by Sida as crucial for achieving sustainability. Evidently, evaluations are not strongly urged to address how ownership is being implemented in evaluation. While some departments do make an effort to organize discussions of evaluations and Sida staff do attend meetings outside of Sida, we could not find a strong, department-wide effort to learn from the formal evaluation process. And, finally, the Sida staff members who we sampled do not find formal evaluations to be useful or that serious attention is paid to them.

The evidence reviewed on incentives for both individual and organizational learning at Sida still does not answer the question: How *do* Sida officers learn about sustainability? Our team asked representatives from each of Sida's departments to what extent they engage in learning about sustainability and how they would characterize this learning process in terms of both its prevalence and content.[13] Based on their responses, we found that representatives from all of the departments recognized the central importance of having a common understanding of sustainability and a plan for how to ensure that it is considered in all phases of the project cycle. No department, however, reported having a particular forum dedicated *exclusively* to sustainability issues. Most departments said the topic permeates the entire work program and that discussions of the topic are frequent whenever discussing specific project activities or potential Sida-supported activities. According to the respondents, most discussions on sustainability are associated with the preparation of project designs. For instance, the screening process often generates discussions among Desk Officers about how to assess the conditions for sustainability from the perspective of a project design. Several department representatives stressed that these discussions, often informal in character, may be the most important opportunity for learning about sustainability at Sida. Lunch seminars, staff meetings, and coffee break discussions all provide a forum for learning about sustainability.

Opportunities do exist for Sida personnel to discuss sustainability issues with their colleagues, but the frequency of such opportunities varies greatly from one department to another. Some departments reported on discussions on issues related to sustainability in one way or another at weekly staff meetings, but most claimed that attention to the issue of sustainability is either "rare," "inconsistent," or "nonexistent." While most of the respondents mentioned discussions of sustainability taking place during the project preparation and screening phase of the project cycle, only one department head mentioned sustainability being discussed in relationship to evaluations, and none of the departments reported on efforts to learn about sustainability from monitoring ongoing project activities.

7.9. BUDGETARY PROCESSES ORIENTED TOWARD SUSTAINABILITY

All government agencies, not just aid organizations, face pressures to disburse their funds within the budgetary year in which they are appropriated. This often leads to a preference for larger projects that enable staff "to move the money" as rapidly as possible. The incentives to "move the money" tend to be enhanced when an organization has few employees to handle a large budget or a large number of individual projects. If an organization had created positive incentives to resist "moving the money" and instead focused on the conditions for achieving sustainable development outcomes, one would expect to find that (1) few staff would perceive pressure from management to disburse and (2) a variety of informal and formal strategies would exist to discourage a resource-focused aid program.

Sida management has made considerable formal efforts to counteract the pressure to disburse. It was repeatedly stressed to us by senior levels within Sida's management that official policy does not stress disbursement over other goals. Most of the Desk Officers we interviewed, however, noted that they do feel pressure to disburse fully their projects' annual allocations. Some Desk Officers noted that as much as 40 per cent of the year's disbursement for their department takes place in the November to December period. (Sida's fiscal year coincides with the calendar year.)

In Table 7.1, we present the quarterly disbursement data for the years between 1997 and 2000. As can be seen from this table, heavy disbursements took place during the fourth quarter of 1997. Some respondents mentioned a panic atmosphere at the end of the budget year. A few noted that some Division Chiefs took a detailed interest of the progress in funds disbursement by Desk Officers working under them. These Division Chiefs would ask for frequent updates of the projects they were receiving and approving. Moreover, they would provide their superiors with project proposals that they had drummed up themselves.[14] These events have created the impression among many Desk Officers that there is a push to disburse and that their superiors would look upon them favorably if they were able to meet such unofficial targets.

Empirical evidence suggests that this impression among Desk Officers—to disburse allocated budgets efficiently—is widespread. Sida employees feel that they are under pressure to spend money, especially at the end of the budget year. Among the 46 randomly selected staff who had been at Sida long enough to discuss their perceptions of what was actively monitored by the section and division managers, two-thirds indicated that disbursement rates (at Sida headquarters or in the recipient country) were actively monitored in the day-to-day business of aid administration. We believe this push to disburse draws from a combination of constraints at the constitutional and policy levels. We noted earlier that Sida is responsible for disbursing a large portion of Sweden's foreign aid budget and that the public is eager to see that this budget approaches the 1 per cent of GNP target and that the money is well spent. In addition, there is pressure from Parliament, whose members find it hard to understand why Sida is unable to use up the allocated funds.

The combination of expenditure ceilings and the prohibition to carry over unspent funds to the following year favors patterns of disbursement that are not supportive of a sustainability-focused program. This combination of conditions has the potential to cause staff to worry that, unless budgeted amounts are fully disbursed, the unspent funds will be lost. This leads to incentives for staff to identify and fund those projects that they can disburse quickly and most reliably. Projects that promise effectiveness and sustainability, but which are not as fast disbursing, can be overlooked within such a regime. More nonconventional and innovative project ideas from new partners represent higher uncertainty and might therefore not be funded under such a regime. Administrative pressures to disburse fully allocated funds can thus act as an incentive that places internal short-term, administrative targets over long-term objectives in sustainable development.

This pressure can lead to a funding bias of renewal of ongoing projects, rather than the initiation of a long process to approve an entirely new project. To examine this hypothesis in more depth, we randomly selected 21 ongoing Sida-supported development projects from Sida's database of all its funded projects and studied the history of each project. We found that 16 of these projects (or 76 per cent) were indeed continuations of earlier Sida support to the same recipient organization. This result confirms our earlier stated impression: the way for a Desk Officer to succeed is to spend money; the way to spend money with any level of responsibility is to spend money on renewal of existing projects.

The effort to realize sustainable development outcomes requires budgetary flexibility. In order to enhance their success and sustainability, aid projects need to fine-tune to local realities. This, in turn, means that disbursement timetables have to be adaptable. To be effective, therefore, aid agencies must continuously monitor the recipient's actions and adjust its support accordingly. Strict budget ceilings, without the flexibility of reserve funds, foster a resource-focused, rather than content- and quality-driven, management of development cooperation initiatives. Budgetary pressures do not seem to be congruent with efforts to stress incentives for sustainability. Many of the staff we interviewed felt strong pressures to disburse—especially toward the end of the year. Few efforts seem to have been made—except for strong denials of its existence— to counteract the pressure to disburse.

7.10. CONCLUSIONS

How does an agency's internal organization influence the sustainability of aid? The institutional analysis in this chapter has shown that despite the large distance between donor agencies and recipient organizations, the broader institutional context of the donor agency has profound effects on the relationships between recipient and beneficiary organizations, contractors, and the individuals working with the aid agency. The origins of many of the institutional incentives that shape the agency staff's decisions about their interactions with the actors in the field can be traced back to several constitutional and collective-choice institutions. As illustrated by the case of Sida in this chapter, some of the most influential constitutional and collective-choice institutions include the rules governing the size of the total aid budget, how the agency may or may not spend the budget, as well as the conditions for agency staff employment.

This means that some of the incentive problems in the development aid process are beyond the immediate control of the development agency. Yet, one should not underestimate the influence of the aid agency's decisions on the prospects for sustainability in the recipient country. The institutional analysis in this chapter showed that one of the critical challenges for aid-supported activities is to overcome the severe information asymmetries that exist between the agency staff and the multiple actors in the field. Even though the constitutional constraints imposed on most aid agencies may limit their influence over some of the institutional arrangements that govern the development aid process, the way that the agency staff members address the information asymmetries is likely to have the biggest impact on aid outcomes. To overcome such asymmetries, agency staff rely on mechanisms for individual and organizational learning about field activities.

Our applied institutional analysis of Sida's collective-choice institutions illustrated the importance of identifying and understanding the incentive structures within the agency that either help or hinder agency staff to engage in such learning activities. We found that many of the incentives that officials working for Sida face—a pleasant atmosphere that is respectful of the views of all, opportunities for overseas travel, association with a well-educated and informed set of colleagues, and an opportunity to do something that staff view as important—help to create a highly motivated staff. Some of the other incentives that Desk Officers face may lead them to invest less in careful planning and preparation of aid-supported activities. For instance, we did not find any mechanisms in place that connect a staff member's performance with activity outputs in the field. We also found clear incentives for agency staff to signal to superiors that one is clever and able to prepare good documents. Preparing good documents, however, is not synonymous with devising good project designs or strategies. This is especially relevant given the lack of opportunities for in-depth discussion of what makes a project design potentially more likely to lead to sustainable outcomes.

Our incentive analysis concluded that although many aspects of Sida's organizational structure and personnel policies encourage a learning environment, we did not find many inducements to engage in individual or organizational-level learning about sustainability as such. While it would be an extraordinary challenge to change the existing incentive structures for learning about sustainability, the institutional context at Sida is probably more amenable for such change than at most other donor agencies. The relative autonomy of Sida regarding the content of its aid portfolio, and the extensive freedom given to agency managers to organize each department's work plan, are two factors that make changes in the agency's collective-choice institutions possible.

The broader implication of this finding is that, under some circumstances, donor agency managers may improve the conditions for sustainability by supporting their colleagues in efforts to learn about the underlying processes that generate the institutional incentives conducive to productive development outcomes.

While every international aid agency faces its own unique mix of institutional rules, we also think there are many lessons from this institutional study of Sida that apply to other bilateral and multilateral aid agencies. Perhaps the most important lesson is that if donor agencies are really serious about reforming the institutions of recipient countries so that the performance of aid-supported activities improve, they should also consider the reforms within their own agencies that would encourage their own staff to learn from past aid interventions.

NOTES

1. Anna Wieslander (2000: 250) reflects on her own experience in the following manner:

   After eighteen months of administrative work for Sida in Tunisia in the late 1960s I returned home, rather humble. I had learnt a lot about the aid relationship between "donor" and "recipient," and the relationship between "us" and "them." First of all, I realized that I had not, as I had hoped, much to contribute to Tunisian society. Secondly, I found that most of the Swedish experts in our small community had little contact with the surrounding society. Thirdly, and maybe most important, I realized that aid was granted according to the plans and preferences of the donor, not of those in need.

2. Excerpts from Sida personnel statistics 2000, courtesy of Sida's Human Resources Department.
3. The Desk Officer, as we shall see in the following section, makes many of the crucial operational-level decisions.
4. One of the advantages of the IAD framework, as opposed to other modes of analysis, is that it allows for dynamic analysis of interactions. As the contextual variables change, so do the configuration of variables in the action arena. When changes occur, a modified outcome can be expected. The actors evaluate these outcomes and may adjust their behavior in future interactions on the basis of their individual or collective perceptions. And, they may move up a level to change the structure itself.
5. For more details on the changes in the constitutional budget regimes and how they affected Sida decision making during this period, please see E. Ostrom *et al.* (2002: 132–5).
6. Our findings are somewhat more positive than the study of learning within Sida conducted by the Swedish National Audit Bureau in 1988 as summarized by Weislander (2000: 255–6). Referring to the 1988 Audit Bureau findings, Weislander concludes

   that while there is an obvious interest in learning, Sida is better at changing its thinking than its acting. Among the problems mentioned is that Sida is incapable of describing "good aid projects." Expressed goals are conflicting, and one goal—disbursement—is not even included. . . . Evaluations are not effectively used, the rate of internal staff turnover precludes learning, and there are no useful routines for transferring the experience of TA. Learning at Sida is said to take place mainly by doing, it is top-down, and promoted primarily through changes in routines. (ibid.)

7. We conducted semi-structured interviews with over 60 staff members using the Study Guide reproduced in E. Ostrom *et al.* (2002: appendix C, 330–47). Interviews with the senior staff, and with those directly involved with the Indian and Zambian projects described in the following chapters, focused on specific substantive questions rather than following the same semi-structured interview schedule for each interview.
8. An initial report of the responses to this survey was sent to us in the Winter of 2000. We appreciate having access to this data very soon after it was collected. Krister Andersson translated the questions from Swedish to English.
9. A general request was sent to all current staff members at Sida to answer a set of questions on a Web-based survey instrument. A total of 308 Sida staff members responded, of which 102 (one-third) were male and 206 (two-thirds) were female. Although the survey was not given to a random sample, respondents were well distributed across age groups as well as departments within Sida. It is reasonable to assume that the most committed employees were the most likely to respond to this voluntary survey. Moreover, it would be natural for some staff members to worry about the possibility that their responses would be traced back and linked to them personally. One should therefore be careful about drawing general conclusions from this nonrandom sample of respondents.
10. This may be a rather surprising finding since many departments say they have problems recruiting staff for field posts. Sida's own Web survey confirms our data: an overwhelming 77 per cent of the respondents said they were interested in taking a field assignment of some sort during the next few years (Sida 2001: 14).
11. All interviews reported in this paragraph were conducted in March 2000.
12. The 10 evaluation documents were: 97/25, 98/21, 96/13, 99/5, 97/12, 97/17, 98/32, 97/11, 99/10, 97/3.

13. The UTV sent the following question via e-mail to all Sida department representatives (12 representatives responded): "How does your department address sustainability issues in its daily work program, and, in your opinion, how has the frequency of your department's discussions of sustainability issues changed over time?"

14. One Desk Officer told us how the Department Head, from mid-November until the closing of the books on December 17, requested daily updates of disbursements so as to ensure that no resources were lost. We were also told about another Department Head who had promised a champagne toast to those colleagues who managed to disburse their entire annual budget by December 17.

8

Incentives for Contractors in Aid-Supported Activities

KRISTER ANDERSSON AND MATTHEW R. AUER

8.1. INTRODUCTION

In 2001, a major American newspaper remarked on the vast sums of aid intended for Poland that, in a strictly financial sense, traveled no farther than to the headquarters of an American consulting firm (Dobbs 2001). Quoting from the US Agency for International Development's (USAIDs) Web site, the *Washington Post* noted that some 80 per cent of all USAID contracts and grants go "directly to American firms" (ibid.: A1). Years later, the London *Guardian* queried about a partisan lobby group in Britain that "received more money from Britain's Department for International Development (DFID) than Liberia or Somalia, two of the most desperate nations on earth" (Monbiot 2004: 23).

Critics from both ends of the ideological spectrum complain that foreign aid too often benefits an industry of aid contractors and grantees, including professional for-profit and not-for-profit consulting firms, NGOs, universities, think tanks, independent consultants, lobbyists, commodity vendors, and recipient country professionals—all at the expense of poor people who are the intended beneficiaries. After stripping away the biases of the critics, an inviolable fact remains: aid contractors are key players in the development and delivery of aid and their choices and actions determine aid outcomes for recipient governments, recipient organizations, and the world's poor.

In the scholarly literature, perspectives diverge on the efficacy of aid consultants, divisible into optimistic and pessimistic camps. The former group finds contractors making vital contributions to aid projects and programs (Deininger *et al.* 1998; Markusen and Rutherford 2002). Consider, for example, advocates of the World Bank's economic analysis and advice (known as 'ESW' or Economic and Sector Work), which is performed both by Bank staff and contractors. Deininger *et al.* (1998: 415) found that a dollar of ESW yields four to eight dollars in development impacts. Indeed, they urge that this rate of return underestimates total benefits for borrower countries because ESW advances not one but myriad projects and influences policy formulation too.

Pessimists, including some former aid consultants, hue more closely to the views of skeptical journalists. Hancock (1989), for example, goes so far as to suggest that aid experts have an incentive not to excel for fear of working themselves out of a job. In a similar vein, and in the context of US aid to Russia, Wedel (1998) portrays aid consultants as avarice rent-seekers. James Jones (1997) attributes American aid advisers' repeated failures to their reliance on standardized, acontextual policy remedies. He sympathizes with George Kennan's observation of "the incurable tendency of Americans to do everything by uniform categories rather than by careful and discriminate attention to the requirements of the individual case" (Kennan quoted in J. Jones 1997: 114). He also speaks of a "development industry" of consultants who ardently cultivate intra-industry and donor contacts so as to ensure long-term business relationships (ibid.: 117).

There are ample hints, then, that donors as well as recipient organizations and beneficiaries would be interested in *discovering what incentives drive contractors' behavior*. This chapter views contractors as key actors in the aid octangle. The forces that influence them, and their own influence over aid processes and outcomes, require formal examination. Many donor agencies increasingly rely on contractors for a wide variety of services, including project design and planning, project implementation, short- and long-term monitoring, evaluation, and expert advice on technical issues (USGAO 1993: 9). Under these circumstances, the contractors' roles are pivotal in determining short- and long-term impacts of aid, for in many instances, they—and not the donor agency staff—have the closest and most regular contact with recipient organizations. Determining prospects for aid sustainability, then, requires a clear understanding of the incentives that contractors face.

Our analysis of consultants' incentives draws on interviews with representatives from 10 large Swedish firms that administered large Swedish International Development Cooperation Agency (Sida) contracts in the 1999–2000 period. It also makes use of data collected from five Sida-supported field projects in India and Zambia.[1] Our analysis finds that there are inherent contradictions between the incentives that consultants face in promoting ownership and the incentives they face in retaining control of a project. Control over project decisions may produce positive short-term project results that please Sida. But contractors' control may also compromise the prospects for sustainability.

This chapter begins by identifying positive incentives generated by the competitive bidding process, followed by a discussion of how such incentives can affect sustainability. The chapter ends with an assessment of factors that motivate high contractor performance. In concluding, we contend that donor agencies can improve aid sustainability by combining consultant expertise with the local knowledge of local beneficiaries— knowledge that donors frequently declare to be critical, but nevertheless, tend to neglect or underutilize. This, in turn, calls for assigning a greater role to beneficiary organizations in the design, implementation, and evaluation of donor-financed field activities.

8.2. THE PLACE OF CONTRACTORS IN AID PROGRAMS

A look at the Octangle presented in Chapter 4 reveals the central importance of contractors. Contractors are involved in essentially all stages of international development cooperation programs. Figure 8.1 expands on the earlier Octangle representation to

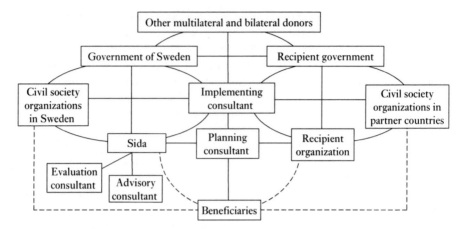

Figure 8.1. *The place of contractors in the development octangle*

account, more completely, for contractors' different roles and contributions, including planning, implementation, monitoring, and evaluation of field activities as well as providing expert advice to the donor agency headquarters.

In Sweden's aid program, the proliferation of consultants is a relatively recent development. Traditionally, government agency staff members were responsible for implementing development assistance activities themselves. This changed in the 1980s because of a public inquiry on Swedish governmental roles and responsibilities (Sida 1989). The report concluded that some types of foreign assistance could be performed more cost-effectively if they were contracted to private actors through a competitive bidding process. This policy has since become Sida's modus operandi.

8.3. INCENTIVES FOR CONTRACTOR PERFORMANCE

Swedish firms are disproportionately represented among winners of Sida contracts, including contracts that are openly bid. However, this is in keeping with procurement trends in most, if not all, Development Assistance Committee member countries. Indeed, there are clear incentives for Sida to favor Swedish consultants. First, contracting domestically helps to strengthen the Swedish human resource base for international development cooperation. Second, compared to consultants from other OECD countries, Swedish consultants tend to be better versed with Sida's development cooperation missions, its operating procedures, and projects in the field. Third, Swedish contractors—particularly those with Sida project experience— already understand Sida organizational cultures, competencies, modes of doing business (including contracting methods and contract renewal rituals), while Sida understands theirs. Veteran Swedish contractors enjoy advantages over new competitors. Long-standing relationships between Sida and older, established, and primarily

Swedish consulting firms lower the transaction costs for both parties in contracting new assignments. Monitoring costs—that is, monitoring by the donor of the contractor—tend to be lower in long-standing contracting relationships, as the donor is comparatively more familiar and perhaps more trusting of oft-awarded contractors. We do not believe these incentive structures to be unique to Sida, but would expect these to be present in all aid agencies that rely on contractors for tasks associated with development aid in general.

According to Sida's Division for Legal Services and Procurement Advice, the international bidding processes for Sida contracts are increasingly open and competitive, with the share of contracts awarded to international firms on a steady rise. In fact, a new trend seems to be emerging whereby Swedish firms lacking certain sets of needed skills are increasingly nudged aside by foreign firms. Sida's procurement experts indicate that the proportion of non-Swedish firms appears to be increasing in areas such as comprehensive evaluation studies and macro-economic analyses. This increased competition for contracts is a healthy development as it may inspire Swedish firms to develop additional competencies with long-term advantages for Sweden's technical assistance resource base. This trend notwithstanding, Sida's legal department informed us that Swedish firms continue to land the vast majority of what consultants consider the most lucrative contracts, those involving implementation of Sida-supported activities.

Incentives, present in particular phases of the aid project cycle, can and do inspire some contractors to perform at a high level. However, there are constraints on the overall effect of these incentives on sustainability—the core concern of sections below. First, we identify the main sets of incentives affecting contractors' behavior. Later, we address how those incentives give consultants potential rent-seeking opportunities while presenting ownership problems for recipients and moral hazard problems for Swedish taxpayers.

8.3.1. *Pre-Design Phase*

The textbook version of how a given Sida project begins is with a request from the recipient organization (Sida 1997c). Both staff members within Sida and consultants interviewed, however, indicated that *consultants* are frequently involved in the project development process *even before* an initial inquiry is made from the recipient. Consultants may seek opportunities for prospective Sida contracts by "helping" the recipient to formulate a project inquiry. These initial inquiries by consultants usually involve problem areas where the consultant has special expertise. Our interviews and some project tender documents also indicate that it is not uncommon for project *design* consultants and project *implementation* consultants to be one and the same firm. Not only does this system potentially favor consultants' interests over the needs of recipients and beneficiaries, it probably undermines recipients' sense of project ownership because the consultant (rather than the recipient or the beneficiary) is the project instigator.[2]

8.3.2. *Design Phase*

Sida policies attempt to discourage consultants from competing for projects that the same consultant has already had a hand in designing. The incentives for consultants to participate in project formulation and subsequent project implementation are clear. Consultants who are invited to help formulate new projects often know the recipient actors, the latter's needs, and the peculiarities of local, institutional contexts. To the extent that Sida preferentially awards contracts for both project design and project implementation to Swedish firms, the likelihood of a project designer winning a project implementation contract is relatively high. This is so since the pool of qualified Swedish consultants is quite small. Such a system generates ownership-related risks for both the recipients and for Sida.

8.3.3. *Implementation Phase*

Our interviews with consultants found that during project implementation, both recipients and consultants perceive a great vesting of power in the Sida Desk Officer. That perception is evident in the triangle of communications among the Desk Officer, the recipient organization, and the consultant (Figures 8.2(a) and (b)).

Many donors urge that recipient organizations take ownership—that is, responsibility for project goals, project administration, and project resources. In theory, a Sida Desk Officer could advance this policy objective by insisting that recipient organizations make key project decisions and that recipients constitute the contractors' primary point of contact for negotiating project issues. Our interviews reveal an important caveat to this otherwise praiseworthy system—namely that the Sida Desk Officer is most often the *de facto* principal. This can be the case when the consultant perceives that it is Sida's evaluation of the consultant's work "that counts most." Figure 8.2(b) illustrates the *de facto* principal–agent relationship between Sida-contractor and recipient organization. The incentives for the consultant to perform are quite different in the *de jure* and *de facto* situations. The implications of these differences merit a more in-depth discussion.

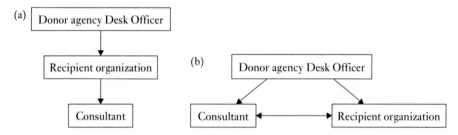

Figure 8.2. *(a) The* de jure *principal–agent relationship of implementation (b) The* de facto *principal–agent relationship of implementation*

8.4. INCENTIVE INCOMPATIBILITIES: CONTROL VERSUS OWNERSHIP

According to Sida's official stance, the recipient organization is formally the principal, and the consultant the agent in the recipient organization–consultant relationship. However, typically, project funds are not administered by the recipient organization, but are disbursed directly by Sida to the consultant. Given this structure, it is natural for the contractors to strive primarily to satisfy Sida, fostering a *de facto* principal–agent relationship between Sida and consultants.

One might expect the consultant's incentive to perform to depend on (1) the importance of the contract and donor relationship to the portfolio of the consultant, (2) the nature of the good being contracted (which determines the profit margin), and (3) the extent to which aid is tied and the competitiveness of the bidding process. We discuss each of these incentives below.

1. *The importance of the donor to the portfolio of the consultant.* The more the consultant depends on Sida for its business, the stronger the incentive to perform well on Sida contracts. A "preferred" client is often one who represents a major income source for the contractor. Consultancies that depend on a few preferred clients rue the day they let down, not to mention lose, such clients. In these contexts, contractors are especially eager to please donors. But as we argue above, pleasing donors and pleasing aid recipients are not necessarily one and the same.

2. *The nature of the good that is contracted.* The indicators of performance that the consultant pays closest attention to vary by the nature of the good. Gauging the quality of the contractors' work varies by task. At times, results from capital-intensive projects—for example, installation of a power plant turbine—are easier to measure than are technical assistance efforts, for example, outcomes from educational reform advice (Auer 1998). If the project outcomes are not easy to measure and evaluate, it is easier for the consultant to hide project misperformance or failure. This condition suggests that consultants have weaker incentives to perform at a high level when project outcomes are difficult to appraise. Moreover, cunning consultants who expect to perform at a low level of competence have an incentive to prescribe difficult-to-measure project outcomes.

3. *Open or restricted bidding procedures.* Tied-aid that "ties" particular contracts to particular contractors may reduce the consultant's incentive to perform. Contractors may grow complacent about the inevitability of winning or being re-awarded contract work. To illustrate, in the case of Sida's portfolio of industrial energy projects, there are only two major contractors (Swedpower and Sweco). Even these actors are units of the same parent company. As we see in the case studies from Zambia in Chapter 10, this situation can create incentives for the consultant to underperform. Several Zambian officials with experience in Sida projects indicated that a more competitive bidding process, open to non-Swedish firms, would inspire better consultant performance. Consultants operating in a

more competitive environment, and who value future business with particular donors, have stronger incentives to perform.

8.5. CONTRACTORS' INCENTIVES AND THE PROSPECTS FOR SUSTAINABILITY

Figure 8.2(b) shows that the contractor commonly interfaces with two counterparts—the donor agency and the recipient organization. In the field, consultants often have an incentive to take control—that is, to dominate the project's management. In some cases, a creative and proactive consultant may be able to convince the donor agency of the feasibility of a certain project, even though the recipient organization may not share enthusiasm for or even accept the goals of such a project. Here, the incentive for the consultant to take control creates an ownership problem, thus jeopardizing prospects for sustainable outcomes.

8.5.1. *Is a Consultant-Directed Project Likely to be Sustainable?*

A consultant preoccupied with forging a long-term relationship with a donor agency is likely to maximize his or her control over a project and not pass along control to the intended beneficiaries. Inculcating a sense of ownership among beneficiaries may be risky if the beneficiary does not perform in ways that the donor prefers. By retaining control, the contractor reduces uncertainty and maximizes expected returns from future contracts. A contractor that is concerned about minimizing uncertainty may therefore be reluctant to promote active participation by stakeholders in aid program decision making, even though such participation may be critical for the beneficiary ownership and thus long-term sustainability of the development outcomes.

8.5.2. *What is the Role of the Consultant in Ownership?*

Within the *de facto* relationship among Sida, contractors, and recipient organizations (Figure 8.2(b)), there are aspects of project ownership. Consultants often are able to exercise choice over the disposition of the assets involved in the donor's project. These choices, however, can be constrained by the terms of the contract, the ability of the donor to monitor performance, and by the nature of the good. In many cases, consultants will have more control than will the intended beneficiaries: sometimes it is even possible for the consultant to choose which groups, among the larger set of beneficiaries, will be targeted. Ownership, in this way, can rest more with the contractor than with the donor, and certainly more so with the contractor than with the beneficiary. However, finding constructive ways to promote direct participation of beneficiaries in the bidding process can be a challenge. As our interviews with several Swedish consultant firms revealed, it is often not easy to secure the recipient organization's involvement in decision making. Involving final "end users" of aid, that is, ordinary beneficiaries, can be even more difficult.

In this latter regard, a Swedish consultancy with experience in both South Africa and Southeast Asia noted the difference in the attitudes of recipient organization representatives. While recipient organization officials in Vietnam consistently asserted their management authority and emphasized the advisory role of the Swedish contractor, officials in a comparable recipient organization in Namibia were more passive in the recipient–contractor relationship. The Namibian recipient organization did not insist on retaining control over project decisions. In fact, Namibian counterparts often referred to the consultant as "the boss."

Recipients' participation in decision making can be further complicated in cases where recipients are reluctant to acknowledge ownership. Especially in cases where there are multiple recipients, various obstacles to participation arise: Should the contractor include them all, or should he/she make a selection? What are the constitutive rules for making selections? If the recipients are not formally organized, how can their input into decisions be incorporated? These questions have no pat answers and they are highly context-specific. Nevertheless, these are "must ask" questions, given the oft-mentioned problem of foreign aid (including consultant-led aid) failing to promote ownership among recipients and beneficiaries.

The discussion of the contractor's incentives, so far, has relied primarily on theory and general information from our in-depth interviews and less so on practical examples. We now turn to case material revealing how Swedish aid contractors, confronted with particular incentives, act in particular ways. Here is a test of the tripartite model described in Figure 8.2(b), where the agent (consultant) makes choices vis-à-vis a formal principal (recipient organization) and *de facto* principal (donor). In our interviews, we asked the consultants for whom they felt they actually worked. The following section reports our results.

8.6. THE SIDA CONTRACTORS' PERCEPTIONS

8.6.1. *"For Whom Do We Work?"*

Sida policy prescribes that consultants who help implement projects should be appointed by recipient organizations. The latter include host country ministries or other relevant agencies. However, both Sida staff and consultants whom we interviewed concur in that undertaking contractual obligations, consultants are often more preoccupied with what they perceive are Sida's concerns than with what they perceive are the recipients' needs. This sentiment varies by project and country. In some instances, a contractor seeking to change a salary provision in a contract might expect to deal principally with the Sida Desk Officer rather than the contracting recipient organization. One consultant suggested that host-country counterparts in South Africa tended to be quite passive about personnel and technical resource-related contractual matters. According to this consultant, the South African counterpart's attitude is that: "This project involves Sweden's money, not ours. What is the purpose of aggravating a consultant who seeks to change a salary condition? If we irritate him, he may do his job less competently. Perhaps the changes that the consultants seek are not what we desire, but it is better to get some assistance than no assistance at all."

The interviewee added that accounting procedures in South Africa are sufficiently poor that the recipients probably would not detect changes to financial provisions of contracts. The consulting firm claims that if it sought to make changes to a contract, and to be honest about these changes, it would raise the issue first with a Sida Desk Officer.

By contrast, in an instance in Vietnam, a consultant sought changes to a salary line in a contract. The consultant approached a Sida Desk Officer with this request, who referred the consultant to the project's host country client—the Vietnam's General Statistics Office. According to the consultant, in Vietnam, recipient organizations genuinely behave like "the boss." The contractor added that Vietnamese recipients are "obsessed" with budgets and contract details and Sida contractors should expect to deal with the counterpart agency first and foremost. These two anecdotes suggest that recipient organizations' ownership over project resources depends on country contexts and the level of institutional development in the recipient country or region.

8.6.2. *Contractors' Perceptions of Relationship to Sida*

Several consultants expressed frustration with the quality of technical expertise at Sida. Some questioned whether Sida's technical prowess had declined in recent years and they regretted a trend toward "generalization" rather than "specialization" in Sida's skill base. Others surmised that while many Sida staff members were competent in a variety of technical areas, growing administrative workloads at Sida discouraged the use of technical skills. Disadvantages of the demise of specialization at Sida and loss of technical knowledge entail more than just Sida's increasing dependence on skilled contractors. In some cases, it also includes a dependence on skilled evaluators because Sida officials who lack technical skills are less capable of evaluating project performance or the quality of work performed by consultants.

On the other hand, consultants recognized that an older system—where Sida officials performed most of the in-country logistical operations, staffing, and implementation—was impractical, and that efficiency was gained by outsourcing these tasks to consultants. Nevertheless, technical consultants bemoaned the fact that their work was not necessarily understood or appreciated by Sida staff. This problem might manifest itself in subtle ways. In one case, technical passages in a report prepared by a consultant specializing in natural resource management received no comments from the relevant Sida project manager. From the consultant's perspective, the client failed to appreciate the subtlety and quality of project methods and results. This problem may be symptomatic of Desk Officers' heavy workload. Further, it is indicative of a potentially more serious problem—inadequate monitoring of consultants' work. Sida and recipients are susceptible to moral hazard because consultants might exert too little effort and produce results whose low quality is obvious only at project's end.

In addition to concerns about Sida personnel's technical expertise, some consultants complained about the lack of uniformity in Sida's ways of conducting business with consultants—a problem that consultants assume is a remnant of Sida not having fully assimilated the various organizational cultures, rules, and procedures of the different previously independent agencies that merged into Sida in 1995.

Some consultants urge that Sida do a more thorough job of providing information about the work that other contractors are undertaking for Sida. Contractors believe that workshops where contractors share experiences and discuss ongoing and planned activities are worthwhile.

8.6.3. *What Makes a Consultant Tick?*

Some of the consultants we interviewed indicated that one of their primary goals was to secure well-paying work for their firm. They assume that by performing well on current Sida tasks, additional and perhaps larger and more lucrative Sida contracts might be obtained in the future. Consultants indicated, however, that profit-orientation is only one motivator for doing good work, and is not even necessarily the most important one. This is a salient finding for Sida as it encourages contractors to perform well even as Sida searches for low-cost ways to motivate its consultants. Interviewees stress the importance of being able to develop meaningful, productive partnerships with counterparts overseas. Developing and refining skills and implementation models through long-term projects are also mentioned as key aspirations.

Consultants also express a desire to receive public praise for their work—a source of pride and also a means for advertising their skills and experience. Consultants feel that their profession is a noble and rewarding one in that their work leads directly or indirectly to improved economic and living conditions for the poor. It is interesting to note that many of the "core values" that "make people tick" are manifested in consultants' remarks (above), including wealth, enlightenment, skill, well-being, respect, righteousness, and affection. These remarks also suggest that while consultants need to be paid fairly for their work, they can be motivated to foster worthy projects by using relatively low-cost measures. Nonmonetary awards for successful projects (public praise, certificates of appreciation, or other commendations) and invitations to relevant convocations (e.g. professional speaking engagements where skill and respect values are indulged) are important ways to increase motivation for learning and high performance (e.g. Frey 1997; Lasswell 1971).

While the recent tendency to rely less on donor agency personnel and more on contractors for the production of several services within international aid programs may lead to more cost-effective short-term results, our analysis suggests that the increased reliance on contractors presents it own set of problems—some of which manifest themselves in the long-term. The incentive structures that exist within the donor agency–contractor relationship create conditions for moral hazard, and moral hazard problems often do not emerge until a project concludes and the contractor's poor work outputs are finally recognized. By then, it is too late: scarce aid resources are spent, recipient organizations and beneficiaries are short-changed (and perhaps reluctant to participate in future rounds of aid cooperation), and consultants have squandered the very thing they so covet: high marks from the donor. Competitive bidding may help mitigate the risk of moral hazard, but this instrument is only a necessary—and not sufficient—condition to encourage high consultant performance. Additional institutional arrangements are needed to ensure high quality outputs that yield real benefits to intended beneficiaries.

One potential scheme may be the use of *performance-based measures*. Such indicators tie consultants' rewards to their job performance. A carefully designed performance measurement and other types of "result-oriented management" incentives may help improve contractor performance. A complementary approach involves reducing knowledge asymmetries. Since many consultants have worked in a particular country or region for many years, they frequently have a thorough understanding of what has or has not worked in the past. These individuals have specialized knowledge about sustainability that may even exceed that of donor agency staff members. Designing ways of drawing more effectively on that knowledge, while encouraging more effective exercise of ownership by the target beneficiaries, are substantial challenges facing all donors.

These challenges notwithstanding, enhancing recipient organization and beneficiary participation is critical. Donors can encourage recipients to open up their decision-making processes and to be more directly accountable to beneficiary groups that are outside the formal government structure. One plausible way of achieving this would be for donors and recipient organizations to assign more significant roles to beneficiaries and beneficiary organizations (as opposed to recipient organizations within government) in the hiring, monitoring, and releasing of consultants. The empowerment of beneficiary organizations to be more active in both the provision and production of contractors' work will strengthen contractor incentives to contribute to sustainable outcomes.

NOTES

1. We interviewed a total of 21 consultants working at the consulting firms with the largest Sida contracts in 1999, and who were based at their firms' headquarters in Stockholm. In addition to the Stockholm-based contractors, we also interviewed 13 representatives of both Swedish and international consulting firms in India and Zambia who were or had been involved with any of the five field projects that we studied there.
2. Consistent with the conceptualization of the actors in the aid Octangle, it is important to distinguish between "recipient organizations" and "beneficiaries." A recipient organization is often a government agency that administrates the support from a donor country. The support is often intended for a particular target group outside the recipient organization, but within the recipient country society. It is this target group that we refer to as "beneficiaries."

9

Sida Aid in Electricity and Natural Resource Projects in India

9.1. USING INSTITUTIONAL ANALYSIS

We now apply the ideas developed in previous chapters to specific aid projects in India and Zambia. To facilitate comparative analysis, we examine five projects that were in either public infrastructure or natural resources sectors in countries of high and low aid-dependence (see Chapter 1, Figure 1.1). While the short-term nature of our fieldwork for each case prevents a fine-grained analysis of these five cases, the cases nevertheless illustrate the central theoretical findings of our earlier chapters with reference to extant development aid projects.

In this chapter, we examine two development assistance projects undertaken by Swedish International Development Cooperation Agency (Sida) in India—"The Capacity Building for Participatory Management of Degraded Forests in Orissa" and "The Chandrapur–Padghe High Voltage Direct Current (HVDC) Converter Terminal Project" in Maharashtra.[1] These case studies demonstrate the use of institutional analysis as a diagnostic tool and illustrate how problems of motivation and asymmetric information arise within the complex mix of actors involved in a project, presenting distinct challenges for sustainable development.[2]

These cases also reveal two larger themes derived from our earlier analysis. The first theme relates to *the nature of the underlying collective-action problem* that gives rise to the existing incentive problem. Here, we need to ask why existing institutions have failed, how those trapped in social dilemmas can overcome this failure, and (only then) how development assistance can help. Both cases provide examples in which the underlying collective-action problems are not addressed successfully.

The second major theme relates to *ownership*. Ownership of an asset refers to participation in provision, production, consumption, and decision making related to its continued use. In the field, these attributes are often dispersed among the donor, the consultant, and the formal owner or recipient. The actual beneficiaries, who often have an enormous stake in the outcome of a project, however, are often excluded from the prerogatives and privileges of ownership. Poorly defined and improperly vested ownership can hamper the success and sustainability of an aid project.

Before we turn to the specific case studies in Orissa forestry and the Maharashtra power sector, we will first provide background on the framework of Sweden's overall development cooperation with India.

9.2. SWEDEN'S DEVELOPMENT COOPERATION WITH INDIA

Sweden's development cooperation with India is framed by policy guidelines set out by the Department for International Development Cooperation at the Swedish Ministry of Foreign Affairs. Country Strategy documents, developed almost exclusively through internal consultations within the Ministry of Foreign Affairs, set out the scope and expected outcomes of Swedish aid support. While Country Strategy documents do not generally specify the particular projects to be implemented, they do define priorities, provide directives on how to make development cooperation operational, and set out budget limits.

While Sida officially emphasizes recipient ownership, the policy dialogue between the Swedish Ministry of Foreign Affairs and the Government of India (GoI) appears to be a largely donor-driven affair. Folke (1998) notes that the Swedish government effectively decides what the scope, content, and modalities of its development assistance in India will be. On the Indian side, officials at the Department of Economic Affairs (DEA) at the Ministry of Finance negotiate with Sida's representative (and those of other bilateral and multilateral donors) based on internal assessments of stated national needs and priorities. Their focus is on securing untied concessional loans or grants. DEA officials hold that India, as a relatively aid-independent country, can extract the best deal for itself through international competitive bidding for projects.

Donor contributions to Project Aid continue to be of interest to the Indian Ministry of Finance since it is concerned with the state of India's foreign exchange reserves—this concern being more acute when these reserves are low (as they were in the early 1990s). Donor financing raises net reserve levels when donor financing substitutes for a project that would have been undertaken by the recipient government.

9.2.1. *Changing Strategic Interests in Bilateral Development Assistance*

Sweden's strategic priorities in its development cooperation with India have changed since its inception in the 1960s. Edgren (1995) identifies two basic periods in Swedish assistance to India. The first occurred roughly from the mid-1960s through the 1970s. Aid in this period was motivated by a need to *strengthen alliances* between the two nations, which had both adopted a policy of nonalignment in the Cold War standoff, and to *respond to public concerns* raised by the Swedish mass-media's interest in India and its poverty. In addition, the Swedish Ministry of Finance had endorsed the then-prevailing model of comprehensive development planning, with its emphasis on filling in the gaps in investment and trade. Reflecting these interests, the objectives of Swedish aid in this first period focused on raising the standard of living and held that the priorities of the recipient country should guide the selection and design of particular aid interventions. In line with these priorities, aid to India was structured mainly in the form of grants for import support.

The second period of Swedish assistance to India, noted by Edgren (1995), lasted through the 1980s and 1990s. By the mid-1970s, the Swedish media began to stress that the persistence of poverty in India, despite the sums of development aid provided, was related to poor governance. In reaction, Sweden's Parliament and Sida's Board insisted that Swedish aid should more directly target the poor. The Swedish government also demanded that a larger share of Project Aid disbursements target specific poverty groups.

Concurrently, as India's commercial potential was being recognized, an interest in expanding commercial contacts "prompted the selection of energy production as a concentration sector and the very unusual measure of 'double-tying' Swedish aid in the mid-1980s, i.e., tying it both to the sector (energy) and to the country of procurement" (Edgren 1995: 12). Swedish policymakers found that sectoral cooperation with India in energy provided opportunities for employing Swedish technology. By the early 1990s, loan-financed energy projects made up the largest component of Swedish aid to India followed by poverty-related Social Forestry projects.[3] By this time, import support programs had all but disappeared (IIED 1994: annex 1: 15).

Sida's 1996 Country Strategy shows another shift in these priorities, emphasizing "Poverty Reduction" over "Infrastructure Development" as an overall direction for bilateral assistance to India. This change of focus reflected OECD regulations that limited subsidized aid credits to projects that are otherwise commercially viable, as well as Sweden's own learning from executing projects in energy development (OECD 1996).

9.2.2. *Aid and Institutional Reform in the States*

India's federal structure affects the content, type, and implementation of aid. Many states in the Indian Union themselves are of a size and population equivalent to the larger countries of Europe. It thus makes sense for Sida and other smaller donors to focus development efforts on particular states as this provides a greater focus and potential for impact. Historically, Sida has concentrated its assistance to the states of Rajasthan and Orissa. Given that bilateral aid must be structured on the relation between sovereign states, however, Sida faces a situation where overall aid negotiations and disbursements are conducted by the DEA while the operational details of the project are discussed with officials at the state level.

Although disbursements made by Sida and other bilateral and multilateral donors for Project Aid in various states are provided under various terms and conditions, the DEA transforms them all into a standard 70 per cent credit: 30 per cent grant facility. (In fact, until 1989, the GoI passed on only 70 per cent of the allotted aid amount to the state hosting the project as per the 70/30 formula, with the remainder distributed among all the states.) Further, as noted by former Finance Ministry officials, the GoI has, in the past, cut funds that it had allocated for projects in the face of replacements drawn from donor funding. In such cases, as a consequence of fungibility, recipient states would see little or no net added incentive from the donor-derived funding.[4]

While the DEAs role dilutes the influence that donors have over state governments, the DEA argues that its actions are well-founded since it bears the risk of currency fluctuations in paying back donor loans, that it strives to develop all the states of India on an equal footing, and that it helps defend Indian sovereignty against foreign pressures. Sida's staff note that this GoI involvement limits possibilities of tailoring the terms and modalities of aid as rewards and incentives to particular states.

State governments have an incentive to obtain foreign assistance when, as in some cases, the funds introduced by a donor represent a real addition to the state's plan and budget—that is, they enable the state to undertake activities that it otherwise could not support. Once accepted, however, donor funds are indistinguishable from other funds disbursed by the state. In such circumstances, states have occasionally reduced their own financial commitment to an aid project. This again reflects the problem of fungibility. If additional funds are finally made available for the donor project, this creates more room for activities by the department in charge.

In sum, by the time a project grant passes from the donor to the owner in India, it changes modality. The net addition to the owner is prone to be reduced by the Union Finance Ministry and the State Finance Ministry. Finally, the fungibility of donor funds vis-à-vis other accounts in the state budget means that the aid itself does not represent an incentive to modify the behavior of the project owner. The prospect of a grant from a foreign donor can act as a spur for change within an agency in the recipient country when the offer is made—formally or informally—conditional upon a required change. The incentive effect of such a grant on a project owner's performance, however, is nearly vitiated when it is processed through the many transactions within the Indian federal system.

Project Aid is also seen as useful by the GoI in pushing for reforms that it favors in various sectors and various states. The DEA sees itself, at least in theory, as matching donors' interests with particular initiatives that they would like to pursue in the course of promoting the nation's development. Large donors, like the World Bank, are thus employed to initiate reform in particular sectors of the economy—such as in the power sector, as we will review. Smaller donors, like Sida, are seen as useful in initiating change in more focused areas and projects—such as in the forest sector in Orissa. Let us now turn to an examination of this case.

9.3. CAPACITY BUILDING FOR PARTICIPATORY MANAGEMENT OF DEGRADED FORESTS IN ORISSA

Sida's project for Capacity Building for Participatory Management of Degraded Forests in Orissa (or the Capacity Building Project) was designed to support the natural regeneration and restoration of degraded forests in the Indian state of Orissa. It attempted to involve the forest communities directly in the protection and management of the areas that the communities relied on for their own livelihoods, but for which they often lacked legal rights of access. To this end, the project sought to put into practice the concept of Community Forest Management (CFM) by restructuring the Orissa Forest Department, the existing owner of the state's forests.

Forest Department officials, however, did not find it in their interest to devolve this ownership with the forest communities, making the project (at the time of this assessment) vulnerable to failure.

9.3.1. *History of the Project*

Sida's Capacity Building Project in Orissa followed an earlier Sida project, called the Social Forestry Project, which was conducted in the early 1980s. Perceiving the threat to forests as coming from the overexploitation of products by rural communities, the Social Forestry Project sought to supplement supplies of fuelwood, fodder, and small timber through the plantation of seedlings in community and private lands.[5] Holding that a shortage of fuelwood was the major problem in rural development, and that cooperatively managed plantations could be a response to this situation, the Social Forestry Project was designed to increase the availability of fuelwood. This project, however, did not lead to sustainable harvesting and replanting of the social forestry plantations. Moreover, the aid-sponsored planting scheme was largely unneeded since most forests are able to regenerate from rootstock.

The Social Forestry Project nevertheless offered important lessons to Sida staff, who learnt of the role that traditional communities play in the protection of forest areas, the role played by the consultants, and the limitations of the Orissa Forest Department as the project owner. Sida staff found that the Forest Department would make promises, year after year, only to break them. They were determined to structure the Capacity Building Project so that additional disbursements would be conditional on performance.

The Capacity Building Project was broken into two phases to create incentives for reform, with the second phase contingent on the Forest Department fulfilling the commitments of the first phase (Ingevall-Memorandum, July 22, 1997, Embassy of Sweden, New Delhi). Phase I (budgeted at Swedish Kronor (SEK) 13.5 million) commissioned preparatory studies by Scandiaconsult Natura[6] on how to enhance the capacity of the Orissa Forest Department and local forest protection organizations. The contractor was also charged with conducting qualitative assessments of community initiatives in forest management, and to propose the development of a legal framework to govern the new relationship anticipated between the Forest Department and the forest communities. Phase I also required the Forest Department to reorganize internally in order to be ready to carry out the consultant's recommendations. Phase II (budgeted at SEK20 million annually over 3–5 years following the completion of Phase I) was to implement the recommendations determined in the earlier phase. The project was thus designed with built-in incentives for the Forest Department to follow through on its program for reform.[7]

In project negotiations, the Forest Department argued that breaking up the project into two separate sections would lead to discontinuities and gaps in execution. Sida, however, held that preparatory work on the second phase could begin even as the first was ending and that such discontinuities should therefore not occur.

9.3.2. *An Institutional Analysis of the Orissa Capacity Building Project*

To assess the project, we begin by identifying the action arena, the rules-in use, and the principal actors (see Figure 9.1).

The action arena

The state of Orissa, one of the least developed in India, lies on the upper eastern peninsular coast of India. Of the total population of 31.5 million, about 22 per cent are identified as tribal. The state's forests account for 36 per cent of its area, though about half of these forests are severely degraded. These forests vary from coastal mangrove swamps to village woodlots to dense jungles of the Eastern Ghats. A variety of communities—each of different size and social composition—directly or indirectly rely on various near or adjoining forests for their livelihood and survival. The tribal populations strongly rely on the gathering and sale of minor forest products as a primary means of subsistence (Saxena 1999).

The rural population of Orissa relies heavily on forests for fuelwood and other nontimber forest products (NTFP) such as *kendu* leaf, which are gathered and used to roll *bidis*—a type of cigarette. For most rural people in forest regions, NTFP provide for 10 to 40 per cent of their annual income (ibid.). As a common-pool resource, such forest resources can easily become degraded (Agrawal 2002; Agrawal and Yadama 1997; Baland and Platteau 1996). When one individual or group gathers *kendu* leaves, for example, this means that there is less available for others at any one time. In the absence of appropriate rules governing such common-pool resources, individuals or particular forest communities face incentives to harvest as many forest products as they can for fear that others may do the same and that such products will then not be available later. Sustainable forest use requires that the rate of extraction from a forest not exceed the rate at which the forest regenerates itself.

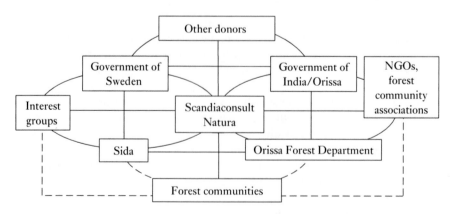

Figure 9.1. *Octangle diagram of the Capacity Building Project*

Rules-in-use—A return to community-based forest management

Overcoming such social dilemmas, forest communities have long managed their forest resources in a sustainable way, both with respect to their own use and with respect to the access rights of individuals in nearby communities. Kant *et al.* (1991: 42) note that village-level organizations in Orissa often possess "tremendous organizational and managerial capabilities in managing community resources," though this varies depending on the degree of community homogeneity and prior experience in problem solving.[8]

In many cases, however, these institutional capabilities have been undermined by the Orissa Forest Department, whose officials see the state's forests more as a source of revenue than as a basis for livelihood. As the state's agents, Forest Department officials arrange contracts with timber companies, the paper industry, and other intermediaries and end-users. Given the objective of maximizing the state's revenue (and often their cut in such deals), Forest Department officials tend to be less attentive to the interests of the tribal and other poor forest communities. In fact, the Orissa Forest Development Corporation and the Tribal Development Cooperative—public sector corporations that have exclusive rights for buying and marketing many types of NTFP—have high fixed costs of operation (created in part by a huge payroll). They balance their books by marking down the price paid out to tribal groups for NTFP supplies. Since tribal groups and other traditional forest users are, thus, not able to make a living through using the forest, their incentive to conserve the forest diminishes. One result is that practices in the preservation and management of forests by local communities, long established in traditions of sustainable forest use, have been severely eroded over the past few decades under state ownership of forestlands.

Faced with declining forests and recognizing the need for local management of forests, the Government of India, with encouragement by the Ford Foundation, promoted the idea of Joint Forest Management (JFM) in the early 1990s. Demand for forest management reform was also voiced from the grassroots, leading the Government of Orissa to pass four resolutions between 1988 and 1996 to facilitate a JFM system of forest co-management. Under JFM, legal ownership of land would remain with the Forest Department, but village communities would now be officially recognized as co-managers in that they would be entitled to a share of proceeds from the sale of NTFP and timber (Kumar 2000).

JFM can be effective when the local forest department recognizes the traditional prerogatives of forest users, where they do exist (Agrawal 2001; Arnold 1998). In Orissa, however, these rights were seldom effectively recognized, with JFM agreements often a pro forma affair. (In our field visit, we observed that the Forest Department's implementation of JFM involved a village or forest community representative signing a pre-prepared standard Memorandum of Understanding with the Forest Department that was written in English.) By the terms of the MOU, the Forest Department would permit foraging and the harvest of nontimber forest products by the community in village woodlots and other designated forest areas. At the end of a fixed period, when the trees would become viable as timber, the Forest Department and the community are supposed to divide the revenue equally from the harvest and sale of the trees. In practice, villagers had little say in matters relating to the transfer of power, the formation of village committees, or the negotiation of rule changes. As a result, they were prone to see the administration of JFM as arbitrary and biased.[9]

Through their involvement in the earlier Social Forestry Project, Sida officials recognized the importance of community ownership for the new Capacity Building Project. They concluded that JFM, as interpreted by the Orissa Forest Department, would likely not lead to sustainable forest use. They thus sought, instead, to encourage a version of Community Forest Management (CFM) that is legally recognized by the Forest Department. As such, the move from JFM to CFM was to represent a shift along a continuum from greater state control to greater community ownership over forest resources. Whereas JFM rules were defined by the state and interpreted by the Forest Department, the CFM approach sought to invoke collective-choice arrangements based on local conditions, often drawing upon indigenous forest protection practices (Conroy *et al.* 2000: 54; Kumar 2000).

From the point of view of the Forest Department, however, CFM was a less attractive regime as it was financially less lucrative—both in terms of fewer donor funds and less revenue from timber and NTFP—and because it limited the power of the Forest Department.

9.3.3. *The Role of Key Actors*

The Orissa Forest Department

The Orissa Forest Department is charged with protecting the state's forests and with implementing nearly all forestry projects in the state. Officers of the Indian Forest Service, deputed to service in the Orissa cadre, manage the Department, which remains by tradition a rigid hierarchical structure.[10] It is geared toward executing orders from above rather than encouraging a culture of initiative and problem solving. Junior officers rarely express their professional opinions when it contradicts that of their superiors. As a result, senior echelons often become remote from field realities and problems (Saxena 1995).

The ethos of the Forest Service continues to reflect its founding purpose when, in 1864, it was developed by the British as a way to collect revenue from forest contractors. The Forest Department, in essence, regards the forests as its own property and values them primarily for their commercial value. It continues to see its role as protecting and managing the forests for this purpose with little or no recognition of the rights of forest users (Pal 2000; Saxena 1995).

As long as the Forest Department "owns" the forests—in that, it is provided legal monopoly power in protecting (i.e. excluding) and raising revenue from the forests—there is scope to use this power asymmetry to make money on contracts for timber, bamboo, and other NTFP. Initiatives crafted within donor projects that seek to increase the control by tribal groups and other forest users over forest resources (i.e. to redress this power imbalance) interfere with the network of expectations of how the career system in the Forest Service operates. We would expect them to be resisted by the bureaucracy—and this is what is in fact observed.

The government of Orissa

The government of Orissa, like other states in India, is organized according to a parliamentary model of government. The state is headed by a Chief Minister who is assisted by a council of ministers. In this model, the ministers formally set policy within the scope of their various portfolios, and a permanent administrative bureaucracy is to execute these policies for the benefit of the population. Informally, however, there exists a well-entrenched system of patronage and tribute whereby particular political and bureaucratic officeholders provide rewards and protection to those clients who subscribe to them. In this way, as is often found in India, various ministries and departments have become political fiefdoms with strong tendencies toward rent seeking and corruption (Wade 1989). Patron–client relationships are maintained through the particular monopoly power exerted by stewardship of the concerned portfolio (such as for forests). In this context, development aid from abroad is often seen as a resource for patronage.[11]

Sida

As with other bilateral aid organizations, successful projects for Sida must fit well within domestic policy priorities and satisfy Sida's own bureaucratic constraints. In their assessment of Sida's initial Social Forestry program, Mothander and Sassarsson (1992) note that aid to the forestry sector fits in with domestic public priorities in Sweden concerning environmental protection. Aid to this sector, they note, also fits in with Swedish expertise in silviculture. In addition, they note that the Indo-Swedish Forestry Development Program "is large enough to consume funds that can be handled by Sida with limited administrative resources" (ibid.: 44). These considerations apply to the Capacity Building Project as well.

Administratively, the responsibility for the Capacity Building Project is shared between the Sida's Asia department (Asien) and the Department for Natural Resources and the Environment (Natur) in Stockholm, with Sida's New Delhi field office taking the lead in negotiating and overseeing the course of the project. The Capacity Building Project has benefited from a continuous long-term involvement of local staff—a relative rarity given patterns turnover within Sida (see Chapter 7)—who had, as a result, developed a strong understanding of the realities of Orissa forestry.

Scandiaconsult Natura

As discussed in Chapters 4 and 8, the consultant frequently plays a central role in aid projects. The consultant in this project, Scandiaconsult Natura, possessed the required technical skills, demonstrated considerable personal commitment toward their task, and made strong efforts to advance Sida's concerns under difficult local conditions, according to a retired consultant involved with Orissa forestry. As one of the consultants for this project interviewed for this study noted, Sandiaconsult's interest in reputation and the professionalism of its consultants leads to a high quality of service.

While this may have been the case, it is also true that Scandiaconsult Natura's close knowledge of the situation in Orissa and a lack of effective Swedish alternatives made Scandiaconsult Natura relatively indispensable to Sida. Sida could not effectively supervise Sandiaconsult because Sida did not have the manpower to do so. This lack of adequate Sida oversight also meant that the consultant could—and often did— step in to fill administrative and supervisory roles left unattended by Sida. The direction of the project, in this way, may have more strongly reflected some of the near-term priorities of the consultant regarding the completion of contractual terms with Sida over the long-term interests of the beneficiary communities.

NGOs

The role of nongovernmental organizations in Orissa forestry includes the village communities themselves as well as various independent intermediaries that seek to assist these communities in their developmental activities.

Local NGOs working directly with communities and their forests have played an important role in Orissa in highlighting the concerns of village communities to officials at the national and state levels in India, as well as internationally. In their work, they have to be careful not to offend the local police, district administrators, and Forest Service officials. NGOs are required in India to be registered with the central government when they receive funds from foreign sources. The processing of these permits can be stalled by irate government officials if the NGO is not careful to build good relationships with them. Even so, some local NGOs have been vocal in criticizing Sida's Social Forestry project and have sought to bring to Sida's attention the relevance of indigenous institutions to its project design. Sida's shift from Social Forestry to Community Forestry, which involves greater beneficiary ownership, is in part a response to this lobbying effort.

International NGOs also play an important role in representing and fostering forest community interests. Sida, through Oxfam, encourages various village protection groups to federate within a larger movement and thus present a more potent political force with which to assert their traditional ownership claims.

9.3.4. *Interactions Within the Octangle*

The Sida—Orissa Forest Department—forest communities triad

An immediate effect of Sida project funding has been to increase the budget and staff of the Social Forestry Division within the Orissa Forest Department. There is considerable prestige in being associated with a donor-funded project. The increase in staff and budget for the Social Forestry Department increases its director's standing and puts him in serious contention for promotion to higher grades. The personal rewards of a donor-funded program, however, do not percolate much further down the forest bureaucracy since prospects for promotions or other rewards are bound within the bureaucratic rules-in-use already described.

On the other hand, the presence of aid directed toward one division can foster disinterest in other parts of the Forest Department. Since aid funding is organized as reimbursements, the Forest Department's expanding expenditures in the area of community forestry are initially drawn out from spending otherwise budgeted for other divisional activity. Consequently, other conservation work, such as those in reserve forests, is cut back.

Meanwhile, the local communities, whose members' participation is vital to the sustainable management of forests, have not contributed directly to the design or promotion of Sida's community forestry projects in Orissa. There was no involvement of the community, not even in reference to villagers' interests, in Sida's Social Forestry project. Little was done to foster a sense of beneficiary ownership. In the Capacity Building Project, village communities have so far had no input into the design of the project, even though the project seeks to invoke their participation through CFM.

The Forest Department's hesitant response to Sida's Capacity Building Project has to be seen in the context of the political clout that local communities have been gathering in recent years. In many stretches of forests, *de facto* control of forest lands has already passed from the Forest Department to the communities. Promoting CFM effectively, as per Sida's project, is likely to reduce further the Department's powers. The fears of the Forest Service therefore run deep, as they are unlikely to reassert authority over these forests. The Orissa Forest Department is, therefore, very resistant to greater local participation in forest management.

The Sida—Scandiaconsult Natura—Orissa Forest Department triad
In theory, Sida identifies a project owner—the Orissa Forest Department in this case—in which it vests responsibility for a project. Consultants hired as agents to implement aspects of the project are expected to look to this Sida-nominated owner as their principal. The patterns of interaction in Sida's involvement in Orissa forestry, however, reveal a more complicated picture. It shows that the consultants often are able to maximize their own objectives when effective ownership responsibility is not exercised by either Sida or the various Indian actors.

The consultants in the earlier Social Forestry project were very closely associated with Sida.[12] This point is acknowledged by the individuals in the Orissa Forest Department, by Sida personnel, and by some project consultants. This aspect was as well picked up by Mothander and Sassarsson in their review of the Social Forestry project. They note, "the consultant was originally considered more or less as a part of Sida. Their office in New Delhi was in the same premises as the Development Cooperation Office and their project was called the Sida Forestry Coordination Project" (1992: 17). In short, as one former consultant interviewed for this study put it, "the consultants were in bed with Sida."

Mothander and Sassarsson further note that in the Social Forestry case, consultants were even given the authority to pose conditions for financing a project component on behalf of Sida. They conclude by noting that it is "questionable if a consultant should be retained for the purpose of extending ongoing programs. This is basically a Sida task, and if Sida needs consultancy support in this matter, such a consultant should not have an interest in creating work for itself" (ibid.: 35).

From the perspective of the Forest Department, Sida and the consultant are seen as being more or less the same. Yet, if the project is seen as a Swedish undertaking, it risks losing commitment from the project owner. Indeed, a consultant's role should reflect Sida's stated philosophy that the consultant's responsibility is to the project owner. Yet, if the consultant, working for the nominal project owners, while being associated by those owners with the donor, takes up appraisal work on behalf of Sida, then this leads to serious ambiguities, not least those that relate to the independent assessment of the terms of the relationship agreements.

Further, if the Forest Department is not as interested in the reforms implied in a project but faces incentives to make the right noises to keep the donor and its funds engaged, then its relationship as owner to the consultant, particularly when the consultant is allied philosophically with the donor, becomes peculiar. Sida purchases the consultant's services for the project owner, but this owner—assuming it cares— has little control over its supposed agent's efforts and priorities.

Given that Sida normally faces a high rate of turnover in its staff assignments (Chapter 7), the main source of project continuity is frequently the consultant. Sida's staff often has to learn of a project's status from the consultants. This asymmetry in knowledge further compromises Sida's ability to administer the work of the consultants. In such cases, Sida's Desk Officers may find it expedient to extend a consultant's contract without a proper appraisal. Indeed, consultants can have the upper hand in bargaining with Sida when such asymmetries are present. A Sida staff member whom we interviewed for this project recalled an instance in the Social Forestry project where the consultant opposed Sida's initiatives to conclude his firm's participation in a project.

In the Capacity Building case, longer-term involvement by particular Sida staff enabled Sida to manage consultants more effectively through well-specified contracts. Proper use of consultants requires more administrative resources from Sida. However, administrative constraints within Sida means that such learning is not institutionalized within the organization.

9.3.5. *Implications for Ownership and Sustainability*

This study illustrates that practical understandings of project ownership in development cooperation can be nebulous; while the main actors in this aid project exercise or exhibit some features of ownership, none bear the required responsibility.

Sida vests formal project ownership with the Orissa Forest Department. Examining the organization and incentives structured within the Forest Department reveals, though, that this corporate designation of ownership is rarely translated into responsibility on the part of its particular staff members. Next, while Sida provides the funds and sets many of the conditions of the project—and these are ownership attributes—it is not willing, nor is it in practical terms able, to take responsibility for the project. Further, we have seen that consultants often exercise day-to-day ownership but that they have no stake in the communities themselves. Meanwhile, the communities—those who have the greatest stake in responsible management of their forest resources—are themselves rarely accorded any of the privileges of ownership.[13]

To be sure, the Capacity Building Project does seek to gear the Forest Department—the project's Sida-nominated owners—to recognize, foster, and use indigenous capacities among various village communities for sustainable forest use. This, however, confronts Forest Department officials with a dilemma. On one side is their stake in preserving their interests, drawn from a particular interpretation of prevailing JFM arrangements and other rules-in-use. These have to be balanced against those incentives configured within the Capacity Building Project, which brings with it—in the short run—other benefits that derive from a foreign donor's involvement. In the longer run, these donor-derived privileges for Forest Department officials end with the project's termination, as do those advantages that come from their current control of Orissa's forests.

Sustainability, in terms of the long-term effects of the project, is thus not likely to be realized. Given the state's control of the forest and the culture of corruption within the Forest Department, there are incentives to receive aid but not to reform. Meanwhile, Sida's own proclivity in keeping project administration to a bare minimum precludes it from engaging the Forest Department on an alert and ongoing basis. In this environment, the strategy of the Forest Department to stall on reforms, while promising reform in the future, may well succeed.

Forest Department officials note that the bureaucratic reform called for in the transition from Phase I to Phase II cannot be ushered through donor mandates and deadlines but rather through continual engagement. They point out that policy reform in India is a long-term process. It requires, they say, that right-thinking personnel fill the needed sensitive positions. As and when this happens, they note, pieces of the reform process fall gradually into place. They hold that as bureaucracies tend to slip back into passivity in the absence of an outside stimulus such as that which a donor provides, Sida should maintain its presence over the long haul to encourage this process.

Further, these officials point out that while transitioning from JFM to CFM, the viability of the incentives expected within the apparent CFM regime must remain very credible. This can happen only, they say, if Sida remains committed to the process. They point out that if Sida's commitment stalls when the Forest Department's reforms hit a snag, it makes it even more difficult to carry out the needed reorganizations.

While Sida distinguishes itself from other donors by taking a long-term perspective, its project managers have to show results from time to time. Even if Sida officials were sympathetic to the points made by the Forest Service, it is unlikely to fund the project indefinitely without realizing some interim benchmarks of success.

This creates a dilemma for Sida. It risks its credibility if it proceeds to fund Phase II when conditions for the completion of Phase I remain unmet. At the same time, officials at the Forest Department hint that other donors—with fewer conditions—can be found to fund the project if Sida withdraws. In either case, prospects for basic reform of the incentive structure within the organization of the Forest Department look poor. Unless a significant degree of ownership passes on to beneficiary groups of forest users through a CFM regime, the incentives underlying the prevalent collective-action problem will remain unchanged, and the sustainability of Orissa's forests will remain in peril.

9.4. THE CHANDRAPUR–PADGHE HVDC CONVERTER TERMINAL PROJECT

Tied-aid from Sweden financed the purchase and installation of converter terminals (and associated services) for an HVDC transmission line in the state of Maharashtra, India. The equipment for these terminals was procured from Asea Brown Boveri (ABB), a Swedish multinational corporation, and from Bharat Heavy Electrical Limited (BHEL), ABBs Indian partner. The project was intended to improve prospects for sustainable development in India by fortifying the physical infrastructure of the national high voltage grid.

9.4.1. *History of the Project*

Sweden's assistance to develop capacity for power transmission in Maharashtra forms one component of the more comprehensive Second Maharashtra Power Project (SMPP). The SMPP, funded in part by the World Bank, Sida, and the governments of India and Maharashtra, was initiated in 1992. The purpose of the project was to meet the increasing demand for electricity in western Maharashtra, particularly metropolitan Mumbai.

The overall SMPP project was comprised, first, of the construction of an additional 500 MW coal-fired unit to the existing power stations in the town of Chandrapur, which is located in the coal-rich eastern portion of the state. Second, it involved the construction of a 500 kV, 1500 MW HVDC line from Chandrapur across a distance of 735 km to Padghe, which is near Mumbai. Such HVDC lines require specialized terminals at either end of the line to convert power from Alternating Current (AC) as generated to Direct Current (DC) for transmission and back to AC again for distribution.[14] Third, it paired this construction and installation of hardware with a distribution enforcement program aimed at reducing losses in selected areas. Finally, the project called for consultants' studies, financed by the World Bank, on load management, on environmental management, on the preparation of private power projects, and on an institutional review of the power sector in Maharashtra[15] (BITS/SIDA Appraisal Report 1.34/1 IND 32.3 1993, Project Agreement between IBRD and the State of Maharashtra, July 8, 1992). Through these measures, the SMPP sought to increase power supply, enhance service, and strengthen the finances of the Maharashtra State Electricity Board's (MSEB), the state-owned and controlled utility. These reforms were in turn expected to encourage private sector investments in the power sector.

Before Chandrapur–Padghe, ABB and the National Thermal Power Corporation of India had cooperated in the construction of two similar projects. The first, a back-to-back station (which is used to create an asynchronous interconnection between two AC networks), was launched at Vindhyachal in 1985 and commissioned in June 1989. The second project, for which ABB was a subcontractor to the Indian state-owned BHEL, concerned the construction of two converter terminals for a HVDC line between Rihand and Delhi. This project was started in 1986 and put into commercial operation by 1992. In both these cases, the World Bank was the lead agency and main financier, though ABBs contracts were financed through concessionary credits with contributions from the Swedish Agency for International Technical and Economic Cooperation (BITS) and the Swedish International Development Authority (SIDA), both predecessors of today's Sida.[16] These two pioneer projects were then to be followed by the third project—the SMPP, which required the same type of transmission terminal links as the Rihand–Delhi line.

By 1992, the MSEB had retained Hydro-Quebec, a Canadian utility, as its own overall technical consultant for planning the SMPP. Bids were then floated by the MSEB by March 1992 for the HVDC terminals. The bidding was officially arranged according to a two-envelope system, with the technical qualifications and specifications forming one part and the price and financing forming the other. Bidders were required to submit a full financing package, with conditions similar to or better than export guarantees. Bids were submitted by ABB in partnership with BHEL, as well as by Siemens-Germany and GEC-Alsthom. Each in turn had put together a financing package in connection with domestic donor agencies. The MSEB was formally in charge of evaluating the bids, though Hydro Quebec was consulted in judging the technical requirements. The financial details were likely overseen at the political level. By February 1993, the tender put forth by ABB/BHEL was judged the most competitive from this process.

By May 1993, the MSEB conveyed its intentions to the Government of Maharashtra (GoM). After the proposal was parleyed through the state planning and finance ministries, it was passed on to the DEA at the Ministry of Finance. Thus, in coordination with ABBs bid and its liaison with BITS and Sida, a proposal was sent to New Delhi by the MSEB to recover funding from Sweden through the established bilateral aid channels.

The Chandrapur and Padghe terminals were executed through four coordinated contracts entered into operation on October 1, 1993: The first contract was for supply of equipment from ABB Power Systems, Ludvika, Sweden. The second was for its erection by ABB India. A parallel set of contracts was made with BHEL for the procurement of the remaining equipment and its installation. According to the deal, ABB-Sweden had a contract for SEK1 billion, BHEL a contract for SEK800 million, while ABB of Switzerland and ABB of Germany were contracted for SEK200 million for the remaining components (*Development Today* 1994).

Of the Swedish financing of the HVDC project, BITS would provide soft loans of SEK500 million, Sida would provide a grant of SEK175 million, while the Swedish Export Guarantee Board was to guarantee the remaining SEK325 million that was raised in the capital market by the Swedish Export Credit Board. ABBs other European subsidiaries correspondingly were able to secure additional sources of soft loan financing from the governments of Germany and Switzerland. The bilateral agreement between Sweden and India regarding the financing of this project contained a tied-aid proviso—that the Swedish contributions were to be used only for the financing of goods and services of Swedish origin. The contract made no mention of reforms to be undertaken to enhance the sustainability of the power sector

(Project Agreement between the President of India and the Government of Sweden, June 24, 1993).

Meanwhile, in March 1993, the HVDC project, due to its high value, came under automatic consideration in Paris by the Consultation Group of the OECD. Under the so-called Helsinki Package, a project that is otherwise commercially viable is not eligible for soft loan financing. The Helsinki Package seeks to ensure fair competition among OECD countries for tied-aid related exports to the developing world. Based on this criterion, the Paris Group turned down Sweden's financing of the HVDC project. BITS, however, argued that the Paris Group's judgment of commercial viability was based on estimates of electricity tariffs that were higher than that which MSEB could charge and was therefore not sound. It also argued that the project would take a long time to phase in and could not become financially viable until 1997. Concluding otherwise, the Paris Group found BITS' price estimates unrealistically low and its time estimates unrealistically long (*Development Today* 1994).

Sweden, however, chose to override the OECDs consensus and proceeded to provide subsidized concessionary credits for the HVDC project. In a letter dated May 24, 1993, to the OECD Secretary-General, the Swedish Minister for European Affairs and Foreign Trade pointed out that Sweden's decision was taken to enhance India's developmental potential and to further Sweden's solidarity with India. Reporting on this story, the trade newspaper *Development Today* (1994) noted that, according to ABB, this contract would save 2,500 jobs that year in Sweden. It implied that this was an important political motivation behind Sweden's action.[17]

The World Bank, meanwhile, had urged the state of Maharashtra to undertake in-depth reforms of its power sector within the framework of its loan for the SMPP. The World Bank stipulated *inter alia* that the state readjust its level of power tariffs, that it reorganize the MSEB's financial and administrative and public utility practices, and that the MSEB reduce its total commercial accounts receivable. As of October 1996, the World Bank, citing noncompliance with the above terms, threatened to suspend further withdrawals of project loans (Letter of Joseph Wood, Vice President, The World Bank to Mr. V. Govindarajan, Joint Secretary to the Government of India, October 22, 1996).

In response, the state attempted to comply with some of the terms though, in the World Bank's judgment, with little improvement, particularly with respect to the MSEBs accounts receivables. The suspension thus stayed in place and the remainder of the loan (US$237.7 million) was cancelled as of June 1998. Some remaining parts of the projects were then completed with funds provided by the governments of India and Maharashtra. The World Bank's objective of strengthening the institutional base of the power sector in Maharashtra, therefore, was only partially met.

Despite the World Bank's decision, Sida concluded that it was worth completing the link needed to transfer generated electricity to the Mumbai area. Work on the HVDC terminals has been completed, though after delays caused by an unrelated dispute over the contract for insulation materials used on the transmission wires. The transmission lines were tested in July 1999 and finally handed over to the MSEB by ABB/BHEL in November 1999. The lines now carry power generated at Chandrapur as well as from the National Thermal Power Corporation's Korba Super Thermal Station. As the supply of electricity has increased, the power situation in the Mumbai area has improved, for now.

9.4.2. *An Institutional Analysis of the Chandrapur–Padghe Project*

The action arena

The western Indian state of Maharashtra, which incorporates metropolitan Mumbai, faces an acute shortage of power. This region is one of the most important load centers in the country, taking up about 6 per cent of India's total electricity demand. Maharashtra has a high concentration of industry that depends on reliable power to become more productive and internationally competitive. Increasing power production and distribution through more investment is thus critical for development.

Indeed, the need for additional capacity in generating and distributing reliable electricity throughout India is very clear: The per capita consumption of electricity, at 380 kW h per annum, is among the lowest in the world, demand exceeds supply by more than 20 per cent at peak times, and the current installed capacity is working only at 60 per cent efficiency.

With the population of the country over one billion and the near-term economic growth projected at the rate of 6–7 per cent per annum, massive investments in additional capacity need to be made just to keep pace. Today, commercial and residential consumers face frequent and often-unanticipated brownouts and blackouts. Even when the electricity is on, it is of poor quality as the voltage fluctuates widely. Apart from disrupting industrial production, the lack of reliable power has also led to worsened air pollution as countless individual generators start when the lights go out (*The Economist*, March 4, 2000).

The lack of adequate power, a serious condition affecting India's developmental potential, is rooted in a problem of collective action. To understand how, we look at the formal structure of India's power sector and the cultural context in which it operates. We then examine the nature of this collective-action problem as the context for the aid project under study.

Rules-in-use: Governance in the power sector

The development of the power sector as well as power production, transmission, and distribution of electricity has been viewed traditionally as a governmental responsibility in India, with this responsibility divided between the central and state governments. The GoI, through the Ministry of Power, oversees the central Electricity Authority, the National Thermal Power Corporation (NTPC), the National Hydroelectric Power Corporation, the Northeastern Electric Power Corporation, and the National Power Transmission Corporation. The operations of Regional Electricity Boards and Power Finance Corporation (PFC) and the Rural Electrification Corporation are also supervised by the Department of Power with the stated aim of developing a national power policy and coordinating development in the power sector. Of these, the National Thermal Power Corporation and the National Hydroelectric

Power Corporation are bulk suppliers of power to State Electricity Boards (SEB), while the Power Finance Corporation provides loans to the SEBs.[18]

The state governments, in turn, control their respective SEBs—in effect, utility companies—and the State Generation Companies. These agencies provide about three-quarters of the electricity that finally reaches consumers. While nominally independent, as based on the Electricity Supply Act of 1948, SEBs and State Generation Companies need to obtain approval from the state government (often at ministerial level) for all major decisions involving investments, tariffs, borrowings, salary, and personnel practices. Legislation that, in 1953, set up the SEBs also entrusted them with regulating the private utilities. Subsequently, most private utilities were taken over by the SEBs. Today, only a handful remains, including the Bombay Suburban Electric Supply Limited.[19] Even these utilities are at least partly dependent on the SEBs for the power they distribute.

In the power sector as elsewhere, a patron–client culture underlies the *de facto* governance structures. Politicians hand out favors in return for tribute in the form of electoral support and/or (legal and illegal) financial contributions. Doling out patronage depends upon the state holding the reins over critical resources. Thus, control of the MSEB—that is, over the regulation, generation, transmission, and distribution of power—enables state politicians in Maharashtra to hand out electricity connections and subsidies to favored electoral clients—rich farmers, organized urban slum dwellers, and others. Control of the MSEB also enables politicians to award jobs at the MSEB to supporters. In 2000, the MSEB counted about 125,000 personnel on its payroll.

Flows of patronage down from the political level are balanced by those of tribute. For example, a portion of the illegal charges for connections collected by some MSEB staff is transmitted through the system and on to the political levels. Political control over the SEBs implies a role in awarding contracts for expanding the infrastructure of power generation and distribution. Here, ministers—personally involved in the final selections within the tendering process—take a direct cut of large infrastructure projects. In fact, as we were informed in confidence by several of those interviewed, the practice of paying the so-called "success fee"—about 5 per cent of the size of the deal—by the winning contractor is well-established. Since infrastructure projects can run into hundreds of millions of US dollars, these fees are large.

Senior officials interviewed at the MSEB referred to a "cross-subsidization" of the "winners"—politically well-connected groups of farmers, slum dwellers, etc.—at the expense of the "losers"—industrial and residential customers—and said that this is perpetuated through political interference. They held that such practices have prevented the MSEB from organizing itself more efficiently and this has had a negative effect on power management and investment in capacity. These officials favor greater independence from political control, but remain unsure of the likelihood of such a prospect.

A free-rider problem

As noted, the power sector in India has traditionally been viewed as a natural monopoly. Policymakers in India have, until recently, held that only the state is capable of marshalling the large investments in facilities needed in power generation, transmission, and distribution. However, given the prevailing patron–client culture of government, its ownership of this sector has led to pervasive free-riding. As we saw, politicians, particularly at the state level, have used their control to provide, as a form of patronage, free or subsidized power to well-connected interest groups. Power tariffs remain low since revising them is politically unpopular. Further, given that utility workers can be tipped to look the other way, theft of power is rampant and bill collection inadequate. The state, in short, has failed, due to the incentives structured within its own organization, to exclude beneficiaries who fail to contribute to the provision of electricity.

With so many free-riders, the MSEB is not able to recoup the costs of producing and providing power. It is thus not able to pay private companies for producing and providing power. In turn, private investors have few incentives to offer such goods and services on their own initiative. Excludability problems, rooted in the poor discharge of ownership responsibilities by the state, have thus led to the problem of free-riding, which in turn has led to chronic underinvestment in capital and maintenance.

In 1991, the GoI, citing the need to expand power capacity and noting the financial limitations of the SEBs in this regard, opened ownership of power generation to private investment. However, the poor fiscal condition of the SEBs left them unable to pay for power purchased from private sources. As a result, there has been little increase in private investment in power generation capacity. The GoI has since recognized the need to put the SEBs on a more sound financial footing. In this regard, it has urged greater autonomy for SEBs from their respective state governments.

9.4.3. *Interactions Within the Octangle*

The SMPP is a complex project with multiple actors, including various personnel in departments within Sida, the World Bank, various ministries, and agencies within the governments of India and Maharashtra, contractors, as well as power consumers in Maharashtra. Figure 9.2 focuses on Sida's contribution to the SMPP in terms of the Octangle.

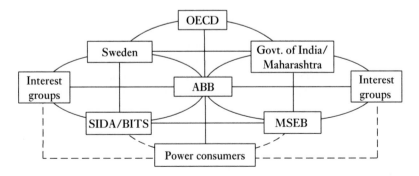

Figure 9.2. *Octangle diagram of the Chandrapur–Padghe Project*

The recipient government—MSEB—interest group triad

The relationship between the recipient government, the "owner" agency, and the interest groups, as identified in the Octangle, is complicated by the nature of India's federal system. The impetus for reform in India's power sector, as in many others, comes from the GoI. The GoI, seeing that achieving growth requires relieving the bottleneck of power supply, has encouraged the states to reform their power utilities. It has urged them to (1) improve metering, billing, and collection through the use of new metering technology, computerization, and enforcement; (2) advance the professionalism of power utility staff through training; (3) create more autonomy for the SEBs from the state governments; and (4) raise power tariffs to reflect costs of production and transmission.

These objectives are being pursued through various strategies. First, states have been encouraged by the Power Finance Corporation of India to reform their SEBs through the award of study grants, attractive loan terms, and large-scale loans for new investments. Second, the GoI has promoted foreign donor participation as a way of accelerating reform. The World Bank's Second Maharashtra Power Project, for example, set conditions for changes in the regulatory structure as a condition for its loans. Third, the Indian Parliament enacted in 1998 the Electricity Regulatory Commission Act requiring states, such as Maharashtra, to set up independent power utility regulatory bodies that will set tariff rates, regulate purchase and procurement processes, and promote competition and efficiency.

Other reforms—including the unbundling of monopoly utilities, corporatization, and privatizing distribution—are being ushered in such states as Orissa, Haryana, and Andhra Pradesh. In Maharashtra, as elsewhere, such initiatives have met opposition from the state government and from SEB unions.

One example is the Maharashtra Electricity Regulation Commission (MERC), made up of retired senior civil servants and judges. The Commission has attempted to force the MSEB to revise and publish its tariff rates and to come up with a plan to install and read meters. It has also chastised the state energy minister and the MSEB for waiving unpaid arrears by politically well-connected power-loom operators in Bhiwandi and elsewhere (*Times of India*, March 1, 2000). The minister, in turn, has attempted to dilute the influence of the MERC by packing the Board with his sympathizers, and by starving it of budgeted funds (*The Economic Times*, July 5, 2000).

Also, the over 125,000 employees of MSEB have threatened repeatedly to go on strike to protest any state government's decision—following the directive of the MERC—to divide the MSEB into three separate corporations, each handling generation, transmission, and distribution. Employees feared that this would lead to the eventual privatization of the utility and the loss of their jobs (*Times of India*, June 12, 2000; *The Economic Times*, July 21, 2000).

Meanwhile, distributing electricity as patronage to powerful special interests remains entrenched within the state's political system. As a state utility regulator interviewed for this study noted, "for politicians, the SEBs are too big a cash cow to be spun off as independent entities; they are likely to remain a while longer under some form of political control." These recent events suggest that the creation of a more viable institutional environment for the power sector, one that can attract investments by independent power producers, is actively opposed by those who benefit greatly from the present system of patronage and tribute.

Development of Maharashtra's capacity in power production requires not only investments in infrastructure but also changes to the incentives prevailing within extant political institutions. If aid investments made by donors in productive capacity are to maintain their momentum, such institutions that foster these incentives must be restructured, even though such changes may not be in the interest of Maharashtra's politicians.

The donor government—Sida—special interests triad

In addition to reflecting the genuine and deep belief among the Swedish people of their moral responsibility to aid in the development of less fortunate societies, Swedish aid has always reflected significant commercial motivations. Sida's own publication, *Sida at Work* (1997c), notes that about 60 per cent of Swedish development assistance ultimately benefits Swedish industry and service providers. Aid expenditures on the part of the government of Sweden are thus of interest to Sweden's industry and services.

Bilateral aid is conducted between two sovereign states. This means that aid is mediated through the agents of those states. Governments of donor countries thus can use funds derived from broad-based taxation and that are earmarked for development assistance to support particular domestic industries by enabling poor countries to purchase the capital goods that they manufacture and the services that they deliver. When differential advantages can be secured through the political process, special interest groups—representing those who benefit from such directed public expenditure—often arise (P. Jones 1995). In the case of aid, the potential for realizing commercial gain from such differential advantages is limited within the scope of procurement procedures of the donor country's aid agency and the level of immunity these procedures enjoy from political influence.

The level of influence that a large Swedish multinational company, such as ABB, can bring to bear in lobbying for differential advantages in procurement of manufactured goods and services used in Swedish development assistance thus has to be gauged carefully in terms of prevailing and practiced donor agency procedures and immunities. Like similarly sized corporations in Sweden, ABB has extensive influence within the Swedish government. (The same may be said of large corporations in other OECD countries.) The exercise of such lobbying power and the limited extent to which it can be exercised bear importantly in evaluating the incentives and sustainability of Sida-funded investments in infrastructure.

Our interviews with diverse individuals with knowledge of this case show that Sida's financing of the HVDC project owes much of its existence to intervention from the Swedish Ministry of Foreign Affairs and its clear intent to promote development of the Swedish industry. Members of the Swedish Parliament also faced incentives to protect jobs in Sweden. In this regard, ABBs award of contract for the HVDC terminals both furthered Sweden's commercial interests and preserved employment for 2,500 workers at ABB (*Development Today* 1994). For its part, ABB lobbied skillfully at all levels within both Sida and the Ministry of Foreign Affairs, as well as with the Swedish Embassy in New Delhi and with local authorities in Maharashtra.

The donor—other donors—recipient triad

Various OECD commitments strive to encourage donors, in solidarity with each other, to promote institutional reform in recipient countries. To the extent that commitments among donors, such as that which the Helsinki Package represents, create an aid cartel to usher institutional changes among recalcitrant aid recipients, cracks in this front weaken all donors' hands in future aid negotiations. Sida officials view their organization's breach of the Helsinki Package in this case to be a singular occurrence, and pledge it will not be repeated.[20]

Further, Sweden did not stop its own funding of the completion of the ABB part of the project even though Sweden supported the Bank's suspension of SMPP funding.[21] In considering this point, Sida's managers pointed out that while the suspension would not have any impact on the behavior of officials in the Maharashtra government—since only a small part of the Swedish financing remained—suspending the Swedish component of the overall project would have increased costs due to delays in completion.

To be sure, Sida, as a small donor with a project in a relatively aid-independent country, would likely have not succeeded where the World Bank failed in reforming politics in Maharashtra. Nevertheless, Sida's action may well have signaled to Maharashtra's politicians that power sector reform can be put off when commercial motivations drive donor interests more than considerations of sustainable development.

The contractor at the center

ABB is interested in maintaining a long-term relationship with the NTPC, MSEB, and other national- and state-level power agencies in India. ABB continues to see the power infrastructure development in India as an important business opportunity.[22] As a competitive for-profit firm, ABB has clear incentives to seek profits in markets where risks might otherwise preclude participation. Sida helps ABB by mitigating the risk it faces and by financing the purchase of products sold by ABB, which would otherwise not be affordable to the recipient.

ABB managers noted to us that while they are internationally competitive in terms of quality, their products are often more expensive. Linking sales of their products with attractive financing from donors is one way to overcome this disadvantage. Sida's financing of ABB sales, for example, has helped ABB to secure future business and to move into a key developing country market.[23] The role of a donor such as Sida in offering tied concessionary credits and/or guarantees—while meeting the stated objective of improving economic and diplomatic cooperation between Sweden and the recipient country—is all the more important to a contractor like ABB. This is because doing business directly with the financially weak Third World agencies, like the SEBs, is risky.

Sida's role in fostering sustainable development has to be distinguished from ABBs natural proclivity to seek profit. Within this case study, Sida's role as the MSEBs "development partner" is less clear given its simultaneous function as ABB's financier. Sida and ABB risk being seen as having common purposes and interests by the project owner-MSEB—a view encouraged by close informal linkages between Sida staff and ABB.[24]

Sida officials suggested that Sida's procurement rules, which at that time permitted semi-closed bidding, might have been a further factor helping ABB secure the contract. Indeed, the administration of a project is made easier when procurement can be limited to those firms with which officers at Sida are already familiar. Sida staff thus may have an incentive to favor this system. Officials at Sida assured us that such semi-closed bidding is unlikely to happen in the future, as Sida's formal procurement procedures are being reassessed, consistent with an internal auditor's report.

In this particular case, however, ABB had informally sounded out its financing from BITS and Sida even as the formal request was being channeled through the Indian Finance Ministry. From this, it would appear that the procurement of the equipment and services from ABB, as against from some other firm, was never in question. Thus, existing procurement rules in Sida did not serve to insulate the primary developmental objectives of aid from those of promoting Swedish commercial interests. These objectives need not be in conflict. Still, Sida, as a leading development agency, bears a responsibility to make sure that Sweden's commercial advantage does not overwhelm the objective of sustainable development.

Recipient beneficiaries

There are two basic sets of power consumers in Maharashtra—those who pay, and those who free-ride by receiving free or subsidized electricity. These "winners" include politically well-organized farmers, mill operators, and slum dwellers. The "losers" include residential customers and other small- to medium-sized commercial and industrial consumers. (Most of the larger industrial consumers have installed their own generating capacities.) Given that the MSEB imposes its losses on the state's budget, the cost of power is also being borne by those who pay taxes and those who might otherwise benefit from state services and investments.

In such a situation, those receiving power for free or at nominal rates have no immediate incentive to change the status quo. They often act in league with corrupt MSEB officials to tap power illegally.[25] These losers have an interest in reform but, as they are numerous and scattered, are unable to coordinate a sustained articulation of their interests (see Olson 1965). The solution to this free-rider collective-action problem remains elusive.

9.4.4. *Implications for Ownership and Sustainability*

The MSEB, the nominal owner of the Chandrapur–Padghe Converter Terminal project, is financially and politically weak. Extensive subsidies and illegal tapping of electricity undermine its revenue base. As long as the MSEB is not able to pay reliably for power production and transmission, private investment to address critical problems in undercapacity will not be forthcoming. The MSEB is not able to assert its proper ownership prerogatives as a regulated utility due to gross interference from the GoM, the *de facto* owner. Responsible ownership—whether by a regulated MSEB or an alternative competitive arrangement—is vital for sustainable private investment in India's power sector.

We noted in Chapter 1 that ownership is meaningful only when placed in the context of the institutional resolution of the underlying collective-action problem. Our case study in Maharashtra reveals a rampant free-rider problem. The system is plagued with extensive subsidies, illegal taps into power lines, and nonpayment of power bills. Donor funding of capital assets for the MSEB increases the capacity of the utility to access and distribute power, but does not resolve the basic free-rider problem. The World Bank's attempt, in this regard, to wrest effective ownership from the GoM through loan conditionalities has failed.

The SMPP has increased the power supply. However, since the underlying free-rider problem remains unsolved, adequate private investment in enhancing power capacity has not materialized. In this way, donor intervention has not helped to sustain investment in India's energy sector.

The core issue in this case is the sustainability of investment in the energy sector rather than the sustainability of particular donor-financed hardware. From an engineering viewpoint, the HVDC terminal project has been successfully implemented. ABB managers maintain that their products are of exceptional quality and endurance, though it is presently too new to report problems related to the reliability and maintenance of the HVDC terminals. They point out that the Rihand–Delhi terminals built earlier are also functioning well. Finally, they point out that the local technical capacity, such as possessed by BHEL, is sufficient to maintain the lines and stations.

Aid-based finance can add to the capacity of the Indian grid by putting physical assets on the ground. Sida's managers argue that the developmental rationale of this case has to be seen in terms of the overall continued progress of India, and that Sweden can help to relieve the immediate bottlenecks in power generation and delivery systems that threaten this process. They see donor assistance as a critical component in building up India's national high voltage grid infrastructure.

While donor investments in expanding the availability of power through the SMPP has helped, *in the short run*, to stanch some of the discontent among those being poorly served, it has also potentially created a bigger pool of patronage. Donor financing in this case may have unwittingly strengthened the role of the GoM. If so, donor investment will have further crowded out private investment. This adversely affects, *over the longer run*, capacities to raise and sustain the financing needed for private sector-led development of the infrastructure required to cope with demands of development.

9.5. CONCLUSIONS

The two case studies in this chapter illustrate that development aid is really a set of linked action situations, with multiple actors and arenas that cross national borders. The way in which these action situations are linked, we find, greatly affects the potential for effective and sustainable project outcomes. In Chapter 4, we identified eight key actors within the development cooperation system. In this chapter, we have shown that the Octangle can be used to untangle the complex relationships involved in aid. This institutional analysis can help clarify the underlying collective-action problem, the meaning of ownership, and the context of sustainability for a project—that is, does the aid project identify and vest responsibility with the appropriate owner as a step towards solving the underlying collective-action problem?

The two Indian cases in this chapter also illustrate how aid independence affects aid negotiation. In the Capacity Building Project, the government of India was using foreign aid from Sweden as a tool to promote reform at the state level. At the same time, state officials in Orissa could threaten to abandon aid from Sweden for aid from Japan, if the former imposed too many conditions on its assistance. In the Chandrapur–Padghe case, we saw that conditional aid from the World Bank failed to crack open an entrenched free-rider problem that continues to preclude sustainable investments in India's energy sector. As an aid-independent country, India (and the state of Maharashtra) could step in and complete the financing of a large power project even though the World Bank stopped its lending, citing failures in power sector reforms. The case also showed how Sweden's interest in promoting its domestic industries through its foreign aid, through loosening short-term bottlenecks in power production in India, may delay the need for sustained investments in the power sector.

Following our study design, we look next to Zambia, a relatively aid-dependent country, for corresponding case studies in the natural resources and infrastructure.

NOTES

1. As noted in Chapter 7, SIDA (Swedish International Development Authority), BITS, and other Swedish aid-related agencies consolidated in 1995 into "Sida," the Swedish International Development Cooperation Agency. We use the term Sida throughout Chapters 9 and 10 to refer to SIDA and Sida for the sake of simplicity.

2. The authors are grateful to Sida for their cooperation in these cases. Sida, in many respects, represents best practice among aid agencies, and its willingness to initiate and participate in this inquiry is a credit to the organization. The chapter is based on interviews conducted with Sida officials as well as officials of the governments of India, Maharashtra, and Orissa. Also interviewed were consultants involved in the projects and NGO representatives involved or interested in the projects. The case studies of Sida projects presented in this and the next chapter reflect events up to July 2000.

3. "Moving the money": As the form of cooperation changed from general import support of the first period to sectoral project grants and tied commodity aid of the second, administrative problems in disbursing committed aid amounts grew. This led to a backlog in unspent monies that, as an IIED report argues, led to the approval of the Uri power project as a way to spend the balance:

   Another major factor in the decision to go ahead with the Uri project seems to have been the huge carry-over of funds—some SEK700 [million]—which had developed by the late 1980s in the tied aid via country budget frames. These reserves were the result of bureaucratic delay and the rejection of Swedish bids and projects by the Indian government because they were too expensive. Arguments in Sweden emerged to the effect of "millions of poor people in India and we cannot spend our money." A quick solution could thus be provided by the Uri scheme. (IIED 1994: annex 1: 29)

4. See Swaroop *et al.* (2000). The authors find that the central government's expenditures are unaffected by external assistance. Thus, state governments may not be reaping the full benefits of foreign aid.

5. The Indian Commission of Science and Technology had developed in the early 1980s the concept of Social Forestry.

6. Swedforest Consulting AB was established in 1973 by the Swedish National Forest Enterprise (Domänverket). In 1992, the company was renamed Swedforest International AB. Scandiaconsult AB purchased Swedforest International AB in 1996; Swedforest International AB became a subsidiary company—focusing on the organization and management of the better land and water-based natural resources—to Scandiaconsult AB. Swedforest International AB kept its name for 2 years after the purchase. In 1998, it was renamed to Scandiaconsult Natura AB, which is the company's present name. As we discuss the consultant's role at various periods, we use "Scandiaconsult Natura" throughout for the sake of simplicity.

7. At the time of the case study, the Capacity Building Project had been interrupted by the Swedish government's suspension of the bilateral Development Cooperation Agreement with India following the Indian government's explosion of nuclear devices in May 1998. As a result, all projects in India were terminated, aside from those that had fresh agreements for a limited period. The preparatory phase of the Community Building Project was completed in June 1999 through this exception.

8. At present, Kant *et al.* (1991) estimate that nearly 6,000 communities are protecting and managing up to 500,000 ha of Orissa's state-owned forests, representing about 10 per cent of the total forest area in the state.

9. Sundar (2000) and Kumar (2000), who have documented interest in JFM more thoroughly, show this from the villagers' point of view. We found that very few of these JFM memoranda have been signed in Orissa, as apparently most communities do not see an incentive to do so.

10. The Forest Service, in its modern incarnation, is an All-India organization intended to produce an elite cadre trained for managerial responsibilities related to forestry at the state and national levels. Graduates of the Forest Service institutes are deputed to the forest departments of various states where they serve out their careers. Saxena (1995: 172), while recognizing the presence of many dedicated and capable officers, describes the service as autocratic and alienated from the public. The Forest Service operates within a heavily regulated and complex legal system covering the protection of forests and the sale of timber and other forest products. There are, by the Forest Service's own acknowledgement, significant problems in illegal felling and smuggling of timber throughout India. There are also persistent allegations that the Forest Department is involved in some of these illegal operations.

11. Aid projects are also often viewed by a state's ministry of finance as a way of meeting the state's current fiscal obligations.

12. Understanding the role of the consultants under the old Social Forestry project is relevant since it raises some critical points of more general concern—such as, to whom is the consultant really accountable? As an academic study, this report is interested in understanding incentives structured within the various relationships in development cooperation. Even though the Social Forestry case is closed, it reveals important lessons.

13. A decade ago, Kant *et al.* (1991: 50) pointed out, in the conclusion of their SIDA-sponsored study of community-based forest management systems in Orissa, that "in order to sustain and expand the phenomena of community management of forests, it is vital to increase the community's stake in the continued existence of forests."

14. Transporting power via DC rather than by AC over high voltage lines is advantageous since it suffers smaller transmission losses, requires a smaller right of way for the transmission lines and towers, and reduces power theft. Installing HVDC lines also contributes in part to the infrastructure being developed for an integrated national grid, under plan by the national power ministry, based on HVDC technology.

15. Of the total SMPP project cost of US$1.2 billion, the World Bank provided loans worth $350 million and a soft-credit package of $200 million. The GoI and the MSEB together financed the remainder of the agreement with the Bank (project documents). As we have noted, Sweden contributed to the completion of the SMPP by financing the purchase and installation of two converter terminals, supplied by ABB and its Indian partner BHEL, each at either end of the Chandrapur–Padghe HVDC line.

16. For the sake of simplicity, we refer to both SIDA and Sida as Sida.

17. Some Sida staff have argued that since financing of the project was almost complete by the time of the Helsinki Package, they considered this a borderline case in regard to the OECD.

18. For more information, see: http://www.powermin.nic.in; www.pfcindia.com; www.ntpc.co.in.

19. For more information, see: http://www.bses.com and www.msebindia.com.

20. Further, they note that financing for the project had more or less been committed to when the Helsinki Package was put into place.

21. The BITS/SIDA support to the Maharashtra project was initially approved under the precondition that the reform component would be taken care of by the World Bank.
22. In March 2000, ABB was awarded a contract by the MSEB, valued at about US$10 million, for transmission line substations. This project is funded by the Japanese Bank for International Cooperation.
23. The essential question in this regard is whether donor country taxpayers, under the guise of aid, should subsidize the sale of products of particular domestic firms.
24. Some Sida staff, for example, have previously worked for ABB.
25. The MSEBs metering and monitoring capabilities are poor; for instance, meter readers, when they do have meters to read, often take bribes in exchange for underreporting readings. The MSEB faces enormous problems of power theft and nonpayment. For example, the MSEB estimates a loss of 29 per cent in revenue due to power theft and transmission losses. A recent estimate by the MERC has put this loss at close to 50 per cent (*Times of India*, April 14, 2000).

10

Sida Aid in Electricity and Natural Resource Projects in Zambia

10.1. INTRODUCTION

We now turn to case studies of three Sida (Swedish International Development Cooperation Agency)-supported field projects in Zambia, a relatively aid-dependent country. Using the Institutional Analysis and Development (IAD) framework, we identify the incentive structures for several actors in the action arenas of the three projects to examine how they affect the likelihood of ownership and sustainable project outcomes.

We begin with an overview of Sweden's bilateral development cooperation with Zambia. Zambia's relative dependency on aid, not only from Sweden but also from other countries, has a profound impact on incentive structures conducive to beneficiary ownership and thus also to sustainable outcomes. This is especially true for the government-to-government model of development cooperation, which channels most of Sweden's support to Zambia.

Following this overview, we look in more detail at three selected field projects: (1) The Zambian Energy Regulation Board (ERB); (2) The Kafue Gorge Hydropower Station Rehabilitation Project (KGRP); and (3) The Zambian National Farmers' Union and their Conservation Farming Unit (CFU). Each project's analysis follows the same sequence of a structured institutional analysis: We start by identifying the action arenas, its actors, positions, and the type of situations in which they interact. Because of their influence on each actor's incentive structures, we spend a great deal of time discussing the particular contextual variables that define the characteristics of the action arena. The incentive structures materialize in the "patterns of interaction" and are described explicitly at the end of each section. We end the chapter with a discussion of the implications of our findings regarding incentives found in these cases.

10.2. ZAMBIA'S EXPERIENCE WITH DEVELOPMENT COOPERATION

Zambia's overall economy has generally gone the way of its mineral exports, especially copper. Before the dramatic plunge of the world price for copper in 1974, Zambia's economy boasted one of the highest growth rates and per capita incomes in Africa. The economy and the Zambian government's ambitious development plans, however, depended heavily on copper revenue.[1] When the price of copper fell sharply, the government turned to outside financing, and accumulated debt. The one-party government (in power from 1972–1991) chose deficit financing[2] and policies that favored urban dwellers over farmers, leading to stagnant or negative growth in both the industrial and agricultural sectors.[3] The Zambian economy has suffered from high inflation, enormous budget deficits, and distorted prices. Although many of the policies that generated these outcomes were changed with the end of the one-party state in 1991, even the more open, market-based economy finds the average Zambian as poor as he or she was 20 years ago.

In such a weak economic environment, foreign aid has been an important resource for Zambia. Aid has increased substantially over the years in Zambia, both per capita and as a percentage of GDP. Most aid is bilateral: in the 1970s, the largest donors were the United Kingdom (25 per cent of external aid), the United States (15 per cent), and Sweden (13 per cent). In the 1980s, the list of most important donors changed to Japan (14 per cent), Germany (13 per cent), and Sweden (12 per cent) (Saasa and Carlsson 1996: 48–9). Sweden's share has remained roughly constant over the past two decades. Most bilateral and multilateral aid to Zambia has been predominantly in the form of grants, not loans, and balance of payment supports grew strongly in the late 1980s and 1990s, to as much as 90 per cent of gross aid to Zambia (Mwanawina and White 1995).[4] In fact, White and Edstrand (1994: 286) claim that donors have provided foreign aid so that Zambia may pay its foreign debt. In 1997, aid represented 17 per cent of Zambia's GNP, 107 per cent of its gross domestic investment, and 35 per cent of its imports.

Saasa and Carlsson (1996: 54) note five distinct periods for Zambia's sometimes "rocky" relationship with donors: (1) 1980–1983, before Zambia's first structural adjustment program (SAP); (2) 1983–1987, during the SAP; (3) 1987–1989, when the government defected from the SAP; (4) 1990–1991, when liberal policies were adopted by the new multiparty government; and (5) after 1991, when SAP measures were accelerated by the government. The periods reflect a country that is highly aid-dependent, but whose domestic politics at times foster a break with international donors.

10.2.1. *Sweden's Role in Zambia's Development*

Sweden has been a consistent donor to Zambia since its independence in 1964. In a review of project memoranda from 1965–1993, Öståker (1994) notes that during the first period of Swedish aid to Zambia, one of the main objectives was to support the country's efforts to move away from its colonial past as well as to decrease Zambia's dependence on white minority regimes in southern Africa. In addition to these political and economic goals, Swedish aid featured assistance to food production, poverty reduction in rural areas, and increased participation by local people.

With the decline in the price of copper, Sweden's aid to Zambia grew. As neighboring liberation struggles ended, the assistance focused more on social and economic issues in the 1970s and early 1980s. A proliferation of personnel-intensive—and often uncoordinated—projects emerged. Generally, this aid focused on the health, education, and agricultural sectors.

The mid-1980s saw a reorientation in Swedish assistance: programs were consolidated and moves were made to become less personnel-intensive. Added to Sweden's focus on agriculture, health, and education were import support and a personnel and consultancy fund. Rural development was also emphasized, and a new emphasis was placed on helping women. With the new democratic elections in 1991, Swedish assistance also incorporated the support of democracy and governance into its country strategy (e.g. Embassy of Sweden 2000; see also Adam *et al.* 1994: 28–65). Because of concerns about the newly democratic government's trends toward authoritarian behavior, however, Sweden suspended its long-term "development cooperation agreement" at the end of 1998. Sida launched a new country strategy in January of 1999 that only allows for "specific agreements" with respect to projects and sectors. Most Sida staff we interviewed for this study felt that this lack of a development cooperation agreement did little to affect their projects and sector aid; they view it as a political statement on behalf of the Swedish government that has had little practical implications on decision making in regard to bilateral cooperation.

While an extensive evaluation of Sweden's aid to Zambia reported some positive effects—especially with more recent programs to build institutions (Adam *et al.* 1994)—many experts see problems with Zambia's overall high dependency on aid, especially as they relate to ownership and sustainability. Bräutigam (2000: 31–2) cites an aid official working in Zambia as saying that "most projects are donor-driven" in Zambia, and that "there is little local initiative" in the design and development of aid projects, a view endorsed by several of those we interviewed. Indicative of this observation is that in 1999, Zambia had $500 million in aid projects committed but not yet implemented. Cromwell (1995: 195) claims that the level of aid to Zambia delayed the demise of the one-party state there, and Rakner (1998) argues that it continues to allow the democratically elected president to act like a dictator (see also Bräutigam 2000: 29). While it can be argued that high dependency on aid may weaken the incentives for local initiatives, ownership, and thus also sustainability, these issues are difficult to sort out at the aggregate, national level. How does the general aid dependency in Zambia play out in the decisions of individual projects? What other contextual factors influence the incentives that may enhance collective efforts to achieve sustainable outcomes? To find answers to these and other questions related to the incentive structures of the actors in the development Octangle, we now turn to analyze three specific cases in which Sida aid has been important.

10.3. THE ZAMBIAN ERB

The energy supply sector is critical for the Zambian economy for many reasons. First, the government decisions in this sector affect the performance of virtually all productive sectors in the country because of their varying degrees of dependency on electricity supply. Second, the Government of Zambia (GRZ) sees the exploitation of the country's largely unexplored energy resources as an opportunity for generating desperately needed cash revenue through the exportation of electricity. In an effort to secure these advantages, the GRZ has embarked on a market-friendly liberalization program to attract private participation in the sector. Despite these emerging reforms, the Zambia Electricity Supply Corporation (ZESCO) remains by far the largest operator in the electricity sector and continues to dominate the generation, transmission, and distribution of electricity.

In 1994, the GRZ issued a new National Energy Policy, which set out to deregulate ZESCO, the state monopoly of electricity, a heritage from the pre-1991 one-party government. The core rationale for this set of reforms was to establish a market-based structure that would be more appropriate for improving the economic efficiency of Zambia's energy supply industry. The National Energy Policy noted that in a deregulated, market-based energy market in which private participation is encouraged, there is also a need for an independent regulator. Consequently, the Energy Regulation Act of 1995 provided for an ERB and charged it with the specific task of providing politically independent regulation of the supply of petroleum, electricity, and other forms of energy. The ERB became operational 2 years later, in July of 1997.

The Energy Regulation Act of 1995 defined the official mandate and general ground rules for the ERB. According to the act, the most important functions of the ERB include (1) monitoring the efficiency, performance, and level of competition among the sector operators; (2) investigating complaints from consumers with regard to price adjustments, services received, and the establishment of new entities in the industry; and (3) designing standards with regards to the quality, safety, and reliability of the supply of energy. The principal instrument by which the ERB can impose these rules on sector operators is its power to license. If an operator is found to have violated any of the rules or regulations, the ERB may not only impose fines but also withdraw the firm's or individual's license to operate in the sector.

Another way for the ERB to regulate the sector's operators is through its decisive role in the price adjustment review process. If an operator wants to raise electricity tariffs, for instance, it must file an official application with the ERB who then proceeds to review the motivations for such a request. To make such an application, the operator must show that it has performed according to the standards pronounced in the licensing agreement. A request for a price adjustment can be rejected if these standards have not been met by the operator. Also, before approving a price hike for any operator, a public hearing is organized by the ERB. These are often televised events, in which individuals and organized interest groups may air their views on the proposed price adjustments. The ERB is required to take these publicly expressed views into account when making the decision on whether an adjustment is warranted. The ERB has developed its own procedures for what it considers due process for the review of both applications and complaints from the consumers and the public. According to these—still informal—rules, the ERB places the burden of proof on the plaintiff who needs to present solid evidence for their request. However, the ERB has been criticized by several domestic interest groups for not taking these public hearings as seriously as they should.

10.3.1. *History of the ERB Project*

As part of Sweden's support to Zambia's effort to rehabilitate the electricity sector's infrastructure and policy reform process, Sida provides economic assistance to a 4-year project called *Institutional Capacity Building Project of the ERB*. The project is part of the sector-wide, World Bank-coordinated Power Rehabilitation Program (PRP). The Swedish support consists of financing the services provided by Sweco, a Swedish consulting firm with expertise in electricity regulation.

10.3.2. *An Institutional Analysis of the ERB*

Actors and the action situation
Given that the ERB seeks to regulate the energy sector of Zambia, a great number of actors are interested in its formation and activities. The major actors are the Zambian government (notably, the Ministry of Energy and Ministry of Finance), ZESCO, the World Bank (IDA), and the public. Other actors also play key roles in the ERB, such as Sweco, the consultant paid by Sida to help the ERB, and several interest groups including the Zambian Chamber of Commerce and the Zambia National Farmers Union (ZNFU). This study considers the relationships between these actors and the period of Sida's involvement with the ERB as the *action situation* to be explored; this study also stays mainly at the collective-choice level of analysis (see Figure 10.1 for the case of the ERB).

Influences on the action arena
The ERB is the legal regulator of the energy sector in Zambia. While this means that the ERB deals with all types of energy production and distribution, much of its work—and hence the focus of this section—features electricity, the underlying good of this project. Electricity has long been considered a natural monopoly, and this has been the case in Zambia as well. Until the advent of the ERB, ZESCO had been the sole organization with the authority to generate and distribute electricity in Zambia.

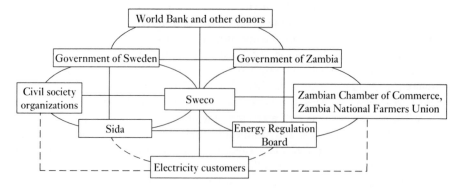

Figure 10.1. *The octangle of actors for the case of the Zambian Energy Regulation Board*

Due to its decades-long preeminent position, ZESCO created a far-flung enterprise that controlled nearly all upstream and downstream linkages in the electricity sector. New thinking about the *nature of the good*—that is, whether or not electricity really is a natural monopoly (a private good with high entry costs)—led the government and World Bank to consider the privatization of the sector (the 1991 government elected in the transitional multiparty elections had considerable support from the private sector, and thus was business-friendly). Sida, likewise, had been thinking about public enterprise reform.

Most important among the *community attributes* that shape the action arena in the case of the ERB is the powerful legacy of the one-party state in Zambia. Bureaucracies and parastatals dominated all major economic sectors in Zambia, resulting in generations of professionals who know few alternatives to one-party state structures. Consequently, there is great reluctance among many, if not most, bureaucrats to move toward any other system (like privatization), especially since Zambia's business arena offers few formal employment options that exist for public employees who are sacked. This former one-party system also distorted market signals to such a great extent that currently operating within any market-like system is new for most Zambian public employees. This is especially true for the electricity sector: for decades, ZESCO has not been charging prices for electricity that were remotely reflective of its costs. As we found, this has also generated expectations on the part of the public for very inexpensive electricity.

Because the ERB is a new agency interacting with more established organizations, the set of rules-in-use that affect the behavior of actors in this action arena reflects both new and old institutions. Formally, the ERB is responsible for issuing licenses to any energy production or distributing entity in Zambia and approving prices for energy. The ERB's revenue consists of the license fees it collects from these entities. The fee that each entity has to pay is defined as a percentage of the entity's gross annual income. Because the foreseen unbundling and privatization of ZESCO has not yet started, the vast majority of the ERB's revenue comes from ZESCO. By law, the ERB is required to deposit all fees collected into the government coffers; the government, in turn, is supposed to remit back to the ERB funds according to the ERB's approved budget. In an effort to acquire increased financial flexibility and to ensure stable cash liquidity for recurrent expenditures, the ERB reached an agreement with the Ministry of Finance to retain 50 per cent of the collected fees in order to prevent delays in paying salaries and other expenses. In actuality, however, the ERB has retained *all* of the fees it has collected, and has petitioned the Ministry of Finance for approval to formally retain 80 per cent of the fees. The informal arrangement that allows ERB to retain complete financial control turns out to be decisive for its incentive structures. As we shall see, these may not always be compatible with the public interest.

The ERB is part of the World Bank-funded PRP. As part of the conditions for the loan, the World Bank insisted on an independent regulatory agency. The continued existence of the ERB is formally necessary for the continuation of the PRP.

Although the government, through ZESCO, had been the source of price changes, both are allowing the ERB to control the process of pricing as per the 1997 Energy

Act. Because the government, through its Minister of Energy, chooses the members of the ERB, however, there are questions about the independence of the board members. For example, the government allowed months to pass before naming the second set of board members.

The structure of financing is an important determinant of the set of rules that the actors in this arena use. Formally, the World Bank has lent money to the government, which, in turn, has lent money to ZESCO at a commercial rate. On paper, ZESCO must repay the money it receives from the PRP to the government. As observed earlier, loans and grants generate quite distinct incentives.

10.3.3. *Patterns of Interaction: Incentives and the ERB*

The characteristics of the action arena, the actors, and their interactions have produced incentives that support the ERB's continued existence and functioning, at least in the short run. Many, if not most observers from within and outside the government, however, doubt the sustainability of the ERB's independence—and therefore its effectiveness, especially if donor support is withdrawn.

Incentives of government
Prior to the agreement to revamp the electricity sector, the government knew well that the electrical generation and production systems in Zambia were at the point of collapse. In addition, members of the government were keen to privatize many sectors of their economy. This position fit with the orientation of the World Bank, which had been active in making loans to update and privatize different sectors in developing countries. The PRP project was the result of this confluence of thinking. As part of the PRP, the World Bank also insisted on institutional reform—especially changes to ZESCO's history of low prices and low rates of collections. Such reform was thought to require an independent regulatory agency like the ERB.

Although they lose some control over the setting of prices and the licensing of energy producers, there were strong incentives for the government to allow the creation of the ERB. First, it met the World Bank demand for some institutional change without wholesale changes to government structures. The ERB would appear less intimidating to the government since it possesses the power to appoint the Board's members. Second, the ERB provides the government with a buffer from the public criticism generated by rate hikes and other privatization actions (such as the selling of the Copperbelt Electricity Company and the lower Kafue Gorge generating station).

The fact that many respondents thought that the government sees ZESCO as a future source of foreign exchange provides incentives that could be at odds with the official position of this sector's privatization and the independence of ZESCO. ZESCO staff and other government officials—especially the Cabinet—believe that Zambia can earn a great deal of money from the exportation of its power; as one respondent put it, "the cash cow that can replace copper."

Incentives of ZESCO

At first glance, the creation of the ERB stripped some powers over the electricity sector away from ZESCO. Long used to setting prices and the condition for electricity supply, ZESCO lost some of this control to the ERB. On balance, however, there are incentives for ZESCO to support the work of the ERB. Since ZESCO desperately needed the funds offered by the World Bank for the rehabilitation of the energy sector, in some ways the ERB was the bitter medicine it had to swallow. But the ERB also provides ZESCO with political cover when it asks for tariff increases: according to ZESCO top-management, the ERB gives legitimacy to ZESCO's demands for the painful but necessary tariff hikes, which it needs to become solvent.

Incentives of the ERB

As a new agency, the members of the ERB have strong incentives to seek support from those individuals or groups that can help sustain them. Even though the ERB is, in part, designed to protect the public interest, the ERB's survival probably depends more on the support of the World Bank, the government, and donors.

Clearly, the World Bank has a strong influence on the incentives of the ERB. In fact, during a public outcry against increases in electricity tariffs, the World Bank took the unusual step of publicly supporting the ERB. Because the World Bank made the ERB part of the conditions for the energy sector loan, and has pushed strongly for the effective functioning of the ERB, the Board's members have had the incentive to live up to their official mandate as an objective, independent arbitrator in the sector that requires them to observe certain standards of performance.

Less clear are the incentives that the government generates for the ERB. The government appoints ERB members, so at a fundamental level the jobs of these individuals depend on meeting what they perceive to be the interests of government. Further, in an era of uncertainty and limited private sector jobs, such a position on the ERB is highly valued. The signals that the ERB get from the government tend to parallel those of the World Bank. Even though different members of the government may complain about the tariff increases—especially legislators who are under pressure from their constituents—the government seems content in the short run to allow the ERB (and World Bank) to bear the responsibility for these unpopular actions.

Members of the ERB have strong incentives to secure aid from donors like Sida. As a new agency, the ERB lacked training, support staff, and basic office supplies to carry out its arguably important role. Sida's help—through Sweco—was considered pivotal by the ERB in electricity (although less so in the petroleum and biomass sectors). Donor support also helps them to travel and to enhance their personal qualifications and thus gain a competitive edge on the job market. One of the ERB's main roles is to bring together the sector's key actors to negotiate proposed regulation decisions and try to build a broad-based consensus with actors before passing regulation. Sweco has been important in training ERB staff and Board in performing this new approach (stakeholder analysis and participatory planning).

Finally, the *de facto* mechanism for financing ERB operations, which lets ERB retain all its revenues, produces perverse incentives for ERB to be agreeable to all solicited price hikes. Since price hikes lead to increased revenues for ZESCO, ERB benefits indirectly from approving these and thereby augmenting ERB revenues from licensing fees. The actual influence of this incentive on decision making at ERB is determined by the strength of counteracting institutions at ERB to serve the public's interest. For instance, ERB board members' commitment to the organization's objectives and the willingness of the GRZs to monitor the ERB behavior may prevent ERB decisions to be biased toward approving price hikes. We found no evidence that ERB is approving price hikes in order to raise more money for its organization. It should be noted, however, that the perverse incentive structures, embedded in the organization's rules in use, do exist and as such constitute a potential risk for the future performance of the ERB.

Incentives for the public and interest groups
The public and special interest groups have incentives to support an independent regulator to monitor political meddling and corruption in the energy sector. The majority of noncommercial electricity users are not organized into any effective group. Lately, however, some commercially oriented interest groups have grown very critical of the ERB's role. The ZNFU and the Zambian Chamber of Commerce and Industry, for example, argue that the Board has become another bureaucracy that is interested in generating more income for itself and the government. Both interest groups and the public object strongly to price hikes, since for decades they have enjoyed subsidized electricity. Additionally, they do not see significant changes in customer service, as mandated by the ERB. Interest groups also accuse the ERB of collecting illegal taxes and swindling, but have not provided evidence nor undertaken any legal action against the Board (although they have lobbied to get a representative on the Board).

Incentives for Sida
There were clear and strong incentives for Sida to support the ERB. First, the World Bank sought donor help to assist the ERB. Second, much of the monitoring of the PRP is to be done by the World Bank, not Sida. Third, such institutional help fits one of the new directions that Sida has been taking in the reform of public enterprise (see Sida/INEC, "Ripe for Change," December 1997). Fourth, Sida had been involved in the energy sector before and had experience with Swedish consultants in this area.

Expected increases in Sida's budget for Africa may threaten support for institution-building projects like the ERB. Institution-building is rarely an expensive effort—the Sida total commitment to the ERB is only SEK7 million over 4 years (Sida, *Semi-Annual Report* 2000). In general, institution-building requires smaller expenditures but usually with higher administrative burdens for the aid agency. When faced with the need to "move the money," aid agencies can face incentives to fund high expense-low administration projects.

10.3.4. *Outcomes: Implications for Ownership and Sustainability*

Sida's support for the ERB has been important. Sida's consultant, Sweco, has given the Board the crucial technical support at the beginning of any new agency. Further, there is evidence that Sida staff took a strong position to support the ERB in discussions with the Zambian government personnel.

An analysis of the incentives at the collective-choice level provides strong reasons to be skeptical about the long-run effectiveness of the ERB, however, if the Board's independence is a crucial part of Sida's goals. ZESCO remains the dominant player in the electricity sector. Although the ERB turned down ZESCO's first attempt to increase rates, the second attempt did go through. The fear remains among nearly all interviewees that since the Ministry of Energy appoints the ERB's members, the government will eventually get its way (and thus ZESCO, through the government, will get its way). When the World Bank finishes with the PRP, and/or when Sida or other donors pull out of their support of the ERB, it is easy to envision the end of its independence. Most interviewees believe the World Bank's policies for the PRP provide the only real incentives that prevented business as usual in a country where a one-party state—and now one-party dominant in a multiparty state—can use the electricity sector to secure political support for itself.

There is no easy translation of the ERB case into Sida concepts of "ownership" and "sustainability." No one interviewed thought that the ERB was likely to be dismantled completely, even though it is one of the conditions of the World Bank funds for the entire PRP. But without continued donor support, few thought the ERB would remain independent. Thus, in one sense, the ERB might be sustainable while being "owned" by Zambia. It is unlikely, however, that this type of survival would include its effectiveness as an independent regulator in the energy sector. Even with donor support, sustaining the existence and independence of the ERB will likely take a long time in a political atmosphere that generally seeks to prevent agency independence.

Strong political incentives exist on the GRZ side to control the ERB. Sida's contributions to the ERB may not prevent this from happening completely. But the support of Sida—especially in partnership with the World Bank—may slow down this process as long as the aid continues flowing.

This case demonstrates that Sida's participation in institution-building can be an inexpensive way to affect an entire sector. Consultants can bring technical assistance to an agency at a relatively low cost. Creating institutions in a very politically sensitive area, however, obviates against a short-term strategy and will most likely require sustained efforts on the part of Sida to make a long-term impact.

10.4. THE KAFUE GORGE HYDROPOWER STATION REHABILITATION PROJECT

10.4.1. *Project History*

The Kafue River drains the central part of Zambia into the Zambezi River. At Kafue Gorge, the river drops vertically about 600 m over a distance of 30 kms, making it an ideal location for a hydro-electrical power-generation station. With credit guarantees from the governments of Yugoslavia, Norway, and Italy, GRZ initiated the construction of the Kafue Gorge Hydropower Station (KGS). In 1971, the 600 MW

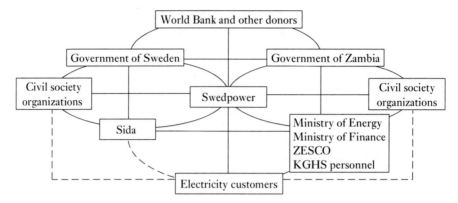

Figure 10.2. *The actors of the Octangle for the Kafue Gorge Power Station Rehabilitation Project*

power station was taken on-line and by 1976, ZESCO (which was established in 1970) had taken over the management and expanded the KGS with two additional 150 MW turbines. This expansion program was supervised by the Swedish Consultant firm, Sweco. In the mid-1980s, the KGS generated more than half of the country's electricity.

On March 26, 1989, a major accidental fire destroyed much of the KGS and caused a complete power outage for about 9 months. To make the KGS operational again, Sida took the lead to provide major economic support (SEK72 million) to an emergency restoration plan. In 1994, all damaged parts had been restored to pre-fire performance levels. Between 1970 and 1994, Sida contributed a total of approximately SEK300 million for the station.

Although the power plant has been up and running at more or less the pre-fire capacity for some time now, the recent World Bank/GRZ policy to rehabilitate and privatize the electricity sector has led ZESCO to design a plan for the complete rehabilitation of the KGS. A technical audit carried out by Swedpower in 1996 concluded that, to make this happen, several civil and electromechanical rehabilitation works needed to be constructed (ZESCO project document 1998). In this new phase, Swedpower is working for ZESCO with funds from Sida to advise and train ZESCO personnel in the management of the rehabilitation project. We focus on this aid by using the IAD framework and staying at the level of collective choice (see Figure 10.2).

10.4.2. *An Institutional Analysis of KGRP*

The action arena

The KGRP is a component of the World Bank-funded PRP. The KGRP involves the rehabilitation of civil, mechanical, and electrical works at the Kafue Gorge Hydropower Station. The main *actors* in this project are the World Bank, the government of Zambia, ZESCO, Sida, and Swedpower, the consultant who is helping ZESCO to manage the project. This study considers the action situation to comprise the period of Sida's support to the KGRP and the actors at the collective-choice level, as highlighted in Figure 10.1.

Influences on the action arena
The KGS produces the majority of the electricity in Zambia. Due to underinvestment in maintenance, the World Bank and the Zambian government identified its rehabil-itation as central to the overall PRP. The station's rehabilitation includes repair and/or renovation of spillways, powerhouse, personnel rooms, and roads, and the provision of goods such as monitoring equipment, spare parts, and surveying tools. Sida's involvement with the KGRP is in paying for the consultant that will help supervise the implementation of this rehabilitation. Thus, the *nature of the goods* directly involved with the KGRP are the standard, private goods common in much development cooperation: hardware and the technical assistance of consultants. The underlying good is electricity.

As in the case of the ERB, the dominance of ZESCO in the production and distribution of electricity in Zambia is one of the most important *community attributes* in the case of the KGRP. The dominance is augmented further in the case of the Kafue Gorge station. As the "backbone of the Zambian network" (ZESCO, Contract for Consulting Services, Kafue Gorge Rehabilitation, appendix B, p. 2), the station has had a privileged position in ZESCO, and even in the government itself. In the discussions of the privatization of the electricity sector, no respondent in or outside of government thought that this station would ever be sold, despite the World Bank's goals. Another important community attribute in this case is the long relationship between the staff at the Kafue Gorge station and the company Swedpower: Swedpower has given technical assistance to the station off and on for decades. (Swedpower also produced the technical audit that assessed the rehabilitation needs of the station in 1993–1994.)

The rules-in-use that affect the behavior of actors in this action arena reflect the history of ZESCO, the Kafue Gorge station, and the new institutions of the rehabilitation project. While ZESCO has long dominated the electricity sector in Zambia, many respondents told us that consultants like Swedpower and the government had more power over ZESCO operations in the past. ZESCO staff said that in previous projects, the consultants would have already been chosen by Sida (tied-aid); the consultants would talk directly with Sida and bypass ZESCO altogether.

This practice has now changed and ZESCO is far more active in the project. ZESCO personnel believe that they are completely in charge of the rehabilitation project. As evidence, they point to the fact of ZESCO's participation in the choice of consultant (while ZESCO believed it still had to be a Swedish consultant, ZESCO did alter some of the terms of reference). Further, the consultant is accountable to ZESCO first, since consultant invoices are not paid by Sida until after ZESCO approves them.

ZESCO's new ownership and actions come from, first, the World Bank's insistence that ZESCO manage the whole PRP, although consultants would be part of each component. In addition, money from the World Bank frees ZESCO from dependence on any one consultant or bilateral donor. Third, since the Sida aid was a grant to the government but a loan (no interest) to ZESCO, the agency is more motivated to see that it gets its money's worth. Finally, ZESCO's power and increased training in the area of procurement through the PRP has changed their understanding and action in that area.

10.4.3. *Patterns of Interaction*

The influences on the action arena, the actors, and their interactions have created clear incentives for Sida's participation and incentives that have empowered ZESCO officials. Thus, KGS is a standard "old-style" development cooperation project with short- to medium-term goals that most respondents think will be met well. The long-run impact of the project—like many projects that feature technical assistance (Sida's part), equipment, and construction—will be more difficult to sustain without additional intervention. This has already been shown in the station's history: the government has continuously underfunded its maintenance, and donors—especially Sida—have continuously stepped in to help.

Incentives of government

The Zambian government knows that the production and distribution systems of the electricity sector are in poor condition. Further, since the Kafue Gorge station is the country's most important producer of electricity, the government was very interested in its rehabilitation.

The government faces few negative incentives with the KGRP. Sida gave a grant for the technical assistance part of the project, which the government has lent to ZESCO. The rest of the project's funding will come either from other donors or from the World Bank (IDA) loan. Almost no reorganization of the Kafue Gorge station was required from any lender (an implementation unit for the project had to be constructed). And given the belief that electricity may be an important export for Zambia in the future, the government is glad to have assistance for the rehabilitation of their most important station.

As mentioned earlier, few respondents believe that the station will be part of any privatization, the goals of the World Bank notwithstanding. The KGS produces the majority of electricity in the country and is seen thus in terms of national security. If electricity does become an important export, the government will also have an incentive to keep ownership of the station in state hands as a means of generating foreign exchange.

Incentives of ZESCO

Like the Zambian government, ZESCO faces generally positive incentives with the rehabilitation of the KGS. It receives much-needed funds to repair various works and has successfully avoided much institutional restructuring. ZESCO officials report that two important institutional changes have, however, changed their incentives. First, employees assert that since the government has lent—not granted—ZESCO the money from Sida, they have stronger incentives to keep track of Sida and other World Bank/PRP money. Second, these incentives are strengthened because ZESCO now has the power to procure for itself (rather than through another unit in the government).

Incentives for Sida
Sida faces strong incentives to support the KGRP. Sida has a long history of supporting this station and with contracting the same consultant for these projects. Sida was asked by the World Bank to support the consultancy for this project. In comparison with a new project, Sida's oversight costs should be far lower in this project since Sida would be working with the same group of people on both the Zambian and consultancy sides.

Incentives for Swedpower
Like Sida and ZESCO, Swedpower possessed strong incentives to be part of the KGRP. They had been helping the station for decades, had close ties with the staff at the station and within Sida, and had the expertise for the job. While some members of Swedpower do not prefer working with the World Bank due to its bureaucratic procedures, Swedpower generally gets along well with Sida personnel.

10.4.4. *Outcomes: Implications for Ownership and Sustainability*

The help provided by Sida for the rehabilitation of the KGS is an example of classic development assistance. Sida has given money for technical assistance, provided by a Swedish firm, which the recipient country needed. As training always has long-term effects, there will be enduring effects at some level from this transfer of knowledge as a result of Sida's contribution (although measuring these effects is always difficult). Without new institutions, however, ZESCO faces the same sets of incentives as it always has—getting donors to pitch in when possible. Sida has been happy to do so over the years, as such support to KGS is clearly important to the country as well as being relatively easy to measure for Sida.

It seems that the structure of the World Bank's PRP has increased the level of ownership for the Zambian ZESCO personnel: they feel empowered by the tendering process. Thus, in the context of Sida's aid, ZESCO felt more control over the process. In this respect, ownership appears higher than in projects past. This empowerment may also endure. Then, one could perhaps say that this aid had an effect on sustainability. The GRZ's continuous need for outside assistance undercuts these effects, however. GRZ remains completely dependent on outside funds for the continued operation of the KGS and Sida's help—both in this instance and over the years—has not generated a way out of this dependence.

10.5. THE CFU

While many of the biophysical conditions, such as soil fertility and climate, are relatively favorable for farming in Zambia, the sector is still far away from its productivity potential (Sida Annual Report 1999). Why might this be so?

Many analyses reviewed for this study seem to agree that one of the main obstacles to a thriving agricultural sector in Zambia is inappropriate farming practices, especially among the sector's smallholders (CFU 1997; ECAZ 1999; MFA 1999; ZNFU 1998). Contemporary agronomic research is making it increasingly clear that the country's predominating, conventional smallholder-farming practices are not well-suited for the existing biophysical context (GART 2000). The conventional practices, which are characterized by extensive tillage methods, have caused severe soil erosion and a decline in soil fertility (ibid.). The apparent mismatch between the biophysical conditions and the existing farming technology has recently become the target of a series of initiatives in Zambia, including several externally funded projects and programs under the auspices of the Ministry of Agriculture, Food, and Fisheries (MAFF).

10.5.1. *History of the Project*

One of the pioneering efforts to introduce better farming practices is a private sector initiative by the ZNFU and their CFU, which they established in 1995. Sida, along with other international development agencies in Zambia, has provided substantial economic support to the activities of the CFU since 1996.[5]

The principal objective of the CFU is to promote smallholder adoption of conservation farming technology, mainly through the development of trainers who work within the existing sector organizations, such as nongovernmental organizations, commercial firms, and MAFF. A recently published econometric analysis of a series of agricultural experiments performed by the Golden Valley Agricultural Research Trust (GART 2000) compared conventional farming with conservation farming practices and concluded that the net economic benefits from conservation farming are, on average, twice as large as those of conventional methods (assuming that the grown crops are actually sold in the market).[6] Despite its relatively small size and limited budget, the CFU has managed to make the conservation farming approach to smallholder farming one of the most promising strategies for combating rural poverty in Zambia (ECAZ 1999). Only 5 years after the introduction of the conservation farming approach into Zambian agriculture, it is estimated that there are approximately 75,000 Zambian farmers who currently practice conservation farming in one way or another (Sida 1998).

Given many international development agencies' frustration with promoting effective poverty reduction strategies in Zambia, the CFU experience can potentially provide useful lessons for the development of future aid programs, especially in the agricultural sector. The CFU is different from many projects, however, in that it is quite small, is not organized through a government ministry, and is run by highly motivated managers. As we will see, these features impact its sustainability and ownership characteristics.

10.5.2. *An Institutional Analysis of the CFU*

Action arena
The promotion of conservation farming in Zambia started in 1995 when the Zambian National Farmers Union invited the "father of conservation farming," Brian Aldrey from Zimbabwe, to present his farming approach at a workshop in Lusaka. After the

workshop, the Zambian National Farmers Union decided to create a special unit dedicated to the promotion of this "new" concept of farming.[7] In October that same year, Peter Aagard and Dutch Gibson were asked to head the new unit, called CFU, and before long the CFU had received enough funds from the European Union and the World Bank to become operational. The objective of the funded CFU activities is to coordinate efforts to promote and demonstrate conservation farming technologies among smallholders in selected regions of Zambia (CFU 1997). Sida first began supporting the CFU in April of 1996 and has, together with NORAD, contributed the largest financial support for the CFU project, with a total amount of about US$600,000 from Sida alone. The CFU is a very small project in Sida's portfolio of support in the area of sustainable agriculture in Zambia as it represents only 2.6 per cent of Sida's total support to the country's agricultural sector during 1998–2000 (Sida 1998). The financial support goes directly to the CFU project managers.

In contrast to most aid-supported projects in the agricultural sector, the CFU is not part of the support channeled through MAFF but is considered a private sector initiative. Nevertheless, MAFF recently adopted conservation farming as one of its main priorities for its extension program, which means that MAFF plays an increasingly important role in the promotion and future success of conservation farming in Zambia. It may have taken only a handful of individuals to create the CFU, but it has required the active engagement and professional commitment of great many more actors in making it a success. The main actors in the current phase of the CFU project are: CFU staff, donors, clients (DAPP, CLUSA, Dunavant, MAFF), individual farmers and organizations participating in the project's coordinating body—the Conservation Farming Liaison Committee.

This study considers the period of Sida's involvement with the CFU, and the actors depicted in Figure 10.3, as the *action situation.*

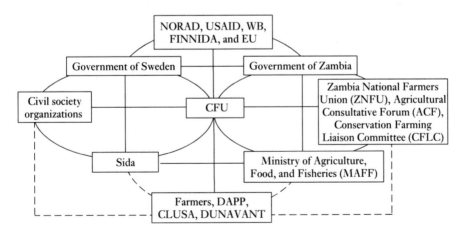

Figure 10.3. *The international development cooperation octangle for the case of the Conservation Farming Unit*

Influences on the action arena

The IAD framework helps us to identify what factors might influence the interactions in the action situation by asking questions about the prevailing *biophysical, socioeconomic,* and *institutional conditions* of the agricultural sector in Zambia. The *biophysical characteristics* help us define the problem of natural resource management in Zambia, providing a rationale for the promotion of the CFU technical package. The semi-arid conditions in the south and central provinces of Zambia make conventional farming techniques inappropriate, mostly because of a popular belief that it is necessary to plow the soil before planting. According to CFU staff, the reliance on oxen-assisted tillage prevents the farmers from doing the "right things at the right time." Since, according to this popular belief, the land cannot be plowed until the rain falls and the seeds cannot be planted until the soils are plowed, farmers are forced to squeeze the whole series of decisive farming activities into a very short period of time, typically a couple of weeks.

The importance of trying to shorten the time lag between plowing and planting is highlighted by the empirical observation that for each day the planting of seeds is delayed after the season's first rainfall, farmers lose 1.3 per cent of their yield (CFU 1997). This means that farmers who are ready to plant two weeks after the first rainfalls lose out on almost a quarter of their potential harvest yields (ibid.: 6). Since the conservation farming approach does not rely on plowing, farmers do not need to wait for the rains to plant, but can already have the seeds in the ground when the first rains come.

Community attributes

For the CFU to be effective in the production of the good, their strategy needs to address sociocultural factors in an explicit fashion. A first factor is that farmers have grown accustomed to not having to repay loans because government officials and politicians have supplied them with fertilizers and seeds in the past. These supplies were often given on loan terms, but since the repayments were seldom enforced, they were *de facto* donations. The CFU addresses this by disallowing participation in the CFU unless farmers honor agreements of paying back the fertilizer and seed inputs that the project offers to farmers as a loan.

Another factor is that during the one-party era, farming—especially the cultivation of maize—was heavily subsidized. These subsidies made the whole sector extremely inefficient. The subsidy culture in turn produced a monoculture of maize production, even in areas where other crops have been grown successfully. Indeed, knowledge of how to grow these other crops is disappearing with the older farmers. One of the main goals of the CFU is to recover this knowledge and diversify smallholder production. The CFU strives to achieve this through a crop diversification program that selects crops with an eye on the market as well as the biological feasibility.[8]

A third factor is that, despite the fact that an epidemic of Corridor disease in the 1980s wiped out the vast majority of cattle for the Zambian smallholder, the reliance on oxen in small-scale farming remains strong. There is a general reluctance to abandon the oxen-draught plowing practices partly because this is regarded as a more "modern" and "developed" way of farming. Using the hoe, as prescribed by the CFU, is associated with a past era when no other farming tools were available. Consequently, a certain degree of prestige is associated with the use of oxen and plow as compared to the technologically less sophisticated hoe. Certainly the hoe is far more onerous to use. Part of the challenge for the CFU is to overcome this cultural discrimination against "going back to the hoe." The CFU addresses this challenge by selecting and working with demonstration farmers who are highly regarded individuals in their communities. If these individuals, who have earned the respect of their neighbors, demonstrate that conservation farming indeed produces better results than using the plow, then neighbors are more likely to start experimenting with conservation farming themselves. The use of demonstration farmers has proven to be an effective way of overcoming the cultural barriers to accepting conservation farming.

Institutional context and rules-in-use

The CFU's success is, in part, attributable to its flexibility. The formal rules of the agricultural sector are not necessarily the rules-in-use; the CFU managers' understanding of this discrepancy has helped its functioning.[9]

Although there are *formal* rules in the bureaucracy that constrain individuals to take advantage of the public provision of goods, a study of the agricultural sector's *rules-in-use* tells a different story. The elites within the government party hold the political authority to control the outcomes of the legislative and judicial processes. The hierarchical structure within the party can stifle all attempts to divert from the officially endorsed party line. The existence of the strong one-party system weakened the accountability mechanisms between politicians, the bureaucracy, and the citizenry, despite the new multiparty democracy. The weak accountability mechanisms are evidenced by repeated interventions in the agricultural sector by politicians. A case in point is the use of fertilizer imports for purposes of political campaigning: while formal rules prohibit this, politicians running for reelection regularly pass out fertilizer to woo voters. Even if the civil servants at MAFF wanted to intervene and put an end to this behavior, it would be difficult if the politicians in question had the support of the party elite.

Even though the formal rules require MAFF to organize meetings and prepare reports for its projects, it has had problems living up to these commitments. Several donors observed that due to shortages of qualified personnel at MAFF, its handling of the reporting to donors is not yet up to par. This has led donors such as the World Bank, Sida, and NORAD to seek alternative ways of supporting activities within the Agricultural Sector Investment Program and, in effect, bypass the administrative bottleneck of MAFF and deal directly with the operational entities of the projects. The World Bank now directs most of its activity support to the district levels, while bilateral donors such as Sida and NORAD provide an increasing part of their support to agriculture through private sector initiatives such as the CFU and the Economic Expansion to Outlying Areas Project.

When the World Bank coordinated the Agricultural Sector Investment Program in the mid-1990s, it was formally agreed by the GRZ and the consortium of donors that a series of sector reforms were to be put in place before the launching of the MAFF-led program. One of the agreements was the retrenchment of half of the existing 6,000 extension officers and the subsequent salary raise for the remaining officers. While the retrenchments were carried out as planned, the promised salary increases were not implemented. The result is that MAFF employees in general continue to be unmotivated and underpaid and are often forced to take on side-jobs to make ends meet. For example, a MAFF employee with a university degree currently makes approximately $45 per month. Extension officers make even less. The current working conditions do not allow MAFF employees to do their jobs properly because they cannot afford to spend the required daily 8 hours at work. These working conditions constitute a breeding ground for rent-seeking and opportunistic behavior, which are difficult for development projects to change. Development projects that do not take these rules-in-use into account make things worse when they inject resources into a rent-seeking bureaucracy. The increased availability of funds tends to fuel the rent-seeking process.

Another less obvious implication of the actual institutional context is the effect it has on the behavior of MAFF employees in the interaction with personnel from externally funded development projects. The differences in salaries (and thus professional status and prestige) may inhibit the development of an environment for mutual learning. Extension workers who earn less than 5 per cent of the CFU directors' salaries might be reluctant to be advised by their well-paid colleagues.

Having noted the difficulties faced by the traditional sector projects channeled through MAFF, the CFU sought an alternative strategy through which it could operate independently from MAFF while, at the same time, collaborate with MAFF in the implementation of activities. Being operationally independent from MAFF, however, does not mean that the CFU operates in isolation from MAFF. In fact, CFU staff have actively worked with MAFF staff at all levels in promoting conservation farming technology primarily through study trips and training activities for staff. One result of this is that the Minister of Agriculture has made the promotion of conservation farming a priority policy for the entire ministry.

10.5.3. *Patterns of Interaction: Incentives and the CFU Project*

Decision making at the collective-choice level involves the planning of CFU activities financed by Sida and other donors. Several forums join the main participants who have a say in the definition of strategies and rules of project implementation. Sida and CFU project managers are the most important actors at this level as Sida's support goes directly from the Swedish Embassy to the CFU. Two other actors play influential roles in the decision making: MAFF and the Sida consultant who is hired to monitor the progress of the project. Other collective-choice forums include Sida's quarterly reviews with CFU project managers, evaluations and mid-term reviews of project activities, informal forums where Sida representatives interact with a broader set of sector actors, for example, the Agricultural Consultative Forum (ACF) and the Conservation Farming Liaison Committee (CFLC).

The CFU project represents a sharp contrast to the traditional government-to-government support. The project's relative decision-making autonomy from MAFF and other government agencies is one of the project's fundamental collective-choice-level rules. This rule of administrative independence makes it possible for the CFU to adopt a flexible and experimental approach that evolves with the challenges that the project faces. Below we outline the incentives faced by each of the four central actors at the collective-choice level.

Incentives of CFU project managers
The historical background of the externally supported activities in the agricultural sector in Zambia explains a great deal of the current funding opportunities for project entrepreneurs. The past failures of the traditional sector support via MAFF have made donors wary of the limitations of this kind of support. Having noted several donors' willingness and even preference to bypass MAFF in agricultural projects, project entrepreneurs have an incentive to develop projects with private sector actors since these are more likely to achieve positive short-term results.

Considering the donors' knowledge of the failures of traditional projects to have an impact at the individual farm level, project entrepreneurs, such as CFU project managers, have an incentive to introduce and promote better farming techniques directly to small-scale farmers.

The CFU strategy to achieve sustainability is straightforward. The project staff maintains that the sustainability lies with the utility of the technical package rather than with the project. In order to achieve sustainability, the project must "do the first things first." This means that the viability of the idea must be tested and validated by farmers before it can be institutionalized by a second- or third-degree organization. The project has been criticized for not having a clear vision of how to institutionalize the technology, but it was not until very recently that the conservation farming technology was recognized as a valid technical package. Now that the technology has been validated, its future institutional home has become a crucial issue. What are the incentives of CFU managers to pursue this strategy of institutionalization? In short, because Sida and other donors demonstrated such a keen interest in the CFU approach, the CFU project managers have a strong professional stake in the success of the project's concept. The managers have been careful to expand slowly, to be highly adaptive, and to work with other organizations on the ground. Further, knowing that farmers may discount the advice given to them by a temporary consultant, the CFU has worked with extant NGOs so as to gain the trust of its target population quickly.

Incentives for MAFF
Although MAFF is only peripherally involved in the decision making at the collective-choice level of the CFU, it remains a central actor in the sector. If the technology is not endorsed by MAFF, its prospects are limited for wider dissemination and adaptation at the national level. The fact that MAFF is being bypassed by an increasing number of externally funded projects, even the ones included under the Agricultural Sector Investment Program umbrella, means that it has lost some of its

importance as a central actor in the sector. While this situation could induce MAFF to attempt to obstruct the projects that do not benefit them directly, MAFF managers have instead decided to recognize its inferior level of performance openly in order to attract funding for sector reform projects. The recent acceptance of the conservation farming technology as a part of MAFF official extension policy follows this logic.

Incentives for Sida
Given the history of meager results of support to the agricultural sector in Zambia, Sida program officers faced incentives to propose that the organization support a new, different, and innovative approach. The relative low cost of the CFU project support reduced Sida's risk. Such a nontraditional project also gives Sida officers an incentive to follow and support it with extra care.

The small size of the project (SEK4.2 million), however, may in and of itself generate a disincentive for Sida to recommend that it be supported. The recent increase in Sida project allocations for Africa and the low-level staffing of field missions generate incentives for Sida management to focus on larger projects. Larger projects may not require much more time to prepare and review than considerably smaller ones but, from the donor's perspective, the larger projects have the advantage of absorbing more money and thus improving disbursement efficiency. Such a focus on efficiency may be in tension with the object of sustainability.

Incentives for conservation farming promoters
The effectiveness of extension officers in promoting the conservation farming technology is likely to be linked to the farmers' perception of the extension workers' vested stake in the program. A short-term consultant will hardly ever be perceived as having the same stake in a project as would an extension officer who will engage in repeated interactions with the farmers and whose future personal well-being is linked to the success of the promoted technology. The result is that the consultants rarely enjoy the same credibility as the national extension workers. The team's assessment of the farmers' perception of CFU staff credibility would suggest that farmers have put a great deal of trust in the people working for the CFU. The sense of trust between farmers and field staff increases the prospects for effective coproduction in the area of conservation farming.

10.5.4. *Implications for Ownership and Sustainability*

The CFU has enjoyed positive reviews and has been endorsed by the Minister of MAFF. They have reached thousands of farmers with their technology package and expect to reach thousands more each year they are in existence. As impressive as the empirical results of conservation farming technology seems, its technology is not by itself sufficient to increase the welfare of Zambian farmers. The knowledge of how to maximize yield is certainly an extremely valuable asset for any farmer, but the farmer is not likely to reach its welfare potential until he or she acquires the knowledge of managing the entire farming system, including choosing the right crops, harvesting and selling at the right time, and to the right price and buyer. It will be the conservation farming farmers' ability to acquire these management skills that will ultimately determine how far the CFU will go to contribute to the overall project objective of poverty reduction in Zambia.

The CFU is not self-sustaining and most likely will never be. While it does garner revenue by working with NGOs, it remains a project based on technical assistance (we found no plans to have the farmers themselves pay for these extension services). Neither is it likely that the government's own agents in MAFF could be as efficient as the CFU, although if MAFF picks up the project it may have a longer shelf life. The impacts of the CFU, on the other hand, could be quite sustainable if farmers see their incomes rise over time, although this depends upon more than CFU technology alone, such as existence and knowledge of markets, weather, etc.

The question of ownership is quite complex when looking at the CFU. Donors, as usual, are part owners of the CFU. The CFU managers themselves have a great deal of the project's ownership: they have designed and implemented the program and have personal stakes in its outcomes. If local farmers do not want to participate, the CFU can move on to another set of farmers who might. Thus, while the targeted populations certainly have a say about whether they will participate in the program, they do not possess any significant management powers within it. Without the strong commitment and vision of the CFU managers, the program would most likely lose steam.

This issue ties directly to the possibility of MAFFs future involvement in conservation farming. There is talk of MAFF adopting the extension of CFU concepts. But many of MAFFs extension personnel, in contrast to the CFU, are not only demoralized and underpaid but have since long promoted the conventional farming practices that conservation farming tries to eliminate. Extension officers who in the past have promoted the conventional practices may be concerned with losing face with their clients, admitting that they had gotten it wrong before but now hold the answer to increasing yields. If the extension officers do as they are told and go along with the prescribed MAFF policy to promote conservation farming, it may create a credibility problem in the relationship to their client farmers. The credibility of the extension officer is a crucial factor for the farmers' incentives to adopt conservation farming. In the field, the farmer's observation of results will determine the incentives to expand, continue as usual, abandon, or only slightly modify the current conservation farming approach. The farmers' incentives to obey the advice given by extension officers will depend on their assessment of the credibility of their advice. This assessment will in turn determine the discount rates (by way of affecting the level of perceived uncertainties) for calculated conservation farming benefits. Thus, expansion through MAFF, one way of sustaining the conservation farming idea, may actually undermine the usefulness of the CFU approach.

10.6. CONCLUSIONS

The three brief cases we explored in Zambia exhibited sets of incentives that had both different and common elements. All three occur in the context of an aid–dependent country: aid is rarely refused by the Zambian government. But it appears that aid only rarely changes the underlying institutions that contribute to poor policy outcomes. In this respect, unfortunately, our Zambian projects appear to resemble our Indian projects examined in Chapter 9.

The Kafue Gorge case exemplifies the traditional way of doing development aid and its subsequent moral hazards: the government continues to underinvest in the electricity sector while many donors keep it going with aid. The CFU is an example of a low-cost project led by highly motivated individuals whose preferences are probably very closely aligned with Sida's, and whose work can be rejected by beneficiaries. These factors help the CFU to achieve the success it has so far enjoyed. The ERB was the strongest case of institution-building we examined in all of our research for this book. Its long-term impact could be enormously important to the effective restructuring of the electricity sectors, given its continued independence. The ERB also shows, however, that institution-building will be as much a political issue as a technical one.

The case studies in India and Zambia reveal that aid projects must address the underlying collective-action problem if they are to be effective and sustainable. Identifying the collective-action problem is a first step in analyzing any proposed aid initiative. Solving these collective-action problems may require efforts in institution-building, which is most often a low-cost but high-effort undertaking. Yet, aid agencies are often poorly matched to the task, given their own budgetary exigencies and administrative constraints. Improving aid effectiveness will require better informed and more long-term staff involvement attention by aid agencies. Given prevailing incentive structures, however, aid agencies may find it as difficult to reform their own ways as it is to reform the ways of others.

NOTES

1. From 1965–1969, copper accounted for 42.3 per cent of Zambia's GDP. That fell to 7.5 per cent in 1990–1993, while still accounting for 82 per cent of the country's exports (Saasa and Carlsson 1996: 35).
2. Zambia was the most indebted country per capita in the world in 1984.
3. Growth in real GDP was negative for 6 years out of 10 from 1982–1992 (Andersson and Ndulo 1994).
4. Zambia was one of the largest recipients of Swedish balance of payments support at the time: SEK600 million from 1990/91 to 1992/93 (Mwanawina and White 1995: 100).
5. Since 1996, CFU has also received economic support from NORAD, USAID, Finnida, EU, and the World Bank in different phases of the project. Currently, the project is in its third phase, which ends in 2002.
6. It should also be noted that labor costs are estimated to be about 50 per cent higher for conservation farming compared to conventional farming methods that use oxen-draught tillage, at least during the early stages of adoption (GART 2000).
7. Arguably, the principle of minimum tillage per se was nothing new to most Zambian farmers since this was the way smallholders farmed long before colonization. However, other components of the conservation farming approach, such as rainfall-harvesting, the timeliness concept, using plant residues to retain moisture and nutrients of the soil, etc., were indeed novel to most Zambian farmers in 1995.
8. Crop diversification is inherent to the conservation farming approach since it requires at least three crops to be annually rotated from one section of the plot to another. Each individual farmer selects a minimum three crops with the advice of the extension officer.
9. For a more thorough discussion of the central importance of rules-in-use, see Chapter 2 on the IAD framework.

PART IV

CONCLUSION

11

What Have We Learnt About Aid?

Studying foreign aid has recently become a "growth industry." In addition to the large traditional literature trying to explain the effect of aid on growth, scholars are now interested in topics including the political effects of aid for recipient governments (Bräutigam and Knack 2004; Coolidge and Rose-Ackerman 1997; Cungu and Swinnen 2003; Gibson and Hoffmann 2005; Kosack 2003; Moore 1998; Robinson 2003), the choices of multilateral donors themselves, especially regarding conditionality (Collier 1997; Easterly 2003; Robinson and Verdier 2002; van de Walle 2001), and the relationship between aid and recipient bureaucracies (Knack and Rahman 2004; Remmer 2004; Werlin 2003). Considering the immense amount of aid given on the world stage—at the time of this writing, for example, the United States is sending billions of dollars for the reconstruction of Iraq, and dozens of countries are contributing to disaster relief following the Southeast Asian tsunami—these studies are important and timely.

In this book we tackled a different issue: how development assistance systems generate particular patterns of incentives that affect sustainable outcomes. In Chapters 1–6, we explored how all collective human endeavors are plagued by incentive problems related to motivation and information. We then investigated how institutions shape the choices of individuals, and how these institutions can lead to better or worse outcomes. In the sphere of foreign aid, these institutions are arranged in a complex set of relationships, which we sought to capture with our International Development Cooperation Octangle. In Chapters 7–10, we employed these theoretical insights to analyze the incentives of individuals in the organization of Sida (Swedish International Development Cooperation Agency)-Stockholm and specific Sida-funded projects in India and Zambia. We found many institutions—some inherent in development assistance and some specific to the structure of Sida—that foster incentives that undermine Sida's goal of sustainable development. In this chapter, we explore some options that may help development assistance agencies mitigate some of the perverse incentives found in the aid system.

In the rest of this chapter, we indicate how things might be done better. We will refer at times to the particular case of Sida, but we hope to provide suggestions that are general enough to be useful enough to any agency concerned with development assistance. We identify six general areas that deserve the attention of all aid agencies, the recipients of international assistance, and those engaged in the analysis of this policy field. These are:

(1) an awareness of the important role of incentives;
(2) paying attention to the nature of the good involved;
(3) focusing on how ownership is related to sustainability;
(4) examining how learning is encouraged at an individual and organizational level;
(5) the role of consultants in development assistance; and
(6) the importance of putting beneficiaries first.

11.1. AWARENESS OF THE ROLE OF INCENTIVES

Most individuals with experience in development cooperation realize that incentives underpin aid effectiveness and sustainability (Wane 2004). Yet, while we may be sensitive to the importance of institutions and the incentives they produce, the knowledge underlying this realization is often tacit. Moreover, tacit knowledge is rarely transmitted in a systematic way. A more explicit and systematic understanding of institutions and the incentives that emerge within particular organizational structures, as well as mechanisms for transmitting this knowledge, are therefore crucial to improve an aid agency's effectiveness. Incentives facing the participants in development assistance, as these affect the incentives of participants in economic and political organizations more generally within the recipient country, are key to understanding the process of economic change (North 2005).

We suggest formalizing an understanding of incentives in the system of aid through an agency's training sessions for its staff. Such training should draw on the experiences of more experienced agency staff members. It should explicitly confront how the institutions of development assistance affect incentives, and hence the sustainability of aid. Such an effort will foster a keener awareness of project and program design and implementation, yielding higher chances of success.

Yet another 2-hour training course for an aid agency's staff on yet another topic—in this case, incentives—is not sufficient to overcome perverse incentives. In fact, we doubt that any development cooperation agency can fully mitigate the structures that produce unwanted sets of incentives. Powerful incentives are built into structures over which a development agency has little control: the structure of political institutions in both donor and recipient countries beget rules that can work directly against effective development aid. We have discussed numerous examples. A low ratio of staff per development aid budget is just one of numerous rules that at best constrain the effective design and delivery of development assistance; at worst, they undermine completely the possibility of success. The structure of the budgetary process also creates the powerful incentive to "move the money" that haunt all bureaucracies.

Indeed, there are also powerful incentives for aid agencies to do nothing. For example, many of the issues that we highlighted in our earlier report to Sida had been identified by others in previous Sida reports and evaluations (although we believe we were the first group to examine fully their theoretical foundations and likely outcomes). Development assistance will continue despite its problems because its funding does not depend on its sustainability. There are no institutions or market mechanisms that ensure the efficient delivery of sustainable aid. The only way that an understanding of incentives will lead to better development assistance is through the determination of an agency's own staff to create rules that promote "good" incentives. Such rules may be costly in terms of an agency's own time and money, may not be supported by the donor country's ministry of foreign affairs, and may not necessarily lead to greater resources from their government. We would argue, however, that this investment to create better incentive structures will lead to better outcomes for development assistance.

11.2. THE NATURE OF THE GOOD

In this book we have emphasized that the "nature of the good"—or, in broader terms, the physical and material conditions affecting any particular aid project—is an important part of the context affecting the incentives of actors in ongoing situations. As our theory and cases have shown, at least two goods are involved in any development assistance project: the specific good involved in the project and the characteristics of aid modalities. Both affect incentives.

First, the underlying goods that are the focus of development assistance have direct impact on incentives. Recipient country actors face collective-action problems when they wish to provide public goods, manage common-pool resources, or reform institutions so as to encourage entrepreneurship, investment, democratic development, and increased economic growth. The complex structure of these collective-action problems must be well-understood for a donor to enter and introduce changes that improve outcomes rather than make things worse. Features of these underlying goods that development aid seeks to affect generate incentives whether a project focuses on electricity, forests, or changes in institutions needed to foster rapid and sustainable development.

Second, the characteristics of different aid modalities produce a variety of incentives to different actors. The effects of the type of aid given clearly matters a great deal to the pattern of incentives facing different actors in the Octangle. The dimensions of moral hazard, adverse selection, and signaling problems differ by modalities as well as by the rules-in-use and by the community involved.

Thus, an aid agency should understand the wider incentives involved in the underlying core good as well as the more narrowly focused incentives related to its specific aid-supported activities. Such an understanding, coupled with a desire for sustainable results, would most likely exclude most projects that primarily involve infrastructure provision and move the agency toward efforts aimed at institution-building. Providing infrastructure or hardware with no realistic plan of maintenance on the part of the recipient is a sure recipe for unsustainability (E. Ostrom *et al.* 1993) and donor dependence (although it allows the donor to monitor immediate outcomes more easily and to move large sums of money).

We suggest that when considering future projects and programs, an aid agency should develop a clear analysis of the underlying collective-action problems that it is trying to ameliorate and how the characteristics of diverse aid modalities affect the incentives of all participants involved in development assistance.

11.3. OWNERSHIP AND SUSTAINABILITY

Many donors have rejected the initial approach of development assistance that argued for a short-term infusion of funds from wealthier to poorer nations. This transfer was to facilitate major investments in infrastructure and was seen as a way to build capacity, allowing poorer nations to take off economically, gain or strengthen democratic procedures, and achieve more equitable distribution of wealth. This approach has not worked well. It has not fostered incentives in recipient countries to build more effective institutions needed to facilitate home growth. In many countries, development assistance has not produced sustainable results.

Many agencies now voice a strong concern for the sustainability of development cooperation. They argue that long-term positive change is a better investment of resources than more temporary results. Such agencies seek to improve the outcomes related to its efforts in development cooperation by giving ownership of aid to recipients. Managers at many development agencies insist that projects belong to the recipient agency, and characterize their agency's role as that of a concerned partner, advisor, and financier. Fostering ownership is thought to promote sustainable outcomes.

The recent stress on ownership is an implicit recognition of the problems that development cooperation generates for provision, production, consumption, and alienation. If recipient agencies (and targeted beneficiaries) are included in these activities, perverse incentives may be ameliorated. Allowing the recipients to participate in the provision process may help align the incentives of donor and recipients as well as make better use of local knowledge and institutions. Participation in the production process may help prevent recipients and beneficiaries from free-riding on the aid. Participation in the consumption of benefits and costs may motivate greater concern for appropriate outcomes. Finally, participation in the alienation of aid may generate information likely to reduce the probabilities of continuing unsuccessful projects or programs. Thus, including recipients and beneficiaries in true ownership can help solve some of the severe information and motivational problems in development cooperation discussed in this book, but, as we have repeatedly stressed, this is not a sufficient condition to ensure sustainability.

Our theoretical findings demonstrate that applying the concept of ownership and sustainability to actual development cooperation relationships is quite difficult. Our analysis shows that motivational and information problems in aid are very deeply embedded. As challenging as these problems are in the context of individuals with full ownership rights in an arena of well-enforced institutions, they pale in comparison with the multi-actor, multi-level, multi-owner characteristics of development assistance. Our representation of the system of aid—the Octangle—illustrates how every dyad and triad in aid are subject to these motivational and information problems. And, our analysis of different aid modalities and characteristics demonstrates that no type of development cooperation is free from powerful perverse incentives.

Furthermore, the difference between a recipient and a beneficiary of development cooperation highlights the difficulty of parceling ownership out to many actors. In some cases, recipients of aid are the targeted beneficiaries; in other cases, the beneficiaries have little or no voice. The official owner is often the national government that may in fact have little knowledge about or interest in the problems facing the targeted beneficiaries. The responsibility and accountability that an owner has, in the conventional meaning of the word, is transformed to nearly unrecognizable forms by the system of development assistance. When the owner is not one of the beneficiaries, endowing a distant government's agent with ownership may do little to change the perverse incentives of the beneficiaries or anyone else involved in traditional development assistance. Nor does it affect the flow and accuracy of information from beneficiaries to the official owner.

Our work in the field supports our theoretical findings. The Orissa Forestry project illustrates how multi-actor, multi-level relationships affect ownership and sustainability. In this case, Sida (Stockholm and India), the national and state governments, the state bureaucracy, and the consultants each shared some type of ownership over the community forestry project. Chapter 9 demonstrated how each of these actors confronts powerful incentives to pursue goals other than those outlined in the project. The result was a project in which responsibilities were not well-understood, different actors were working at cross-purposes, and intended beneficiaries were not well-integrated. The institutions found in this case nearly guarantee that even with full funding, the project will not meet its goals.

The case of Sida's forestry project in Orissa illustrates how incentives created by power asymmetries at the bureaucratic level affect sustainability. The Orissa Forest Department, as other closed-career hierarchical bureaucracies in India and elsewhere, can be depicted in terms of a rent-seeking model. Career aspirants compete in a market for jobs, with desirable postings going to the highest bidder. This structure encourages forest service officers to exploit the forest, forest users, and development cooperation to secure good postings. The incentives spawned by this bureaucratic organization lie at the root of the problem of forest degradation. Sida's attempts to reform the Orissa Forest Department to be more sensitive to community forest management run directly counter to the Forest Department's present set of incentives, making long-term change improbable. Long-existing, indigenous forest institutions have been weakened by the policies of the Orissa Forest Department so that the former stewards of local forests no longer have much voice in the policies affecting the forests upon which they depend for fuelwood, fodder, and timber—indeed, their very livelihood.

Chapter 9 also showed that some types of ownership devolution may have the unintended effect of exacerbating the power asymmetries found within the recipient country. The Maharashtra power project, for example, has increased the power supply in India. However, this has created a bigger pool from which politicians can potentially hand out free or cheap electric power. Since the underlying free-rider problem remains unsolved, private investment in enhancing power capacity has still not materialized. The aid project may have made the free-rider problem even more severe by crowding out the private investment needed to expand the state's power capacity. By inadvertently strengthening the hand of Maharashtra's politicians, the aid intervention undermined indigenous capacities to sustain investment in power production. Much the same long-term consequence can be anticipated for the case of the Kafue Gorge Hydropower Project in Zambia (Chapter 10). And, Sida's effort to foster new organizations and policies by supporting the Zambian Energy Regulation Board does not appear to be sustainable once external financial support to it is withdrawn.

Despite an aid agency's efforts to change the orientation of its development assistance, it remains in many important ways the *de facto* owner of development assistance. Most agencies remain the primary actor in decisions related to the terms of development assistance funding, and they have a large—if not the largest—voice in design of the project. It is also clear that beneficiaries rarely exercise much ownership in most cases, especially when project implementers and project beneficiaries are different groups of people (which is the usual situation). The everyday use of the term "ownership" conveys an individual or organization with clearly defined responsibilities who receives the benefits and pays the costs resulting from its exercise of these responsibilities. Within development cooperation processes, responsibilities and accountability are unclear. Who "owns" the project when things go wrong? The large number of actors within development cooperation allows each actor with partial ownership to deny full ownership, and thereby accountability. The entire Octangle may be filled with actors pointing to each other as the source of the problems.

Given aid's complexity regarding relationships and incentives, it is understandable that the staff and reports of an aid agency should offer various views of ownership and sustainability. As mentioned in Chapter 1, Sida staff, recipient government personnel, and private sector consultants expressed different views of what the concepts of ownership and sustainability mean in practice. Defining these core concepts clearly is far from an academic exercise: in fact, our team would argue that it is an essential first step for any agency that seeks to be more effective in its development efforts.

We suggest that aid agencies revisit their concept of ownership. The common meaning of ownership does not translate automatically to the realities of development assistance. While the term has been fashionable among aid circles, it has rarely led to changes in the incentives facing actors in development assistance situations.

We argue that aid agencies need to allow sufficient opportunities for the owner(s) to contribute to the design, implementation, and mid-course corrections of the project/program. A final step is to allow the owner full participation in the final evaluation of a project/program. We set out four criteria for beneficiary ownership. Beneficiary owners need to (1) enunciate a *demand* for aid, (2) allocate at least some of their own *assets* to the project or program so that they have a real stake in the way their own and other actors' assets are used, (3) obtain real net benefits, and (4) have clear-cut responsibilities and be able to participate in decisions regarding continuance or ending of a project. Part of the success of the CFU project in Zambia is related to the fact that it allows beneficiaries a greater role in these actions. Farmers possess some input in the design of how CFU technologies will be used on their lands. Farmers must participate in the production of crops, and they consume all of its benefits and nearly all of its costs. And, farmers can choose not to participate in the project at any time. As a result, better chances exist for longer-term impacts of this project than for most.

Genuine devolution of ownership may mean less control for an aid agency and its consultants. While less control is not without its attendant risks, we argue that it is necessary to achieve more sustainable results. Less control, however, does not mean less aid agency involvement in ongoing activities in partner countries. In fact, agency personnel should play a crucial facilitative role to ensure that ownership of activities is anchored primarily with beneficiaries, and not taken over by consultants or individuals within recipient organizations. The incentive structures that emerge in each donor-supported undertaking are greatly influenced by an agency's interventions, or lack thereof. In general, we think that many aid staff in the field are too overstretched in their work to gather and evaluate information about their projects and programs. And, devolving ownership may increase monitoring costs.

We recommend that aid agencies focus on the concepts of responsibility and accountability as they relate to ownership (Grant and Keohane 2005). Agency staff should articulate which specific responsibilities they seek to devolve to which actors, and how such actors can be held accountable for their actions. Such an exercise should include an examination of the institutional context and the incentives it generates, as well as the incentives produced by different aid modalities.

As ownership is thought to affect sustainability, we also suggest that aid agencies revisit its idea of sustainability in development cooperation. As discussed in this study, the imprecision of the ownership concept and its loose application to many different arrangements has left it without much meaning. An agency should make clear, in each project or program of development cooperation, precisely what is intended to be sustainable, how development assistance helps produce sustainability, what time frame is being used, and how sustainability will be measured. Project planning documents should clearly identify the intended owners and include an analysis of the anticipated impact that this designation of ownership will have on sustainability. Such documents should also detail how meaningful ownership will be vested and what evidence will be gathered to ascertain success in these goals. In designing its projects/programs, aid agency staff must also keep in mind that the greater the number of owners, the smaller the stakes will likely be for any particular owner to ensure success.

These recommendations should not be viewed as easy palliatives. To implement them effectively will be, in fact, incredibly challenging. The experience of our team members is that development agencies do a poor job of developing, requiring, collecting, and evaluating such evidence. This task is also challenging since donors finance projects and programs and thus always remain a *de facto* owner; donors may find themselves in a Samaritan's Dilemma. Further, aid agencies must operate within the political logics of its own and a recipient country, which may not be amenable to the aim of promoting sustainable development. Even so, steps can still be taken to improve the conditions for real ownership by recipients and beneficiaries.

11.4. ENCOURAGING LEARNING AT THE INDIVIDUAL AND ORGANIZATIONAL LEVELS

Most aid agencies can boast of a deep reservoir of knowledge and expertise in development cooperation. Even so, the institutions of most agencies fail to make use of this knowledge. Given the high rate of turnover of staff dealing with any one project or program, and the lack of a link between career advancement and participation in sustainable projects, few incentives—besides personal motivation—exist for individuals within most agencies to be involved with a project after reassignment. These institutions detract from any agency's potential for organizational learning and ability to create better projects and programs.

At a minimum, staff who have been reassigned after they participated in the early design efforts for a project should be included in mid-term evaluations of that project so as to offer their knowledge of original conditions and design. A more challenging, though ultimately fruitful, approach would be to reward staff, especially at the manager level, for more sustainable projects. Like most of the recommendations in this chapter, there are incentives for an agency to do little about creating institutions that record and distribute information from field activities. Tying individuals to the design and implementation of programs and projects in addition to their basic administrative duties is a sensitive and difficult endeavor. Most staff would want to avoid the risk that this might pose to their professional position.

Perverse incentives thrive in the absence of information. The motivation and information problems of development cooperation create sets of perverse incentives for the actors involved. In many, if not most, instances of development cooperation, actors within the Octangle are not fully motivated by achieving sustainable outcomes. Or, if they are, there are still other benefits that they prefer more. It is not that accountability does not exist. It is that most Octangle actors are generally not directly accountable for producing *sustainable* results. Aid agencies seek first to meet the demands of their own country's government, legislatures, foreign ministries, staff, and organized interest groups. Recipient governments first attempt to remain in power by targeting resources to constituents. Consultants and NGOs seek to please their donor–employer (albeit this may include successful, sustainable projects). Highly critical evaluations can upset these actors' abilities to achieve their immediate goals. In other words, no effective demand exists for meaningful evaluations of development assistance.

These incentives often lead to watered-down evaluation processes (Martens 2000). Evaluations come late in a project or program's life, are not linked to the career paths of the agency staff, and generally do not include the views of the intended beneficiaries. Further, if consultants are the actors who perform evaluations, incentives may exist that mitigate against making suggestions to end of donor assistance to any particular project/program. Evaluations provide a critical feedback mechanism between beneficiaries and donors. When evaluations are casually or irresponsibly conducted, the likelihood of sustainable outcomes decreases.

The incentives and outcomes of evaluations as currently being performed are generally well-known (Carlsson *et al.* 1994; Cracknell 2001; Gordillo and Andersson 2004; Picciotto 2003). A system of evaluations is one of the few ways available to increase the level of information for all participants in development cooperation. And with increased information comes a chance to learn and thus improve outcomes. We also recommend that aid agencies consider mid-term evaluations so that all actors involved in a project can learn and adjust during the second half of a project. Mid-term formal evaluations are particularly critical to improving sustainability, since they would allow project participants to learn more effectively about their own activities and, if needed, adjust strategies mid-project in order to enhance sustainability. This also may mean they disinvest in projects that are not expected to be sustainable.

All those affected by projects—particularly the beneficiaries—should be involved in the evaluation of projects. This will encourage beneficiaries, donor officials, and contractors to learn of each other's concerns and from each other's experiences. In cases where beneficiaries are numerous, random samples can be done with a survey tool. For some projects, focus groups may be more appropriate. Projects across any aid agency should also be randomly selected to study thematic issues raised in these evaluations. To increase learning within an aid agency, staff with past involvement with the project or program should be invited to project evaluation discussions.

Evaluators should be instructed to examine the level of ownership in a project or program and the impact of ownership on sustainability should be seriously discussed. Evaluations should be read and discussed formally both with recipient country officials, with beneficiaries where possible, and at the aid agency. They can then be used as guides to future projects. Staff no longer working on a particular project should be encouraged to participate in the discussion of these evaluations. To support this practice, evaluations should be reviewed in conjunction with staff performance reviews.

11.5. THE ROLE OF CONSULTANTS

Many aid agencies over the last decade have reduced the number of staff in the field and have become more reliant on consultants. This shift has important consequences for the ownership and sustainability of aid. Consultants clearly possess some level of ownership over a donor's projects and programs. Their choices are constrained by the terms of the contract and the ability of the donor to monitor performance. Consultants also possess important informational advantages with respect to a donor. Consultants often have greater knowledge about project realities in the recipient country than the aid agency's staff, particularly given the latter's turnover rate; consultants clearly have more information about their own sector. Usually, consultants also have more control than the intended beneficiaries. After all, consultants can choose their target populations, but the reverse rarely happens.

If we assume that consultants seek long-term relationships with donors, then they will worry about their reputations and will try to please their donor–employer. This yields two effects. First, given the information asymmetry about how the project is actually working, consultants have incentives to provide information about the project that agency staff want to hear (part of the principal–agent problem). In the absence of well-executed evaluations, this information asymmetry can lead to the continuation of projects that do not produce sustainable outcomes.

Second, a consultant concerned with possible future contracts with a donor agency is likely to maximize control over a project, rather than pass control on to the targeted individuals for aid. Giving up control to the beneficiaries can be risky—they may not perform in the ways that a consultant or donor wants. Reducing this uncertainty by retaining control, the consultant maximizes expected returns from future contracts. Such control is also affected by the nature of the good. The provision of physical goods is less affected than the provision of less measurable goods. The more difficult the measurement of the good being provided, the more likely the consultant attempts to control its provision so that donors are satisfied.

Inclusion of consultants in the pre-design and design phases of projects also produces incentives to prioritize the needs of the consultant over the recipient or beneficiary. Tied-aid can reduce the recipient's level of ownership and decrease a consultant's incentive to perform since this can reduce the competition for the contract with Sida. This depends on the extent of competition in particular areas of expertise within the donor country. In the energy cases we examined, there are only two major Swedish consultants (Swedpower and Sweco), and even these are part of the same parent company.

We suggest that contracts to consultants should specify outputs that the aid agency believes are important, measurable, and less subject to information asymmetries and manipulation. These measurable outputs should be clear enough to be used in any subsequent evaluation. All aid agencies try to get around missing and asymmetric information problems by contracting consultants they know well. Reputation effects do help mitigate uncertainty and some of the principal–agent problems discussed in Chapters 3 and 4. But rather than depend on reputation alone, the agency should establish formal understandings with its consultants regarding exactly what it considers as success, especially for its major goals of ownership and sustainability.

11.6. PUTTING BENEFICIARIES FIRST

Effective and sustainable development assistance must center on beneficiaries and the problems they face. Evaluations of projects and programs with a focus on beneficiary incentives can help a concerned donor to address how individuals in the action situation relate to each other and how they might overcome their problems and dilemmas through institutional change. This process requires that beneficiaries take ownership of their developmental prospects in all four senses of that term (i.e. provision, production, consumption, and alienation). The tools developed in this report can help. They allow the analysis of the institutional change that will be required to allow beneficiaries to overcome their collective-action problems and realize their own developmental potential. Supporting research on indigenous institutions, norms, and local knowledge systems also provides essential understanding for helping to build contemporary institutions on the healthy roots of earlier normative systems used to solve collective-action problems. This requires, as well, that donors rethink their own role.

Development assistance should focus on the intended beneficiaries and the problems they face. To be sustainable, aid should address how beneficiaries relate to each other in dealing with diverse collective-action problems. Without this deeper analysis and programs focused on institutional change to facilitate the long-term improvement in the lives of beneficiaries, aid is likely to provide only short-term benefits. As part of the design phase of any project or program, we suggest that questions like the following be asked:

✓ What underlying collective-action problem(s) do beneficiaries face?
  • Is it a public good problem/free-rider problem/Tragedy of the Commons problem? (For example, the Indian power case is at root a free-rider problem.)
  • What are the basic incentive problems facing beneficiaries at an operational level? Motivational? Missing information? Asymmetric information? Other?
  • What are the developmental implications of this collective-action failure?
  • What rules or norms have been used in this cultural tradition in the past that may be the source of modern rules that resonate with beneficiaries as fair and can be understood easily?
  • What incentives have precluded beneficiaries from resolving their own collective-action problem at a collective-choice level in the absence of aid? How would they be affected by a proposed aid project or program?
  • Are needed institutions missing or weak, or are perverse institutions in place?
  • Would a modification in rules affecting this underlying problem be threatening to the power elite of this country?

✓ In what ways have previous aid interventions altered similar collective-action problems?
  • Did aid abet or exacerbate power or information asymmetries or adverse selection?
  • What ownership attributes do the targeted beneficiaries possess?
  • Have aid interventions affected the capacity of the beneficiary group to address the collective-action failure?
  • Have they exacerbated existing perverse incentive structures (as is the situation in the Indian power case)?

✓ What are the implications for sustainability?
  • How have the underlying collective-action problems been addressed by the aid intervention?
  • In what ways are such issues included in the feedback loops of the Octangle?
  • Given the roles of the contractor and the recipient, are the prospects for an appropriate solution to the underlying collective-action problem enhanced or reduced?

The aid agency Desk Officer and the intended beneficiaries are separated by many intermediary actors; each dyad harbors incentives to select and transmit only the information that is likely to benefit the participants privately. The information asymmetries in this multilayered arena make it very difficult for the Desk Officer sitting in the donor's capital city to appreciate the reality on the ground.

Some aid agencies—and we note that Sida is among them—have taken important steps to address the information asymmetry problem. We were particularly pleased to learn about the encouraging results of Sida's pilot efforts to decentralize a wide range of management responsibilities to selected embassies. The experiment may serve to reduce the number of intermediary layers. While such structural modifications might improve the possibilities for decision makers to acquire essential beneficiary-level information, it will hardly be sufficient to generate stronger incentives for an aid agency to seek out information about sustainability issues in ongoing field activities. As suggested by the evidence in Chapter 7, Sida and other donor agencies can improve the conditions for learning about sustainability by addressing current constraints in both organizational and individual learning.

The practice of development assistance is very difficult. It is comprised of complex relationships between many different actors, each possessing different preferences and varying levels of information and resources. It is often directed to areas with the most intractable problems. And, it is haunted by perverse incentives at every turn. We hope that this book has provided an analysis of development assistance that helps those involved in its creation and delivery to reach better outcomes. We believe such a goal is more possible now than it was a generation ago. The political considerations that constrained much of development cooperation during the Cold War have disappeared. That does not mean that political considerations have disappeared altogether: political actors in donor and recipient governments still have tremendous influence over the way that development assistance is allocated. What it does mean, however, is that there are more opportunities to get aid right.

Bibliography

AAPAM (African Association for Public Administration and Management) and the Dag Hammarskjold Foundation. 1995. *Report of the Expert Consultation on the Role of Autonomous Funds as Intermediaries in Channeling Money for Social and Economic Development in Africa.* Kampala, Uganda, April 4–6, 1995.

Adam, Christopher S., Arne Bigsten, Paul Collier, and Stephen A. O'Connell. 1994. *Evaluation of Swedish Development Cooperation with Zambia.* Stockholm: SASDA, Ministry for Foreign Affairs.

—— and Stephen A. O'Connell. 1999. "Aid, Taxation and Development in Sub-Saharan Africa." *Economics and Politics* 11(3): 225–53.

Agrawal, Arun. 2001. "State Formation in Community Spaces?: Decentralization of Control over Forests in the Kumaon Himalaya, India." *Journal of Asian Studies* 60(1) (February): 1–32.

—— 2002. "Common Resources and Institutional Sustainability." In *The Drama of the Commons*, National Research Council, Committee on the Human Dimensions of Global Change, eds. Thomas Dietz, Nives Dolšak, Elinor Ostrom, Paul Stern, Susan Stonich, and Elke Weber, 41–85. Washington, DC: National Academy Press.

—— and Clark C. Gibson. 1999. "Enchantment and Disenchantment: The Role of Community in Natural Resource Conservation." *World Development* 27(4): 629–49.

—— and Gautam N. Yadama. 1997. "How do Local Institutions Mediate Market and Population Pressures on Resources? Forest *Panchayats* in Kumaon, India." *Development and Change* 28(3) (July): 435–65.

Akerlof, George A. 1970. "The Market for 'Lemons': Qualitative Uncertainty and the Market Mechanism." *Quarterly Journal of Economics* 84: 488–500.

Alchian, Armen A. 1950. "Uncertainty, Evolution, and Economic Theory." *Journal of Political Economy* 58(3): 211–21.

—— and Harold Demsetz. 1972. "Production, Information Costs, and Economic Organization." *American Economic Review* 62(5) (December): 777–95.

Andersen, H. 1996. *Vietnam 1995: Sustainable Growth and the Issue of Capital.* Stockholm: SIDA, Macroeconomic Report.

Andersson, Krister P. 2003. "What Motivates Municipal Governments? Uncovering the Institutional Incentives for Municipal Governance of Forest Resources in Bolivia." *Journal of Environment and Development* 12(1): 5–27.

—— 2004. "Who Talks with Whom? The Role of Repeated Interactions in Decentralized Forest Governance." *World Development* 32(2): 233–49.

Andersson, Per-Åke and Manenga Ndulo. 1994. "Hyperinflation, Stabilization and the New Economic Recovery Program." Stockholm: University of Gothenburg, Department of Economics. Mimeo.

Andreoni, James. 1990. "Impure Altruism and Donations to Public Goods: A Theory of Warm-Glow Giving." *Economic Journal* 100: 464–77.

Arnold, J. E. M. 1998. *Managing Forests as Common Property.* Rome: FAO.

Arrow, Kenneth. 1951. *Social Choice and Individual Values.* 2nd edn. New York: Wiley.

—— 1985. "The Economics of Agency." In *Principals and Agents: The Structure of Business*, eds. J Pratt and R. Zeckhauser, 37–51. Boston, MA: Harvard Business School Press.

Ashby, W. Ross. 1960. *Design for a Brain: The Origin of Adaptive Behavior*. 2nd edn. New York: Wiley.

Auer, Matthew R. 1998. "Agency Reform as Decision Process: The Reengineering of the Agency for International Development." *Policy Sciences* 31(2): 81–105.

Baland, Jean-Marie and Jean-Philippe Platteau. 1996. *Halting Degradation of Natural Resources: Is There a Role for Rural Communities?* Oxford, UK: Clarendon Press.

Bates, Robert H. 1981. *Markets and States in Tropical Africa: The Political Basis of Agricultural Policies*. Berkeley, CA: University of California Press.

—— 1998. "Institutions as Investments." In *The Political Dimension of Economic Growth*, eds. Silvio Borner and Michael Paldham, 272–87. New York: Macmillan.

Bauer, Peter T. 1971. *The Economics of Under-Developed Countries*. New York: Cambridge University Press.

Baumgartner, Frank and Bryan D. Jones. 1993. *Agenda and Instability in American Politics*. Chicago, IL: University of Chicago Press.

Bell, Simon and Stephen Morse. 1999. *Sustainability Indicators: Measuring the Immeasurable*. London: Earthscan Publications.

Bickers, Kenneth N. and John T. Williams. 2001. *Public Policy Analysis: A Political Economy Approach*. Boston, MA: Houghton Mifflin.

Bigsten, Arne. 1999. "Can Aid Generate Growth in Africa?" In *Foreign Aid: New Perspectives*, ed. Kanhaya L. Gupta, 173–90. Boston, MA: Kluwer.

Blomstrom, Magnus and Mats Lundahl, eds. 1993. *Economic Crisis in Africa: Perspectives on Policy Responses*. New York: Routledge.

Boone, Peter. 1994. "The Impact of Foreign Aid on Savings and Growth." Working Paper. London: London School of Economics.

—— 1996. "Politics and the Effectiveness of Foreign Aid." *European Economic Review* 40: 289–329.

Bosc, Pierre-Marie and Ellen Hanak-Freud. 1995. *Agricultural Research and Innovation in Tropical Africa*. Paris: Centre de Coopération Internationale en Recherche Agronomique Pour le Développement.

Bossert, Thomas J. 1990. "Can They Get Along without Us? Sustainability of Donor-Supported Health Projects in Central America and Africa." *Social Science Medical* 30(9): 1,015–23.

Bossuyt, Jean, Tehri Lehtinen, Anne Simon, Geert Laporte, and Gwénäelle Corre. 2000. "Assessing Trends in EC Development Policy: An Independent Review of the European Commission's External Aid Reform Process." ECDPM (European Centre for Development Policy Management). Discussion paper 16. Maastricht: ECDPM.

Boyd, Robert and Peter J. Richerson. 1985. *Culture and the Evolutionary Process*. Chicago, IL: University of Chicago Press.

Bräutigam, Deborah. 2000. *Aid Dependence and Governance*. Stockholm: Almqvist & Wiksell International.

—— and Stephen Knack. 2004. "Foreign Aid, Institutions, and Governance in Sub-Saharan Africa." *Economic Development and Cultural Change* 52(2): 255–85.

Breton, Albert and Ronald Wintrobe. 1982. *The Logic of Bureaucratic Conduct: An Economic Analysis of Competition, Exchange, and Efficiency in Private and Public Organizations*. Cambridge, UK: Cambridge University Press.

Bromley, Daniel W., David Feeny, Margaret McKean, Pauline Peters, Jere Gilles, Ronald Oakerson, C. Ford Runge, and James Thomson, eds. 1992. *Making the Commons Work: Theory, Practice, and Policy*. San Francisco, CA: ICS Press.

Brunetti, Aymo and Beatrice Weder. 1994. "Political Credibility and Economic Growth in Less Developed Countries." *Constitutional Political Economy* 5(1): 23–43.

Buchanan, James M. 1977. "The Samaritan's Dilemma." In *Freedom in Constitutional Contract*, ed. James M. Buchanan, 169–80. College Station, TX: Texas A&M University Press.

—— and Gordon Tullock. 1962. *The Calculus of Consent: Logical Foundations of Constitutional Democracy*. Ann Arbor, MI: University of Michigan Press.

Bueno de Mesquita, Bruce and Hilton L. Root, eds. 2000. *Governing for Prosperity*. New Haven, CT: Yale University Press.

Burnside, Craig and David Dollar. 1997. "Aid Spurs Growth—in a Sound Policy Environment." *Finance & Development* 34(4) (December): 4–7.

—— and —— 2000a. "Aid, Growth, the Incentive Regime, and Poverty Reduction." In *The World Bank: Structure and Policies*, eds. Christopher L. Gilbert and David Vines, 210–27. Cambridge: Cambridge University Press.

—— and —— 2000b. "Aid, Policies, and Growth." *American Economic Review* 90(4): 847–68.

Camerer, Colin. 2003. *Behavioral Game Theory: Experiments in Strategic Interaction*. Princeton, NJ: Princeton University Press.

Campbell, Donald E. 1995. *Incentives: Motivations and the Economics of Information*. Cambridge, UK: Cambridge University Press.

Campos, Ed and Sanjay Pradhan. 1996. "Budgetary Institutions and Expenditure Outcomes: Binding Governments to Fiscal Performance." Policy Research Working Paper No. 1646. Washington, DC: World Bank.

Carlsson, Jerker, Gunnar Köhlin, and Anders Ekbom. 1994. *The Political Economy of Evaluation: International Aid Agencies and the Effectiveness of Aid*. London: Macmillan.

—— and Lennart Wohlgemuth, eds. 2000. *Learning and Development Co-Operation*. Stockholm: Almqvist & Wiksell International.

Cashel-Cordo, Peter and Steven Craig. 1990. "The Public Sector Impact of International Resource Transfers." *Journal of Development Economics* 32(1): 17–42.

Cassen, Robert. 1994. *Does Aid Work?* Oxford, UK: Clarendon.

Catterson, Julie and Claes Lindahl. 1999. *The Sustainability Enigma: Aid Dependency and the Phasing Out of Projects—The Case of Swedish Aid to Tanzania*. Stockholm: Almqvist and Wiksell International.

Cernea, Michael. 1987. "Farmer Organization and Institution Building for Sustainable Development." *Regional Development Dialog* 8(2): 1–24.

CFU (Conservation Farming Unit [Zambia]). 1997. *Proposal for Support to the ZNFU Conservation-Farming Unit from January 1998 to December 2000*. Lusaka, Zambia: ZNFU.

Chambers, Robert. 1988. *Managing Canal Irrigation: Practical Analysis from South Asia*. New York: Cambridge University Press.

Chenery, H. B. and A. M. Strout. 1966. "Foreign Assistance and Economic Development." *American Economic Review* 56(4) (September): 679–731.

Cohen, John M., Merilee S. Grindle, and S. Tjip Walker. 1985. "Foreign Aid and Conditions Precedent: Political and Bureaucratic Dimensions." *World Development* 13(12): 1211–30.

Collier, Paul. 1997. "The Failure of Conditionality." In *Perspectives on Aid and Development*, eds. Catherine Gwin and Joan Nelson, 51–77. Washington, DC: Overseas Development Council; Baltimore, MD: Johns Hopkins University Press.

—— 1999. "Consensus-Building, Knowledge, and Conditionality." Paper presented at the International Symposium on Global Finance and Development, Tokyo, Japan, March 1–2, 1999.

——, Patrick Guillaumont, Sylviane Guillaumont, and Jan Willem Gunning. 1997. "Redesigning Conditionality." *World Development* 25(9): 1,399–407.

Conroy, Czech, Abha Mishra, and Ajay Rai. 2000. "Learning from Self-Initiated Community Forest Management in Orissa, India." *Forests, Trees, and People* 42: 51–61.

Coolidge, Jacqueline and Susan Rose-Ackerman. 1997. "High-Level Rent Seeking and Corruption in African Regimes: Theory and Cases." Policy Research Working Paper No. 1780. Washington, DC: World Bank.

—— and —— 2000. "Kleptocracy and Reform in African Regimes: Theory and Examples." In *Corruption and Development in Africa*, eds. Kempe Hope, Sr. and Bornwell Chikulo, 57–86. New York: St. Martin's Press.

Cracknell, B. E. 2001. "Knowing is All: Or is it? Some Reflections on Why the Acquisition of Knowledge, Focusing Particularly on Evaluation Activities, Does Not Always Lead to Action." *Public Administration and Development* 21(5): 371–79.

Crawford, Sue E. S. and Elinor Ostrom. 2005. "A Grammar of Institutions." In *Understanding Institutional Diversity*, ed. Elinor Ostrom, 137–74. Princeton, NJ: Princeton University Press. Originally published in *American Political Science Review* 89(3) (1995): 582–600.

Cromwell, E. 1995. "Zambia: A Wind of Change in Expenditure Management?" In *Votes and Budgets: Comparative Studies in Accountable Governance in the South*, eds. John Healy and William Tordoff. New York: St. Martin's Press.

Cungu, Azeta and Johan F. M. Swinnen. 2003. "The Impact of Aid on Economic Growth in Transition Economies: An Empirical Study." Working Paper. Leuven, Belgium: Catholic University of Leuven, LICOS Centre for Transition Economies.

Debreu, G. 1951. "The Coefficient of Resource Utilization." *Econometrica* 19: 273–92.

Deininger, Klaus, Lyn Squire, and Swati Basu. 1998. "Does Economic Analysis Improve the Quality of Foreign Assistance?" *World Bank Economic Review* 12(3): 385–418.

de Soto, Hernando. 2000. *The Mystery of Capital: Why Capitalism Triumphs in the West and Fails Everywhere Else*. New York: Basic Books.

de Waal, Alex. 1997. *Famine Crimes: Politics & the Disaster Relief Industry in Africa*. London: African Rights & The International African Institute, in association with James Currey (Oxford) and Indiana University Press (Bloomington and Indianapolis).

Devarajan, Shantayanan, David Dollar, and Torgny Holmgren, eds. 2001. *Aid and Reform in Africa: A Report from Ten Countries*. Washington, DC: World Bank.

—— and Vinaya Swaroop. 1998. "The Implications of Foreign Aid Fungibility for Development Assistance." Policy Research Working Paper. Washington, DC: World Bank.

Development Today. 1994. "Sweden Over-rides OECD Aid Subsidy Regulations—Saves 2500 Jobs and SEK 1.2bn Power Project for ABB. OECD Secretary-General Regrets Decision." Vol. 4, No. 10, July 6.

Dietz, Thomas, Elinor Ostrom, and Paul Stern. 2003. "The Struggle to Govern the Commons." *Science* 302 (December 12): 1907–12.

Dobbs, Michael. 2001. "Aid Abroad is Business Back Home." *Washington Post*, January 26: A1.

Dollar, David and William Easterly. 1999. "The Search for the Key: Aid, Investment and Policies in Africa." Policy Research Working Paper 2070. Washington, DC: World Bank.

—— and Victoria Levin. 2004. "The Increasing Selectivity of Foreign Aid, 1984–2002." Washington, DC: Work Bank Policy Research Working Paper 3299.

—— and Jakob Svensson. 2000. "What Explains the Success or Failure of Structural Adjustment Programmes?" *Economic Journal* 110 (October): 894–917.

Drazen, Allan M. 1999. "What is Gained by Selectively Withholding Foreign Aid?" Working Paper. College Park, MD: University of Maryland.

Easterly, William. 1999. "The Ghost of Financing Gap: Testing the Growth Model Used in the International Financial Institutions." *Journal of Development Economics* 60: 423–38.

—— 2001. *The Elusive Quest for Growth: Economists' Misadventures in the Tropics*. Cambridge, MA: MIT Press.

—— 2002*a*. "The Cartel of Good Intentions: The Problem of Bureaucracy in Foreign Aid." *Policy Reform* 5(4): 223–50.

—— 2002*b*. "What Did Structural Adjustment Adjust?: The Association of Policies and Growth with Repeated IMF and World Bank Adjustment Loans." Working Paper No. 11. Washington, DC: Institute for International Economics, Center for Global Development.

—— 2003. "Can Foreign Aid Buy Growth?" *Journal of Economic Perspectives* 17(3) (Summer): 23–48.

ECAZ (Environment and Conservation Association of Zambia). 1999. *Evaluation and Impact Monitoring of Development and Adoption of CF Practices in Agro-Ecological Region I and II of Zambia*. Vol. 1. Lusaka, Zambia: USAID.

Edgren, Gus. 1995. "Indo-Swedish Development Cooperation: Objective, Issues and Achievements." In *Sharing Challenges: The Indo-Swedish Development Cooperation Programme*, ed. V. Sahai, 8–46. Stockholm: Ministry for Foreign Affairs.

Eggertsson, Thráinn. 1990. *Economic Behavior and Institutions*. New York: Cambridge University Press.

—— 2005. *Imperfect Institutions: Possibilities and Limits of Reform*. Ann Arbor: University of Michigan Press.

Elgström, Ole. 1992. *Foreign Aid Negotiations*. Aldershot, England: Avebury.

Ellis, Peter and Cameran Hill. 2003. *Review of Incentives and the Australian Aid Program*. Evaluation and Review Series No. 32. Canberra, Australia: Australian Agency for International Development.

Embassy of Sweden. 2000. "Strategy for Sweden's Support to Democratic Governance in Zambia 2000–2002." Lusaka: Embassy of Sweden.

Epstein, T. Scarlett. 1988. "Macro-Planning Versus Micro-Needs." In *The Hidden Crisis in Development: Development Bureaucracies*, eds. Philip Quarles van Ufford, Dirk Kruijt, and Theodore Downing, 195–210. Tokyo: United Nations University Press.

Erikson, J. et al. 1995. *Hifadhi Ardhi Dodoma (HADO) Regional Soil Conservation Project— Report by a SIDA and GoT Mission*. Stockholm: Sida.

Eriksson Skoog, Gun. 2000. *The Soft Budget Constraint: The Emergence, Persistence and Logic of an Institution*. Dordrecht, the Netherlands: Kluwer.

Feyzioglu, Tarhan, Vinaya Swaroop, and Min Zhu. 1998. "A Panel Data Analysis of the Fungibility of Foreign Aid." *World Bank Economic Review* 12(1): 29–58.

Fisher, Ian. 2001. "Can International Relief Do More Good than Harm?" *The New York Times Magazine*, February 11, 2001, pp. 72–77.

Folke, Sten. 1998. "Swedish Development Cooperation with India—In a Poverty Reduction Perspective." CDR Working Paper 98.1. Copenhagen: Center for Development Research.

Forss, Kim, Lars Bjern, Jerker Carlsson, and Tove Strömberg. 1996. "A Review of the Programme for Technical Cooperation; Organization, Implementation, and Results." Consultant's report for a study commissioned by Sida, February 15, 1996. Stockholm: Sida.

Frey, Bruno. 1997. *Not Just for the Money: An Economic Theory of Personal Motivation*. Cheltenham, UK: Edward Elgar.

Gardner, Roy. 2004. *Games for Business and Economics*. 2nd edn. New York: Wiley.

GART (Golden Valley Agricultural Research Trust). 2000. *Golden Valley Agricultural Research Trust's 2000 Yearbook*. Lusaka, Zambia: GART.

Geddes, Barbara. 1994. *Politician's Dilemma: Building State Capacity in Latin America*. Berkeley, CA: University of California Press.

Gibson, Clark C. 1999. *Politicians and Poachers: The Political Economy of Wildlife Policy in Africa*. New York: Cambridge University Press.

—— and Matthew Hoffmann. 2005. "Making Democrats of Dictators: Foreign Aid and Africa's Political Liberalization." Working Paper. San Diego, CA: University of California.

—— and Fabrice Lehoucq. 2000. "Linking National and Local Level Politics: Deforestation in Guatemala." Working Paper. Bloomington: Indiana University, Workshop in Political Theory and Policy Analysis.

——, Margaret McKean, and Elinor Ostrom, eds. 2000. *People and Forests: Communities, Institutions, and Governance*. Cambridge, MA: MIT Press.

Gilbert, Christopher C., Andrew Powell, and David Vines. 1999. "Positioning the World Bank." *Economic Journal* 109(459): 598–633.

Goldsmith, Arthur A. 2001. "Foreign Aid and Statehood in Africa." *International Organization* 55(1): 123–48.

Gordillo, Gustavo and Krister Andersson. 2004. "From Policy Lessons to Policy Actions: Motivation to Take Evaluation Seriously." *Public Administration and Development* 24: 305–20.

Government of France. 2002. *La Biodiversité et nous, dix ans après Rio* (Biodiversity and Us: Ten Years after Rio). Paris: Ministry of Foreign Affairs.

Government of Japan. 2002. "Environmental Conservation Initiative for Sustainable Development." <http://mofa.go.jp/policy/environment/wssd/2002/kinitiative3-2.html>.

Government of Sweden. 1982. *Lagen om Anstäellningskydd*. Stockholm: Sveriges Riksdag.

Grant, Ruth W. and Robert O. Keohane. 2005. "Accountability and Abuses of Power in World Politics." *American Political Science Review* 99(1): 29–43.

Grindle, Merilee S., ed. 1997. *Getting Good Government: Capacity Building in the Public Sectors of Developing Countries*. Boston, MA: Harvard University Press.

Grossman, Sanford and Oliver Hart. 1986. "The Costs and Benefits of Ownership: A Theory of Vertical and Lateral Integration." *Journal of Political Economy* 94: 691–719.

Güth, Werner. 1995. "An Evolutionary Approach to Explaining Cooperative Behavior by Reciprocal Incentives." *International Journal of Game Theory* 24: 323–44.

Hammerstein, Peter. 2003. *Genetic and Cultural Evolution of Cooperation*. Cambridge, MA: MIT Press.

Hancock, Graham. 1989. *Lords of Poverty: The Power, Prestige, and Corruption of the International Aid Business*. New York: Atlantic Monthly Press.

Hansen, Henrik and Finn Tarp. 2000. "Aid Effectiveness Disputed." *Journal of International Development* 13(3) (April): 375–98.

—— and —— 2001. "Aid and Growth Regressions." *Journal of Development Economics* 64(2): 547–70.

Hardin, Garrett. 1968. "The Tragedy of the Commons." *Science* 162: 1,243–48.

Hayek, Friedrich A. von. 1948. *Individualism and Economic Order*. Chicago, IL: University of Chicago Press.

—— 1952. "Scientism and the Study of Society." In *Essays on Hayek*, ed. Fritz Machlup. New York: New York University Press.

Hayter, Teresa and Catherine Watson. 1985. *Aid Rhetoric and Reality*. London: Pluto Press.

Hermes, Niels and Robert Lensink, eds. 1999. *Financial Development and Economic Growth: Theory and Experiences from Developing Countries*. Oxford, UK: Routledge.

Herr, Andrew, Roy Gardner, and James M. Walker. 1997. "An Experimental Study of Time-Independent and Time-Dependent Externalities in the Commons." *Games and Economic Behavior* 19: 77–96.

HIID (Harvard Institute for International Development and World Economic Forum). 1999. *World Competitiveness Report*. New York: Oxford University Press.

Hilton, Rita M. 2002. "Institutional Incentives for Resource Mobilization in Farmer-Managed and Agency-Managed Irrigation Systems." In *Improving Irrigation Governance and Management in Nepal*, eds. Ganesh P. Shivakoti and Elinor Ostrom, 150–76. Oakland, CA: ICS Press.

Hodgson, Geoffrey. 2004. "What are Institutions?" Working Paper. Hertfordshire, UK: University of Hertfordshire, The Business School.

Holmstrom, Bengt. 1982*a*. "Managerial Incentive Problems: A Dynamic Perspective." *Essays in Economics and Management in Honor of Lars Wahlbeck*. Helsinki: Swedish School of Economics.

—— 1982*b*. "Moral Hazard in Teams." *Bell Journal of Economics* 13 (Autumn): 324–40.

—— and Paul R. Milgrom. 1991. "Multi-Task Principal Agent Analyses: Incentive Contracts, Asset Ownership and Job Design." *Journal of Law Economics and Organization* 7 (Spring): 24–52.

Huntington, Samuel P. and Myron Weiner, eds. 1987. *Understanding Political Development*. Boston, MA: Little, Brown.

Hyden, Goran. 1990. "Reciprocity and Governance in Africa." In *The Failure of the Centralized State: Institutions and Self-Governance in Africa*, eds. James Wunsch and Dele Olowu, 245–69. Boulder, CO: Westview Press.

IIED (International Institute for Environment and Development). 1994. "Swedish Aid and UNCED: Case Study of India and Zambia." London: IIED.

Isaac, R. Mark and James M. Walker. 1988. "Communication and Free-Riding Behavior: The Voluntary Contribution Mechanism." *Economic Inquiry* 26: 585–608.

Jepma, Catrinus J. 1991. "The Tying of Aid." Paris, France: Development Center Studies, Development Center of the Organization for Economic Co-operation and Development.

JICA (Japan International Cooperation Agency). 2001. *The Second Study on Development Assistance for the Environment: Practical Approaches towards Environmental Challenges*. Tokyo: Japan International Cooperation Agency.

Johnson, John H. and Sulaiman S. Wasty. 1993. "Borrower Ownership of Adjustment Programs and the Political Economy of Reform." Discussion Paper No. 199. Washington, DC: World Bank.

Jones, James C. 1997. "Development: Reflections from Bolivia." *Human Organization* 56(1): 111–20.

Jones, Philip R. 1995. "Rents from In-kind Subsidy: 'Charity' in the Public Sector." *Public Choice* 86: 359–78.

Joseph, Richard. 1987. *Democracy and Prebendal Politics in Nigeria: The Rise and Fall of the Second Republic*. Cambridge, UK: Cambridge University Press.

Kanbur, Ravi and Todd Sandler with Kevin Morrison. 1999. *The Future of Development Assistance: Common Pools and International Public Goods*. Policy Essay No. 25. Washington, DC: Overseas Development Council.

Kant, S., N. M. Singh, and K. K. Singh. 1991. *Community Based Forest Management System (Case Studies from Orissa)*. Bhopal and New Delhi: IIFM, SIDA, and Swedforest.

Keen, David. 1994. *The Benefits of Famine: A Political Economy of Famine and Relief in Southwestern Sudan, 1983–1989*. Princeton, NJ: Princeton University Press.

Killick, Tony, Ramana Gunatilaka, and Ana Mar. 1998. *Aid and the Political Economy of Policy Change*. London and New York: Routledge Press.

Kiser, Larry and Elinor Ostrom. 1982. "The Three Worlds of Action: A Metatheoretical Synthesis of Institutional Approaches." In *Strategies of Political Inquiry*, ed. Elinor Ostrom, 179–222. Beverly Hills, CA: Sage.

Klitgaard, Robert. 1988. *Controlling Corruption*. Berkeley, CA: University of California Press.
—— 1995. "National and International Strategies for Reducing Corruption." Paper presented at AECD International Symposium on Corruption and Good Governance, Paris, March 13 and 14.
Knack, Stephen and Aminur Rahman. 2004. "Donor Fragmentation and Bureaucratic Quality in Aid Recipients." Washington, DC: World Bank Policy Research Working Paper No. 3186.
Knight, Jack. 1992. *Institutions and Social Conflict*. Cambridge: Cambridge University Press.
Kosack, Stephan. 2003. "Effective Aid: How Democracy Allows Development Aid to Improve the Quality of Life." *World Development* 31(1): 1–22.
Kreps, David M. 1990. "Corporate Culture and Economic Theory." In *Perspective on Positive Political Economy*, eds. James E. Alt and Kenneth A. Shepsle, 90–143. New York: Cambridge University Press.
Krueger, Anne O. 1993. *Political Economy of Policy Reform in Developing Countries*. Cambridge, MA: MIT Press.
——, Constantine Michalopoulos, and Vernon Ruttan, eds. 1989. *Aid and Development*. Baltimore, MD: Johns Hopkins University Press.
Kuhnert, Stephan. 2001. "An Evolutionary Theory of Collective Action: Schumpeterian Entrepreneurship for the Common Good." *Constitutional Political Economy* 12: 13–29.
Kumar, Neeraj. 2000. "All is Not Green with JFM in India." *Forests, Trees and People Newsletter* 42: 46–50.
Lachmann, Ludwig. 1971. *The Legacy of Max Weber*. Berkeley: University of California Press.
—— 1978. *Capital and Its Structure*. Kansas City, MO: Sheed, Andrews, and McMeel, Inc.
Laffont, Jean-Jacque and Jean Tirole. 1993. *A Theory of Incentives in Procurement and Regulation*. Cambridge, MA: MIT Press.
Lam, Wai Fung. 1998. *Governing Irrigation Systems in Nepal*. San Francisco, CA: ICS Press.
—— Forthcoming. "Reforming Taiwan's Irrigation Associations: Getting the Nesting of Institutions Right." In *Asian Irrigation in Transition: Responding to Challenges*, eds. Ganesh Shivakoti, Douglas Vermillion, Wai Fung Lam, Elinor Ostrom, Ujjwal Pradhan, and Robert Yoder. New Delhi, India: Sage.
Lancaster, Carol. 1999*a*. *Aid to Africa*. Chicago, IL: University of Chicago Press.
—— 1999*b*. "Aid Effectiveness in Africa: The Unfinished Agenda." *Journal of African Economies* 8(4): 487–503.
Larson, B. A. and Daniel W. Bromley. 1990. "Property Rights, Externalities, and Resource Degradation: Locating the Tragedy." *Journal of Development Economics* 33(2) (October): 235–62.
Lasswell, Harold D. 1971. *A Pre-View of Policy Sciences*. New York: American Elsevier.
Lavergne, Réal P. 1988. "The Management of Canadian Foreign Aid: Structure, Objectives, and Constraints." In *The Hidden Crisis in Development: Development Bureaucracies*, eds. Philip Quarles van Ufford, Dirk Kruijt, and Theodore Downing, 57–74. Tokyo: United Nations University Press.
Lensink, Robert and Howard White. 1999. "Aid Dependence Issues and Indicators." EGDI Study 1999: 2. Stockholm: Ministry for Foreign Affairs, EGDI (Expert Group on Development Issues).
Levy, Victor. 1987. "Anticipated Development Assistance, Temporary Relief Aid, and Consumption Behavior of Low-Income Countries." *The Economic Journal* 97(386): 446–58.
Lindahl, Claes, Elin Björkman, Petra Stark, Sundeep Waslekar, and Kjell Öström. 1999. "Managing the NGO Partnership: An Assessment of Stakeholder Responses to an Evaluation of Development Assistance through Swedish NGOs." Sida Studies in Evaluation 99/4. Stockholm: Sida.

Lipton, Michael. 1993. " 'Urban Bias': Of Consequences, Classes and Causality." *Journal of Development Studies* 29: 229–41.

Lumsdaine, David H. 1997. *Moral Vision in International Politics*. Princeton, NJ: Princeton University Press.

MacRae, Joanna and Anthony B. Zwi with Mark Duffield and Hugo Slim, eds. 1994. *War and Hunger: Rethinking International Responses to Complex Emergencies*. London and New Jersey: Zed Books, in association with Save the Children Fund (UK).

Maipose, Gervase, Gloria Somolekae, and Timothy Johnston. 1997. "Effective Aid Management: The Case of Botswana." In *Foreign Aid in Africa: Learning from Country Experiences*, eds. Jerker Carlsson, Gloria Somolekae, and Nicolas van de Walle, 16–35. Uppsala: Nordic Africa Institute.

Mansuri, Ghazala and Vijayendra Rao. 2003. "Evaluating Community Driven Development: A Review of the Evidence." Washington, DC: World Bank, Development Research Group.

Maren, Michael. 1997. *The Road to Hell: The Ravaging Effects of Foreign Aid and International Charity*. New York: Free Press.

Markusen, James R. and Thomas Rutherford. 2002. "Developing Domestic Entrepreneurship and Growth through Imported Expertise." Frederiksberg, Denmark: Centre for Economic and Business Research (CEBR) Discussion Paper, CEBR DP 2002–12.

Martens, Bertin. 2000. "The Institutional Economics of Foreign Aid. How Donor Country Aid Institutions, Rather than Beneficiary Country Policies, Affect the Performance of Foreign Aid Programmes." Paper presented at the Annual Conference of the International Society for New Institution Economics (ISNIE), Tübingen, Germany, 22–24 September.

—— 2002. "Introduction." In *The Institutional Economics of Foreign Aid*, eds. Bertin Martens, Uwe Mummert, Peter Murrell, and Paul Seabright. Cambridge, UK: Cambridge University Press.

——, Uwe Mummert, Peter Murrell, and Paul Seabright. 2002. *The Institutional Economics of Foreign Aid*. Cambridge, UK: Cambridge University Press.

Mayhew, David. 1986. *Congress: The Electoral Connection*. New Haven, CT: Yale University Press.

McCay, Bonnie J. and James Acheson, eds. 1987. *The Question of the Commons: The Culture and Ecology of Communal Resources*. Tucson: University of Arizona Press.

McGinnis, Michael D., ed. 1999a. *Polycentric Governance and Development: Readings from the Workshop in Political Theory and Policy Analysis*. Ann Arbor, MI: University of Michigan Press.

——, ed. 1999b. *Polycentricity and Local Public Economies: Readings from the Workshop in Political Theory and Policy Analysis*. Ann Arbor, MI: University of Michigan Press.

—— 1999c. "Conflict Dynamics in a Three-Level Game: Local, National, and International Conflict in the Horn of Africa." Presented at the 33rd North American meeting of Peace Science Society (International), University of Michigan, Ann Arbor, October 8–10, 1999.

—— 2000. *Polycentric Games and Institutions: Readings from the Workshop in Political Theory and Policy Analysis*. Ann Arbor, MI: University of Michigan Press.

McGuire, Martin and Mancur Olson. 1996. "The Economics of Autocracy and Majority Rule: The Invisible Hand and the Use of Force." *Journal of Economic Literature* 34: 72–96.

MFA (Ministry for Foreign Affairs). 1999. *Zambia Country Strategy for January 1999–December 2001*. Stockholm: Regeringskansliet.

Milgrom, Paul and John Roberts. 1992. *Economics, Organization and Management*. Englewood Cliffs, NJ: Prentice Hall.

Miller, Gary. 1992. *Managerial Dilemmas: The Political Economy of Hierarchy*. New York: Cambridge University Press.

Moe, Terry M. 1984. "The New Economics of Organization." *American Journal of Political Science* 28(4): 739–77.

—— 1990*a*. "Political Institutions: The Neglected Side of the Story." *Journal of Law, Economics, and Organization* 6: 213–66.

—— 1990*b*. "The Politics of Structural Choice: Toward a Theory of Public Bureaucracy." In *Organizational Theory from Chester Bernard to the Present*, ed. Oliver Williamson, 116–53. Oxford, UK: Oxford University Press.

Mohiddin, Ahmed. 1998. "Towards a New Partnership: Assessment of Government Performance." ECDPM Working Paper No. 55. Maastricht, The Netherlands: ECDPM (European Centre for Development Policy Management).

Monbiot, George. 2004. "On the Edge of Lunacy." *The Guardian*, January 6: 23.

Monroe, Burt. Forthcoming. *Electoral Systems in Theory and Practice: Toward an Empirically Relevant Theory of Social Choice*. Ann Arbor, MI: University of Michigan Press.

Moore, Mick. 1998. "Death Without Taxes: Democracy, State Capacity, and Aid Dependence in the Fourth World." In *Towards a Democratic Developmental State*, eds. G. White and M. Robinson. Oxford: Oxford University Press.

Morss, Elliott R. 1984. "Institutional Destruction Resulting from Donor and Project Proliferation in Sub-Saharan African Countries." *World Development* 12(4): 465–70.

Mothander, Bjorn and Pia Sassarsson. 1992. "The Forestry Coordination Programme." Consultant's Report. Stockholm: Sida.

Mule, Harris. 1996. "Partnership for Capacity Building in Africa. A Report of the Working Party on the Impact of Bank Policies, Instruments and Operational Practices on Capacity Building in Africa." Washington, DC: World Bank.

Murrell, Peter. 1999. "The Interactions of Donors, Contractors, and Recipients in Aid Projects: Improving the Effectiveness of Contracting and Project Evaluation." Working Paper. College Park, MD: University of Maryland, IRIS Center.

Mwanawina, Inyambo and Howard White. 1995. "Swedish Balance of Payments Support to Zambia: Final Report." Mimeo.

Narayan, Deepa. 2000. *Voices of the Poor: Can Anyone Hear Us?* London: Oxford University Press for the World Bank.

Ngaido, Tidiane and Michael Kirk. 2001. "Collective Action, Property Rights and Devolution of Rangeland Management: Selected Examples from Africa and Asia." In *Collective Action, Property Rights and Devolution of Natural Resource Management*, eds. Ruth Meinzen-Dick, Anna Knox, and Monica Di Gregorio. Feldafing, Germany: Deutsche Stiftung für Ernährun and Landwirtschaft.

NORAD (Norwegian Agency for Development Cooperation). 2000. *Corruption—A Selected and Annotated Bibliography*. Oslo: NORAD.

North, Douglass C. 1990. *Institutions, Institutional Change, and Economic Performance*. New York: Cambridge University Press.

—— 1994. "Economic Performance Through Time." *American Economics Review* 84: 359–68.

—— 2005. *Understanding the Process of Economic Change*. Princeton, NJ: Princeton University Press.

Norton, Andrew and Bella Bird. 1999. "Social Development Issues in Sector Wide Approaches." DFID Social Development Working Paper No. 1. London: DFID.

Oakerson, Ronald J. 1992. "Analyzing the Commons: A Framework." In *Making the Commons Work: Theory, Practice, and Policy*, eds. Daniel W. Bromley *et al.*, 41–59. San Francisco, CA: ICS Press.

—— 1993. "Reciprocity: A Bottom-Up View of Political Development." In *Rethinking Institutional Analysis and Development: Issues, Alternatives, and Choices*, eds. Vincent Ostrom, David Feeny, and Hartmut Picht, 141–58. San Francisco, CA: ICS Press.

ODI/ECDPM (Overseas Development Institute/European Centre for Development Policy Management). 1995. *Study of European Union Aid Agencies: Comparative Management and Effectiveness*. Project Summary, December.

OECD (Organisation for Economic Co-operation and Development). 1992. *DAC Principles for Effective Aid*. Paris: OECD, Development Assistance Committee.

—— 1996. *Ex Ante Guidance for Tied Aid*. Paris: OECD/GD (96)180.

—— 2002. *Working Together Towards Sustainable Development: The OECD Experience*. Paris: OECD Policy Brief, July.

Olsen, Gorm Rye and Lars Udsholt. 1995. "The Danish Aid Administration: Between Politics and Technical Rationality." Working Paper 95.12. Denmark: Center for Development Research.

Olson, Mancur. 1965. *The Logic of Collective Action*. Cambridge, MA: Harvard University Press.

Öståker, Emma. 1994. "Swedish Development Assistance to Zambia." SASDA Working Paper No. 8. Stockholm: SAU/SASDA (Secretariat for the Analysis of Swedish Development Assistance).

Ostrom, Elinor. 1990. *Governing the Commons: The Evolution of Institutions for Collective Action*. New York: Cambridge University Press.

—— 1996. "Incentives, Rules of the Game, and Development." In *Proceedings of the Annual World Bank Conference on Development Economics 1995*, 207–34. Washington, DC: The World Bank.

—— 1999. "Social Capital: A Fad or a Fundamental Concept?" In *Social Capital: A Multifaceted Perspective*, eds. Partha Dasgupta and Ismail Seraeldin, 172–214. Washington, DC: World Bank.

—— 2000. "Collective Action and the Evolution of Social Norms." *Journal of Economic Perspectives* 14(3) (Summer): 137–58.

—— 2005. *Understanding Institutional Diversity*. Princeton, NJ: Princeton University Press.

—— and Roy Gardner. 1993. "Coping with Asymmetries in the Commons: Self-Governing Irrigation Systems Can Work." *Journal of Economic Perspectives* 7(4) (Fall): 93–112.

——, Clark Gibson, Sujai Shivakumar, and Krister Andersson. 2002. *Aid, Incentives, and Sustainability: An Institutional Analysis of Development Cooperation. MAIN REPORT*. Sida Studies in Evaluation No. 02/01. Stockholm: Sida.

——, Larry Schroeder, and Susan Wynne. 1993. *Institutional Incentives and Sustainable Development: Infrastructure Policies in Perspective*. Boulder, CO: Westview Press.

——, Roy Gardner, and James M. Walker. 1994. *Rules, Games, and Common-Pool Resources*. Ann Arbor, MI: University of Michigan Press.

——, Wai Fung Lam, and Myungsuk Lee. 1994. "The Performance of Self-Governing Irrigation Systems in Nepal." *Human Systems Management* 13(3): 197–207.

Ostrom, Vincent. 1986. "A Fallabilist's Approach to Norms and Criteria of Choice." In *Guidance, Control, and Evaluation in the Public Sector*, eds. Franz-Xaver Kaufmann, Giandomenico Majone, and Vincent Ostrom, 229–49. Berlin and New York: Walter de Gruyter.

—— 1987. *The Political Theory of a Compound Republic: Designing the American Experiment*. 2nd edn. Lincoln: University of Nebraska Press.

—— 1997. *The Meaning of Democracy and the Vulnerability of Democracies: A Response to Tocqueville's Challenge*. Ann Arbor, MI: University of Michigan Press.

—— 1999. "Cryptoimperialism, Predatory States, and Self-Governance." In *Polycentric Governance and Development: Readings from the Workshop in Political Theory and Policy Analysis*, ed. Michael McGinnis, 166–85. Ann Arbor, MI: University of Michigan Press.

——, David Feeny, and Hartmut Picht, eds. 1993. *Rethinking Institutional Analysis and Development*. San Francisco, CA: ICS Press.

Pack, Howard and Janet Rothenberg Pack. 1990. "Is Foreign Aid Fungible? The Case of Indonesia." *Economic Journal* 100(399) (March): 188–94.

—— and —— 1993. "Foreign Aid and the Question of Fungibility." *Review of Economics and Statistics* 75(2) (May): 258–65.

Pal, Sarthak K. 2000. "Community Based Forest Management (CFM) in Orissa; A New Way Forward." *Forests, Trees, and People* 42: 62–8.

Pedersen, Karl R. 1996. "Aid, Investment and Incentives." *Scandinavian Journal of Economics* 98(3): 423–38.

—— 1998. "Incentives and Aid Dependence." EGDI Working Paper 1998: 1. Stockholm: Ministry for Foreign Affairs.

Picciotto, R. 2003. "The Logic of Mainstreaming: A Development Evaluation Perspective." *Evaluation* 8(3): 322–39.

Platteau, Jean-Philippe. 2003. "Community Based Development in the Context of Within Group Heterogeneity." Paper presented at the Annual Bank Conference on Development Economics, Bangalore, India.

Prebisch, Raul. 1970. *Change and Development: Latin America's Great Task*. Washington, DC: Inter-American Development Bank.

Pritchett, Lant and Michael Woolcock. 2004. "Solutions When the Solution is the Problem: Arraying the Disarray in Development." *World Development* 32(2): 191–212.

Putzel, James. 1998. "The Business of Aid: Transparency and Accountability in European Union Development Assistance." *Journal of Development Studies* 34(3): 71–96.

Quarles van Ufford, Philip. 1988. "Development Bureaucracies in between Intentions and Outcomes." In *The Hidden Crisis in Development: Development Bureaucracies*, eds. Philip Q. van Ufford, Dirk Kruijt, and Theodore Downing, 9–38. Tokyo: United Nations University Press.

——, Dirk Kruijt, and Theodore Downing. 1988. *The Hidden Crisis in Development: Development Bureaucracies*. Tokyo: United Nations University Press.

Rakner, L. 1998. "Reform as a Matter of Political Survival: Political and Economic Liberalisation in Zambia 1991–1996." Ph.D. dissertation. Bergen, Norway: University of Bergen.

Rasmusen, Eric. 1989. *Games and Information: An Introduction to Game Theory*. Oxford: Basil Blackwell.

Remmer, Karen L. 2004. "Does Foreign Aid Promote the Expansion of Government?" *American Journal of Political Science* 48(1): 76–91.

Riker, William H. 1982. *Liberalism Against Populism: A Confrontation between the Theory of Democracy and the Theory of Social Choice*. San Francisco, CA: W. H. Freeman.

Roberts, John. 1979. "Incentives in Planning Procedures for the Provision of Public Goods." *Review of Economic Studies* 46: 283–92.

Robinson, James A. 2003. "Politician-Proof Policy?" Working Paper. Washington, DC: World Bank.

Rogers, A., A. Chadwick, and K. Oglesby. 1997. *TANDEM Project with the Folk Development Colleges in Tanzania 1990 to 1996*. Stockholm: Sida Evaluation 97/22.

Romer, Thomas and Howard Rosenthal. 1978. "Political Resource Allocation, Controlled Agendas, and the Status Quo." *Public Choice* 33(4): 27–43.

Rostow, Walt W. 1960. *The Stages of Economic Growth: A Non-Communist Manifesto*. London: Cambridge University Press.

Saasa, Oliver and Jerker Carlsson. 1996. *The Aid Relationship in Zambia: A Conflict Scenario*. Lusaka: Institute for African Studies; and Uppsala, Sweden: The Nordic Africa Institute.

Sachs, Jeffrey. 2004. "How to Halve World Poverty." *The Economist—The World in 2005*, November, p. 96.

Salanié, Bernard. 1997. *The Economics of Contracts: A Primer*. Cambridge, MA: MIT Press.

Salmi, Jyrki. 1996. "Economics of Sustainability: Neo-Classical Viewpoint." Helsinki: Department of Economics, University of Helsinki. Unpublished ms.

Sandler, Todd. 2004. *Global Collective Action*. New York: Cambridge University Press.

Saxena, Naresh C. 1995. "Policies, Realities and the Ability to Change." *Sharing Challenges, The Indo-Swedish Development Cooperation Programme*. Stockholm: Ministry for Foreign Affairs.

—— 1999. "Forest Policy and the Rural Poor in Orissa." Unpublished manuscript. New Delhi: National Planning Commission.

Schedvin, True. 2001. "Contract Financed Technical Cooperation (KTS)—A Background Paper." Sida/UTV document. Stockholm: Sida.

Schlager, Edella and Elinor Ostrom. 1992. "Property-Rights Regimes and Natural Resources: A Conceptual Analysis." *Land Economics* 68(3) (August): 249–62.

Schmidtchen, Dieter. 2002. "To Help or Not to Help: The Samaritan's Dilemma Revisited." In *Method and Morals in Constitutional Economics: Essays in Honor of James M. Buchanan*, eds. Geoffrey Brennan, Hartmut Kliemt, and Robert D. Tollison, 470–84. Berlin: Springer-Verlag.

Schraeder, Peter, Steven Hook, and Bruce Taylor. 1998. "Clarifying the Foreign Aid Puzzle: A Comparison of American, Japanese, French, and Swedish Aid Flows." *World Politics* 50(2): 294–320.

Scott, James C. 1998. *Seeing Like a State: How Certain Schemes to Improve the Human Condition Have Failed*. New Haven, CT: Yale University Press.

Seabright, Paul. 2002. "Conflicts of Objectives and Task Allocation in Aid Agencies." In *The Institutional Economics of Foreign Aid*, eds. Bertin Martens, Uwe Mummert, Peter Murrell, and Paul Seabright. Cambridge: Cambridge University Press.

Shepsle, Kenneth A. 1979. "The Role of Institutional Structure in the Creation of Policy Equilibrium." In *Public Policy and Public Choice*, eds. Douglas W. Rae and Theodore J. Eismeier, 249–83. Sage Yearbooks in Politics and Public Policy, Vol. 6. Beverly Hills, CA: Sage.

Shivakoti, Ganesh, George Varughese, Elinor Ostrom, Ashutosh Shukla, and Ganesh Thapa, eds. 1997. *People and Participation in Sustainable Development: Understanding the Dynamics of Natural Resource Systems*. Proceedings of an international conference held at the Institute of Agriculture and Animal Science, Rampur, Chitwan, Nepal, March 17–21, 1996. Bloomington: Indiana University, Workshop in Political Theory and Policy Analysis; Rampur, Nepal: Tribhuvan University, Institute of Agriculture and Animal Science.

Shivakumar, Sujai J. 2003. "The Place of Indigenous Institutions in Constitutional Order." *Constitutional Political Economy* 14: 3–21.

—— 2005. *The Constitution of Development: Crafting Capabilities for Self-Governance*. New York: Palgrave Macmillan.

Shleifer, Andrei and Robert W. Vishny. 1998. *The Grabbing Hand. Government Pathologies and Their Cures*. Cambridge, MA: Harvard University Press.

Sida. 1989. *Rollutredningen*. Stockholm: Sida.

—— 1996a. *Aid Dependency: Causes, Symptoms, and Remedies: Project 2015*. Stockholm: Sida.

—— 1996b. *Bistånd på Kredit*. Stockholm: Sida.

—— 1996c. *Landstrategi Indien*. Stockholm: Sida.

—— 1997a. *Development Cooperation in the 21st Century*. Stockholm: Sida.

—— 1997b. *Sida Looks Forward*. Stockholm: Sida.

—— 1997c. *Sida at Work: Sida's Methods for Development Cooperation*. Stockholm: Sida.

—— 1997d. *Using the Evaluations Tool*. Sida Studies in Evaluation 97/1. Stockholm: Sida.

Sida. 1997e. *Swedish Humanitarian Assistance—Annual Report 1997*. Stockholm: Sida.

———1998. *Bedömningspromemoria 1998–03–26: Stöd till uthålligt Naturbruk i Zambia 1998–2000*. Stockholm: Sida.

———1999a. *Are Evaluations Useful? Cases from Swedish Development Cooperation*. Sida Studies in Evaluation 99/1. Stockholm: Sida.

———1999b. *Dollars, Dialogue, and Development: An Evaluation of Swedish Program Aid*. Stockholm: Sida.

———1999c. *Human Resources Report: Annual Report 1999 of the Department of Personnel and Organisation Development*. Stockholm: Sida.

———1999d. *Sida: Developmental Humanitarian Assistance: Ten Emerging Examples*. Stockholm: Sida.

———1999e. "Financing of Infrastructure—Guarantees." Sida/Inec document. Stockholm: Sida.

———2001. *Sida's Organisationsmätning 2000*. Stockholm: Sida.

Simon, Herbert A. 1965. *Administrative Behavior: A Study of Decision-Making Processes in Administrative Organization*. New York: Free Press. Originally published in 1947.

———1972. "Theories of Bounded Rationality." In *Decision and Organization: A Volume in Honor of Jacob Marschak*, eds. C. B. McGuire and Roy Radner, 161–76. Amsterdam: North Holland.

———1985. "Human Nature in Politics: The Dialogue of Psychology with Political Science." *American Political Science Review* 79 (June): 293–94.

———1997. *Models of Bounded Rationality: Empirically Grounded Economic Reason*. Cambridge, MA: MIT Press.

Smith, Alan. 1994. "Incentives in Community Forestry Projects: A Help or Hindrance?" ODI Rural Development Network Paper 17c. London: Overseas Development Institute.

Sowerwine, Jennifer, Ganesh Shivakoti, Ujjwal Pradhan, Ashutosh Shukla, and Elinor Ostrom, eds. 1994. *From Farmers' Fields to Data Fields and Back: A Synthesis of Participatory Information Systems for Irrigation and Other Resources*. Proceedings of an International Workshop held at the Institute of Agriculture and Animal Science (IAAS), Rampur, Nepal, March 21–26, 1993. Colombo, Sri Lanka: International Irrigation Management Institute (IIMI), and Rampur, Nepal: IAAS.

Spence, A. Michael. 1973. *Market Signalling: Information Transfer in Hiring and Related Processes*. Cambridge, MA: Harvard University Press.

Spiller, Pablo T. and Mariano Tommasi. 2004. "The Institutional Foundations of Public Policy: A Transactions Approach with Application to Argentina." Working Paper. Berkeley, CA: Department of Economics.

Stein, Robert M. and Kenneth Bickers. 1995. *Perpetuating the Pork Barrel: Policy Subsystems and American Democracy*. New York: Cambridge University Press.

Sterkenburg, Jan and Arie van der Wiel, eds. 1999. "Area Development: Experiences with Netherlands Aid in Africa." Focus on development No. 10. The Hague, Netherlands: Ministry of Foreign Affairs.

Stiglitz, Joseph. 1997. "Can Aid Facilitate Development? A New Vision for Development Cooperation in the 21st Century." Public lecture, Tokyo, Japan, September 17, 1997.

Stone, Randall W. 2004. "The Political Economy of IMF Lending in Africa." *American Political Science Review* 98(4): 577–92.

Sundar, Nandini. 2000. "Unpacking the 'Joint' in Joint Forest Management." *Development and Change* 31: 255–79.

Svensson, Jakob. 2000a. "Foreign Aid and Rent-Seeking." *Journal of International Economics* 51: 437–61.

———2000b. "When is Foreign Aid Policy Credible? Aid Dependence and Conditionality." *Journal of Development Economics* 61: 61–84.

Swaroop, Vinaya, Shikha Jha, and Andrew Sunil Rajkumar. 2000. "Fiscal Effects of Foreign Aid in a Federal System of Governance: The Case of India." *Journal of Public Economics* 77(3) (September): 307–30.

Tanzi, Vito and Hamid Davoodi. 1998. "Roads to Nowhere: How Corruption in Public Investment Hurts Growth." IMF Economic Issues No. 12. Washington, DC: International Monetary Fund.

Tendler, Judith. 1975. *Inside Foreign Aid*. Baltimore, MD: John Hopkins University Press.

The Economic Times. "Maharashtra Power Regulator Under Siege." July 5, 2000.

—— "MSEB Unions Call for Strike." Friday, July 21, 2000.

The Economist. "Thoroughly Modern Mercantilists." February 1, 1997.

—— "Many Obstacles Still Ahead." March 4, 2000.

—— "Letter from Maldives—Not Sinking but Drowning." May 13, 2000.

—— "The Kenya-Fund Dance." August 5, 2000.

The Times of India. "MSEB Told to Revise Tariff Proposal." March 1, 2000.

—— "MSEB Losing Revenue Due to Power Theft." April 14, 2000.

—— "MSEB Employees to Go On Indefinite Strike." June 12, 2000.

Thomson, James T. 1992. *A Framework for Analyzing Institutional Incentives in Community Forestry*. Rome: FAO.

Tirole, Jean. 1986. "Hierarchies and Bureaucracies: On the Role of Collusion in Organizations." *Journal of Law, Economics, and Organization* 2(2) (Fall): 181–214.

—— 1994. "The Internal Organization of Government." *Oxford Economic Papers* 46: 1–29.

Tsikata, Tsidi M. 1998. "Aid Effectiveness: A Survey of the Recent Empirical Literature." IMF Paper on Policy Analysis and Assessment. New York: IMF, Policy Development and Review Department.

Ueda, Yoshifumi. 2001. "Collective Action and Political Entrepreneur: An Incomplete Contract Approach to Collection Actions." Paper presented at the Annual Meeting of the Public Choice Society, New Orleans, Louisiana, March.

United Nations. 2002. *Report of the World Summit on Sustainable Development: Johannesburg, South Africa, 26 August–4 September 2002*. New York: United Nations.

USAID (United States Agency for International Development). 2000. "USAID's Strategy for Sustainable Development: An Overview." USAID Policy Directive 200sai. Washington, DC: USAID. <http://usaid.gov/policy/ads/200/200sai.pdf>.

—— 2004. "Functional Series 200—Programming Policy." Washington, DC: USAID. <http://usaid.gov/policy/ads/200/200.pdf>.

USGAO (United States General Accounting Office). 1993. *Foreign Assistance: Reforming the Economic Aid Program*. GAO/T-NSIAD-93-20. Washington, DC: GAO.

—— 1994. "International Trade: Combating US Competitors' Tied Aid Practices." GAO/T-GGD-94-156. Washington, DC: GAO.

USGAO/NSIAD (United States General Accounting Office/National Security and International Affairs Division). 1995. "Foreign Assistance: Selected Donors' Approaches for Managing Aid Programs." United States General Accounting Office Letter Report, 02/23/95, GAO/NSIAD-95-37.

van de Walle, Nicolas. 1999. "Economic Reform in a Democratizing Africa." *Comparative Politics* 10: 21–41.

—— 2001. *African Economies and the Politics of Permanent Crisis, 1979–1999*. New York: Cambridge University Press.

—— and Timothy A. Johnston. 1996. *Improving Aid to Africa*. Washington, DC: Overseas Development Council.

Vermillion, Douglas L. 2001. "Property Rights and Collective Action in the Devolution of Irrigation System Management." In *Collective Action, Property Rights and Devolution of*

Natural Resource Management, eds. Ruth Meinzen-Dick, Anna Knox, and Monica Di Gregorio, 183–220. Feldafing, Germany: Deutsche Stiftung für internationale Entwicklung.

Wade, Robert. 1985. "The Market for Public Office: Why the Indian State is Not Better at Development." *World Development* 13(4): 467–97.

—— 1989. "Politics and Graft: Recruitment, Appointment, and Promotions to Public Office in India." In *Corruption, Development and Inequality: Soft Touch or Hard Graft?*, ed. Peter M. Ward, 73–109. London and New York: Routledge.

—— 1995. "The Ecological Basis of Irrigation Institutions: East and South Asia." *World Development* 23(12): 2,041–49.

Waller, Christopher J., Thierry Verdier, and Roy Gardner. 2002. "Corruption: Top-Down or Bottom-Up?" *Economic Inquiry* 40: 688–703.

Wane, Waly. 2004. "The Quality of Foreign Aid: Country Selectivity or Donor Incentives?" Washington, DC: World Bank Policy Research Working Paper No. 3325.

WCED (World Commission on Environment and Development). 1987. *Our Common Future*. New York: Oxford University Press.

Wedel, Janine R. 1998. *Collision and Collusion: The Strange Case of Western Aid to Eastern Europe 1989–1998*. New York: St. Martin's.

Werlin, Herbert H. 2003. "Poor Nations, Rich Nations: A Theory of Governance." *Public Administration Review* 63(3): 329–42.

White, Howard. 1992. "The Macro-Economic Impact of Development Aid: A Critical Survey." *Journal of Development Studies* 21(2): 163–240.

——, ed. 1998. *Aid and Macroeconomic Performance*. London: Macmillan Press.

—— 1999. *Dollars, Dialogue and Development. An Evaluation of Swedish Programme Aid*. Stockholm: Sida.

—— and Tove Edstrand. 1994. "The Macroeconomic Impact of Aid to Zambia." SASDA Working Paper No. 19. Stockholm: SAU/SASDA (Secretariat for the Analysis of Swedish Development Assistance).

WHO (World Health Organization). 1999. "Lessons of Experience from Sector-Wide Approaches in Health." September.

Wieslander, Anna. 2000. "When Do We Ever Learn?" In *Learning in Development Co-Operation*, eds. Jerker Carlsson and Lennart Wohlgemuth. Stockholm: Almqvist & Wiksell International.

Wildavsky, Aaron B. 1984. *The Politics of the Budgetary Process*. 4th ed. Boston, MA: Little, Brown.

Williamson, Oliver E. 1967. "Hierarchical Control and Optimum Firm Size." *Journal of Political Economy* 75(2): 123–38.

—— 1973. "Markets and Hierarchies: Some Elementary Considerations." *American Economic Review* 63(2) (May): 316–25.

—— 1975. *Markets and Hierarchies*. New York: Free Press.

—— 1979. "Transaction Cost Economics: The Governance of Contractual Relations." *Journal of Law and Economics* 22(2) (October): 233–61.

—— 1985. *The Economic Institutions of Capitalism*. New York: Free Press.

—— 1994. *Institutions and Economic Organization: The Governance Perspective*. Washington, DC: World Bank.

Wilson, Maureen G. and Elizabeth Whitmore. 1995. "Accompanying the Process: Principles for International Development Practice." *Canadian Journal of Development Studies* (Special Issue): 61–77.

World Bank. 1997. "Annual Review of Development Effectiveness." Report 17196. Washington, DC: World Bank, Operations Evaluation Department.

—— 1998. *Assessing Aid: What Works, What Doesn't and Why.* Written by David Dollar and Lant Pritchett. Oxford, UK: Oxford University Press.

Wunsch, James. 2000. "African Political Reform and International Assistance: What Can and Should Be Done?" In *Handbook of Global Political Policy,* ed. Stuart S. Nagel. New York: Marcel Dekker.

ZNFU (Zambia National Farmers Union). 1998. *Zambia National Farmers' Union. What is it?* Lusaka, Zambia: ZNFU.

Index

Lightning Source UK Ltd.
Milton Keynes UK
30 October 2009

145647UK00001B/10/P